Archetypes and the Fourth Gospel

Archetypes and the Fourth Gospel

Literature and Theology in Conversation

Brian Larsen

LONDON • NEW YORK • OXFORD • NEW DELHI • SYDNEY

T&T CLARK
Bloomsbury Publishing Plc
50 Bedford Square, London, WC1B 3DP, UK

BLOOMSBURY, T&T CLARK and the T&T Clark logo are trademarks of Bloomsbury Publishing Plc

First published in Great Britain 2018
This paperback edition first published 2020

Copyright © Brian Larsen, 2018

Brian Larsen has asserted his right under the Copyright, Designs and Patents Act, 1988, to be identified as Author of this work.

For legal purposes the Acknowledgements on p. ix constitute
an extension of this copyright page.

All rights reserved. No part of this publication may be reproduced or transmitted in any form or by any means, electronic or mechanical, including photocopying, recording, or any information storage or retrieval system, without prior permission in writing from the publishers.

Bloomsbury Publishing Plc does not have any control over, or responsibility for, any third-party websites referred to or in this book. All internet addresses given in this book were correct at the time of going to press. The author and publisher regret any inconvenience caused if addresses have changed or sites have ceased to exist, but can accept no responsibility for any such changes.

A catalogue record for this book is available from the British Library.

A catalogue record for this book is available from the Library of Congress

ISBN: HB: 978-0-5676-7647-4
PB: 978-0-5676-9289-4
ePDF: 978-0-5676-7648-1
eBook: 978-0-5676-7649-8

Typeset by Deanta Global Publishing Services, Chennai, India

To find out more about our authors and books visit www.bloomsbury.com
and sign up for our newsletters.

Contents

Acknowledgments			ix
Preface			x
I	Introduction		1
	I. A	Opening remarks	1
	I. B	Experience, archetype, and archetypal literary criticism	2
	I. C	Theology, archetype, and conceptual prefigurement	11
	I. D	Archetypal criticism and the Fourth Gospel	17
	I. E	Goals, objectives, and qualifications	20
II	The Fourth Gospel, Jesus, and Romance		23
	II. A	Introduction	23
	II. B	Romance, the Fourth Gospel, and Jesus	24
		II. B. 1 The Fourth Gospel as romance in critical opinion	24
		II. B. 2 Basic elements of romance	26
	II. C	Romance motifs and the Fourth Gospel	32
		II. C. 1 Dramatic qualities of marvel, risk, and triumphant adventure	32
		II. C. 2 Emphasis on generation differences	33
		II. C. 3 Abundant use of pageantry	33
		II. C. 4 Claims to historical relevancy	34
		II. C. 5 The wandering journey toward "home"	34
		II. C. 6 The essential piety of the main character	34
		II. C. 7 The idealized male–female relationships	35
		II. C. 8 The protagonist's mental agility	35
		II. C. 9 Ever-present mingling of blessings and sorrows	35
		II. C. 10 The directing influence of a supernatural higher power	36
		II. C. 11 A distinguishing token or scar by which the hero or heroine will eventually be recognized	36
		II. C. 12 Shipwreck or apparent loss	37
		II. C. 13 Magical wonders	37
		II. C. 14 Interlacing narrative	37
		II. C. 15 An ending when the disparate strands are drawn together in a final reunion scene	38

	II. D	Structural/conceptual elements: Setting, plot/story, character		38
		II. D. 1 Setting: Romance and realism in the FG		38
		II. D. 2 Plot and story in romance		44
		II. D. 3 Characters in romance		51
			II. D. 3. a Identity and self-determination	51
			II. D. 3. b Representation	55
			II. D. 3. c Other characters in the FG: Personal and theological encounters	58
	II. E	Conclusion		66
III	Tragedy and Pilate			67
	III. A	Introduction		67
	III. B	Pilate in the Fourth Gospel		69
		III. B. 1 Pilate as a dynamic character		69
		III. B. 2 The trial narrative as interpretative paradigm		71
	III. C	Narrative analysis 18:15–19:22		73
		III. C. 1 Preface: The narrative context: 18:15-27		73
		III. C. 2 Scene 1: Judicial concerns: 18:28-32		74
		III. C. 3 Scene 2: From politics to truth: 18:33-38a		75
		III. C. 4 Scene 3: Return to innocence: 18:38b-40		76
		III. C. 5 Scene 4: Desperate measures: 19:1-3		77
		III. C. 6 Scene 5: Revelation of divinity: 19:4-8		78
		III. C. 7 Scene 6: Confirmation of divinity: 19:9-11		79
		III. C. 8 Scene 7: Capitulation: 19:12-16		80
		III. C. 9 Epilogue: 19:22		82
	III. D	Tragedy and Pilate		82
		III. D. 1 Elements of audience reaction		83
			III. D. 1. a Fear and pity	83
			III. D. 1. b Catharsis	87
		III. D. 2 Structural elements of tragedy		88
			III. D. 2. a Plot	89
			III. D. 2. b Character	95
			III. D. 2. c *Hamartia*	97
		III. D. 3 Tragedy in Greek and Christian perspective		99
	III. E	Conceptual elements of tragedy		100
		III. E .1 Introduction		100
		III. E. 2 The tragic clash		103
		III. E. 3 Relative values: Knowledge and ignorance in tragedy		112
		III. E. 4 Absolute values: Moral order in tragedy		114
	III. F	Conclusion		119

IV	Irony, Thomas, and the Jews		121
	IV. A Introduction		121
	IV. B Thomas and the Jews in the Fourth Gospel: Variations on the ironization of irony		122
	IV. B. 1 Thomas and the ironization of the ironist: Seeing and not seeing and seeing		122
	IV. B. 2 The Jews and the ironization of irony: Seeing without seeing		128
	IV. B. 2. a The Jews and symbolic narrative		128
	IV. B. 2. b The Jews in 4:43–6:71: The ironization of irony		130
	IV. C Conceptual issues in irony		136
	IV. C. 1 Survey and classification of studies of irony in the FG		136
	IV. C. 2 Values and beliefs in irony		140
	IV. C. 3 Positive, equivocal, and negative irony		142
	IV. C. 3. a Positive irony		142
	IV. C. 3. b Equivocal irony		143
	IV. C. 3. c Negative irony		146
	IV. D Conclusion		151
V	Comedy and Peter		153
	V. A Introduction		153
	V. B Peter in the Fourth Gospel		153
	V. B. 1 Peter as follower		153
	V. B. 2 Peter as leader		156
	V. B. 2. a Peter in chapter 13		156
	V. B. 2. b Peter in chapter 18		159
	V. B. 2. c Peter in chapter 20		161
	V. B. 3 Peter as follower and leader		162
	V. B. 3. a Peter in chapter 21		162
	V. B. 3. b Peter and the status of chapter 21		164
	V. C The comic and Peter		165
	V. C. 1 Introduction		165
	V. C. 2 Elements of audience reaction		167
	V. C. 2. a Comic emotions: Sympathy and ridicule		167
	V. C. 2. b Laughter		168
	V. C. 3 Structural elements of comedy		169
	V. C. 3. a Character		169
	V. C. 3. b Plot		176

	V. D	Conceptual elements of comedy		179
		V. D. 1	Introduction	179
		V. D. 2	Beliefs and frames of reference	181
		V. D. 3	Frames of reference in conflict	182
		V. D. 4	Comic reality	186
		V. D. 5	Comedy and Christianity	190
	V. E	Conclusion		192
VI	Conclusion			193
	VI. A	Retrospect		193
	VI. B	Review		194
	VI. C	Results		195
	VI. D	Prospects		196
Bibliography				199
Index				210

Acknowledgments

I wish to acknowledge with thanks the assistance and advice of Professors Trevor Hart and Richard Bauckham, who, together with Professors Alan Torrance and Chris Seitz, did so much to make the Institute for Theology, Imagination and the Arts at the University of St. Andrews a stimulating environment for study. I also wish to note with appreciation and thanks the contributions, social, academic, and spiritual, of the many postgraduate students who enriched my life in a variety of ways: Bob Winchell, Todd Pokrifka-Joe, Steve Guthrie, James Bruce, Dave Hogg, Jane Rowland, Jack Wisemore, Al Baker, and Lindsay Sullivan.

With thanks I wish to gratefully acknowledge the assistance of Jeremy and Jan Peckham, financially through the Fraser-Peckham Trust and personally through prayer, friendship, and example. Many thanks and much love are to be extended to Adrian, Jenny, Edward, Henry and Cathy Gratwick; Jim[†] and Grace Clark; Rev. George and Jan Fairlie; Winston and Olga Kilfetter; Alison Anderstrem and Gill Craig for their kindness to me and, especially, to my family during our stay in Crail. Thank you to Peter Knight, Geoff Holt, Rev. Tom Ruhlman, and Rev. Dr. Peter Thomson for providing encouragement and/or direction when either or both were in short supply. I would be remiss not to mention the congregations of Buckhaven Baptist Church; Anstruther Baptist Church; Largo Baptist Church; Pittenweem Baptist Church; Crail Parish Church; the Parish churches of Flotta and Hoy, Orkney; the Parish churches of Carbost and Dunvegan, Isle of Skye; and the Church of Scotland Department of National Mission, who provided opportunities for me to minister and thus allowed me to keep my feet more firmly on the ground than they would have been otherwise.

I am most grateful for the efforts of teaching assistants Hannah Richards, Kalie Kreischer, Claire Broberg, and Sarah Blumert and my colleague Alan Rose for their cheerful and diligent work in preparation of this manuscript. Many thanks to Ron Fay, Stanley Porter, and Leland Ryken for their interest and support of my work.

Most of all, I wish to thank and dedicate this work to my wife, Elaine, shining in beauty always, and our children, Adrianne, Celeste, and Christian, who challenged, encouraged, endured, laughed, cried, and smiled.

Preface

The story of this work began some time ago when I was an undergraduate student at a small Christian liberal arts college in the United States. As it relates to this work, my story there can be summarized by two approaches to the Bible. Interested in the Old Testament, I began my studies as a Biblical Languages major, having been advised that the way into the Old Testament was background studies and working with Biblical and ancient near eastern languages, but I found this method too removed from the dynamics and drama of the text. At the same time, I encountered an English professor who had far more interesting things to say about the Bible than I had encountered elsewhere. Although I later left that school for a variety of reasons, I made a perhaps greater move—I changed my major from Biblical Languages to English.

The story picks up again sometime later. After a ten-year hiatus from the academic world spent ranching and farming among the rocks and sagebrush of the family farm in Eastern Washington State, I hit the books again at a major American Evangelical seminary. While I greatly respect this institution and very much share its general ethos and outlook, here I increasingly came to see an inadequate appreciation of the Bible as a work of literature, particularly its narrative portions. Perhaps the motivation stemmed from an aversion of allegorical readings, the excesses of many current literary readings, and a laudable desire to read the Bible, as history where appropriate, in its historical context. Yet this seemed to me to lead to a kind of blindness to certain aspects of the Bible. Ascending the soapbox for a moment, the gathering around the fire in John 21 cannot be confined to the dustbin of "local color" and its resonances, however sentimental, of the warmth of the presence of Jesus must be taken into account. Likewise, the deaths of Elimelech, Mahlon, and Killion in Moab in the opening verses of Ruth offer, at least minimally, an invitation to associate these deaths with Moab and judgment rather then, as I heard in one memorable lecture, bare details with which to begin a story. However trivial, these examples represent a clash of methodologies and modes of thinking of no small importance when, especially, preaching from one or the other is taken into account.

To some extent, this work represents an attempt to explore and, if possible, come to terms with these tensions for myself, for my Evangelical fellow travelers, and possibly for others. Two strains of my life and interests, the Bible and theology on the one hand and literature and literary analysis on the other, are here placed in a sustained dialogue that attempts to give full weight to what each has to offer in a way that, it is hoped, is mutually beneficial. While some might have reservations of the place given to theology with respect to literature, doubtless others may have equal reservations of the reverse.

As regards this work itself, several things may be helpfully noted. The chapters are relatively independent, partly because they interact with different bodies of critical literature that are relatively independent of each other and partly because the subject matter of each chapter raises its own issues and challenges. Each chapter, therefore, has its specific concerns, and chapters do not so much build sequentially on each other as they build the collective case for which the work is arguing. At the same time, they nevertheless relate to each other and are approached from and within the archetypal framework governing the entire work. Additionally, while writing some chapters, I was continually met by the challenge of presenting the material in a coherent order when everything related to that chapter needed to be explained at once. The main arguments are summarized in the conclusion, and readers may wish to take advantage of this fact as they begin reading.

In any case, the subject matter presented here has been a reward in itself, full of discoveries, holding my interest, deepening my appreciation for the Fourth Gospel, and indeed for the Gospel itself.

Subsequent to the original completion of this work, I have had many opportunities to share this material at conferences and with my literature students. Others have certainly provided useful input and helped me to clarify a few matters, and my sense is that this study, rooted in a few basic Christian beliefs, focused on a classic text (the Fourth Gospel), and utilizing a classic literary approach (Northrop Frye's archetypal criticism), has stood the test of time.

All scripture quotations, unless otherwise indicated, are taken from the Holy Bible, New International Version®, NIV®. Copyright ©1973, 1978, 1984, 2011 by Biblica, Inc.™ Used by permission of Zondervan. All rights reserved worldwide. www.zondervan.com The "NIV" and "New International Version" are trademarks registered in the United States Patent and Trademark Office by Biblica, Inc.

1

Introduction

I. A Opening remarks

The Bible itself is manifestly a work of literature and a work of theology. As such it offers a distinct perspective on the relationship between God and the created order. Christian theology usually includes significant reflection and reliance on the Biblical texts and some significant attempt to address issues of life arising from the experience of human beings living within the created order. Given the enormity and scope of the issues, it is not surprising that much of world literature attempts to articulate, express, or reflect on the meaning of human life with respect to the existence of God and his interactions with human beings and the temporal order. The relationships between beliefs and experience and between immanence and transcendence endure as perennial issues in both literature and theology. While these fields of study often explore the same issues, works of literature and the Bible may themselves be studied as literary locations at which and by which the issues pertaining to theology and experience themselves are given artistic form.

The Fourth Gospel (hereafter FG) is just such a location, arguably the most transparently literary and theological of the four Gospels. Using the FG and with reference to specific characters in the FG, the present work will seek to outline and explore the relationship between literature and specifically Christian theology by holding each up for comparison and contrast in a sustained interaction that will prove mutually illuminating and contribute to the field of literary studies applied to the Bible.

Because of their mutual concern with expressing and evaluating human experience with reference to God or the transcendent, literature and theology may be assumed to be in some relationship to each other, related on an explicitly theistic basis rooted in the Biblical teaching that God is the Creator or for no other reason than that both simply form part of the phenomena of human history and experience. This is not, however, to equate religious experience and literary experience;[1] it is to note that some similarities exist. The nature, content, and limits of that relationship are unclear, nor is

---

[1] For a critique of this tendency, see Leland Ryken, *Triumphs of the Imagination: Literature in Christian Perspective* (Downers Grove, IL: InterVarsity Press, 1979).

there any readily apparent systematic means or method by which such a relationship might be explored.

Therefore, it will be necessary to first outline the way in which literature and theology will be placed in dialogue here, an interaction based on four elements: (1) the principle of interaction—human experience; (2) the means of interaction—archetypal criticism; (3) the location of interaction—characters in the FG; (4) the ideology and governing principle of the interaction—Christian theology. Human experience and Christian theology, on a Christian understanding, very much interact and connect and form something of a circle or totality of which archetypal criticism and the characters in the FG form a part. Time and reading being linear, however, these elements will be introduced below by moving from #1 to #4 in progressive and overlapping fashion, concluding with a statement of objectives and qualifications.

I. B Experience, archetype, and archetypal literary criticism

The concept of archetype as a way of categorizing and explaining human experience rose to prominence through the work of Carl Jung in the field of psychology. Jung defines archetype as follows:

> The primordial image or archetype is a figure, whether it be a daemon, man, or process, that repeats itself in the course of history wherever creative phantasy is freely manifested. Essentially, therefore, it is a mythological figure. If we subject these images to a closer investigation we discover them to be the formulated resultants of countless typical experiences of our ancestors. They are, as it were, the psychic residua of numberless experiences of the same type. They depict millions of individual experiences in the average, presenting a kind of picture of the psychic life distributed and projected into the manifold shapes of the psychological pandemonium.... Each of these images contains a piece of human psychology and human destiny, a relic of suffering or delight that has happened countless times in our ancestral story, and on the average follows ever the same course. It is like a deeply graven river-bed in the soul, in which the waters of life, that had spread hitherto with groping and uncertain course over wide but shallow surfaces, suddenly become a mighty river. This happens when that particular chain of circumstances is encountered which from immemorial time has contributed to the laying down of the primordial image.[2]

Archetypes, Jung believes, appear in a variety of intellectual contexts, ranging from Plato's concept of forms to Kant's categories of human cognition and beyond. But rather than logical or metaphysical categories, Jung finds archetypes rooted in depth

---

[2] Carl Jung, *Contributions to Analytical Psychology*, trans. H. G. Baynes and C. F. Baynes (London: Kegan Paul, 1928), 246–47.

psychology.[3] For Jung, archetypes are visible manifestations of something rooted in the deepest soil of human experience.[4] Frasier's influential *The Golden Bough* pursues a similar line of thought from an anthropological perspective.[5] Whatever its source, in general terms the concept of archetype has a long history and has been widely used in a number of disciplines.

One of those disciplines is literary criticism. Lee offers the following definition of archetypal literary criticism:

> Archetypal criticism focuses on the generic, recurring and conventional elements in literature that cannot be explained as matters of historical influence or tradition. It studies each literary work as part of the whole of literature. This kind of criticism accepts as its informing principle that archetypes—typical images, characters, narratives designs, themes, and other literary phenomena—are present in all literature and so provide the basis for study of its interconnectedness.[6]

Or plainly, "The archetype is simply the typical at the highest power of literary generalization."[7]

The application of archetypal analysis to literature received its most comprehensive and influential treatment in Northrop Frye's *Anatomy of Criticism* (1957). Indeed, perhaps no work of literary criticism produced in the middle of the twentieth century has had the impact of Frye's *Anatomy of Criticism*, specifically his third essay "Archetypal Criticism: Theory of Myths."[8] While indebted to Jung and Frazer, Frye is by no means bound by a link between archetype and anthropology and depth psychology.[9] For Frye, archetypes are simply typical and recurring elements of literature, something resembling a convention, a way in which literary experience, itself a social fact and mode of communication, may be unified.[10] Frye believed that all literature represented the interaction with the upper world of idealized experience and the lower world of non-idealized experience. According to Frye, each of his four archetypes represented a certain type of viewpoint or experience within these two poles of existence. Frye develops a comprehensive theory of literary criticism based on four enduring literary *mythoi* or generic plots: romance, tragedy, satire and irony, and comedy. This diagram illustrates their relationships:

---

[3] Jung, *Contributions*, 278–79.
[4] Ibid., 118–19.
[5] For a psychological perspective see Joseph Campbell, *The Hero with a Thousand Faces*, 2nd ed. (Princeton: Princeton University Press, 1968).
[6] Alvin Lee, "Archetypal Criticism," in *Encyclopedia of Contemporary Literary Theory*, ed. Irena Makaryk (Toronto, Buffalo, and London: University of Toronto Press, 1993), 3.
[7] Geoffrey Hartman, "Ghostlier Demarcations: The Sweet Science of Northrop Frye," in *Beyond Formalism: Literary Essays 1958–1970* (New Haven and London: Yale University Press, 1970), 25.
[8] Northrop Frye, *Anatomy of Criticism: Four Essays* (Princeton, NJ: Princeton University Press, 1957), 131–242.
[9] Lee writes, "So far as Frye's account of archetypal criticism is concerned, it is important to recognize that he disengaged the concept of the literary archetype from its anthropological and psychological beginnings." Lee, "Archetypal Criticism," 4.
[10] Frye, *Anatomy*, 99.

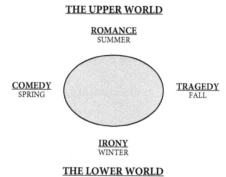

For Frye, in common with other forms of archetypal analysis, these four *mythoi* transcend time, place, and genre; they are simply the enduring patterns of all narrative literature.[11] He outlines the four primary *mythoi* as follows:

> The four *mythoi* that we are dealing with, comedy, romance, tragedy, and irony, may now be seen as four aspects of a central unifying myth. *Agon* or conflict is the basis or archetypal theme of romance, the radical of romance being a sequence of marvelous adventures. *Pathos* or catastrophe, whether in triumph or in defeat, is the archetypal theme of tragedy. *Sparagmos*, or the sense that heroism and effective action are absent, disorganized or doomed to defeat, and that confusion and anarchy reign over the world, is the archetype of irony and satire. *Anagnorisis*, or recognition of a newborn society rising in triumph around a still somewhat mysterious hero and his bride, is the archetypal theme of comedy.[12]

Defined simply by Frye, these universal categories enjoy broad popular recognition and command wide recognition among literary critics. In addition, Frye identifies each archetype with a specific season of the year—romance/summer, tragedy/fall, irony/winter, and comedy/spring—and thus links these archetypes to patterns in the natural world that reinforce the strength and universality of his system. By organizing these literary categories into a comprehensive scheme of interpretation, Frye has created a program that enables systematic comparison and contrast.

As a way of limiting the scope of the inquiry into literature and theology and to avoid a discussion of the romance, tragedy, irony and satire, and comedy abstracted from any specific text or applied generally to a specific text, these literary archetypes will be applied to characters in the FG who, it will be argued, embody the salient features of each archetype: Jesus, an innocent and virtuous man acting on behalf of

---

[11] "The archetypal view of literature shows us literature as a total form and literary experience as a part of the continuum of life, in which one of the poet's functions is to visualize the goals of human work." Frye, *Anatomy*, 115.

[12] Frye, *Anatomy*, 192. The classifications adopted here will follow Frye with the exception of triumph in defeat being always seen as tragedy. Triumph in defeat, as in the case of Jesus, is more in keeping with romance.

others embodies much of the heroic pattern characteristic of romance; Pilate, unable or unwilling to act justly in an unwanted and unavoidable particular circumstance, as tragic; Thomas and the Jews, as representatives of the ironic and skeptical point of view; and Peter, who denies Christ and later recovers, as comic. Thus, these characters who exemplify a specific archetype will serve as a way to bring literature into Biblical studies and theology, and, conversely, these characters will serve as focal points for bringing Biblical studies and theology into literature. Frye's system will serve as the conduit by which literature and theology may be in dialogue at the specific location of these characters in the FG.[13]

The advantages of Frye's system are that it is comprehensive and straightforward, encompassing a large portion of imaginative literature without being simplistic. And Frye's classification system offers the advantage of explaining the relationships of one type of literature with another, as a way of putting the whole of literature in dialogue with itself. For example, Frye's system places romance and irony as opposites and rightly predicts that irony is not usually present in romance and that the heroic innocence typical of romance does not usually appear in irony. In another example, irony can be found in both tragedy and comedy, but to the degree that comedy and tragedy contain irony, they move further from romance. Tragedy and comedy are obvious opposites because one moves from success to failure and the other moves from confusion to success. Frye's statement of archetypal criticism endures, in no small measure, because it is explanatory, predictive, and flexible.

Additionally, Frye makes a critical distinction between archetype and genre that also expands the applicability of his system. For Frye, archetype precedes and transcends genre, allowing Frye to sidestep pedantic concerns as to whether, for example, a novel can be tragic because it is a prose narrative rather than a dramatic production.[14] Genre, on the other hand, refers to the specific form in which the literary work actually appears, such as a novel, play, poem, or motion picture.[15] For example, the form and presentation of Thomas Hardy's *The Return of the Native* is in the genre of a novel, yet it follows many of the conventions of Greek tragedy and may be considered, like Greek tragic drama, as archetypal tragedy. A novel might conceivably contain elements of all four archetypes.[16] Finally, Frye's system itself, like the Jungian archetypal analysis to which it owes some debt, is applicable beyond literature and, for example, has been usefully applied to the narrative forms of history writing by Hayden White.[17] Later,

---

[13] By *mythoi* or *mythos*, Frye essentially argues for a mode or meta-archetype, the basic idea being the same in both cases. Since the current discussion is largely confined to character and for simplicity and ease of reference, "archetype" will generally be used in place of Frye's *mythoi*.

[14] See Frye, *Anatomy*, 162.

[15] For example, Reardon observes, "The 'novel' is undoubtedly a major literary genre. The broader term 'romance' may well signify something bigger and more important than a mere literary genre. It may constitute a whole mode of thought, a frame of reference, an authority for our behavior: Frye's term 'secular scripture' is a singularly felicitous formula." B. P. Reardon, *The Form of Greek Romance* (Princeton: Princeton University Press, 1991), 12.

[16] For example, Jane Austen's *Mansfield Park* features characters that can be interpreted according to Frye's four archetypes: the protagonist Fanny Price as heroic in the manner of romance, Maria Bertram as tragic, Henry and Mary Crawford as ironic, and Edmund Bertram as comic.

[17] Hayden White, *Metahistory: The Historical Imagination in Nineteenth-Century Europe* (Baltimore and London: The Johns Hopkins University Press, 1973).

elements of White's work will be employed to a limited extent as it relates to literary and conceptual issues.

But Frye has his critics. Frye often interchanged the terms *systematic* and *scientific*[18] and proposed his system as a means of establishing literary criticism on a scientific basis. For this "scientific" claim, it has drawn criticism and time has shown this to be a false hope.[19] However, this flaw has by no means decreased its explanatory usefulness as a self-coherent system. Reflecting the difficulty of relating universals to particulars, any classification system tends to clarify and obscure by virtue of the fact that the universals do not always illuminate a particular work.[20] An additional related criticism is that Frye's system with its emphasis on universal themes of literature is notably synchronic rather than diachronic. Flack observes,

> A classifying theorist such as Northrop Frye, while being intimately familiar with the history of literature, has no way of making sense of the familiarity within his classificatory scheme. Much of the argument of Frye's *Anatomy of Criticism* rests on generalizations which beg the main questions at issue, and he has only the most improvisational things to say about why our literary conventions have changed as they have. The flaw in Frye's approach is that it is standpointless and unhistorical rather than based in a present-day creative sensibility, and that it can therefore offer us little more than an academic exercise in literary taxonomy.[21]

What Flack says, while generally true, need not be taken as a disadvantage and can be taken just as easily as an advantage. Indeed, the very purpose of archetypal criticism of any sort is to be "standpointless and unhistorical" and to focus on perennial themes regardless of when and where they occur. What Flack views as a fatal flaw is little more than stating the obvious. Frye did not conceive *Anatomy of Criticism* as a literary history. Furthermore, diachronic analysis of any kind must recognize the persistence of a given form through time and, therefore, unavoidably pays some attention to the synchronic aspect of literature. In many ways, the synchronic approach of Frye's *Anatomy* provides the natural counterpoint to Auerbach's *Mimesis*, a work that might easily and unfairly be criticized as being too wedded to a diachronic approach. Criticism of Frye or Auerbach on the grounds of being synchronic or diachronic, or stressing the universal or the particular, is equally correct and equally misguided.[22]

---

[18] John Casey, "A 'Science' of Criticism: Northrop Frye," chapter VII in *The Language of Criticism* (London: Methuen & Co., 1966), 140.
[19] Casey, "Criticism," 140–51.
[20] See Wayne Booth, *A Rhetoric of Irony* (Chicago and London: The University of Chicago Press, 1974), 100–01, note.
[21] Colin Flack, *Myth, Truth, and Literature: Towards a True Post-Modernism*, 2nd ed. (Cambridge: Cambridge University Press, 1989), 89.
[22] The diachronic and synchronic methods can profoundly critique each other; indeed, a synchronic approach to the FG may expose interpretative myopia within diachronic criticism as diachronic criticism. Although beyond the scope of the present work, it is worth noting that to the extent that the FG exhibits the use (conscious or not) of recognized literary techniques and archetypes in a sophisticated way, this undermines the notion that the FG is to be interpreted with reference to an isolated and sectarian community within the early church.

Flack also notes that the *Anatomy of Criticism* "rests on generalizations which beg the main questions at issue." Booth makes a similar observation on Frye, commenting, "I find myself again and again unable to guess 'how he knows' a particular assertion."[23] Likewise, Borkland points out, "Frye's 'method'—his constant dependence on simile and analogy to make his main points—raises some serious questions. The analogies are often striking, but whether or not they have much logical validity is another matter."[24] The issue here is Frye's method of argumentation. The simple fact of the matter is that Frye's method is self-justifying and self-evident; he makes no strictly formal attempt at proof. In common with all analogical reasoning, strictly speaking it has no "logical" validity. For Frye, and for the present work, this aspect must be laid bare and kept in mind from start to finish. Like any argument from analogy, connections can only be suggested, not "proved." Arguments from analogy can be better or worse and must be evaluated on the basis of what analogy is and does. The authority available is implicit, one relying on an imaginative sense of the authoritative similitude of things and the inherent appropriateness of various generalizations and specific connections. Archetypal criticism in any form in any discipline relies on assumptions of similarity.

But rather than being a conspicuous exception, Frye is well within the tradition of literary criticism as interpretation, of reasoning by analogy and speaking for literature as its interpreter. Frye has simply taken a common method of interpretation, fashioned it into a system, and made it something of a target by doing so. Interpretation of this sort performs a function similar to that which historians often do for the facts of history. Indeed, in his analysis of forms of history writing, White favorably observes,

> Romantic historians, and, indeed, "narrative historians" in general, are inclined to construct generalizations about the whole historical field and the meaning of its processes that are so extensive that they bear very little weight as propositions that can be confirmed or disconfirmed by appeal to empirical data.[25]

The issue can hardly be confined to the humanities. As Polanyi has shown, "there is nothing in any concept that points *objectively* to any sort of reality."[26]

Additionally, any coherentist effort, including Frye's or the one offered here, suffers from the need to explain the parts in terms of the whole and *simultaneously* the whole in terms of its parts. Part of the difficulty here may be traced to problems related to finding a way between induction and deduction, a problem Kuhn, like Polanyi, observed with regard to the "difficulties often encountered in developing points of contact between a theory and nature"[27] and a difficulty noted by Frye himself.[28] The unavoidable result

---

[23] Booth, *The Rhetoric of Irony*, p. x.
[24] Elmer Borklund, *Contemporary Literary Critics* (London: St. James Press, 1977), 212–18.
[25] White, *Metahistory*, 15.
[26] Michael Polanyi and Harry Prosch, *Meaning* (Chicago and London: The University of Chicago Press, 1975), 61, his emphasis.
[27] Thomas Kuhn, *The Structure of Scientific Revolutions*, 2nd ed. (Chicago: The University of Chicago Press, 1970), 30.
[28] Frye, "The Archetypes of Literature," in *Fables of Identity: Studies in Poetic Mythology* (New York: Harcourt, Brace & World, 1963), 7–20.

is some form of circular reasoning. Criticism on this ground alone, however, is banal; any scientific or historical theory of any scope manifests the same inherent difficulty.[29] A coherentist system does not exist in isolation and must be judged on the basis of its overall explanatory value of the data it seeks to explain. A coherentist system offers the advantage of placing the parts in relation to a whole and constructing a whole in relation to its parts rather than isolating the parts or abstracting the whole. Historical/critical studies and theological studies tend, at least superficially, to be at opposite ends of the part/whole continuum. Reflecting the difficulty of relating universals to particulars, any classification system, especially one as universal as Frye's, can clarify but can also obscure by virtue of the fact that the universals do not always illuminate particular works.[30] Like the four points of a compass, Frye's four archetypes do not always reflect the direction traveled or the lay of the land, but they do serve as valuable reference points for making one's way. As with the synchronic/diachronic dilemma, the liabilities of Frye's archetypal criticism must be acknowledged, but need not be taken as fatal and perhaps not even as serious.

The advantage is that Frye's archetypes are general and flexible yet maintain an explanatory value. A practical disadvantage of Frye, one that reflects the partial validity of the above criticisms, is that a portion of the minutia of Frye's analysis seems little more than esoteric mumbo jumbo. On archetypal criticism Hartman remarks, "Archetypal analysis can degenerate into an abstract thematic where the living pressure of mediations is lost and all connections are skeletonized."[31] In consequence, the present work will make use of Frye's four archetypes as an overall explanatory system and refer to Frye as appropriate, but will in no way be bound to everything he says. Significantly, an attempt will be made to go beyond Frye and offer an explanation of each archetype that even if less nuanced and erudite than Frye, is at least more specific and better defined. The clearer definitions offered here may help make archetypal criticism more useful in Biblical studies. Yet the basic validity of Frye's system will simply be assumed as a given, a system that provides the basic framework for the classification of literature on which the present work is based. If Frye has failed to establish literature on a scientific basis, a designation of waning authority and desirability, a state of affairs equally true for historians in their discipline, he in large measure succeeded in providing a self-coherent and widely applicable framework of interpretation.

A key feature of Frye's archetypal system is that it is intended to be nonideological, and Frye wrote his opening "Polemical Introduction" to insure that it stays that way.[32] Frye views literary criticism as a discipline in search of some kind of unifying theory, still in its infancy at the naive induction and classification stage. *Anatomy of Criticism* represents Frye's attempt to fill this void. Literary criticism, for Frye, must be autonomous and develop its own theories and practices like history or science. Frye believes that the importation of sets of values or a conceptual framework, be it Christian or Marxist,

---

[29] This is Kuhn's essential point in *Revolutions*. Interpretation of the FG in terms of the "Johannine community" is essentially a coherentist approach, although, unlike the present work, one that purports to establish historical fact.
[30] See Booth, *A Rhetoric of Irony*, 100–01, note.
[31] Hartman, "Ghostlier Demarcations," 30.
[32] Frye, *Anatomy*, 3–29.

or whatever, must be avoided and that evaluation of literature must take place on its own terms derived from literature itself. Frye responds to the criticism that literature must deal with the larger world in some way and thereby be potentially open to outside evaluation by insisting that literature creates an autonomous world of its own. Literary criticism proceeds, like math, hypothetically and is verified by its internal consistency and application to its subject matter. For Frye, literature is primarily a verbal structure. In its own way, Frye's nonideological system was revolutionary and prefigures much of later structuralism and deconstruction[33] but without the sterility of the former or the reader-centered tendencies of the latter.

But there is no reason, other than Frye's own polemical assertions to the contrary, to accept Frye's rejection of ideology.[34] Just as Frye himself developed his criticism shorn, perhaps incompletely, of the wool of its psychological and anthropological ancestry, Frye's four archetypes are readily suited for some kind of ideological or theological analysis. By setting the ideological element aside—if this were ever a realistic possibility—Frye paradoxically rendered his work more open to the very thing he sought to avoid. Frye's polemics are a line in the sand and nothing more. The present work will give an applied theological interpretation to the basic outlines of Frye's archetypes as they appear in the FG with reference to specific characters. Since the present work is a dialogue, Christian theology will also speak to literature by integrating theology and a Christian meta-narrative into literature by way of Frye's archetypal framework, in this sense taking to heart Eliot's statement, that, "Literary Criticism should be completed by criticism from a definite ethical and theological standpoint."[35] To the extent that this interpretative completion proves to be valid, both literary criticism and a theological standpoint are reinforced by the other's perspective. Depending on one's point of view, Frye may perhaps gain more than he loses.

The same method of Frye's ahistorical reasoning by analogy, or the authoritative similitude of things, will be employed in the present work, albeit one with an explicitly theological basis—that all of reality as the creation of God may be interpreted within the framework of Christian theology. At its most basic level, traditional Christian theology holds that all things were created by God (Gen. 1:1, Jn 1:3, Col. 1:16) and that all of creation exists within a meta-narrative in which God is actively involved (Acts 17:28, Col. 1:16). Although the fall of humanity and the transcendence of God impose limits on our understanding, it does not follow that an assumption of relatedness is unjustified.[36] Any attempt to integrate (or contrast) two or more works

---

[33] Richard Stingle, "Northrop Frye," in *The Johns Hopkins Guide to Literary Theory and Criticism*, eds. Michael Groden and Martin Kreiswirth (Baltimore and London: The Johns Hopkins University Press, 1994), 318.

[34] Jameson faults Frye's definition of romance at this very point. He notes, "Frye's account . . . fails to come to grips with the conceptual categories which inform and preselect the attributes and qualities by which those states [of being in romance] are characterized." Fredric Jameson, "Magical Narratives: Romance as Genre," *New Literary History* 7 (1975): 139–40.

[35] T. S. Eliot, "Religion and Literature," in *Selected Essays* (London: Faber, 1951), 388.

[36] This is not in any way an attempt to prove the existence of God or predicate something about God by reference to the temporal order after the manner of natural theology; rather the present work assumes a Christian point of view and is an attempt to relate that point of view to imaginative attempts to express significant and enduring patterns of human experience as found in literature.

of artistic creation by the same artist assumes a relatedness whether anything is known about the artist or not. Archetypal study of any variety rests on the observance of the recurring or typical in human experience as reflected in the wide variety in artistic creations. Archetypal study is simply the attempt to make some sense and use of these observations, whether on nontheistic or on theistic assumptions, as done here.[37] On an analogical basis by means of archetypal criticism, whether theistic and Christian or nontheistic, elements of the FG may be compared to Shakespeare or Homer or Sophocles with absolutely no account of historical influence offered or assumed even though these four archetypes certainly appear in the literature written before, during, and after the New Testament (NT) era.[38]

At the same time, by relating the four archetypes to characters in the FG, a vital connection to experience and the particular will be maintained. Rather than being only abstract locations of interaction, these characters, like any characters, serve as human invitations into the world of the text, points of contact, and imaginative identification with that brave new world of the FG, and points of location defining the reader's location within that world. Through character identification, a kind of "aesthetic encounter"[39] or reader response occurs, one traditionally recognized, but perhaps near or outside the bounds of how that discipline is normally understood.[40] And, the FG is nothing if it is not the story of one character, Jesus. By focusing on character, some account is given to that "surplus of meaning" wherein it is acknowledged that analysis, definitions, and archetypes can only take us so far. Character, then, offers an appropriate meeting place between literature and theology within the field of experience—ours and theirs.

By using these characters in the FG as representative of Frye's four archetypes, the disciplines of literary studies and Christian theology meet on something approaching a common ground. The Bible stands as a great cultural and literary document and is of crucial importance for its role in shaping Christian theology. The choice of Jesus, Pilate, the Jews and Thomas, and Peter offers the advantage of examining characters who correspond to a different literary archetype and who reach their defining literary climax during the theologically laden events of the crucifixion and resurrection of Christ. In the FG, theology and literature meet in a profound and dynamic set of circumstances.

---

[37] If the world is viewed on a theistic basis as the creation of God, to that extent, it might be expected to find and even assert analogical relationships.

[38] Comedy and tragedy are well known to predate the NT and irony is certainly a feature of the FG itself. Less familiar perhaps, is romance, on which Reardon remarks, "Above all, it is now beyond question that romance constituted, in antiquity, a veritable genre." Reardon, *The Form of Greek Romance*, 10. It may be remarked that most study of the NT in its historical setting operates on the principle that similarity implies influence. The historical critic of the FG arguing for a particular historical influence can usually do no more than reason by analogy, the results of such analogical relations advanced here being qualified and modest in comparison.

[39] Stephen Wright, "An Experiment in Biblical Criticism: Aesthetic Encounter in Reading and Preaching Scripture," in *Renewing Biblical Interpretation*, The Scripture and Hermeneutics Series, volume 1, eds. Craig Bartholomew, Colin Greene, and Karl Moller (Carlisle: Paternoster Press, 2000), 240–67.

[40] The approach here is theological and vertical, in contrast to a tendency of much of reader response criticism toward a problematic emphasis on a horizontal and linear perspective. Stephen Moore remarks, "The more the temporality of the reading experience is stressed—its cumulative, successive side—the more the Bible sheds its familiar image a meaning-ful object." *Literary Criticism and the Gospels: The Theoretical Challenge* (New Haven, CT: Yale University Press, 1989), 120.

I. C Theology, archetype, and conceptual prefigurement

As a way of initially integrating archetypes and theology on conceptual grounds, some elements of Hayden White's *Metahistory* will prove useful to clarify and illustrate relationships between archetypes and ideas. White's project is to clarify and categorize various ways in which the study of history may be approached, especially with regard to a work of history as "a verbal structure in the form of a narrative prose discourse that purports to be a model, or icon, of past structures and processes in the interest of *explaining what they were by representing* them."[41] For White, the "method of emplotment" employed is fundamentally linked to the conceptualization and interpretation offered for a given subject matter. He writes,

> Providing the "meaning" of a story by identifying the *kind of story* that has been told is called explanation by emplotment. If, in the course of narrating a story, the historian provides it with the plot structure of a Tragedy, he has "explained" it in one way; if he has structured it as a Comedy, he has "explained" it another way. Emplotment is the way by which a sequence of events fashioned into a story is gradually revealed to be a story of a particular kind.[42]

Although it is beyond the scope and object of this work to examine the relationship between the FG and the historical data it re-presents, significantly, according to White, history and literature make use of the same narrative structures and conceptual prefigurements. For the present work, however, it is more important to note White's observation that the method of emplotment employed for a particular story entails a certain point of view inherent in a particular method of emplotment.[43] For White, form and meaning are inseparable. And, to the extent that an archetype refers to human experience, general or specific, an archetype is both centrifugal and centripetal, simultaneously conveying and creating meaning.[44]

As another way of conceiving and introducing the four archetypes and observing the connection between content and form, White's analysis of the tropological function of language may be employed.[45] White argues that the four tropes of language recognized by traditional poetics and modern language theory—metaphor, metonymy, irony, and synecdoche—function as precognitive and precritical ways of prefiguring the way in which the writer (White means the historian) conceives the subject matter. He writes,

> These tropes permit the characterization of objects in different kinds of indirect, or figurative, discourse. They are especially useful for understanding the operations by which the contents of experience which resist description in unambiguous prose presentations can be prefiguratively grasped and prepared for conscious

---

[41] White, *Metahistory*, 2, his emphasis.
[42] White, *Metahistory*, 7.
[43] Similarly, Frye observes, "The *mythos* is the *dianoia* in movement; the *dianoia* is the *mythos* in stasis." Frye, *Anatomy*, 83.
[44] In this sense Jung is correct. See above.
[45] The study of the tropological elements of language is immense and contains a number of conflicting definitions of even the most basic terms, especially metonymy and synecdoche. White's definitions will be accepted.

apprehension. In Metaphor (literally, "transfer"), for example, phenomena can be characterized in terms of their similarity to, and difference from, one another, in the manner of analogy or simile, as in the phrase "my love, a rose." Through Metonymy (literally, "name change"), the name of a part of a thing may be substituted for the name of the whole, as in the phrase, "fifty sail" when what is indicated is "fifty ships." With Synecdoche, which is regarded by some theorists as a form of Metonymy, a phenomenon can be characterized by using the part to symbolize some *quality* presumed to inhere in the totality, as in the expression "He is all heart." Through Irony, finally, entities can be characterized by way of negating on the figurative level what is positively affirmed on the literal level. The figures of the manifestly absurd expression (catachresis) such as "blind mouths," and of explicit paradox (oxymoron), such as "cold passion," can be taken as emblems of this trope.[46]

Most important is White's analysis of the relationship of the literal to the figurative in each trope. He writes,

> Irony, Metonymy, and Synecdoche are kinds of Metaphor, but they differ from one another in the kinds of *reductions* or *intergrations* [sic] they effect on the literal level of their meanings and by the kinds of illuminations they aim at on the figurative level. Metaphor is essentially *representational*, Metonymy is *reductionist*, Synecdoche is *integrative*, and Irony is *negational*.[47]

Although White does not make any such connections, archetypal modes of emplotment may also be related to the four basic tropes on the basis of their figurative/literal relationships that obtain within a work of literature itself. What White uses to characterize each trope also describes the fundamental quality of each archetype and the mode of linguistic prefigurement it entails. Mode of archetypal emplotment, which possesses a figurative quality in itself, may be matched with the conceptual prefigurement manifest in the use of poetic or figurative language. Romance as an archetype may be characterized tropologically and conceptually by *representation*, tragedy by *reduction*, comedy by *integration*, and irony by *negation*.[48] The following chart will illustrate this characterization.

Literal/Figurative or Belief/Reality

Archetype	Trope	Relationship	Example	Relationship
Romance	Metaphor	Representation	My love, a rose	Belief = Reality
Tragedy	Metonymy	Reduction	All people = all hands	Belief < Reality
Comedy	Synecdoche	Integration	He is all heart	Belief > Reality
Irony	Irony	Negation	Cool passion	Belief < > Reality

Each archetype may be further identified by a conception of reality's relationship to a belief, an ideal, or the transcendent manifest within a work of literature itself. *The*

---

[46] White, *Metahistory*, 34, his emphasis. White differs from Jakobson and others who adopt a dualistic conception and see synecdoche and irony as variations on metonymy.
[47] White, *Metahistory*, 34, his emphasis.
[48] On irony and negation, see Paul Duke, *Irony in the Fourth Gospel* (Atlanta: John Knox, 1985), 15–16.

fundamental ideological or theological variable between each archetype or trope is the relationship assumed between reality and experience, on the one hand, and some ideal, transcendent belief, or imaginative conception of things on the other. While the specific belief or ideal can vary, the presence of a belief or ideal and its perceived relationship to reality within a work of literature provides the common ground of conceptual exchange between theology and the four archetypes.[49] In other words, the difference between belief and reality is the critical variable between Frye's four archetypes. Thus, in romance a belief or ideal is held up for representation or display; in tragedy a reduction of that ideal is effected as the ideal no longer adequately corresponds to reality; in irony reality and an ideal are separated; and in comedy reality and an ideal progress toward some form of integration. While by no means identical, the relation of reality to a belief or ideal in literature is in theology analogous to the relationship between reality and belief in God and establishes a point of exchange between them. Thus, for example, Peter is comic in his relation to his partially erroneous theological understanding of Jesus and discipleship, and Peter is comic strictly in literary terms without reference to the theology of the FG. Thus, Peter's theological problem mirrors his problem as a comic character. The differences between belief and reality in each trope and archetype are exemplified in characters in the FG.

The relation of belief to reality, whether in literature or theology, will serve as the essential variable to compare and contrast each archetype with the others. The chart below will illustrate many of the items discussed above.[50]

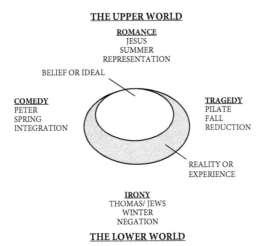

---

[49] Similarly, Cahill develops the idea of a "center" as a point of exchange in, P. J. Cahill, "The Johannine Logos as Center," *Catholic Biblical Quarterly* 38 (1976): 54–72.

[50] While the chart's main purpose is to illustrate the synchronic relationship of belief/ideal to reality/experience, it may be noted that this pattern is diachronically analogous to the Biblical meta-narrative of innocence, fall, experience, redemption, and consummation. The movement through representation, reduction, and negation parallels the history of Biblical studies (itself a mirror of intellectual history) since the Middle Ages as outlined by Hans Frei in *The Eclipse of Biblical Narrative: A Study in Eighteenth and Nineteenth Century Hermeneutics* (New Haven, CT, and London: Yale University Press, 1974). Frei's own work on narrative is an attempt at integration of some kind. Although it will not be attempted in detail here, Biblical studies of most kinds may be broadly classified according to ideas and relationships shown on the chart.

In romance, the representation of one thing in terms of another is assumed to be adequate; the knight is an adequate representation of his ideals and his life is a virtual embodiment of some ideal, the representation of an ideal being the theme of romance. In the FG, Jesus as man is assumed to represent the qualities of love and obedience, and as a man Jesus also represents God himself. Likewise, when Jesus speaks of being "born again" or "living water," he assumes a theological reality cast in metaphorical language and invites his listeners to move away from a literalistic way of thinking toward a way of thinking that is at once metaphorical and equally theologically meaningful. In romance, reality is assumed to be infused with meaning, giving rise to expectations that objects and events carry meanings larger than themselves. Metaphor and symbol, so common in romance and the FG, are the inevitable result.

In metonymy a fundamental reduction takes place. "All people" are reduced to a constituent part by the expression "all hands." Conceptually the part stands for the whole with an emphasis on the part. "All people" are reduced to "all hands," the people being reduced by being characterized through their implied function as workers. In metonymy, the more or less integrated conception of metaphor gives way to a fractured part/part or whole/part relationship wherein one element stands in a relationship of *reduction* to the other. Likewise, in tragedy a reduction takes place wherein the integrated world and ideals and beliefs held by the protagonist are exposed as inadequate. The protagonist is seen to be reduced by being separated from his/her ideals. Further, the protagonist is seen to have a representative function for humanity in that the protagonist stands as a part in relation to the whole of humanity, giving rise to the theme of sacrifice implicit in tragedy even though, by reduction, the sacrifice of the tragic protagonist is viewed as inadequate. Conceptually, the tragic protagonist moves to a position in which beliefs and ideals are reduced and exceeded by the demands of reality. However, the validity of those ideals remains, even if vestigially, however much particular circumstances call the enactment of those ideals into question. Metonymy and tragedy stand between metaphor and romance on the one hand and between irony as a trope and irony/satire as an archetype on the other.

In synecdoche a fundamental integration takes place. In White's example, "he is all heart," qualities represented figuratively by "heart" become integrated as a conceptual description of what is intrinsic to the person as a whole. In synecdoche, the part is seen as integrated with a whole greater than the sum of the parts, yet the part retains its own integrity. For example, "crown" in synecdoche stands conceptually for rulership or kingship or authority rather than simply for a ruler as it would in metonymy. "Crown" implies more than a king or queen in a way opposite to the way "all hands" stands for "all people." Comedy as an archetype displays the living movement of an individual's or group's integration with a larger whole, whether marriage, society, self-knowledge, salvation, or some other laudable goal. Misunderstandings, obstacles, and mistakes typify the comic movement toward integration. In the FG, Peter struggles to integrate his belief in Jesus with what his belief means in terms of practical experience.

White characterizes metaphor, metonymy, and synecdoche as naive in the sense that "they can be deployed only in the belief in language's capacity to grasp the nature of things in figurative terms."[51] In contrast, irony stands as the mode of negation. White observes, "The trope of Irony, then, provides a linguistic paradigm of a mode of thought which is radically self-critical with respect not only to a given characterization of the world of experience *but also to the very effort to capture adequately the truth of things in language.*"[52] Metaphor, metonymy, and synecdoche lend themselves to the expression of some ideal or belief in a way that the negation characteristic of irony does not. Irony as an archetype relies on two levels of perception, as do the other tropes, but its characteristic negation works against any kind of integration. Irony *as a mode of thinking* (as opposed to a literary structure) emphasizes the difficulty or impossibility of reality being integrated with a belief or ideal in a way that is not illusory, where one level cannot be integrated with another. In the FG, irony as an archetype and literary structure is employed in a sophisticated way to ironize irony as a way of thinking by negation characterized in different ways by Thomas and the Jews. To Nicodemus and the Samaritan woman, references to "born again" and "living water" begin in literalism and misunderstanding and invite a move through synecdoche to metaphor in its fullest sense, or, in other words, from irony to comedy to romance. The archetypes may be viewed by analogy as narrative extensions of the various tropes or, conversely, the tropes as tropological compressions of the various archetypes embodied in specific characters in the FG.

Frye associates each archetype with a particular season of the year and thus reinforces the power of his archetypal system by connecting it to the symbolism of the natural world and to the natural world itself. To illustrate the relationship between the four archetypes and their respective seasons and to their implicit relationship of belief and reality, the chart below uses the relationship of a leaf to a tree.

Archetype, Season, and Belief/Reality Relationship

Archetype	Season	Explanation
Romance	Summer	The leaf in living union with the tree in full representation of itself as a complete and living whole.
Tragedy	Fall	The leaf still attached to the tree, but reduced from its living symbiotic union to an altered and dying form of its former self.
Irony	Winter	The realized negation of a living relationship between leaf and tree.
Comedy	Spring	The promise of renewed integration between leaf and tree.

Significantly, the seasons of the year, the stages of the leaf, the four tropes, and the four archetypes all blend into each other in a circular continuum with each perhaps best defined in relation to its opposite.[53] Although fixed by planetary activity, calendar dates as definitive markers of the seasons often seem arbitrary when applied to today's

---

[51] White, *Metahistory*, 36.
[52] Ibid., 37, my emphasis.
[53] Frye notes, "If we think of our experience of these *mythoi*, we shall realize that that they form two opposed pairs. Tragedy and comedy, contrast rather than blend, and so do romance and irony, the champions respectively of the ideal and the actual. On the other hand, comedy blends insensibly into satire at one extreme and into romance at the other; romance may be comic or tragic; tragic extends from high romance to bitter and ironic realism." Frye, *Anatomy*, 162.

weather, as, for example, when a day in fall seems like summer. Yet definite seasonal characteristics exist that allow us to say that spring is not summer and winter is not fall. This blend of continuity and distinction and opposites in relation will be helpful to keep in mind. Frye tends to be more concerned with continuity within and between archetypes, whereas in order to more fully define Frye's archetypal criticism the present work will focus on distinctive feature of each archetype. As shown on the chart above, the relation of belief to reality, whether in literature or theology, will serve as the variable and overall guide to trace continuity, distinction, and relationships within Frye's archetypal system.

Archetype and the specific characters may thus be viewed in parallel according to their conception of the relationship between experience and some belief or ideal. Each archetype may be characterized by the implicit relationship between a belief or ideal on the one hand and reality and experience on the other, a relationship that governs the actual form of a work of literature in terms of plot, character, and setting. Form and meaning, or form and ideology, are linked in a way that is not casual; rather, they are linked in a way that both artist and reader implicitly sense to be true. The difference between an archetypal comic plot and a tragic plot, for example, reflects a fundamental difference in worldview. Each archetype represents a particular point of view or frame of reference that forms the basis for an implicit, common understanding with the reader.

Beliefs comprise part of what has been termed more generally as a "frame of reference." A frame of reference or paradigm is a system or way of thinking about reality that includes active, consciously held beliefs and tacit assumptions about life. Language itself involves a frame of reference or script in which it is to be interpreted. Victor Raskin observes,

> The script is a large chunk of semantic information surrounding the word or evoked by it. The script is a cognitive structure internalized by the native speaker and it represents the native speaker's knowledge of a small part of the world. Every speaker has internalized rather a large repertoire of scripts of "common sense" which represent his/her knowledge of certain routines, standard procedures, basic situations, etc.[54]

Beyond the semantic level, a frame of reference is the ideological, physical, historical, sociological, and psychological context in which a given individual or group interprets reality. In developing his ideas of paradigms and paradigm shifts, Kuhn applies a similar notion to science and scientific revolutions and stresses the idea that science advances only insofar as adequate paradigms arise to facilitate progress.[55] Following a broad but generally sociological approach to what he terms "frame analysis," Goffman notes, "a primary framework is one that is seen as rendering what would otherwise be a meaningless aspect of the scene into something that is meaningful."[56] Life itself, then, involves interpretation, and interpretation is inevitably done through a frame of reference. In literature, the author or narrator provides a frame of reference for the

---

[54] Victor Raskin, *Semantic Mechanisms of Humor* (Boston and Lancaster: D. Reidel Publishing Company, 1985), 81.
[55] Kuhn, *Structure*.
[56] Erving Goffman, *Frame Analysis: An Essay on the Organization of Experience* (Cambridge, MA: Harvard University Press, 1974), 21.

reader and supplies a frame of reference for each character within the narrative. The two may or may not correspond. Here, "frame of reference" will be used primarily in regard to the relationship of a belief or ideal with reality or experience as a convenient way of referring to these issues.

In the FG, the narrator and Jesus generally share a frame of reference not normally shared fully by the other characters. By asserting that "in the beginning was the Word, and the Word was with God, and the Word was God,"[57] the prologue of the FG places the context of the FG in terms of both story and discourse as beginning in eternity past, beyond the creation events narrated in Genesis 1 on which language they draw. The proper context or frame of reference of the FG, and by implication, all of reality, lies beyond temporal creation with God himself. The prologue of the FG thus establishes a conceptual paradigm by which Jesus and the FG are to be interpreted.[58] Comparing the Johannine prologue to its contemporary literature, Harris concludes,

> It is to be remembered that the evangelist, by beginning his work with a prologue, placed the entire work within the literary sphere of Greek religious drama. Consequently it was directed to a widespread readership. . . . The introduction of the Logos into a literary construction which follows the convention of certain ancient Greek prologues in that preparation is vital for a correct understanding of the Johannine gospel. From the prologue onwards the evangelist skillfully unveils the full identity—the metaphysical identity, one might say—of the protagonist of this cosmic drama, the Logos μονογενης θεος, Jesus Christ.[59]

The prologue also informs the reader that the "Word became flesh and made his dwelling among us" (1:14). The context is at once universal and particular. Whatever is said about the Word applies to the flesh and must be taken together in what Culpepper calls a "stereoscopic" reading,[60] however much a rebellious world remains in darkness on this matter.

In summary, each archetype has its own implicit point of view or frame of reference, and each character herein analyzed represents a particular archetype and literary/theological frame of reference within a literary and theological context established by the prologue of the FG.

I. D Archetypal criticism and the Fourth Gospel

However uneasy the relationship may be to its older cousins, the fact remains that in recent years literary studies play a prominent role in Biblical studies. The appearance

---

[57] Unless noted, all scripture quotations are taken from the New International Version.
[58] C. K. Barrett notes, "John intends that the whole of his gospel shall be read in the light of this verse. The deeds and words of Jesus are the deeds and words of God; if this be not true the book is blasphemous." Barrett, *The Gospel According to John: An Introduction with Commentary and Notes on the Greek Text* (London: SPCK, 1978), 156.
[59] Elizabeth Harris, *Prologue and Gospel: The Theology of the Fourth Evangelist*, JSNTSS 107 (Sheffield: Sheffield Academic Press, 1994), 195.
[60] R. Allan Culpepper, *Anatomy of the Fourth Gospel: A Study in Literary Design* (Philadelphia: Fortress Press, 1983), 33.

in 1983 of *The Anatomy of the Fourth Gospel* by Robert Culpepper, who had previously approached the FG very much in the historical/critical tradition, established literary approaches to the FG in the mainstream and granted them status not previously attained. Although criticized by some as anachronistic,[61] Culpepper's *Anatomy* is generally a modest and straightforward work, employing such traditional features of literary criticism as plot and character, along with the more recent concerns of narrator and point of view, narrative time, implicit commentary, and the implied reader. Culpepper makes limited and cautious use of Frye's archetypes and will be referred to later. Culpepper's main purpose in *Anatomy* is simply to make known and explain certain literary features of the FG with an emphasis on reader response criticism. As such, it tends to be more of a literary handbook to the FG and less of a sustained argument or work of theology, a limitation that is at once an asset and arguably contributes to the timeless quality and enduring influence of this landmark book.

While Culpepper's *Anatomy* remains the classic, perhaps no other writer has written as extensively on literary approaches to the FG than Mark Stibbe. Stibbe's *The Gospel of John as Literature: An Anthology of Twentieth-Century Perspectives* offers a valuable historical survey of the field as well as representative examples of various methodologies and perspectives, from reader response and structural criticism to the more ideologically inclined feminist criticism. In *John as Storyteller* (1992), Stibbe attempts to integrate literary criticism of the FG with historical/critical concerns as well as covering the gamut from an emphasis on the author, the text, and the reader. *John's Gospel* (1994) is an effort to read the FG through various literary methodologies. Stibbe is impressively eclectic in the approaches he employs.

More than anyone else, Stibbe has attempted to apply Frye's archetypal approach to the FG.[62] Rather than connecting archetype to character, as Frye tends to do and will be done here, Stibbe relates Frye's archetypes to discrete sections of the FG,[63] a proposal that, Murphy believes, undermines the unity of the FG.[64] Unfortunately, this difference aside, much of Stibbe's use of archetypes is often mistaken, resulting from an inadequate understanding of the archetypes combined with haphazard application.

---

[61] Mark Stibbe, *John as Storyteller: Narrative Criticism and the Fourth Gospel*, SNTSMS 73 (Cambridge: Cambridge University Press, 1992), 11.

[62] Mark Stibbe, *John's Gospel* (London and New York: Routledge, 1994), 62–72; Stibbe, *John as Storyteller*, 121–47.

[63] Stibbe, *John's Gospel*, 67–70. Stibbe makes good use of this method in applying the archetype of satire to an analysis of 8:31-59. *John's Gospel*, 105–31.

[64] Francesca Murphy observes, "Mark Stibbe claimed that the plot of John's Gospel ultimately obeys the U-shaped curve of comedy. But he does not rest content with this suggestion: he has found all four of Frye's genres in successive stages of the Gospel. Stibbe thinks that we may discover in John the plots of Romance, Tragedy and Satire; it concludes with the 'mythos of comedy' in the Resurrection. It beggars credulity to believe that John's Gospel contains four generic plots, each projecting its own world, and yet converging to create a dramatic and harmonious whole. Shakespeare suggested the possibility, but he was joking." Francesca Murphy, *The Comedy of Revelation: Paradise Lost and Regained in Biblical Narrative* (Edinburgh: T&T Clark, 2000), 229. Perhaps failing to consider the closed nature of drama as compared with the open narrative of the FG, Murphy's dismissal is more cavalier than careful. Unlike the more nuanced if mistaken Stibbe, Murphy reads the parts of the Bible she deals with exclusively and aggressively in terms of comedy. Against Murphy, it will be argued here that the FG contains the four archetypal plots, but as applied to characters rather than discrete sections. Jesus's story certainly differs from that of Pilate and Peter.

In a particularly egregious example, Stibbe designates the narrative of the Samaritan woman as romance because in Frye's conception of things romance relates to summer, and the encounter by the well takes place at noon in the hot sun.[65]

Significantly, use of Frye's archetypes and the use of "comedy" and "tragedy" as generic terms are common in literary criticism of the Bible.[66] "Comedy" and "tragedy" are often used to refer to little more than the shape of the plot as it relates to a happy or sad ending.[67] "Comedy" is also made to refer to any reading of a Biblical text seen to contain humor, even if such humor owes its existence to a reading strategy that is conceptually ironic and parasitic.[68] Additionally, comedy and/or tragedy, unless stretched to the breaking point and beyond, cannot account for much of the data.[69] And, as opposites, no accounting is offered of possible forms existing between them.[70] If archetypal criticism is to have significant explanatory value whether specifically designated "archetypal criticism" or not, it must be established on a more definitive basis than at present. One of the goals of this work will be to examine and clarify the basic components of Frye's archetypes in greater depth than has been previously attempted, especially as they relate to theology and Biblical studies, and thus provide a much needed stabilization of the four points of the archetypal literary compass. As noted, in Frye's case some of the confusion may be traced to Frye's allusive method of argument combined with an emphasis on continuity between and within the four archetypes.[71] The present work differs from Frye in this respect and will attempt to offer a more fixed accounting of the salient features of each archetype, a clarification that, it is hoped, will prove useful to literary studies applied to any portion of the Bible.[72]

Stibbe closes *John as Storyteller* with the following remarks:

> Of particular value will be studies devoted to the revelatory function of the narrative form. The next step from a book such as this must surely be to ask the following question: "If John's story is revelatory, then how much of that sense of disclosure is due to John's exploitation of the narrative form?"[73]

Part of the answer to this very large question will be to examine archetypes in the FG and relate them to their theological significance. Previous literary treatments of the FG

---

[65] Stibbe, *John's Gospel*, 67.
[66] Besides Stibbe and Culpepper, see Leland Ryken, *Words of Delight: A Literary Introduction to the Bible*, 2nd ed. (Grand Rapids: Baker, 1992).
[67] For a balanced but skeptical assessment, see Yair Zakovitch, "and in the Bible," *Semeia: Tragedy and Comedy in the Bible* 32 (1984): 106–14.
[68] For a representative of this the approach, see William J. Whedbee, *The Bible and the Comic Vision* (Cambridge: Cambridge University Press, 1998).
[69] The remarks on Murphy, (see note above) also apply to the point.
[70] For example, Good reads Dan. 1-6 as comedy when it is better taken as romance, or, as Ryken does, as a hero story. See Edwin Good, "Apocalyptic as Comedy: The Book of Daniel," *Semeia: Tragedy and Comedy in the Bible* 32 (1984): 41–70; Ryken, *Words of Delight*, 109–114. Ryken observes (109) that the story of Daniel (1-6) is "thoroughly governed by the principle of heroic narrative."
[71] Frye divides each archetype into six phases, a subtlety not attempted here.
[72] For example, Good mistakenly reads Daniel as comedy whereas Ryken correctly identifies it as "hero story," a designation much more in keeping with romance. See Good, "Apocalyptic as Comedy"; Ryken, *Words of Delight*, 109–25.
[73] Stibbe, *John as Storyteller*, 199.

offer no integrated literary or theological cosmos and are generally piecemeal attempts at applying particular approaches to particular texts. Unlike Stibbe's gentle probing of the FG's soil with a variety of tools, certainly valuable, the present effort is an attempt to utilize one approach, archetypal criticism, to maximum effect and do so with a view toward synchronically comparing the FG with other literature. Although conceived with different methodology with respect to its analysis of discrete narrative units, Dorothy Lee's *The Symbolic Narratives of the Fourth Gospel* is an impressive effort to integrate narrative analysis with the FG's theology,[74] an effort that in this work is hoped to be carried on in a different but related way. The present work is to a great degree an attempt to clarify and expand the FG's use of the narrative form by way of a comparison with other forms of literature by means of Frye's formulation of archetypal criticism.

I. E Goals, objectives, and qualifications

The goal of this work is a sustained, rigorous, and mutually illuminating dialogue between literature and theology facilitated by the four archetypes of romance, tragedy, irony, and comedy within a dialogue to be conducted specifically with reference to Jesus, Pilate, Thomas and the Jews, and Peter as they appear in the FG. Christian theology will be brought to bear on literature and, conversely, literature and literary studies may be seen as a legitimate avenue for exploration of certain enduring theological themes. This dialogue will cross barriers between literature and theology in a way that, it is hoped, will prove mutually illuminating for archetypal criticism, for understanding of Jesus, Pilate, the Jews and Thomas, and Peter as literary characters in the FG, and for literature and theology as separate but related disciplines.

Along the way, a number of goals or benefits may be suggested: (1) to suggest a way ahead for the comparison and/or integration of literature and theology by means of archetypal criticism; (2) to demonstrate the validity and usefulness of archetypal criticism in Biblical studies; (3) to establish the correct archetype for each of the five characters examined; (4) to define archetypes in relation to an inherent and variable relationship between belief or ideal and reality and experience; (5) to define these archetypes from a theological point of view in relation to readily recognizable specific reference points; and (6) to point to a manner, mode, or habit of reading the Bible theologically and literarily as a way of moving toward a fuller appreciation of these two disciplines as opposed to applying literary analysis of the Bible without reference to its theology.

These goals will, however, be limited and defined by the methodology and ideology employed. There are three important elements: the limits of analogy and comparison, the strength of each individual analogy and comparison, and the limits of suggested theological conclusions. First, by using analogical reasoning in terms of comparison and contrast, "proof" can only be relative; there can be no conclusive proof as such. With any such undertaking, it is difficult to say "this proves that." True or false is possible only in the sense that analogies and comparisons are appropriate and

---

[74] A less successful attempt is Gail O'Day's *Revelation in the Fourth Gospel: Narrative Mode and Theological Claim* (Philadelphia: Fortress Press, 1986). See Chapter 3 below.

illuminating rather than inappropriate and misleading. It is not so much the intention of the present work to "prove" that, for example, Peter is a comic character as much as it is to show that Peter can be best interpreted as a comic character and that a valuable and illuminating comparison can be made. Although the FG is most like a romance, in no way is it argued or implied that the FG *is* a romance, tragedy, anti-romance (irony and satire), or comedy. It is asserted only that certain elements of the FG, namely, Jesus, Pilate, the Jews and Thomas, and Peter as they appear in the FG, may be analyzed and illuminated in terms of their respective archetypes and by being compared to other literature and characters typified by the same archetype. Archetype, then, is a means of comparison, a point of exchange. The present work is conceived in view of the limitations of comparison and analogy, and these must be kept in mind as a general principle. The very nature of analogy demands the imaginative and poetic. Jasper's comment that "literary readings of the Bible hover between the imaginative and poetic, and the academic" is quite appropriate here.[75]

Second, any analogy or comparison is not above evaluation by virtue of being an analogy or comparison, but must be evaluated in terms of analogy and comparison. Thus, for example, if Jesus is better explained with reference to tragedy rather than romance or if Pilate is unconvincingly compared to Oedipus, the analogy and comparison is weakened or rendered invalid. On this ground, there is ample space for analysis. As a practical consideration, rather than tediously evaluating the strength or weakness of each element of each comparison and subjecting the reader to the death of a thousand qualifications, except at points of obvious contention, comparisons will be offered and presented as if valid, legitimate, or true. The same goes for qualifications related to the principle of analogy: the limitations of analogy have been noted.

The strength of the connections between literature and theology will depend on the principle of analogy, the strength of those analogies, and, third, the faith commitments brought to bear on the principle of analogy with respect to a Christian worldview. However much a work of this kind invites a provisional assumption of its own point of view, the goal at present is not to "prove" a Christian point of view. Rather, it is written with a Christian point of view as its primary and governing point of reference. Additionally, as a coherentist effort, the conclusion of the argument is the same as the premise; the strength of the "argument" can only be the strength of the connections made from and within such a worldview according to tacit assumptions of their validity. It is the limitation of the principle of analogy applied to interpretation from and within a particular worldview. The validity of the principle analogy and the validity of a Christian point of view are mutually interpenetrating assumptions in the present work. The middle ground on which evaluation of the components of this interaction leading to an increased understanding between literature and theology is to occur is the particular and comprehensive strength of its many analogies and comparisons. By conjoining archetypal criticism and characters in the FG, the twin visions of literature and theology will be focused close and distant, however well or poorly, into a single vision of a single cosmos.

---

[75] David Jasper, "Literary Readings of the Bible: Trends in Modern Criticism," in *The Bible and Literature: A Reader*, eds. David Jasper and Stephen Prickett (Malden, MA: Blackwell, 1999), 52.

2

The Fourth Gospel, Jesus, and Romance

II. A Introduction

The relative unfamiliarity of romance as a term designating a recognized body of literature with certain distinctive qualities is a fact of life. At the same time, the commonness of romance and its qualities and themes is surprising, finding present-day expression in westerns and science fiction, both in fiction and in film, and other venues where imaginative and heroic qualities predominate. Like tragedy and comedy, romance cannot be confined to any one genre (drama, novel, etc.). Significant elements of romance can be found in works as diverse as *The Odyssey*, *The Tempest*, *Pilgrim's Progress*, *Moby Dick*, and Tolkien's *Lord of the Rings* trilogy. Indeed, in viewing fiction as a "total verbal order," Northrop Frye holds that "romance is the structural core of all fiction."[1] For the moment, a romance can be defined as an episodic hero story or quest that features a conflict between an ideal and its opposite within a context of signs, wonders, and the marvelous. Another reference point for understanding romance is *The Chronicles of Narnia*: when Peter, Susan, Edmund, and Lucy pass through the wardrobe into Narnia, they move from the world of the novel into the world of romance.

The ubiquity of romance as an archetype has much to do with its being expansive, open, and inclusive. Consequently, it often goes unrecognized. Conversely, tragedy is characterized by concentration and a definitive ending, while comedy is characterized by confusion and misunderstanding moving toward integration and a realization of a desired goal. Romance both ends where tragedy begins and picks up where comedy leaves off and assumes from the start an integration and an openness to all things imaginative and fantastic. Romance tends to move through something more than moving toward something else. Romance, it will be argued, is the archetype that applies best to Jesus and the FG as a whole.

---

[1] Northrop Frye, *The Secular Scripture: A Study of the Structure of Romance* (London: Harvard University Press, 1976), 14.

II. B Romance, the Fourth Gospel, and Jesus

II. B. 1 The Fourth Gospel as romance in critical opinion

As might be expected, controversy surrounds the archetype that best fits the FG. Following Frye's method of classifying literature in terms of four *mythoi*, Culpepper cautiously designates the FG as being most like a romance. He observes,

> As romance inclines towards myth the hero may possess attributes of divinity, but the conflict "takes place in, or at any rate primarily concerns, *our* world."[2] The relevance of a *mythos* [romance] so described is obvious. In the Gospel of John, Jesus, who has descended from the world above, is unrecognized except by a privileged few. As he strives to fulfill his mission, preliminary minor "adventures" (i.e., signs and conflicts with opponents) begin to reveal his identity. He is faced with a crucial struggle, his own death, which he accepts and thereby finishes his task successfully: "It is finished" (19:30). Although triumph takes the form of apparent defeat, he is recognized by his followers as "my Lord and God" (20:28).[3]

Culpepper's discomfort with the romance designation wins out in the end. He notes that "the fit is certainly not perfect. The gospels are clearly very different from other members of this genre or *mythos*. Only when the general shape of the *mythos* is considered somewhat abstractly do the gospels begin to fit in."[4] Culpepper's hesitation is well founded, but perhaps he sees more problems than possibilities.[5] No work of literature fits any genre or *mythos* exactly, and only when considered somewhat abstractly does any work (or object; trees, for example) fit into any classification, a qualification that applies to reading the Gospels as Greek *bioi* (biography) as well.[6] Classification of any kind is an exercise in comparison and as such it is an exercise in exploring similarities and differences. In the case of the FG, the differences present challenges as much as the similarities present opportunities; the struggle is to illumine rather than obfuscate through the process of comparison and contrast.

Stibbe rejects the designation of the FG as romance. Instead, he finds the closest parallel, especially to the passion narrative, in the *mythos* of tragedy and offers Euripides's *Bacche* for comparison. Significantly, both *The Bacche* and the FG feature a God appearing on earth in the form of a man who remains unrecognized by those

---

[2] Frye, *Anatomy of Criticism*, 187.
[3] Culpepper, *Anatomy*, 83.
[4] Ibid., 84.
[5] Culpepper might well have followed through his flirtation with labeling the plot of the FG as romance. His actual analysis of the plot of the FG fits very well with the plot of a romance and seems only to lack a systematic study and comparison with salient features of romance plot. See Culpepper, *Anatomy*, 84–98.
[6] See, Richard Burridge, *What Are the Gospels? A Comparison with Greco-Roman Biography* (Cambridge: Cambridge University Press, 1992). While Burridge's approach is historical and empirical, it is nonetheless analogical and comparative.

to whom he appears, giving rise to a number of striking parallels.[7] But in terms of the final shape of the plot and the character of the god/God involved, there are radical differences that Stibbe fails to take into account. Whereas Dionysus resorts to deception and guile and is vindictive and spiteful, Jesus comes to reveal and is full of mercy and love. Rejection brings out the best in Jesus, the worst in Dionysus, and here is where the two plots are crucially different. The mercy and self-sacrifice of Jesus at the point when Dionysus is most revolting prompts Stibbe to observe that the story of Jesus subverts the conventions of tragedy.[8]

But this comment begs the question of how much the FG and the story of Jesus conform to the *mythos* of tragedy and whether or not Jesus is a tragic figure in chapters 18 and 19 or anywhere else. Stibbe does not explicitly say Jesus is a tragic *figure*, but implies as much when he states, "The death of Jesus in John's gospel is archetypally tragic." Elsewhere he endorses the views of "very influential secular literary critics and theorists who have regarded the gospel story of Jesus as the archetypal tragic story."[9] Furthermore, the FG is manifestly about Jesus, and, as Stibbe himself notes, "the identification of the genre of John 18–19 depends therefore on our ability to identify the basic image of Jesus, the hero of that story."[10] Much is therefore at stake in the identification of the story of Jesus.

Stibbe's confusion results from inaccurately identifying several elements taken from Aristotle's analysis of tragedy in his *Poetics* with this or that group in the FG. For example, he applies Aristotle's notion of *hamartia* to the Jews and their rejection of Jesus.[11] But *hamartia* is properly a quality applied to the protagonist of a tragedy, who in this case would be Jesus, impossible on the terms of the FG because Jesus is nowhere seen as fallen, sinful, or mistaken. Elsewhere Stibbe applies the term *anagnorisis*, or recognition, to the fact that neither Pentheus from *The Bacche* nor the people of Jesus's day recognized who Jesus was. Again, *anagnorisis* properly applies to recognition on the part of the protagonist who remains ignorant of certain facts or perceptions until a moment of recognition or *anagnorisis* that comes too late to alter the course of events. Jesus is hardly ignorant of anything and the Jews never recognize Jesus. Pilate, as will be argued later, is a tragic character complete with *hamartia* who undergoes precisely such an *anagnorisis*. In tragedy, recognition and reversal are consequent on the protagonist undergoing a destruction of self in terms of circumstance and self-identity.[12] While doubtless there are elements of tragedy in the FG in general and specifically in chapters 18 and 19, the tragic character and the center of the tragic story in this passage is Pilate and not Jesus. Rather than subverting the *mythos* of tragedy as Stibbe argues, Jesus is not a tragic figure nor is his story best identified with the tragic archetype. Stibbe's analysis of Jn 18–19 in comparison with *The Bacche* illuminates

---

[7] Stibbe, *John as Storyteller*, 134–35.
[8] Ibid., 144.
[9] Ibid., 138. Stibbe cites Frye (*Anatomy*, 36) in his defense. Frye, not always consistent, has been cited in the present work as designating Jesus as corresponding to the archetype of romance.
[10] Stibbe, *John as Storyteller*, 123.
[11] Ibid., 137.
[12] See Chapter 3 for a full discussion of Pilate and tragedy.

because it is ever so close to being right, yet obfuscates much by making a fundamental category mistake and by a lack of precision in applying the details of tragedy.

As Culpepper notes, Jesus and his story in the FG most closely resemble romance with its pattern: "the preliminary minor adventures; the crucial struggle, usually some kind of battle in which either the hero or his foe, or both, must die; and the exaltation of the hero."[13] Responding to Culpepper, Stibbe objects that "there is a sense of dreamy wistfulness in romances like *The Faerie Queene* which we certainly do not sense in John's gospel."[14] But this is a matter of presentation and tone rather than archetypal pattern or what Culpepper refers to as the "general shape" of the story. Stibbe also notes that "Jesus' conflicts with the Jews are nothing like the knight's adventures with dragons and other fictive creatures. They are concrete, flesh-and-blood encounters with real, societal evils."[15] But this curiously literal criticism overlooks the representative and symbolic nature of dragons and other obstacles as standing for real dangers met with real selflessness and courage, precisely the qualities evident in Jesus as he met the dragons of his day. Nowhere does Jesus exhibit ignorance, hubris, or character flaws necessary for a figure to be tragic.[16]

Nor can Jesus in the FG be read as comic.[17] In comedy the need typically arises for some outside agency or "miraculous" turn of events to make things right. Jesus is fundamentally the agent of such change rather than its recipient, although Jesus is the recipient of such an action in the resurrection. But the singular fact that Jesus rises from the dead does not make his story a comedy. The comic hero is one whose understandings and pretensions are at some distance from reality, one who stumbles forward in the darkness of misunderstanding. Self-imposed incongruity with one's surroundings and ignorance of a contingent sort moving to some kind of integration are the hallmarks of the comic hero and in no way apply to Jesus.

II. B. 2 Basic elements of romance

Given Frye's four archetypes, the story of Jesus and the FG most nearly resembles romance. There are three important considerations under which romance may be broadly defined. First, the basic archetype of romance consists of a story of a hero[18] who embodies and displays some ideal, a characteristic it shares with epic.[19] The story of the hero takes the form of a quest, an episodic account of the hero's identity with

---

[13] Culpepper, *Anatomy*, 83.
[14] Stibbe, *John as Storyteller*, 126.
[15] Ibid.
[16] Margaret Davies notes, "In spite of the Gospel's tragic elements, therefore, they are not tragedies. Jesus' martyrdom is the unjust humiliation of an innocent man but it is also his final act of obedience to God and it is the way which leads through death to eternal life." Davies, *Rhetoric and Reference in the Fourth Gospel*, JSNTSS 69 (Sheffield: Sheffield Academic Press, 1992), 108.
[17] For a reading of John's Gospel in terms of comedy, see Murphy, *The Comedy of Revelation*, 226–49.
[18] "Hero" will be used in the sense defined in this paragraph, as opposed to the more neutral term "protagonist."
[19] "The main emphasis of Homeric criticism, down to about 1750 at least, has been overwhelmingly thematic, concerned with the *dianoia* or ideal of leadership implicit in the two epics." Frye, *Anatomy*, 53.

that ideal and the maintenance and display of that identity and ideal in the face of challenges and difficulties. Frye gives the following account of romance:

> The complete form of the romance is clearly the successful quest, and such a completed form has three main stages: the stage of the perilous journey and the preliminary minor adventures; the crucial struggle, usually some kind of battle in which either the hero or his foe or both, must die; and the exaltation of the hero. We may call these three stages respectively, using Greek terms, the *agon* or conflict, the *pathos* or death-struggle, and the *anagnorisis* or discovery, the recognition of the hero, who has clearly proved himself to be a hero even if he does not survive the conflict.[20]

The hero is identified with the ideal such that representing and maintaining the ideal is synonymous with preservation of the self. Rather than being selfish, the hero embodies a kind of universal selflessness. The hero exceeds the pressure of circumstances and maintains an ideal worthy of death. White observes,

> The Romance is fundamentally a drama of self-identification symbolized by the hero's transcendence of the world of experience, his victory over it, and his final liberation from it—the sort of drama associated with the Grail legend or the story of the resurrection of Christ in Christian mythology. It is a drama of the triumph of good over evil, of virtue over vice, of light over darkness, and of the ultimate transcendence of man over the world in which he was imprisoned by the fall.[21]

Although subject to changing external circumstances, the hero tends to be essentially a static character, one who remains the ideological and narrative center of the story, a character who is revealed and reveals. Culpepper notes,

> The plot [of the FG] is a plot of action in the sense that Jesus achieves his goals while his fortune apparently changes for the worse. It is a plot of character only in the sense that it is bound up with his moral character and the threats to it, for Jesus is a static character.[22]

In romance, the hero is, poetically speaking, without or very nearly without flaws but is subject to tests and challenges in the course of events. As such, romance is fundamentally related to epic and shares these qualities with the FG. The hero is tempted and tried, but the struggle is to maintain an ideal that is readily apparent, not to struggle toward integration or destruction in doubt and perplexity as is typical of comedy and tragedy. To view the FG and the story of Jesus as comedy or tragedy is to mistakenly view a particular phase of Jesus's changing external fortunes as definitive of the whole.

---

[20] Frye, *Anatomy*, 187.
[21] White, *Metahistory*, 8–9.
[22] Culpepper, *Anatomy*, 88.

While epic and romance share the fundamental characteristics of a hero who embodies and represents an ideal, the former gave way to the latter in historical development. Ker observes,

> The victory of the Norman knights over the English axemen has more than a fanciful or superficial analogy to the victory of the new literature of chivalry over the older forms of heroic narrative. The history of those two orders of literature, of the earlier Epic kinds, followed by the various types of medieval Romance, is parallel to the general political history of the earlier and the later Middle Ages, and may do something to illustrate the general progress of the nations. The passage from the earlier "heroic" civilisation to the age of chivalry was not made without some contemporary record of the "form and pressure" of the times in the changing fashions of literature, and in successive experiments of the imagination.[23]

Ker's analysis points to a substantial development but at the same time demonstrates a fundamental link between the two. However much they may have developed and differ in outward trappings, both function as imaginative projections of the ideals of a particular society, public, and/or private. Noting their differences, Ker continues his comment stating, "Whatever Epic may mean, it implies some weight and solidity; Romance means nothing, if it does not convey some notion of mystery and fantasy."[24] Although Ker shows a marked preference for epic over romance, his comment points to the epic tendency toward the objective as compared to the tendency in romance for the subjective, differences that might be termed, respectively, "landscape" and "soulscape." And, traditionally but not exclusively, the epic portrays the destiny of a nation as embodied in its heroes, for example, Aeneas of Virgil's *Aeneid*, whereas in romance the focus tends to be more on the individual.[25] Yet, to use an analogy from cathedral architecture reflecting something of the change from "solidity" to "fantasy," the change from Romanesque to Gothic style by no means implies a change in essential form, purpose, or motivation of the building itself.[26] It need not be assumed, as Ker seems to imply, that mystery and fantasy, taken on their own terms, exclude weight and solidity, however much they may tend in that direction.

In Clara Reeve's *The Progress of Romance*, an old (1785) but still significant work, a central theme is that romance, despite the tendency to decry romance and venerate epic, deserves to be taken seriously in its own right, is fundamentally related to epic, and may seriously be compared to it. The common ground between them is the hero who embodies some virtue or virtues. She writes,

> By fixing a clear and certain meaning to it [romance], not of my own invention or judgment; but borrowing the idea of the Latinists, I would call it simply an *Heroic*

---

[23] W. P. Ker, *Epic and Romance: Essays on Medieval Literature* (London: Macmillan and Co., 1926), 4.
[24] Ker, *Epic and Romance*, 4.
[25] *The Complete Romances of Chretien de Troyes*, trans. with an introduction by David Staines (Bloomington and Indianapolis: Indiana University Press, 1990), xxvii.
[26] Commenting on Ker's point, Eugene Vinaver writes, "What distinguishes one literary generation or one epoch from another is surely not the stories they tell but the way they tell them." *The Rise of Romance* (Oxford: The Clarendon Press, 1971), 1-2.

fable—a fabulous Story of such actions as are commonly ascribed to heroes, or men of extraordinary courage and abilities.—Or if you would allow of it, I would say an Epic in prose.[27]

They [romance and epic] spring from the same root—they describe the same actions and circumstances—they produce the same effects, and they are continually mistaken for each other.[28]

More recently, Burrow links epic and romance under the term *epic romance* and employs the treatment of pity and sympathy as a common ground for study.[29]

If romance is taken as the story of a hero who embodies and represents an ideal, the range of subject matter can be as light as *Daphnis and Chloe*, an early Greek romance wherein the two main characters embody the pastoral ideals of chastity (for the most part) and innocence, to the weight, solemnity, and scope of *The Song of Roland*, a twelfth-century French epic featuring the heroic stand of the Christian Roland in the face of certain defeat by the Saracens. The basic format thus extends from the lighthearted tone and subject matter typical of comedy to the heaviness of tone and subject that extends through epic and into tragedy.[30]

The hero in romance must face real situations and in this sense suffers real consequences; but to the extent that the hero maintains the ideal, the exigencies of circumstance are of secondary importance. Heroes thus preserve their identity and determine their ultimate destiny because that identity is fundamentally about adherence to an ideal rather than contingent circumstances. As a realized, embodied ideal generally free from doubt and perplexity acting in accordance with an ideal, the hero is an active, causal agent rather than the hapless victim of the impersonal causal forces of chance and fate. In contrast, the tragic protagonist is destroyed through adherence to a set of beliefs proven by events to be flawed or unworkable in a particular circumstance and thus something of the tragic protagonist's identity is destroyed as well. The beliefs and actions of the comic protagonist are self-caused, but assumed to be false or deficient, although ultimately harmless. In their own way, tragedy and comedy feature an ideal, but one qualified by circumstance. In contrast, an ironic

---

[27] Clara Reeve, *The Progress of Romance*, Colchester edition of 1785N (New York: The Facsimile Text Society, 1930), 13.

[28] Reeve, *Progress of Romance*, 16. These two quotations are offered in place of the following one supplied virtually any time Reeve is quoted; "The Romance is an heroic fable, which treats of fabulous persons and things. The Novel is a picture of real life and manners, and of the times in which it is written. The Romance in lofty and elevated language, describes what never happened nor is likely to happen" (*Progress*, 111). Taken by itself, this quotation connotes a negative view of romance very much at odds with the overall theme of the book. Similar to her treatment of romance, Reeve's concern with the novel relates to its portrayal of virtue, a standard employed to judge the merits of numerous individual works.

[29] Colon Burrow, *Epic Romance: Homer to Milton* (Oxford: Clarendon Press, 1993).

[30] Indeed, a similar point extends to *The Iliad* and *The Odyssey*, the former tending toward tragedy the latter toward comedy. Frye remarks, "I shall begin with a similar dichotomy about literary criticism. I may express it, in the manner of Coleridge, by saying that all literary critics are either Iliad critics or Odyssey critics. That is, interest in literature tends to center either in the area of tragedy, realism, and irony, or in the area of comedy and romance." Frye, *A Natural Perspective: The Development of Shakespearean Comedy and Romance* (San Diego, NY, and London: Harvest/Harcourt Brace Javonovich, 1965), 1.

perspective is one characterized by negation, a perspective ranging in scope from one in which a departure from an ideal is recognized to one in which any ideal is held to be false and illusory.

In addition to the portrayal of Jesus as a heroic character, another reason why romance is the archetype closest to and most appropriate for the FG as a whole is that romance features an open and inclusive narrative pattern. Dean observes,

> The narrative multiplicity of romance, each tale bound within terms of its own continuity and defined by the separate character of its interaction with the surrounding tales, creates a dynamic and unresolved pattern.[31]
>
> Romance is not a genre confined to one literary technique, such as prose or poetry, nor is it strictly confined to a set number of stylistic features, such as the use of irony or ornate diction. The generic quality of romance is far too diverse, too rich in contrast, to tie it down to a fixed set of ordering principles. It is the supreme example of a literary genre which achieves unity in multiplicity and full expression as a genre by utilizing a wide variety of literary forms.[32]

Ker makes a similar statement about epic:

> Epic poetry is one of the complex and comprehensive kinds of literature, in which most of the other kinds may be included—romance, history, comedy; *tragical, comical, historical, pastoral* are terms not sufficiently various to denote the variety of the *Iliad* and the *Odyssey*.[33]

This point is important. Romance and epic can entertain the surrounding tales of tragedy and comedy in a way that comedy and tragedy (especially) cannot. The relationship is not reciprocal in any straightforward way. Tragedy and comedy are not archetypes of diversity after the manner of romance and are simply unable to host all the same literary guests with quite the same grace. Significantly, material provided by the epics of Homer is expanded and developed by the later tragic poets and not the reverse. The issue is not simply one of chronology. It is difficult to imagine how *The Iliad* and *The Odyssey* could have arisen from Greek tragedy. According to Aristotle, "Again, the poet should remember what has been often said, and not make an Epic structure into a Tragedy—by an Epic structure I mean one with a multiplicity of plots—as if, for instance, you were to make a tragedy out of the entire story of the *Iliad*."[34] The open and expansive nature of romance and epic is a point that bears some emphasis and will be discussed below in relation to story and plot. Apart from accepting the complexity, diversity, and interwoven and episodic nature of this style of narrative—a narrative that at the same time achieves a fundamental unity on its own terms—romance will

---

[31] John Dean, *Restless Wanderers: Shakespeare and the Pattern of Romance* (Salzburg: Salzburg Studies in English Literature 86, 1979), 9.
[32] Dean, *Wanderers*, 87.
[33] Ker, *Epic and Romance*, 16, his emphasis.
[34] Aristotle, *Aristotle's Poetics*, trans. S. H. Butcher, Introduction, Francis Fergusson (New York: Hill and Wang, 1961), XVIII.4, 91.

remain elusive. At the same time, any attempt to view the narrative of the FG as comic or tragic fails to account for the diversity of its narrative.[35]

Finally, while the FG is primarily the story of Jesus, it is also the story of Peter, Pilate, the Jews, and many others. Each of these characters corresponds in varying degrees to different archetypal patterns. Jesus is best described by the basic pattern of a romance, Pilate by tragedy, and the Jews and Thomas by anti-romance, or satire and irony, and Peter by comedy, designations forming much of the substance of the present work. The FG presents these characters swirling in different patterns, at cross-purposes and often in conflict with one another and, most importantly, in conflict with Jesus. As Fletcher notes, "A systematically complicated character will generate a large number of other protagonists who react against or with him in a syllogistic manner."[36] Significantly, conflicts with Jesus are not all of the same type and reflect characteristics and patterns of specific archetypes. To say that the FG follows the tragic or comic archetype is to be partly correct. But to do so will inevitably result in confusion as elements of tragedy, comedy, or romance, certainly present are applied indiscriminately to the wrong person or group, or extended to the FG as a whole. Clarity of category and application is crucial.[37]

What is meant in the present work as romance is broadly defined by these elements: (1) the story of a hero who embodies and represents an ideal who (2) embarks on a journey or quest and undergoes a series of tests (3) portrayed in an expansive, interlacing, and episodic narrative that often includes other stories and characters. Additionally, because beliefs and ideals are usually connected with the transcendent, romance and epic typically include elements of the marvelous. Adopting a term like *heroic romance*, or *epic romance, epic-heroic-romance*, or simply *heroic* or *hero story*, is tempting, but the term *romance*, whatever its inadequacies, in the sense given here will suffice if *romance* is broadly defined as an umbrella term very much related to epic. If the two are not siblings, they are at least first cousins. Given the definition offered here, romance and epic may be seen as variations on the hero story. Whatever the outward trappings of tone and presentation, be they Odysseus's journey toward home, the preservation of life and chastity, or tales of knights and chivalry, or the faithfulness of Jesus to his mission, the archetypal pattern of the story is essentially the same. To focus on the tone or the narrative trappings of a particular time, the armed knights and chivalry of Medieval romance, for example, is to mistake armor and lance for what is really at stake: loyalty to and representation of an ideal under the pressure of circumstance. In this respect, romance assumes the values and ideals it projects, and, whatever the departures from its ideals, offers its own vision of a unified and coherent cosmos.

---

[35] Stibbe rightly argues for the diversity of archetypes in the FG but mistakenly does so on the basis of sections or episodes of the FG rather than as embodied in character. See Stibbe's *John's Gospel*. Frye connects archetype with character.

[36] Angus Fletcher, *Allegory: The Theory of a Symbolic Mode* (Ithaca and London: Cornell University Press, 1964), 35.

[37] Dean comments, "The distinctiveness of romance depends upon its special ability as a genre to absorb and synthesize other literary forms. Regarding romance in terms of only one of its narrative components inevitably leads to a critical distortion of the fine balance of parts which a successful romance must maintain." Dean, *Wanderers*, 221.

In the FG, Jesus defines reality; the world is in darkness, under judgment, and Jesus is the light. Remaining obedient to the Father, Jesus enters the world but does not partake of its sin. Jesus does not need to be integrated into the world and its way of doing things. Rather, the world stands in need of salvation and Jesus, the hero of a different order than comedy and tragedy, the person at one with the ideal represented—the Word made flesh—is the one who accomplishes its redemption.

II. C Romance motifs and the Fourth Gospel

As a way of facilitating a comparison and treating numerous features of Jesus and romance in the FG in a relatively compact fashion, recurring motifs of romance will be examined.[38] This kind of comparison is limited in that it merely attempts to note the existence of features common to both the FG and romance, but at the same time this method offers many striking similarities. In any case, this list and comparison is intended to be illustrative and not definitive or exhaustive. A more in-depth analysis will follow in Section III.

Although his primary concern is Shakespearean romance, Dean begins his *Restless Wanderers: Shakespeare and the Pattern of Romance* with *The Odyssey* and offers a comprehensive and detailed survey of romance. The inclusion of *The Odyssey* is significant in that it gives Dean's analysis wider applicability that extends to epic as well. He lists the following motifs as characteristic of romance: the dramatic qualities of marvel, risk, and triumphant adventure; the emphasis on generation differences; the abundant use of pageantry; the claims to historical relevancy; the wandering journey toward "home"; the essential piety of the main character; the idealized male-female relationships; the protagonists' mental agility; the ever-present mingling of blessings and sorrows; the directing influence of a supernatural higher power; a distinguishing token or scar by which the hero or heroine will eventually be recognized; the shipwreck or apparent loss; and the magical wonders—all of which are bound within an interlacing narrative, ending when the disparate strands are drawn together in a final reunion scene.[39] An analysis of the FG in light of these motifs will highlight a number of similarities.

II. C. 1 Dramatic qualities of marvel, risk, and triumphant adventure

The prologue initially establishes the theme of the marvelous in the FG's discourse through its emphasis on the God of creation being incarnate in the world. In the FG, the marvelous is fundamentally related to risk. Risk becomes important when the

---

[38] In future chapters, close readings of relevant passages will be offered. Given the length of the FG and the amount said about Jesus, this is not possible here.
[39] Dean, *Wanderers*, 3–4. Dean's specific concern here is applying these motifs to *The Odyssey* as a means of demonstrating the Odyssey's qualities of romance. However, Dean intends this list to be representative.

Jews threaten to kill Jesus following his claims to be equal with God arising from the Sabbath healing of the paralytic (5:18). Popular attempts to make him king resulting from the feeding of the five thousand (6:15) present another risk. Jesus risks being misunderstood, whether he was a "good man" or "deceives the people" (7:12) or even demon-possessed (7:20, 8:49), a misunderstanding that is at bottom related to misunderstanding who Jesus really is. The link between risk and the marvelous is most clearly seen in the connection between the raising of Lazarus, a marvelous event, and Caiaphas's declaration that "it is better for you that one man die for the people" (11:50). The raising of Lazarus is thus a key background event for the risk of the triumphal entry and the supreme risk of death itself. Without the marvelous in the FG, either in deeds or theological claims, there is no risk. Adventure implies risk, and the triumphant adventure of the FG originates in Jesus's divine claims as these claims become subject to risk and real consequences in a world that fails to accept them.

II. C. 2 Emphasis on generation differences

The generation differences in the FG involve differences between the new, announced and represented by Jesus, and the old, represented and defended by the Jews. The miracle at Cana in John chapter 2 both affirms the old—marriage and the continuation of life—and announces the new, as seen in the implicitly theological action of the new wine of Christ being created in the jars used for ceremonial washing. While some of the old will be preserved, much will be removed and replaced as the temple cleansing makes clear. Jesus's statement "destroy this temple, and I will raise it again in three days" (2:19) implies a replacement theology where one temple will be replaced by another. Nicodemus, by birth and privilege the quintessential insider of the old generation, must become a member of the new generation by being "born again," this time in a spiritual rebirth. The new generation will be comprised of those who believe, children born "not of natural descent" but "born of God" (1:13). Lazarus is the eschatological prototype of the age to come, an age entered through faith in Christ (11:25-26). Rejection of Lazarus relates to rejection of Jesus and his subsequent death, but only through his death, resurrection, and going away can the next generation be fully realized.

II. C. 3 Abundant use of pageantry

Pageantry and festivals impart a sense of wonder and extraordinariness to quotidian life. Because of the prominent inclusion of Jewish festivals and because it is set primary around Jerusalem, the FG emphasizes this inherently religious aspect. Weddings are a social and religious festival, the latter aspect being especially prominent and employed for thematic purposes in the wedding at Cana. The temple, the primary location of Jewish ceremonial life, is dramatically cleansed at Passover of money changers and sellers of cattle and sheep, those traps and trappings of everydayness that festival and ceremony attempt to overcome. Much of the FG's organization revolves around festivals. Jesus's appearance at the unnamed festival in 5:1 among the blind, the lame, and the paralyzed, itself a carnival of paralysis, leads to the healing of the paralytic, a miracle characterized by a sterile response and opposition. The feeding of the five thousand during the second Passover (6:4) gains additional festive force by the attempt to make him king (6:15) and its association with the provision of manna in the wilderness (6:25ff). Jesus next attends the festival of Tabernacles (7:2, 14) and then the Feast of Dedication (10:22). Having been lavishly anointed, Jesus enters Jerusalem before the final Passover in festive triumph. But Jesus's greatest glory occurs during the humiliation of the passion, presented in the FG with a motif of royal enthronement. Jesus's burial is lavish and moving. Finally, the resurrection appearances speak of the resurrection as a sublime event, a kind of pageantry without ostentation.

II. C. 4 Claims to historical relevancy

Unlike fantasy, which may be set somewhere else in a galaxy far away or a world unlike our own, romance is set in a world like our own. While it is beyond the scope of the present work to debate the historicity of the FG, however present the marvelous, the FG presents the world of its setting as real and historical. Jesus travels around a historically recognizable Palestine and authentically encounters the people, politics, and religion of his day. Any treatment of the FG in terms of the history or society of its day assumes as much. Rather than narrating events for their own sake, the concrete events of the FG are viewed as meaningful and significant within and beyond their specific historical context. In any case, the emphasis falls more on the fact *that* the "word was made flesh and dwelt among us" and its implications rather than emphasizing the facts *of* the flesh dwelling among us.

II. C. 5 The wandering journey toward "home"

The theme of descent (1:10-11, 14, 51) and ascent (7:33, 16:5) is a well-noted feature of the FG.[40] Related to this are references to being sent (5:37; 6:57; 7:29; 8:18, 42) or from above (8:23). Jesus's journey in the FG has two aspects: the journey to the cross and his journey back to the Father. In this sense, the journey of Jesus is both horizontal and vertical; he must return to the Father by way of the cross (13:1a). Yet, like Odysseus's wandering journey toward home, Jesus's journey is purposeful. Jesus's departure is meaningful because he goes "to prepare a place for you" (14:2) so that the Holy Spirit can be sent.

II. C. 6 The essential piety of the main character

The most prominent features of Jesus's piety are love and obedience, qualities that must be manifested in concrete acts. Jesus, the light of the world, does what the Father does. Jesus's love is clearly demonstrated in the raising of Lazarus, the footwashing, comforting his disciples, and supremely on the cross. He is loved, honored, and worshipped by those around him. Even amid an honor and shame culture, the FG presents Jesus as

---

[40] Most notably, Wayne Meeks, "The Man from Heaven in Johannine Sectarianism," *JBL* 91 (1972): 44–72.

preserving his honor in shameful circumstances.[41] Although possessing power to do otherwise, Jesus suffers unjustly and is rejected by friend and enemy alike.[42] Jesus is the theological, ethical, and narrative center of the FG.

II. C. 7 The idealized male–female relationships

The male-female relationships in the FG are more developed than in the Synoptics. To the extent that Jesus's relationships with women can be said to be idealized, such idealization is done in a profoundly real way. As the disciples' reaction indicates (4:27), the most noteworthy aspect of Jesus's conversation with the Samaritan woman is that it occurs at all. On Lazarus's death, Martha and Mary both display faith and disappointment, disappointment seemingly consequent on their brother's death and Jesus's absence. Jesus's relations with the sisters are intimate and genuine; displaying the full depth of his humanity, he shares their suffering and grief. Jesus's encounter with Mary Magdalene is at once close and distant; he approaches her with sensitivity but, on being recognized, eschews sentimental and/or physical attachment and insists that his mission is primary.[43]

II. C. 8 The protagonist's mental agility

Often in romance, mental agility allows the protagonist to escape from some danger, as, for example, the "resourceful" Odysseus. Jesus's encounters with Nicodemus, the Samaritan woman, and Pilate are in a sense clever in that he moves from one level of understanding to another. Many of Jesus's disputes with the Jews are clever, but mostly concern a conflict between two different ways of thinking. If teaching has anything to do with mental agility, the Jews are amazed (7:15). The best example of Jesus's mental agility is perhaps 10:33-39, where Jesus uses the Old Testament (OT) reference to men being called "gods" (Ps. 82:6) to support his claim to be one with the Father (10:30). Although the account of the woman caught in adultery (7:53–8:11) lacks early manuscript support, Jesus soundly (silently?) defeats those attempting to trap him. Pilate's encounter with Jesus shows the latter's mental mastery of the situation even while suffering defeat. Jesus is supremely in control of conversations throughout the FG.

II. C. 9 Ever-present mingling of blessings and sorrows

First introduced by John's statement, "Look, the Lamb of God, who takes away the sin of the world" (1:29): the death of Jesus is a theme throughout the FG. The proleptic

---

[41] See Jerome Neyrey, "Despising the Shame of the Cross: Honor and Shame in the Johannine Passion Narrative," *Semeia* 68 (1994): 113–37.

[42] For a discussion of Jesus as seen positively by elements of Hellenistic culture, see Josephine Massyngbaerde Ford, "Jesus as Sovereign in the Passion According to John," *BTB* 25 (1995): 110–17.

[43] For Lindars, "The desire to hold Jesus must be restrained, because it is an attempt to recapture the conditions of the incarnate life in place of the universal and abiding relationship which is the object of his mission." Barnabas Lindars, *The Gospel of John* (London: Oliphants, 1972), 607.

statement of 2:22 "after he was raised from the dead" makes clear that the death implicit in being "the lamb of God" did in fact occur. But the occurrence of Jesus's death is more than a brute fact: it is a deeply felt loss, a loss given emotional depth by being set generally against the beauty of Jesus's life and specifically set against the presence of Jesus's mother and the other women at the crucifixion (19:25-27) and the lavish anointing by Nicodemus. The wedding at Cana and the incident of the Samaritan woman show Jesus as someone deeply involved in human life. He is someone who in obedience to the Father proclaims himself to be from the Father, and yet is rejected by his own. The raising of Lazarus is as remarkable for its picture of humanity as it is for the raising itself, an event made all the more poignant by its juxtaposition against those coldly planning his demise. Mary's anointing shows that Jesus is deeply loved and worshipped, yet the event signals that the sensibilities and loyalties of Judas are elsewhere. The incident of the footwashing places the pathos of the footwashing itself and Jesus's command to love one another against the background of his betrayal and impending death. Jesus later prays for all believers, yet he is abandoned by two of his inner circle and later abandoned by the wavering Pilate. As he is put to death, Jesus sees to the care of his mother. Jesus's post-resurrection appearance to Mary mixes profound human sorrow with the highest of joys. These incidents–full of love, loss, and joy–create a mood of authentic feeling and pathos characteristic of romance all too easily overlooked in historical/critical analysis.

II. C. 10 The directing influence of a supernatural higher power

The prologue places the mission of Jesus in a profoundly theological context with reference to his earthly ministry, the Word made flesh. Conversely, the witness of John the Baptist (1:19-34) places Jesus in a historical context with reference to his theological identity: the Son of God (1:34) who "comes after me" but was "before me" (1:30). Jesus adds much understanding to the nature of his mission in 5:19ff. Doing nothing by himself, Jesus does only what he sees the Father doing. Thus, Jesus is directed by a "higher power" but not in any mechanistic sense. Having been granted "life in himself" by the Father, Jesus acts on his own but does so in submission to what the Father does, even to the point of rejecting Peter's sword in favor of the cup of the Father. Further, the work of Jesus is frequently seen in light of the scriptures, implicitly affirming the divine ordering of earthly events.

II. C. 11 A distinguishing token or scar by which the hero or heroine will eventually be recognized

The importance of a distinguishing token or scar arises when a period of time or some event separates and casts doubt on the authentic identity of a character which must be established with certainty. The famous scar of Odysseus analyzed by Auerbach serves this function.[44] In a larger sense, the miracles and signs provide "tokens" by which Jesus

---

[44] Erich Auerbach, *Mimesis: The Representation of Reality in Western Literature* (Princeton: Princeton University Press, 1953), 1–20.

might be recognized. These aside, the obvious example of a scar or token is the incident of Thomas being shown the hands and side of Jesus. For Thomas, as for countless others, a mark or token authenticating the identity of someone who reappears is not simply a detail of plot. Rather, the mark or token provides an entry into a world transformed by that person's reappearance. The marks and tokens are real enough, but also serve as real and imaginative links to the marvelous connections between events where no connection seems likely or possible. Conversely, as in the story of Judah and Tamar, the tokens of identity serve as transforming reminders of a concrete past event. However, in the end, the token or mark may establish the identity of the hero, but more importantly, it also vindicates the values and ideals for which the hero stands.

II. C. 12 Shipwreck or apparent loss

The death of Jesus is the central loss in the FG, a loss that does not occur in isolation and, without the resurrection, suggests the following scenarios. For the disciples, the crucifixion is the death of their leader and friend, with whom Peter can never be reconciled. The death of Jesus reverses the clever irony of the incident of the man born blind as the Pharisees, for the moment, were right after all. The life of the resurrected Lazarus becomes a mocking reminder of what might have been or never was. The triumphal entry becomes a foolhardy display of mass optimism. The footwashing becomes a moving farewell instead of a living example. The death of Jesus becomes a kind of shipwreck, the destruction and loss of something good at the hands of forces hostile and capricious. At the same time, the death of Jesus vindicates his enemies. Judas appears to have bet on the winning team. For the Jews, loyalty to Caesar promises to be an effective strategy for the future. The apparent loss of Jesus is a moving story in its own right.

II. C. 13 Magical wonders

Miraculous wonders of various kinds characterize all the four Gospels. However the FG designates some occurrences as "signs." Unlike most romances, however, the miracles and signs of the FG are connected with Jesus as being the agent of their occurrence. Jesus performs the miracle of the turning of the water to wine, feeds the five thousand, and so forth, whereas Odysseus or King Arthur merely participates in the magical wonders within a magical landscape. The miracles are intimately connected with Jesus as the one sent from the Father and bound up with his Christological identity.[45] Others experience the miracles through provision, healing, omniscient knowledge, and raising of the dead.

II. C. 14 Interlacing narrative

The FG contains a variety of characters and a variety of incidents, the structure of which does not resemble the highly ordered plots of, for example, Ruth and Esther

---

[45] See R. Schnackenburg, *The Gospel According to John*, vol. I. trans. Kevin Smyth (London and New York: Burns & Oates, Crossroad, 1980): 515–28; Barrett, *The Gospel According to John*, 75.

or a tragedy like *Oedipus*. Characters come and go; some appear again while others do not. In addition to FG being a mixture of narrative and discourse, the narrative emphasis changes between public and private: the public ministry of 2:1–12:50 gives way to the private emphasis of 13:1–17:26 only to reappear in the crucifixion narratives (18:41–19:42), then returns to the private emphasis as the Gospel closes (20:1–21:25). The interlacing nature of the narratives has been mentioned and will be treated in more depth later.[46]

II. C. 15 An ending when the disparate strands are drawn together in a final reunion scene

The final reunion scenes of the FG are mixed and tenuous; these scenes are not final. The visit to the empty tomb and appearances to Mary, the ten, and finally to the eleven establish the fact of Jesus's resurrection, but the story does not end there. The fishing expedition of chapter 21 is a bit of an anti-climax, a descent into the real world, or, rather, a reminder that the real world and its demands need to be taken seriously. The grand story and events of previous chapters culminate in the resurrection and inaugurate an eternal eschatological reality, an age to come that in the meantime remains in tension with temporal reality as it presently exists. The story of the FG is at once closed, insofar as it concerns Jesus's earthly ministry, and it is also open-ended: the story continues into the present, its characters empowered by the promised Holy Spirit.

In summary, assuming the validity of Dean's characteristics and allowing for a range of similarity with specific characteristics, these parallels between romance and the FG nevertheless indicate a more than passing correspondence and establish a basic plausibility for the more developed comparison between the FG and romance and conceptual analysis to follow.

II. D Structural/conceptual elements: Setting, plot/story, character

II. D. 1 Setting: Romance and realism in the FG

Analogous to the interpenetrating style of narrative characteristic of romance and the overlapping of many of the above characteristics, structural elements of romance very much tend to overlap with conceptual elements. Distinctions between setting, plot/story, and character are useful but often difficult to maintain, a circumstance related to the fact that romance, more than any other archetype, presents a unified vision of a coherent cosmos. The prologue of the FG assumes a coherent cosmos "in the beginning" but notes the present darkness.

As the narrative moves beyond the prologue, John the Baptist announces Jesus to the world, which is followed by his meeting with the disciples. When the first disciples

---

[46] The nature of the FG narrative is discussed under "story and plot" below.

meet Jesus (1:35-51) and begin to follow him, a sense of their being drawn into another reality occurs wherein following Jesus as his disciples is synonymous with a change of perception. Nathanael's ruthlessly horizontal perception of anyone from Nazareth ("Can anything good come from there?") changes radically on experiencing the wonder of being seen under the fig tree ("You are the Son of God."). The assumption of the narrative is that Nathanael, however widespread or justified or mistaken in his opinion of Nazareth, fails to perceive things as they really are. Although Nathanael believed "because I told you I saw you under the fig tree" (1:50), he will see "greater things than that." Jesus's initial contact with the disciples in chapter 1 culminates in the promise that "you will see heaven open, and the angels of God ascending and descending on the Son of Man" (1:51). Recalling Jacob's dream, this reference to heaven being opened indicates that the disciples and readers will, like Jacob, be caught up in events wherein the presence and activity of God will, in the manner of romance, blur the distinction between heaven and earth. Jacob thought "surely the Lord is in this place, and I was not aware of it . . . . How awesome is this place" (Gen. 28:16), yet later wrestled with God in blindness. The angels of God will ascend and descend on the Son of Man; Jesus will become a kind of living ladder, a new Israel, a connection between heaven and earth, making himself more like earth and transforming earth to be more like heaven by virtue of his presence in it.[47]

Following the introductory events of chapter 1, the wedding at Cana is the first miracle and introduces Jesus on the stage of the larger world. The events of the wedding at Cana suggest actual and imaginative links between heaven and earth and exemplify the signs and wonders and atmosphere of the marvelous that is typical of romance. Weddings—then and now—are generally happy and festive occasions full of decoration, costume, ceremony, love, hope, and the promise of human life, and weddings transfer these best of human aspirations to the bride and groom. In a very real way, weddings are those occasions where human life comes closest to the imaginative fullness of heaven, the union of Christ and his bride being cast in precisely these terms. In this context of space and time at a particular wedding where water and six stone jars await, Jesus performs the miracle of turning the water into wine. The wine, the festive drink appropriate for such occasions, runs out. This mundane detail is more than a social gaffe: it is a crack in a crystal glass or a sour note in a symphony, a real and symbolic link to the contingency of quotidian life at a time when the wonder of life is at its fullest. By supplying the wine, Jesus restores some sense of Eden, narrowing the imaginative gap between heaven and earth. And, with consummate grace, Jesus refuses to allow the mere provision of wine to upstage the greater wonder of the wedding. The remarks of the master of the banquet to the bridegroom are as sincere as they are naive; the reader looks on, as the servants do, with wonder and delight. By restoring the wine, Jesus reaches into that highest part of human life and transforms it in a way that slips by so easily unnoticed. The wine is water transformed without fermentation and decay and recalls by contrast another

---

[47] In a context discussing the Jacob's ladder reference of 1:51 and specifically in reference to 3:13, Barrett notes, "The paradox of the Son of man is that even when on earth he is in heaven; the mythical—or historical—descent and ascent is of such a kind that effectively the Son of man is in both places at once: the top and the bottom of the ladder." C. K. Barrett, "Paradox and Dualism," in *Essays on John* (London: SPCK, 1982), 110–11.

product of another fruit, one that rotted in the hands of Adam and Eve. The presence and actions of Jesus at the wedding at Cana, an idealized but still flawed event, suggests an Edenic world, flawed, but restorable at the hands of Jesus.

In the wedding at Cana, the path between heaven and earth is at its smoothest, the link between the two being as seamless as possible. When the incident is subjected to the rigors of interpretation and analysis, it is hard to say exactly when the historical details of the wedding and miracle fade away and when a symbolic theological event begins. The six stone water jars function as containers near at hand, and at the same time, because they are used by the Jews for ceremonial washing, speak of the transformation and fullness of Christ in comparison to the law and possibly of the six days of creation as well. In the manner of romance, the objects, like the event, are at once concretely real and metaphorically and theologically real. In such a context, the meanings of objects, words, and events expand into a greater range of possibilities and associations, coinciding with the FG's propensity for double meaning and with the metaphoric tendency of romance. The wedding at Cana functions as a kind of living hermeneutical paradigm for what follows and sets a tone of grace and innocence.

Frye notes that romance has a "perennially childlike quality . . . marked by its extraordinarily persistent nostalgia, its search for some kind of imaginative golden age in time or space."[48] Significantly, the wedding at Cana occurs at the start of the FG rather than at the end, as is the typical placement of weddings in comedy,[49] an arrangement mirrored in the fact the best wine appears during the banquet and not at the beginning. The wedding functions as a proto-eschatological event, an idealized situation or realized romance, a standard from which the rest of the Gospel must inevitably depart, analogous in romance to the idealized or noble situation set over against its evil or demonic parody.[50] If romance is about the ideal, the wedding at Cana offers a taste of that ideal. The wedding at Cana grounds the ideal in real space and time, an eschatological here and now made so by the presence of Jesus. The marvelous is possible, even probable, now that Jesus is here.

Significantly, then, temple cleansing follows the wedding at Cana. Here the world of romance or the integrated world infused with the ideal and the symbolic is juxtaposed against the world of realism,[51] a world of concrete and specific here and now devoid of reference to transcendent values. As temporal and spatial tokens of the presence of God on earth, the temple and its environs at Passover time should by poetic logic continue the sense of the marvelous and ideal as the social emphasis of the wedding of Cana moves to the religious emphasis of the temple. But Jesus finds the temple courts

---

[48] Frye, *Anatomy*, 186. Compare, for example, the Edenic atmosphere opening Radcliffe's *Mysteries of Udolpho*.
[49] Stibbe notes this feature, but passes by its association with romance. Stibbe also notes the eschatological aspects of miracle. Stibbe, *John's Gospel*, 67. cf. Murphy, *The Comedy of Revelation*, 231.
[50] Frye, *A Natural Perspective*, 110.
[51] Richard Bauckham interprets the demonstration in the temple as being directed against the commercial and exploitative nature of the financial apparatus connected with temple worship. In other words Jesus's actions are directed against realism in its oppressive and exploitative aspects. Bauckham, "Jesus' Demonstration in the Temple," in *Law and Religion: Essays on the Place of the Law in Israel and Early Christianity*, ed. Barnabas Lindars (Cambridge: James Clarke, 1988), 72–89.

filled with the trappings of realism: "people selling cattle, sheep and doves, and others sitting at tables exchanging money" (2:14). The construction of a whip replaces the creation of wine, judgment replaces celebration, and mayhem casts out the marvelous. The ideal suggested by a wedding gives way to the realistic demands of money, markets, and merchandise. The narration of the wedding at Cana incident consists primarily of dialogue or prose describing human social interaction, a narrative strategy that lends a certain distance from the real world. In contrast, the temple cleansing is immersed in realism in all its sights, smells, and objects: a whip, sheep, cattle, coins, tables, men, confusion, overturning, and shouting.[52] The unseen and appreciated miracle of the wine gives way to conspicuous confrontation and public judgment. When Jesus says "get these out of here! Stop turning my Father's house into a market!" (2:16), he asserts the romance-like primacy of the wonder-full and the holy against the all-too-easily accommodated demands of the worldly.

The Jews from Jesus demand a sign, a miraculous warrant to prove his authority for these actions (2:18). Superficially, the Jews seem to be acknowledging that he may be a prophet, but the request for a miracle has an unbelieving, realistic ring to it. Jesus refuses the spirit of the request yet grants its substance when he says, "Destroy this temple, and I will raise it again in three days" (2:19). The literalness of their response exposes a wrong kind of thinking, a response excessively concerned with realistic detail rather than spiritual truth. Yet Jesus utters a truth as real as it is spiritual: that in the destruction and resurrection of his body he will replace the temple. By missing the point, the Jews exhibit, fairly innocently at this point, a propensity for realism over against the freer association of metaphor and romance.

Rather than being an innovation, the mixture of romance and realism appears frequently in OT narrative and is characteristic of the Bible as a whole. Ryken notes, "These [Biblical] stories are both factually realistic and romantically marvelous. They bring together two impulses that the human race is always trying to join—reason and imagination, fact and mystery."[53] Rather than being a characteristic to describe the text, the emphasis on romance and realism makes two theological points: (1) that God is resolutely and personally involved in his creation and in the lives of human beings and (2) that human beings should interpret their ordinary existence with reference to God. By including the marvelous within the "real" and linking it with the activity of God, the emphasis falls on the personal causality of God. As a general observation on the ideological perspective of the OT narrative, Auerbach comments,

> The Bible's [OT] claim to truth is not only far more urgent than Homer's, it is tyrannical—it excludes all other claims. The world of the Scripture stories is not satisfied with claiming to be a historically true reality—it insists that it is the only real world, it is destined for autocracy.[54]

---

[52] A similar progression is seen in Luke, where the prophecy, human interaction, poetry, and idyllic joy of chapter 1 give way to the hard impersonal realism of taxes, Romans, governors, travel, mangers, inns with no room, and ill-timed births in 2:1-7. The account of the angels and shepherds that follows reestablishes the idyllic tone and the presence of the marvelous.
[53] Ryken, *Words of Delight* (Grand Rapids: Baker, 1992), 39, cf. 35–41.
[54] Auerbach, *Mimesis*, 14–15.

The link between realism and romance in the OT is maintained by the ideological pressure of an all-powerful God assumed by the text. The ideological pressure inherent in the OT narrative finds expression in Jesus himself in the story and discourse of the FG, the most narrative Gospel. The realism and romance held together by the presence of God in the OT finds its FG unity in Jesus who is both God and man, making the Father known to the world. Viewed this way, Jesus is "the Word made flesh" in all its fullness. The potential for conflict as romance meets realism is obvious. To a great extent, the FG presents the world of realized romance in mortal conflict with the world of "realism" strictly defined.

Although unique by virtue of its subject matter, the FG's clash of realism and romance occurs elsewhere in world literature. The dynamic appears in Twain's *A Connecticut Yankee in King Arthur's Court* and, to a lesser extent, in *Huckleberry Finn*. In *A Connecticut Yankee*, a time machine transports the iconoclastic American realist Hank Morgan to the world of King Arthur, a world Morgan views as absurd and in need of renovation through pragmatism and common sense. *Huckleberry Finn* displays romance and realism in tension as the realists Huck and Jim, successful escapees from the wrecked steamboat *The Walter Scott*, are juxtaposed against the failed romance of Tom Sawyer, the King and the Duke, and the Grangerford-Shepherdson feud. Like the FG, each in its own way manifests the values and norms of one age or way of thinking set against those of another.

Employing a similar tactic of juxtaposing the values of one age against another, Cervantes's *Don Quixote* is the definitive clash between romance and realism. The errant knight Don Quixote, avid and unstable reader of Medieval romance, crosses the hostile boarder between fact and fiction and invades the modern world of realism with predictable results. In doing so, Don Quixote and Sancho Panza embody what Beer calls "the two permanent and universal impulses of fiction."[55] Beer observes,

> Quixote presents the imagination cut loose from the world of sense and observation, aspiring towards the ideal. This way leads to madness, and to the noble simplification and suggestiveness of myth. Sancho Panza is preoccupied with registering the everyday signs and accepting their authority. His robust life is practicable only in relation to ordinary satisfactions and achievements.[56]

The basic dynamic of *Don Quixote* is the world of romance set in opposition to the world of realism, a clash seen in both Don Quixote's relationship with Sancho and with his encounter with the actual world. In romance, the hero is the center of the world, but in the decentered world of realism and irony, Don Quixote is an eccentric.

The FG and its presentation of Jesus represents a *Don Quixote* in reverse. In *Don Quixote*, the world or realism is the standard by which the wandering knight of La Mancha is judged whereas in the FG Jesus is the norm, the true reality, against whom the world is judged. Jesus's encounters with his foes are not Quixotic encounters of a misguided soul after the manner of a mistaken eschatological Jesus, but heroic

---

[55] Gillian Beer, *The Romance*, Critical Idiom, #10 (London: Methuen & Co., 1970), 43.
[56] Beer, *Romance*, 43.

encounters with real enemies who fail to understand or believe. In so doing, they, like Quixote, fail to understand things as they really are. Jesus extends and potentially makes reality plain in a fuller sense. Jesus does not represent, as Don Quixote does, "the idealization of the self, the refusal to doubt inner experience, the tendency to base any interpretation of the world on personal will, imagination and desire, not upon an empirical and social consensus of experience."[57] Rather, Jesus acts on the will of the Father whom he represents in all His fullness. For Adam and Eve, in both Genesis and *Paradise Lost*, for the Redcrosse Knight in *The Faerie Queene*, and for characters in the FG, the "empirical and social consensus of experience" is a danger, an obstacle and impediment to faith, not the solution.

As representatives or the opposing tendencies of romance and realism, Don Quixote and Sancho Panza are necessary for each other. Beer notes that "they interpret the world for each other. They illustrate the interdependence of the impulse to imitate and the impulse to idealize."[58] In Quixote and Panza, these tendencies are at once juxtaposed and symbiotic, but in a way that resembles how a blind person might combine resources with a deaf person to interpret the world. In Jesus the tendencies unite, not in a tepid middle ground, but in an embracing of both extremes. Jesus both embodies an ideal and is worthy of idealization but does so in a way that is subject to time, space, grief, thirst, and death, preventing abstraction and providing a basis on which he is to be imitated. The love of Jesus is not idealized for its own sake after the manner of courtly and idealized love typical of Medieval romance, but manifested in concrete action in the service of others.

Romance and realism are partners always threatening to go their separate ways. Romance devoid of realism drifts off into an extra-historical reality, an aesthetic treatment of values without practical purpose.[59] The opposite is the realistic—and ironic—tendency to view life without reference to meaningful values by which life transcends time and place. The FG displays these tendencies in the actions of those who surround Jesus. Adherence to realism without due attention to romance results in everything from misunderstanding to rejection and rebellion. Thus, Pilate represents the dawn and premature eclipse of romance in the face of realism. Pilate's attempts to free Jesus are sincere and moving toward true heroism, but flawed, incomplete, and ultimately tragic. The Jews represent the static qualities of realism and resort to employing realistic means for realistic ends. Adherence to romance and its heroic qualities without due attention to the demands of realism results in misunderstanding and folly, as is the case with Peter, a comic figure who displays what is essentially over-realized romance, or romance without reference to Jesus's ideals of humility, service, and sacrifice. When washing the disciples' feet or supremely in the Passion, Jesus transcends the differences between realism and romance by uniting the ideals of one with the praxis of the other.

Mastery of realism and romance in FG allows a full range of humanity to be displayed that at the same time allows for a kind of living theology. Auerbach writes, "It was the story of Christ, with its ruthless mixture of everyday reality and the highest

---

[57] Ibid., 42.
[58] Ibid., 43.
[59] Auerbach, *Mimesis*, 138–42.

and most sublime tragedy, which had conquered the classical rule of styles."[60] Similarly, Smith observes, "It is the genius of the Fourth Evangelist to have created a gospel in which Jesus as the representative of the world above visits and really lives in this world without depriving it of its verisimilitude and without depriving life here of its seriousness."[61] The FG presents the real as the universal and the universal as the real.

Ultimately, in the FG there is no distance between the world of romance and realism or between the ideal and the real insofar as this concerns Jesus himself. Jesus refuses to be accepted on any terms other than what he himself claims to be. Jesus's claims do not allow for either-or as much as they demand both-and. The conceptual and literary challenge for the FG is to hold these opposites of romance and realism in tension.[62] The solution, and paradoxically the problem, is found in the subject matter of the FG: the person of Jesus Christ, the incarnate Logos, both God and man. The prologue is at pains to include both aspects. Jesus is thus simultaneously both a figure of romance and realism in one person wherein these qualities are not in tension, as in Shakespeare's Prospero whose powers are external to himself, but in perfect unity. Typically in romance, heroes struggle to maintain an ideal in a fallen world, and in this respect the FG is no exception. But in the theology of the FG, the struggle is more of a fallen world refusing to accept an ideal and, indeed, lacking the proper mode of thinking or frame of reference within which Jesus must be understood.

II. D. 2 Plot and story in romance

Much can be gained in understanding the nature of the FG narrative by using novelist E. M. Forster's famous distinction between the often interchanged literary terms "story" and "plot."[63] Forster divides life into two spheres, the life of time and the life of value. For Forster, story primarily has to do with events happening in a sequence of time and thus relates mostly to the life of time. Story can be illustrated simply as "the king died and then the queen died." Here, the emphasis falls on sequence rather than causality or value. As such, Forster has a low opinion of story ("this low atavistic form"[64]) for its own sake and notes, "It [story] runs like a backbone—or may I say a tape-worm, for its beginning and end are arbitrary."[65] The appeal of story lies in curiosity and suspense, a natural desire to find out what happens next. Like Twain, Forster enlists Walter Scott, writer of historical romances, as a suitable literary whipping boy.

Plot, on the other hand, is also a narrative of events, but the emphasis falls on causality.[66] In Forster's analysis, "the king died and then the queen died" is a story

---

[60] Ibid., 555. For Auerbach, the story of Jesus as portrayed in the Gospels formed a kind of base line of comparison for *Mimesis*.
[61] D. Moody Smith, "The Presentation of Jesus in the Fourth Gospel," *Interpretation* 31, no. 4 (1977): 367–78.
[62] Although his terms are different and his concerns elsewhere, Lincoln offers a cogent summary of the literal versus metaphorical debate in "The Beloved Disciple as Eyewitness and the Fourth Gospel as Witness," *JSNT* 85 (2002): 17ff.
[63] E. M. Forster, *Aspects of the Novel* (London: Edward Arnold, 1927).
[64] Forster, *Aspects*, 27.
[65] Ibid., 28.
[66] Ibid., 82.

while "the king died and then the queen died of grief" is a plot.[67] Both manifest a time sequence, but in plot a sense of causality and value transcends the temporal sequence. Forster observes, "It is in a story we say 'and then?' It is in a plot we ask 'why?' That is the fundamental difference between these two aspects of the novel."[68] Forster holds that the two primary elements demanded and assumed by a plot are intelligence and memory.[69] Intelligence moves beyond simple curiosity and fosters mystery by raising the question "why?" Memory permits connections to be made with previous events. While Forster is essentially correct in describing a distinction between what he labels story, his evaluation of them is worth a further look: intelligence and memory of a certain type can also function as barriers that inhibit or even prevent understanding. Forster's distinction is not without its detractors but remains helpful, if slightly ambiguous.[70]

If plot and story are seen as tendencies on a continuum and not as complete opposites, romance tends to emphasize story rather than plot. For example, the episodic structure of *The Odyssey* tends much more toward story than to plot. This characteristic relates to Auerbach's claim that Homer tends to use narrative "foregrounding," a style that does not prompt questions about why.[71] Modern readers frequently find Homer frustrating to read because he spends so much time filling out the story with copious details rather than advancing the plot. Shakespeare's romance *Pericles* is very much a series of incidents often linked together by the convention of the storyteller, although its primary coherence rests on the fact that it is the story of one man. Melville's *Moby Dick* is a simple narrative frequently with little or no causal connection between sections; some chapters are purely descriptive and can hardly be termed even minimally as incident. The coherence of *Moby Dick* and similar works rests on their overall success at transfiguring the characters, incidents, and description by ideological or thematic pressure.[72]

Contrary to Forster, an emphasis on story rather than plot creates an expansiveness and inclusiveness in romance not obtainable when the emphasis falls more significantly on plot. An emphasis on plot leads to a corresponding emphasis on causality, self-coherence, and a casting off of all superfluous baggage. As Forster notes, "Unlike the weaver of plots, the storyteller profits by ragged ends."[73] Therefore, if a writer tells a story rather than develops a plot, ample opportunity exists to pause, take side trips, examine the scenery, make speeches, sing songs, or recite poetry, activities less permissible when plot is of primary concern. Likewise, for example, in *Cliges*, a twelfth-century romance by Chretien de Troyes, the story is interrupted, slowed to a crawl, to explore

---

[67] Ibid.
[68] Forster, *Aspects*, 83. This distinction transcends the novel.
[69] Forster, *Aspects*, 83.
[70] Elizabeth Dipple, *Plot* (Critical Idiom, London: Methuen & Co, 1970).
[71] Auerbach, "Odysseus' Scar," chapter 1 in *Mimesis*, 3–23.
[72] *Moby Dick* has met mixed critical success, and some view it as simply bombastic, as if the only thing swelling the sails of the *Pequod* is the huffing and puffing of Melville himself. Others see *Moby Dick* as the great American novel. Forster himself offers a positive assessment of *Moby Dick* under the category of what he terms "prophecy," a work that stretches reality and says something beyond itself. Whatever its evaluation, *Moby Dick* illustrates the risk inherent in such story-driven narratives.
[73] Referring to Scott, Forster observes, "He need not hammer away all the time at cause and effect." Forster, *Aspects*, 34.

the dynamics of being in love.[74] A general tendency of the novel as opposed to the romance is a propensity for a self-contained organic completeness knit together with an emphasis on plot.[75]

By manifesting the characteristics of story, the FG offers a series of incidents and stops along the way and expands on this or that aspect as the occasion demands. In analyzing the FG, Hitchcock follows Aristotle's *Poetics* and reads the FG as a drama but in doing so fails to account for the FG's narrative diversity.[76] Windisch rightly rejects reading the FG as drama in favor of focusing on certain incidents as drama within a loosely structured dramatic whole.[77] Acknowledging a diversity, Windisch proposes three major classifications of dramatic narrative: (1) the broadly elaborated, dramatically presented narratives (the healing of the man born blind, the raising of Lazarus); (2) a connection between narrative and dispute discourse (the healing of the lame man in chapter 5); and (3) the sequence of individual scenes that belong together (the Baptist narratives and the calling of the first disciples in chapter 1). Like Windisch, Stibbe rightly rejects attempts to read the FG as drama in favor of reading the FG as dramatic.[78] But this distinction has little to do with problems caused by reading the FG as drama in the sense of drama characterized by actors on a stage, as Stibbe supposes in making his criticism. Rather, the real issue behind the superficial issue of drama versus the dramatic is the emphasis on the nature of causality inherent in plot and drama as opposed to the episodic and loose organization emphasized in romance and in story.[79]

The emphasis on story over plot in romance and the FG is much more than an empirical fact and much more than a quality that allows for inclusiveness, however important these qualities are important in themselves. By lessening the emphasis on causality, the story is much more able to allow and create a state of marvel and wonder and open the doors to the ideal and transcendent. Beer observes,

> One method of disengaging us from our ordinary assumptions is the swift smooth elision from adventure to adventure. The lack of causal links is again typical of much oral literature or literature based on an oral tradition. What matters artistically, however, is the range of effects which the romance writers create by such means.[80]

---

[74] Vinaver notes the presence of explanation in romance as found in *Cliges* as a key development as compared to the periscope-like format of the earlier *Song of Roland*. Eugene Vinaver, *Rise of Romance*, 15–32. A comparison with the Synoptic's relationship to the FG is interesting.

[75] "But in a Novel, a combination of incidents, entertaining in themselves, are made to form a whole; and an unnecessary circumstance becomes a blemish, by detaching from the simplicity which is requisite to exhibit that whole to advantage." Thomas Holcroft, *Preface to Alwyn: Or the Gentleman Comedian* (1780) in Miriam Allott, *Novelists on the Novel* (London: Routledge and Kegan Paul, 1959): 46–47.

[76] F. R. M. Hitchcock, "Is the Fourth Gospel a Drama," *Theology* 7 (1923): 307–17; reprinted in *The Gospel of John as Literature: An Anthology of Twentieth-Century Perspectives*, ed. Mark Stibbe (Leiden, NY, and Koln: E. J. Brill, 1993), 15–24.

[77] Hans Windisch, "John's Narrative Style," in Stibbe, *Anthology*, 25–64.

[78] Stibbe, "Introduction," *Anthology*, 8.

[79] Forster observes, "The plot is exciting and may be beautiful, yet is it not a fetish, borrowed from drama, from the spatial limitations of the stage? Cannot fiction devise a framework that is not so logical yet more suitable to its genius?" *Aspects*, 92–93. Similarly, for Frye, "The essential element of plot in romance is adventure, which means that romance is naturally a sequential and processional form, hence we know it better from fiction than from drama." Frye, *Anatomy*, 186.

[80] Beer, *Romance*, 28.

For example, Shakespeare's *Pericles* often lacks causal links between scenes.[81] There is no causal transition at all to link Pericles's arrival at Tharsus aboard a ship loaded with wheat for famine relief with anything that preceded it. Rather, this scene serves as emotional relief from previous depressing scenes and enhances the reputation of Pericles. To Cleon, Dionyza, their subjects in Tharsus, and to the viewer, the arrival of the grain is completely unexpected and truly marvelous. Likewise (with exceptions), the events of the FG generally proceed in as if uncaused by previous events, at least insofar as Jesus himself is concerned. Why does Jesus go to the wedding (2:1), or up to Jerusalem (2:13), or to the Judean countryside (3:22), or to Galilee (4:43), or to Cana again (4:46), or up to Jerusalem (5:1)?[82] We are not told. On simply reading through the FG, the effect is striking.[83] We are only told *that* he went, the implication being he went because he chose to go. Throughout the FG, Jesus determines his own destiny and, although he avoids the Jews (7:1), he continues to confront them and places himself at the disposal of the Jews only on his own terms at his own time. Only in the events of the Passion Week does Jesus significantly enter into the causal matrix of circumstances, but even then he maintains control, is steadfast to his mission (18:11), and asserts his control over the trial events[84] (19:11). True to form, the FG closes with its greatest causal aporia, the status of chapter 21 with respect to chapter 20 and the rest of the Gospel.[85] However inviting such source-critical chasms may be to literal-minded scholars, they are perhaps better bridged through imagination and the marvelous.[86]

Marvel and wonder happen best when, like the laws of nature, the laws of causality inherent in plot are lessened or absent. Links between events can be suggestive, imaginative, or thematic rather than being defined and supplied for the reader by means of plot. Breaking free of the iron laws of causality is analogous to the suspension of the laws of realism, resulting in marvelous adventures, angels, fairies, gods, signs, wonders, miracles, and delight. A heavy plot in a closed world is the enemy of wonder, as any reader of Hardy's later novels soon discovers. Equally true, wonder is the enemy of a heavy plot. Tragedy, with its emphasis on plot, leaves little room for the wonderful.

---

[81] Dean, *Wanderers*, 234–38.
[82] The incident of the Samaritan woman is only superficially an exception. Jesus "had to go through Samaria" and this counts as a reason, but it is a reason linked to Jesus's choice and contrary to cultural expectation. In addition, no reason is given for going to his final destination.
[83] Stibbe speaks of much the same thing in his discussions of Jesus as the elusive Christ. *John's Gospel*, 5–31; "The Elusive Christ: A New Reading of the Fourth Gospel," *Anthology*, 231–47. Stibbe also discusses the causal aspects of John's plot, but has in mind something like the progression or stages in the development of the story. See *John's Gospel*, 35–36.
[84] "Jesus does nothing, and nothing happens to him, by chance; and this is nowhere more evident than in the account of his death, whether in the passion narrative proper or in the many references and allusions to it throughout the Gospel. . . . Jesus' own fixity of purpose is contrasted, probably quite deliberately, with Pilate's uncertainty." D. Moody Smith, "Presentation," 371.
[85] See Chapter 4 below.
[86] Wayne Meeks comments "The major literary problem of John is its combination of remarkable stylistic unity and thematic coherence with glaringly bad transitions between episodes at many points. The countless displacement, source, and redaction theories that litter the graveyards of Johannine research are voluble testimony to this difficulty." Meeks, "The Man from Heaven in Johannine Sectarianism," 48. The interpretation of "the glaringly bad transitions between episodes" may be a kind of trap for the unwary or a hermeneutical test: namely, whether to interpret them according to the demands of realism (source criticism) or romance. Perhaps not coincidentally, source criticism has preoccupied both Johannine scholars and scholars of Medieval romance.

The marvelous, and the would-be marvelous—those tragic heroes—die with their ideals on the twin edges of causality and plot.

Suspending or lessening causality fosters the marvelous and wonderful in romance and grants something like a state of grace. Indeed, the connection between a state of grace and the severing of causality claims theological warrant from the NT where, supremely, the resurrection breaks the causal authority of death itself. On this basis, the work of Jesus breaks the causal link between sin and death and allows the believer to live in a state of grace wherein the causal authority of the past is broken. Memory, the past, and intelligence too occupied with the quality of "why," those elements so important to Forster's analysis of plot, simply no longer apply. Grace and forgiveness reduce the authority of the past and allow "why" to take on a marvelous quality free from the kind of "why" fraught with potential negative obsession. In romance, "why" becomes "it is." One enters the state of grace in romance by a step of faith wherein things are allowed to relate to each other outside the bounds of strict linear causality. Romance, then, has its own form of logic or mode of thought.

In romance, the lessening or suspension of causality is an accomplished fact, whereas in comedy it is potential and occurs at or near the end as some sort of integration is achieved. In comedy, the suspension of causality can be confined to something that is technically or realistically possible, as is typical of Jane Austen, or can involve all manner of implausible solutions effected by fairy godmothers and the like. In the FG, the most basic of causal sequences in life—death—is suspended in the end, as might be expected in comedy. But in the FG, the other basic causal sequence of life—birth—is likewise suspended. Jesus, the Word, is already in the world as the Word made flesh, poetically and theologically unborn, begotten not made, and fully realized in a way not linked with the progression of birth and childhood. The "how" of earthly birth is not important; it is significant primarily for its non-occurrence at the beginning. The converse is that spiritual birth is possible, indeed necessary, without reference to previous events.

The link between scenes or adventures in romance is both personal and thematic related to an ideal. And since it is personal, the link between scenes is related to the ideal held by the hero and on this basis the links between scenes are vertical and personal—links that in romance are one and the same.[87] The question "why?" in relation to some sort of linear causality is inappropriate and some other "answer" is waiting to be discovered, an answer that is on its own terms self-evident. The ideal is self-evident; a causal answer on any other terms is incorrect. For the knight in battle or for the chivalrous lover, no explanation is necessary; the presence of the ideal is assumed and is justified on its own terms.

In a discussion of causality and typology in *The Great Code*, a literary analysis of the Bible, Frye notes,

> Causality, however, is based on reason, observation, and knowledge, and therefore relates fundamentally to the past, on the principle that the past is all that we

---

[87] Culpepper states, "The plot of the gospel is propelled by conflict between belief and unbelief as responses to Jesus." *Anatomy*, 97. Disregarding the issue of plot/story, Culpepper's point is not quite correct. By initiating the challenge to believe, Jesus propels the story of the FG.

genuinely or systematically know. Typology relates to the future, and consequently relates primarily to faith, hope, and vision.[88]

Further, causality has to do with locating the causes and effects on the same temporal plane. For example, "Ascribing a disease to the will of God or to the malice of a witch is not causal thinking."[89] To a large extent, *The Great Code* is an attempt to attribute the content and production of the Bible, including its typology, entirely to causation in one sphere, that is, historical, social, cultural, factors, and so on. But, with reference to its own specific purposes, limitation of causation to one sphere is precisely the type of thinking the FG seeks to overcome by virtue of incarnational theology. In the FG and in romance, existence or causality in one sphere has a relationship to another: water can become wine, the lame are healed, dead men rise, Jesus replaces the temple, Jesus works because his Father is working and, most importantly in the FG, believing grants life[90] (20:31). On the FG's conception of things Davies writes,

> The Fourth Gospel differs from modern histories in one major respect. By beginning with the Creator God's plan for creation, and telling the story of Jesus as the most significant contribution to that plan, it not only notices the effect of this belief on people within the story, but asserts that God is the first cause of all things. The Creator God causes the world and history to come into existence and gives eternal life to those people who conform to the divine conception of human life. Compared to this primary cause, the social, economic and political power structures play a less significant role.[91]

A different kind of causality, if it can be called that, is in order, one in which "the Son can do nothing by himself; he can do only what he sees his Father doing, because whatever the Father does the Son also does" (5:19). Rooted in the Word as creator, this kind of "causality" is based on God's present involvement in the world in Jesus and on an interpersonal/inter-Trinitarian relationship manifest in space and time.

In his classic defense of Christianity, *Orthodoxy*, G. K. Chesterton makes a similar point regarding causality. For the materialist or the madman (the two are synonymous for Chesterton), only one form of explanation is available, that of a strict causal progression.[92] But for Chesterton, this is a dangerous limitation, one that he calls "the clean and well lit prison of one idea." He observes,

> But scientific men do muddle their heads, until they imagine a necessary mental connection between an apple leaving the tree and apple reaching the ground. They

---

[88] Northrop Frye, *The Great Code: The Bible and Literature* (London: Routledge & Kegan Paul, 1982), 82.
[89] Frye, *The Great Code*, 82.
[90] "With the miracles, as with other elements of the tradition, John has seized the Christological interpretation which is implicit in the Synoptics, clarified it and stamped it upon the material in such a way that the reader is not allowed to escape it. The miracles of this Gospel are a function of its Christology. Rightly to understand them is to apprehend Christ by faith (10:38, 14:11). The miracles once grasped in their true meaning lead immediately to the Christology, since they are a manifestation of the glory of Christ (2:11)." Barrett, *The Gospel According to John*.
[91] Margaret Davies, *Rhetoric*, 59.
[92] G. K. Chesterton, *Orthodoxy* (London: John Lane, 1909), 40. In large measure, Chesterton argues the case for Christianity by debunking a worldview, frame of reference, or mode of thinking based on realism in favor of one based more on imagination and association akin to romance.

do really talk as if they had found not only a set of marvelous facts, but a truth connecting those facts. They do talk as if the connection of two strange things physically connected them philosophically.[93]

They talked as if the fact that trees bear fruit were just as *necessary* as the fact that two and one trees make three. But it is not.[94]

For Chesterton, the connection between trees and fruit or between the apple falling and hitting the ground is not based on a law, but based upon a continuous, willful act of God. He notes, "The repetition in Nature may not be a mere recurrence; it may be a theatrical *encore*."[95] For the materialist, the mistake is to suppose that a law posited *on* the basis of repetition becomes a law posited *as* the basis of repetition.[96] For Chesterton, the world continues at the pleasure of God and, therefore, it is a place where the marvelous might well be expected because its essential everyday continuation is an ongoing marvelous act in itself.

Analogous to the embodiment of an ideal in romance, in the FG the willful act of God ceases to be an unseen principle and becomes concrete and specific in Jesus. A kind of conflict appears in the FG that might be characterized after the manner of Kuhn as conflicting paradigms of interpretation. Kuhn's remarks with regard to science are appropriate here: "The proponents of competing paradigms are always at least slightly at cross-purposes. Neither side will grant all the non-empirical assumptions that the other needs in order to make its case."[97] To the extent that romance and epic are, as Frye remarks about epic, "the story of all things,"[98] other stories or paradigms are incompatible.

Romance and the FG simultaneously assume and educate in the right paradigm that is for them self-evident.[99] This is the kind of conflict that marks much of Jesus's conflicts in the FG, especially the tenacious opposition of the Jews. For the Jews, the law and Moses have become causal factors sufficient unto themselves without due reference to the action of God. Jesus informs the Jews, "It is not Moses who has given you the bread from heaven, but it is my Father who gives you the true bread from

---

[93] Chesterton, *Orthodoxy*, 90.
[94] Ibid., 88, his emphasis.
[95] Chesterton, *Orthodoxy*, 107, his emphasis. Richard Swinburne has developed a defense of the teleological argument along similar lines. See, "The Argument from Design," *Philosophy* 43 (1968), reprinted in *Readings in the Philosophy of Religion: An Analytic Approach*, 2nd ed., ed. Baruch Brody (Englewood Cliffs, NJ: Prentice Hall, 1992), 189–201.
[96] In a similar way, Kuhn states, "Given the slightest reason for doing so, the man who reads a science text can easily take the applications to be the evidence for the theory, the reasons why it ought to be believed." Kuhn, *The Structure of Scientific Revolutions*, 80.
[97] Kuhn, *Scientific Revolutions*, 148.
[98] Northrop Frye, "The Story of All Things," in *The Return of Eden: Five Essays on Milton's Epics* (Toronto: University of Toronto Press, 1965), 3–31. Reprinted in, *Paradise Lost: An Authoritative Text Backgrounds and Sources Criticism*, ed. Scott Elledge (New York and London: W. W. Norton, 1975), 405–22.
[99] In a similar way, Stanley Fish argues that the "argument" of *Paradise Lost*, or Milton's attempt to "Justify the ways of God to man", is not an argument in the conventional sense. Rather, it is the education of the reader's perceptions such that the line of thought assumed in the work, the argument, will come to be accepted. See Stanley Fish, *Surprised by Sin: The Reader in Paradise Lost*, 2nd ed. (Houndmills, Basingstoke, Hampshire, and London: Macmillan, 1997); "Discovery as Form in *Paradise Lost*," in same 340–56.

heaven" (6:32). The Jews fail to grant the required assumption with the result that the one who said, "I am the living bread that came down from heaven" will intractably remain "Jesus, the son of Joseph, whose father and mother we know" (6:42). A related dynamic is present when Jesus informs Pilate, "You would have no power over me if it were not given to you from above" (19:11). Jesus being glorified through the passion and cross certainly finds no basis within contemporary views of crucifixion.

Point of view with regard to Jesus and scope and limits of perception are of paramount importance in the FG, and the romance-like qualities of the FG present its "argument" and present Jesus in a particular way: in a narrative that eschews linear, cause-and-effect thinking in favor of a narrative that assumes the marvelous because of the presence of Jesus.

II. D. 3 Characters in romance

II. D. 3. a Identity and self-determination

While the story of the FG is closest to the archetype of romance, it differs from romance and defines itself with emphasis on certain key themes, notably on character type. Frye divides characters of all literature into five types that are each characteristic of an archetype:[100] (1) if the hero is superior in kind and environment to others, the story will be a myth, or a story about a god; (2) if superior in degree to other characters and his environment, the hero will be typical of romance, wherein the human hero moves in a world of slightly suspended natural laws; (3) if superior in degree to others in terms of authority, passions, and expression but not to his natural environment and subject to the order of nature, the hero will be typical of tragedy and most epic; (4) if superior neither to others nor to his environment, the hero is of common humanity and typical of comedy and realistic fiction; and (5) if inferior in power or intelligence to ourselves resulting in a sense of looking down on a scene of bondage, ignorance, or frustration, the hero belongs to the ironic mode. Of present concern is the distinction between myth and romance, which Frye summarizes, "We have distinguished myth from romance by the hero's power of action: in the myth proper he is divine, in the romance proper he is human."[101]

In Christian theology, Jesus clearly transcends Frye's categories. He is fully divine, "the Word made flesh," and thus fits the first category as the subject of a myth. But he is also fully human, again "the Word made flesh," and thus fits the category of romance because he is superior in degree to other characters in his environment. In addition, the FG features characters best described by the other three categories. This eclectic mixture of characters and character types and, more importantly, of worldviews associated with these different types combine to make the FG an interesting book. The incarnation itself is theologically rich—profoundly so—but the incarnation allows and even demands the multidimensional literary richness so evident in this Gospel.

One of the ways that the hero of romance is distinguished from others is the hero's power of action. If the hero is to be free and possess the power to act in the sense

---

[100] Frye, *Anatomy*, 33–34.
[101] Ibid., 188.

Frye has in mind, then the hero must be free from being primarily determined by the exigencies of causality and realism in the sense argued above with respect to story and plot. Freedom from linear causality is not to be free from the principle of causality in general; rather, the type of causality in romance is personal causality, freedom to determine one's own destiny in the midst of circumstance and to transcend those circumstances by adherence to an ideal. *In romance, the knight does not meet the enemy to defend himself; he meets the enemy because he is brave.* The former locates motivation in external cause and effect, the latter within one's own self and one's adherence to an ideal or belief.

In romance, the hero's actions are bound up with a character's being what he or she is that excludes acting in any other way. Romance assumes something like a necessary connection between identity and action so that, whatever the external circumstances, the hero cannot but act in accordance with certain character-defining ideals and beliefs. Ideals and character are one and the same. On this topic Auerbach notes,

> Except feats of arms and love, nothing can occur in the courtly world—and even these two are of a special sort: they are not occurrences or emotions which can be absent for a time; they are permanently connected with the person of the perfect knight, they are part of his definition, so that he cannot for one moment be without adventure in arms nor for one moment be without amorous entanglements. If he could, he would lose himself and no longer be a knight.[102]

While the knight meets the enemy because he is brave, his bravery does not allow him to do otherwise. Doubt and duplicity are excluded. While the ideal in a particular romance may vary, the principle remains substantially the same: to be untrue to the ideal is to be false to one's self. Jesus, who does what the Father does (5:19) must drink the cup given to him; he, like Luther, can do no other.

In contrast, in comedy and tragedy, some tension-producing distance always exists between the self with its ideals and its surroundings, a tension that inevitably leads to tension within the self. In *Oedipus*, for example, Oedipus's character requires him to get to the bottom of things in his quest for knowledge and destroys him in doing so. In romance, the source of the conflict is not grounded in the protagonist's struggle with the self coming to terms with some issue or with the world; rather, the struggle is to successfully maintain the self and an ideal against the onslaught of circumstances. The conflict in romance is thus between the integrated and good world of the hero and the values the hero assumes and represents as over against a world of chaos, evil, and darkness. Frye casts this struggle in terms of descent into a lower world followed by an ascent to a higher world.[103] To depart from the ideal is to destroy the self, call the ideal into question, and align the self with the lower world.

The integrity of the self with one's actions may be seen, for example, in the Medieval French epic *The Song of Roland*. The Judas-like treachery of Ganelon places the hero Roland in a Saracen ambush. Outnumbered, Roland's companion Oliver repeatedly

---

[102] Auerbach, *Mimesis*, 140.
[103] This is a central theme of Frye's *Secular Scriptures*.

urges Roland to blow the horn and summon help from Charlemagne and his army some distance ahead. Roland refuses, saying "that would be an act of folly,"[104] citing as reasons the loss of his good name, the reproach to his kinsmen, the reputation of France, and a desire to strike blows against the pagans.[105] Implicitly, for Roland the honor and reputation of Christianity is at stake. Following these interchanges, the poet writes, "Roland is brave and Oliver is wise; both are marvelous vassals."[106] Roland's bravery is incompatible with the wisdom of Oliver and may seem foolhardy to readers not sharing those values. But Roland's judgment on Oliver's advice as folly is significant. While Roland and Oliver do not share the same point of view, each is true to his own values, and this fact matters most of all. And, given the ethos of the poem, the antithetical nature of their respective values to which they remain loyal may actually enhance their stature as heroes rather than call their respective positions into question. Roland dies, but in maintaining bravery in a hopeless situation, he is not only loyal to his ideals and those of his society, but in doing so also determines his own destiny.

In another variation on preserving one's self in bad circumstances, in Shakespeare's *Pericles*, pirates capture Pericles's daughter Marina and sell her into slavery in a brothel. But by asserting the rightness of her cause—a cause at one with her character—she shames her captors, preserves her virtue, works something of a transforming effect on those around her, and vindicates the protection of the gods. The threatened virgin convention common to romance (analogous to Penelope's situation in *The Odyssey*) is not so much an obsession with chastity as it is in essence a test of the survival of the self with its integrity intact. Frye observes, "What is symbolized as a virgin is actually a human conviction, however expressed, that there is something at the core of one's infinitely fragile being which is not only immortal but has discovered the secret of invulnerability that eludes the tragic hero."[107] In the cases of Marina and Roland, both preserve themselves in the midst of circumstances, however different those circumstances and outcomes may be. In the FG, Jesus's struggle is to display and preserve his identity as the incarnate Logos, however much others attempt to define him on other terms. In comedy and tragedy, the protagonist experiences a change, for better or worse, of self and circumstance.

In romance, the aforementioned lessening of linear causality as expressed in plot allows for an imaginative space for the hero to rise to prominence. Likewise, the rise of the hero suspends linear causality, as is the case with the alteration of Marina's destiny in *Pericles*. The hero acting on an ideal is the source and unity of the action, but only to a point. The hero cannot always fashion events and must often endure them, but does so under the eyes of an implicit or explicit divine providence on the terms of which the worthy will be successful, good will triumph, and evil punished. The choice of Arthur is cast in terms of divine approval as evidenced by his removal of the sword from the

---

[104] *The Song of Roland*, translated with an introduction and notes by Glyn Burgess (London: Penguin, 1990), *laisse* 83, line 1053.
[105] Burgess, *Song of Roland*, laisses 83–86.
[106] Burgess, *Song of Roland*, laisse 87, lines 1093–94.
[107] Frye, *Secular Scripture*, 86.

stone and subsequent events. The copious victories of the invincible knight depend upon the same principle as do the successes of Odysseus.

In a study of Shakespeare's romances and their place and time in Shakespeare's development as an author, Mincoff argues that Shakespeare's turn to romance in his later works represents, at least in part, something of a reaction against a decline in faith characteristic of his age.[108] He writes,

> Since in turning to romance Shakespeare did lay considerable stress on "things supernatural and causeless" it thus seems probable that this was at least one of the things that attracted him to the genre. Moreover, it seems he was definitely interested in suggesting that the strange happenings and coincidences one may so easily attribute to a blind fortune are in fact part of a wider scheme of things. It is done very tactfully; we are generally led to believe not so much in chance as in human causation throughout the body of the play, and it is only at a single point in the action, mostly at the very end that the interest of superior powers in things human is made manifest, and with it the obvious suggestion that what we have taken for chance is after all something more than that. Only in *The Tempest* are we faced with the definitely marvelous as a part of the action itself, and there it is a question of magic, not of divine interference.[109]

Whatever the merits of Mincoff's qualified and cautious linking of Shakespeare's use of romance to Shakespeare's attempt to assert something of his own point of view in his own day (a point debated in Shakespearean scholarship), Mincoff rightly highlights the link between romance and divine providence. In a kind of dance between heaven and earth, chance encounters and miscellaneous adventures find a thematic unity, as the preservation of Marina in the brothel shows, that is as much related to character qualities as it is to divine providence. In romance, the waters of miracle, providence, and character, if traced far enough, are seen to flow from the same fountain.

Writing in epic-like tone and, as it were, from the other side of orthodoxy, Thomas Carlyle argues for the great man theory of history and offers an analysis of several figures ranging from Mohammed to John Knox. Carlyle discerns a central quality of sincerity in great men. He writes,

> But [he] is first of all in right earnest about it; what I call a sincere man. I should say *sincerity*, a deep, great, genuine sincerity, is the first characteristic of all men in any way heroic. Not the sincerity that calls itself sincere; ah, no, that is a very poor matter indeed;—a shallow braggart, conscious sincerity; oftenest self-conceit mainly.[110]

---

[108] Marco Mincoff, *Things Supernatural and Causeless: Shakespearean Romance* (London and Toronto: Associated University Presses, 1992). The title is significant and is taken from Lafeu in *All's Well That Ends Well*, 2.3.1–6, who states, "They say miracles are past, and we have our philosophical persons, to make modern and familiar, things supernatural and causeless. Hence is it that we make trifles of terrors, ensconcing ourselves into seeming knowledge, when we should submit ourselves to an unknown fear."

[109] Mincoff, *Supernatural and Causeless*, 25.

[110] Thomas Carlyle, *Sator Resartus and on Heroes and Hero Worship* (London: Dent, 1965), 280.

By sincerity Carlyle means something like "unconscious truthfulness to one's self," a quality that goes beyond merely believing that one believes. For Carlyle, to the extent that the great man cooperates with "the great deep Law of the World,"[111] he is victorious and assured of the rightness of his cause. Religion is important for Carlyle, not in any creedal sense but only insofar as it exhibits sincerity and conviction. Doubt is synonymous with cultural defeat, for "no sadder proof can be given by a man of his own littleness than disbelief in great men."[112] For Carlyle, (1) the rightness of a cause, religion, or god, and (2) acting according to one's beliefs combine to form an indispensable part of life and allow the heroic person to shape events. Significantly, no matter how much his contemporary world viewed heroic culture as a fading if not distant memory, Carlyle grounded the worthiness of the hero in the enduring twin principles of connection with some higher principle and truthfulness to one's self.

In romance, the identity of characters cannot be understood only in terms of the characters themselves; identity must be understood with reference to some greater transcendent ideal.

II. D. 3. b *Representation*

Very much related to the hero of romance as embodied ideal, romance is fundamentally *representational* in character. Romance is representational in *character* in more than one sense: in terms of character (person) as embodied ideal, and character in terms of a quality or property. Since the hero represents an ideal, the archetypal pattern of romance may be viewed tropologically as metaphor in which one thing is represented in terms of another. I. A. Richards offers a widely accepted distinction between "tenor" and "vehicle" in metaphor, and defines tenor as the idea being expressed or the subject of the comparison and vehicle as the image by which this idea is conveyed or the subject communicated.[113] Thus, in the metaphor "family tree," the tenor refers to family relationships through the vehicle of the tree. In romance, there is a high degree of representation or correspondence between tenor and vehicle. The hero represents something in a metaphorical sense; at the same time what the hero represents is bound up with the hero's person and being. And since the ideals are both represented and held by the hero, the hero's actions display that ideal. Opposition to the hero is opposition to the ideal; the triumph of the hero is the triumph of the ideal. Due to the FG's emphasis on realism, history, and the incarnation, tenor and vehicle are united such that characters are at once representational and "real."

The representative quality of romance often leads to an emphasis on the fantastic and marvelous. The marvelous elements common to romance tend to allow the hero greater scope for the exercise and display of ideals by a simultaneous increase in the hero's power to do so. In such contexts, romance is simply being true to what it attempts to do: in romance it is more important that the ideal be represented rather than concrete reality. Odysseus, repeatedly designated as "resourceful," is given ample opportunity to demonstrate his resourcefulness through his actions; in a reciprocal

---

[111] Carlyle, *Heroes*, 291.
[112] Ibid., 250.
[113] "Metaphor," *A Handbook to Literature*, 264–65.

way, his actions display his resourcefulness. The bravery and prowess of the knight is exaggerated in marvelous or improbable circumstances within the framework of a convention that demands to be taken on its own terms. Chretian de Troyes's knight Eric defeats three knights, then five knights, then survives the treachery of a count with one hundred knights, then defeats several giants, and concludes his adventures with the supreme defeat of a previously undefeated knight. The adventures of James Bond or any other superhero follows the same dynamic.

Often in romance, the depiction of a hero triumphing over exaggerated villains in a labyrinth of adventures and difficulties becomes a kind of end in itself. In such cases, self-conscious experiments in form triumph over content. To the extent that the bonds of realism are left behind and the worth of an ideal (or any ideal) becomes questionable, the romance form becomes conventionalized into stock formula and begins the plunge into irony and self-parody. The ideals of love, adventure, and victory degenerate into sex, violence, and incompetence. Thus, the Bond films maintain the adventure and "heroic" conventions of romance but do so ironically and vestigially without serious reference to significant ideals.

The representative principle applies equally as well to the realistic circumstances of characters as diverse as Ruth the Moabitess to the prophet Daniel to Agnes and Mr. Peggotty of *David Copperfield* to Fanny Price of *Mansfield Park*. Oliver Twist and Tiny Tim are variations on the timeless theme of threatened innocence. Whatever the limits of circumstance, the hero as embodied ideal characteristic of the archetype of romance remains as long as a writer or an audience accepts an ideal and its value as possible and worthy of emulation. By way of contrast, in Hardy's *Tess of the d'Urbervilles*, threatened innocence becomes ruined innocence, innocence being an ideal no longer possible under the demands of circumstance. Angel, Tess's ironically named husband, cannot or will not redeem Tess amid circumstances of spiritual sterility.

In the FG, Jesus is the incarnate Word and both operates within and transcends the conventional representational boundaries. Jesus is sui generis—human and divine—and therefore does not correspond precisely to Frye's classification of character types. Jesus enters the world as man in space and time and realism, and in doing so descends from what Frye designates "myth" into romance and beyond. And since Jesus is fully human and subject to the order of nature, classification of his character in Frye's scheme extends to epic as well. While doing so, Jesus maintains his status as divine, and Jesus also claims representative status with respect to the Father. Jesus claims to be at one with the Father (10:30) and thus a full participant in deity. Jesus is the sent one of the Father who performs his mission in obedience to what the Father desires. But Jesus is distinct from the Father while at one with him. In representing the Father, or showing the Father to the world, he displays the Father. Jesus tells Philip, "Don't you know me, Philip, even after I have been among you such a long time? Anyone who has seen me has seen the Father. How can you say, 'Show us the Father?' Don't you believe that I am in the Father, and that the Father is in me?" (14:9-10) Thus, Jesus both represents the Father, acting according to the Father's wishes on the Father's behalf, and, sharing the Father's deity, Jesus represents the Father in a medium not inherent to either.

As a human being and as God and as the Son at one with the Father, Jesus in one sense is, as a man, a metaphor for God, and, as the Son, a metaphor for the Father.

Metaphor is here understood as an imaginative identification of one thing with another. In Jesus's case, an "imaginative identification" is precisely what is necessary; the normal categories of human/divine and God as one in a non-Trinitarian sense have broken down. At the same time, the identification is not imaginative in the sense of not being real; rather imagination (analogous to faith) is the faculty by which the reality is apprehended. To see Jesus is to see God, and to see Jesus is to see the Father. The incarnation reveals God in that Jesus is God, and reveals something about God in that Jesus can claim oneness with the Father and yet maintain a separate identity. Jesus reveals God in the incarnation in a metaphorical or representational way, meaning that he does so in a way that is not inherent in the nature of God, that is, as a human being. At the same time, this does not necessarily mean that, however much it remains a mystery, the claim that Jesus is a human being is incompatible with the claim that he is God. Theologically, Jesus is in one sense the quintessential metaphor, fully one thing and fully another, God and man, the degree of correspondence between tenor and vehicle in his case being absolute. In another sense, nontheologically, Jesus is first cousin to other heroes in romance, heroes who are fully themselves and fully representational of something else.

Metaphor can mean or express much or little, depending on an evaluation of similarities, differences and degree of correspondence between tenor and vehicle. Jesus is both God and man, absolute similarity and absolute difference. Hick's designation of Jesus as "the metaphor of God incarnate" is ironic in that it negates Jesus's unique claim to divinity, the key feature of the way Jesus has been traditionally understood.[114] This view reduces Jesus to a mere ethical illustration or representation in a way detached from his identity. For Hick, tenor and vehicle for Jesus are accidental, not ontological. If Hick's view of things is applied to the conception of the hero as an embodied ideal in the case of Jesus or anyone else, the hero represents something other than what is inherent to the self, and tenor and vehicle threaten to break apart, stay apart, or bang together, a state of affairs more akin to tragedy, irony, or comedy than romance.

The conflict in the FG is not simply one of the fantastic meeting the world of realism in physical or literary terms: it is the conflict of the personal and ideal, God, meeting a fallen world, the integrated meeting the disintegrated, the whole meeting the broken. The worlds of tragedy, irony, and comedy are worlds in which the individual is somehow estranged from the world and estranged from the self in that both the world and the individuals who inhabit it are estranged from God. Jesus is the one who both represents the Father by doing as the Father does (5:19) and does so in submission, obedience, and freedom as one who has been granted "life in himself" by the Father (5:26). Jesus is the living embodiment of a unity of faith and knowledge; faith being understood as volitional commitment related to love and obedience and knowledge understood as complete factual and personal knowledge of God the Father. In the FG, "the evangelist stresses repeatedly that Jesus's knowledge is full and perfect knowledge of the Father . . . of men and of the work which has been given Him to do. Christ's knowledge of the Father is direct and absolute."[115] Jesus knows and "believes" the

---

[114] See John Hick, *The Metaphor of God Incarnate* (London: SCM Press, 1993).
[115] James M. Boice, *Witness and Revelation in the Gospel of John* (Grand Rapids: Zondervan, 1970), 45.

Father; in their intra-Trinitarian fellowship, knowledge and belief are fully realized and perichoretic. Faith and knowledge are not reciprocal or in process for Jesus and the Father as if one built upon and enhanced the other, but faith and knowledge for Jesus and the Father are one, an established state of affairs, an ontological fact. "I and the Father are one" (10:30) is a statement of unity and diversity. Jesus is doubly the ideal in that he is God and obeys God.

In a fallen world, faith and knowledge are at a distance from each other, especially in matters relating to God, something reflected in the endeavor of Christian theology being often designated, following Anselm, as "faith seeking understanding." In this sense, the FG does not so much present Jesus as making an ethical challenge through teaching, as is more often the case in the Synoptics, but as one who is fully integrated and realized being, both in terms of integration of identity and in terms of that identity expressed in love. In this sense, Jesus in the FG follows the romance pattern of identity being at one with ideal. Jesus's challenge to the world is fundamentally ontological. Jesus, as one with the Father, is in this sense a fully realized ideal, not in a platonic sense, but as one who lives what he is, and what he is identical with God. As such, he exposes the darkness and corruption of a world that prefers the darkness of disintegration and rejects the light.

Again, at its dialectical poles, the conflict in the FG displays the antithetical nature of the perspectives of romance and irony as points of view held by various characters. The romance form assumes the possibility and reality of some ideal and the possibility and reality of that ideal actually being worthy of being known, asserted and lived, however difficult and dangerous that may be; irony denies both the ideal and the possibility of knowing and living by them, tending instead toward relativism and a "realistic" concern with the here and now. The ironic perspective, with its characteristic tendency toward detachment and negation, in some formulations very much tends toward faithlessness, accepting as insurmountable the fractured and confused aspects of human existence. In the FG, romance meets irony and realism in a theologically full way.[116]

II. D. 3. c Other characters in the FG: Personal and theological encounters

In romance the hero and all other characters are defined in relation to an ideal. As theological and narrative center of the FG, Jesus defines all other characters in relation to himself. Jesus does not meet the world in abstraction: he meets others, fractured people with varying degrees of faith and knowledge. Faith and knowledge as crucial components of all characters in the FG are challenged and most characters are in flux, a dynamic that gives a certain life to those in transition and produces narrative tension as Jesus opposes those who refuse to be changed. In its characterization, the FG parallels the conventions of romance by giving its characters a universal significance. According to Frye, "the characterization of romance is really a feature of its mental landscape. Its heroes and villains exist primarily to symbolize a contrast between two worlds, one

---

[116] While irony is manifestly a feature of the FG, the FG employs irony as a narrative strategy to make its point *against* a personal perspective that is fundamentally ironic. This will be explored in Chapter 3.

above the level of ordinary experience, the other below it."[117] In the world of the FG, being above or below the level of ordinary experience corresponds to a character's response to Jesus.[118] However, the FG differs from the conventions of romance in that its secondary characters are not static; all must respond to Jesus and neutrality is not an option. The FG is noteworthy for the scarcity of characters indifferent to Jesus.

Beginning, as it were, in the depths of Biblical criticism, the characters in the FG might also be designated minimally as "representative figures." The difference between the two terms lies in the fact that "character" suggests a living quality while "representative figure" suggests a function as a living embodiment of some other concern, although the two overlap. Bultmann saw Peter and the Beloved disciple as representing a conflict between the church in Palestine and the Hellenistic Christian church and in doing so located the representative function in the *Sitz im Leben* of the early church.[119] In its strong form, this type of approach is virtual allegory, positing a reality beyond the text no less fanciful than Origen's platonic excursions, albeit one wearing the fig leaf of a theoretically possible empirical referent.[120] In another guise, this approach attempts to use the NT as a pathway to reconstruct a historical person beyond the text itself.[121]

Collins offers an approach that begins to move from the quicksand of the prehistory of the text to the representative function of the figures within the text itself.[122] He writes,

> It is my conviction that a process of oral tradition similar to that which lay behind the Synoptic Gospels also lies behind the Fourth Gospel. Within this homiletic tradition we should place the development of units of material, pericopes, in which various individuals appear—precisely as types of the point that the homilist was trying to make.[123]

---

[117] Frye, *Secular Scripture*, 53. "There is, first, a world associated with happiness, security, and peace; the emphasis is often thrown on childhood or on an 'innocent' or pre-genital period of youth, and the images are those of spring and summer, flowers and sunshine. I shall call this world the idyllic world. The other is a world of exciting adventures, but adventure which involves separation, loneliness, humiliation, pain, and the threat of more pain. I shall call this world the demonic or night world. Because of the powerful polarizing tendency in romance, we are usually carried directly from one to the other." Criticizing and going beyond Frye at this point, Jameson argues that Frye's upper and lower worlds are conceptually informed by the clash between good and evil in a way characteristic of romance but not tragedy or comedy. See Chapters 2 and 4 below.
[118] On the importance of faith response, see Elizabeth Dawana, *Which Side of the Line: The Non-Jewish Characters in the Fourth Gospel*. Unpublished PhD Diss. University of Durham, 1997.
[119] Rudolf Bultmann, *The Gospel of John: A Commentary*, trans. G. R. Beasley-Murray, R. W. N. Hoare, and J. K. Riches (Oxford: Blackwell, 1971), 484–85.
[120] See Francis Watson in "Toward a Literal Reading of the Gospels," in *The Gospels for all Christians: Rethinking the Gospel Audiences*, ed. Richard Bauckham (Edinburgh: T&T Clark, 1998), 195–217. See also Tobias Hägerland, "John's Gospel: A Two-Level Drama?" *JSNT* 25.3 (2003): 309–22.
[121] For example, see *Peter in the New Testament*, eds. Raymond Brown, Karl Donfried, and John Reumann (London: Geoffrey Chapman, 1974). This book might be better entitled *Peter Outside the New Testament*.
[122] Raymond Collins, "The Representative Figures of the Fourth Gospel," *The Downside Review* 94 (1976): 26–46; 95 (1976) 118–32, reprinted in *These Things Have Been Written: Studies in the Fourth Gospel* (Grand Rapids: Eerdmans, 1990).
[123] Collins, "Representative Figures," 29.

For Collins, the representative figures in the FG are stripped to their essential role and thus function as typecast figures to provoke and confirm faith within the reader. For example, the royal official, who Collins does not believe to represent the gentile world, "stands as a representative of those who believe in Jesus's word, the word which brings life."[124] By stressing the representative or type quality of those appearing within the FG, Collins emphasizes the static quality of each and tends not to explore their dynamic potential.[125]

Coupled with the dynamic nature of the secondary characters, the stress on realism and concrete detail in the FG prevents a given character from being a cipher for abstract values. In other words, characters appear as interesting and differentiated human beings. Various aspects of representative figures can be explored in the case of the Samaritan woman. The narrative begins within the oft-noted framework of the OT-type scene, wherein a man meets a maiden at a well and in so doing tests the waters of courtship.[126] The personal history of the Samaritan woman, being five times married and living with a sixth man, parallels and represents the national history of Samaria as a whole, a country repeatedly colonized by outside powers and religiously corrupt and, like the Samaritan woman herself, is maiden no more.[127] The correspondence of the details of her personal life with her country's history grounds her representative function to a particular people in a particular time and place. Knowledge about the particulars of Samaria and the details of her life helps with understanding her representative function, however difficult that may be 2,000 years later. But within narrative of the FG, her role expands to represent the one who tells others of Jesus and who recognizes Jesus in all his fullness as the savior of the world who transcends national boundaries. The story begins in a Jewish context of the type scene at Jacob's well and ends with universal gospel proclamation.

But in addition, the Samaritan woman, estranged by her race, religion, location, gender, and conduct, is a universal type—the outsider. Yet whatever her liabilities, they present no barriers to faith in the Messiah. In contrast, Nicodemus is an insider, another universal type. His status as a man with all the privileges of race, location, wealth, and social position offers no advantage with regard to God. Fitting his remarks to Nicodemus and his circumstances and aristocratic birth, Jesus tells him, "You must be born again." Their function as universal types keeps the Samaritan woman and Nicodemus from the oblivion of ancient history, while the specific details of their lives and circumstances prevent them from becoming mere docetic placeholders for spiritual values, thus bridging the gap between romance and realism. The fact that they must respond to Jesus challenges their respective points of view and challenges their insider-outsider status with respect to faith in Jesus. Both

---

[124] Ibid., 41.
[125] For clarity, in literary analysis a static character is one who does not change and a dynamic character is one who does. For example, Lot is a static character and Abraham is a dynamic character.
[126] See Robert Alter, *The Art of Biblical Narrative* (Basic Books, 1981): 47–62.
[127] Much of the treatment of the representative role of the Samaritan woman within the FG itself draws on Craig Koester, "The Savior of the World: John 4:42," *JBL* 109 (1990): 665–80. For a helpful treatment of representative figures, see Koester, *Symbolism in the Fourth Gospel: Meaning, Mystery, Community* (Minneapolis: Fortress Press, 1995), 49.

function as characters who speak, think, misunderstand, respond, and act, infusing them with life and vitality.

The FG contains a variety of characters, from the committed to the hostile and all shades in between. The centrality of Jesus and the FG's universal claims about him make the characters of the FG seem to live in a way that defies the lack of historical information about them. Thomas, Peter, Nicodemus, Pilate, Mary and Martha of Bethany, and Mary Magdalene seem more like living beings, particular individuals, yet types of people we know or might know or have met somewhere rather than relics of history whose dust we might comfortably shake off from our garments.[128]

The dramatis personae found in the FG or any other work of literature cannot help but manifest some representative quality. O'Connor states that "any character is . . . supposed to carry a burden of meaning larger than himself."[129] There exist only a finite number of qualities, values, or characteristics of any sort, and any character or person embodies various combinations of them. The particular combination of these makes every person or character unique. On this matter Chatman writes,

> I argue—unoriginally but firmly—for a conception of character as a paradigm of traits; "trait" in the sense of "relatively stable or abiding personal quality," recognizing that it may either unfold, that is, emerge earlier or later in the course of the story, or that it may disappear and be replaced by another.[130]

All characters and all people are representative types of some sort by virtue of a common humanity and common human experience without which communication between individuals ceases to be possible and literature becomes irrelevant.

The function of characters in the FG is, therefore, relentlessly particular and relentlessly theological and universal. The characters may be compared to Auerbach's interpretation of the typical Medieval function of characters as what he terms "*figura*," a quality Auerbach finds not exclusive to but perhaps best seen in Dante's *The Divine Comedy*.[131] Normally, figural interpretation involves viewing one event in light of another, the former prefiguring the latter, the latter expanding and fulfilling all within a vertical structure of divine providence, as, for example, in Adam or Joseph prefiguring Christ. Auerbach acknowledges this aspect but extends its application. In interpreting a character as *figura*, the historical reality of that character or event is maintained and

---

[128] For a discussion of universality and particularity with reference to imagination and the "human" factor in understanding, see Trevor Hart, "Imagination and Responsible Reading," in *Renewing Biblical Interpretation*, eds. Craig Bartholomew, Colin Greene, and Karl Moller (Carlisle: Paternoster Press, 2000), 307–34.

[129] Flannery O'Connor, *Mystery and Manners*, ed. Sally and Robert Fitzgerald (New York: Farrar, Strauss and Giroux, 1957), 167.

[130] Seymour Chatman, *Story and Discourse: Narrative Structure in Fiction and Film* (Ithaca, NY: Cornell University Press, 1978), 126.

[131] Eric Auerbach, "Figura," in *Scenes from the Drama of European Literature; Six Essays*, trans. Ralph Manheim (Gloucester, MA: Peter Smith, 1973), 11–75, esp. 56–76. Auerbach states that his analysis of *figura* in this essay represents a refinement and clarification of an earlier book length analysis of *The Divine Comedy*. Figural interpretation is also discussed in *Mimesis*, 73–76; 156–57; 174–202; 554–57.

seen against a context of the future divine judgment of God, an already realized eternal event. Auerbach observes,

> The figural interpretation of reality which, though in constant conflict with purely spiritualist and Neoplatonic tendencies, was the dominant view in the European Middle Ages: the idea that earthly life is thoroughly real, with the reality of the flesh into which the Logos entered, but that with all its reality it is only *umbra* and *figura* of the authentic, future, ultimate truth, the real reality that will unveil and preserve the *figura*. In this way the individual earthly event is not regarded as a definitive self-sufficient reality, nor as a link in a chain of development in which single events or combinations of events perpetually give rise to new events, but viewed primarily in immediate vertical connection with a divine order which encompasses it, which on some future day will itself be concrete reality; so that the earthly event is a prophecy or *figura* of a part of a wholly divine reality that will be enacted in the future. But this reality is not only future; it is always present in the eye of God and in the other world.[132]

Note that this kind of figural interpretation is not allegory, however easily figural interpretation drifts in that direction or however common allegory was in the Medieval world. For Auerbach, "the literal meaning or historical reality of a figure stands in no contradiction to its profounder meaning, but precisely 'figures' it; the historical reality is not annulled, but confirmed and fulfilled by the deeper meaning."[133]

In the FG, the reality against which other events and characters are defined or judged is the incarnate Logos, the earthly and divine Jesus. The judgment of God is seen as eschatological and already present (3:18ff), and the presence of Jesus presents a living challenge to the status quo, simultaneously bound up in actions and being. A character's historical encounter with Jesus becomes a *figura* of an ultimate encounter with God, the one no less real than the other. The Nicodemus story in its narrative presentation displays the dynamics of a character within the FG being vertically integrated with a transcendent reality. The real encounter of Jesus and Nicodemus moves theologically upward such that Nicodemus fades away, and Jesus and the entire world are placed in a theological relationship with God. Characters can be seen at odds with the vertical dimension, but never outside of it. Since the theological context of the FG is universal, readers participate in the same challenges posed by Jesus in his own particular earthly circumstances.

The universal theological claims of the FG demand that the extraordinary circumstances therein presented remain living with us both theologically and imaginatively, animated in no small measure by those who encountered Jesus in their day. They are caught up in the same matrix as the reader, a matrix that in the FG cannot be limited to a past encounter with the earthly Jesus. The characters of the FG and the reader revolve around a common center: the incarnate word and his universal claims. In this sense, the characters of the FG are infused with life and significance; they are part of

---

[132] Auerbach, "Figura," 72.
[133] Ibid., 73.

the language and grammar by which the FG seeks to convey its message. The characters are at once invitations or entry points into the experience, theology, and world of the FG and points of reference by which to define or change locations within that world.

The FG reflects and Jesus embodies the tendency of romance toward vertical perspective. The resulting tendency is a vertical stratification of characters into heroes and villains[134] and a tendency to set an idealized or noble situation over against an evil or demonic parody of it.[135] Frye notes that "romance avoids the ambiguities of ordinary life, where everything is a mixture of good and bad, and where it is difficult to take sides or believe that people are consistent patterns of virtue or vice."[136] Thus, in order for this polarization to take place, the world of romance correspondingly tends to be idealized, in the fullest sense of that term, and depart from the ambiguities of realism in some way. The tendency is for romance to be set somewhere else, in a world not quite like our own, usually in the sentimental or idyllic past. In the FG, the idyllic past is the eternal past, before creation; the present is the eschatological now, a now that, contrary to a common tendency in romance, takes full account of concrete particulars and the vexing circumstance of earthly life. In order for realism to continue on its own terms without reference to romance, it must focus on the present as it is, get along with the Romans, and cast out the miraculous and ideal; Christ must be crucified and heroes brought into line with the demands of realism.

The hero/villain polarity characteristic of romance and the FG is not established on ethical grounds. Since the hero is the ideal, to the extent that others are at odds with the hero, they are members of the lower world. Everything depends on the relationship to the hero. Jameson writes,

> We have already suggested the constitutive relationship between romance and something like a positional concept of evil, analogous to the function of shifters or pronouns in linguistics, where the person standing opposite me is marked as the villain, not by virtue of any particular characteristics of his own, but simply in function of his relationship to my own place.[137]

Frye makes a similar comment:

> The characterization of romance follows its general dialectic structure, which means that subtlety and complexity are not much favored. Characters tend to be either for or against the quest. If they assist it they are idealized as simply gallant or pure; if they obstruct it they are caricatured as simply villainous or cowardly. Hence every typical character in romance tends to have his moral opposite confronting him.[138]

---

[134] Frye, *Secular Scripture*, 50.
[135] Frye, *Natural Perspective*, 110.
[136] Frye, *Secular Scripture*, 50.
[137] Jameson, *Magical Narratives*, 160.
[138] Frye, *Anatomy*, 195. Similarly, Reardon writes "The numerous episodes, individually attractive, form not simply a linear series but a mounting climax—and they also people the story with a wealth of secondary characters against whom the figure of the hero can be measured." Reardon, *Greek Romance*, 16.

The FG is like romance with respect to all characters being defined in relation to the hero, Jesus, but atypical of romance in that the FG with its emphasis on the realism of a particular time resists the tendency toward caricature and stereotype.

In the FG, a character's "ethical" dimension develops *subsequent* to a response to Jesus. Although the world is in darkness and rebellion (1:5) and the world is under condemnation by virtue of its unbelief and evil deeds (3:18-21), within the confines of the narrative each character begins in a state of poetic innocence. Fairy tales and romances generally hold a sense of good being the norm so that, although evil is present, it is an aberration.[139] In the FG, each character must choose, in the terms of romance, to be part of the upper or lower world. But regarding the phenomena of the narratives as opposed to the overall theological statements of the FG, nobody is a "villain" until choosing to be one. Those who receive him, those who "believed in his name, he gave the right to become children of God" (1:12; cf. 3:16). The Jews, portrayed as questioning but relatively calm bystanders of the temple cleansing in chapter 2, are never denounced as hypocrites or "open graves" after the manner of the Synoptics. The Jews lapse into active opposition with murderous intent only after rejecting Jesus's implicit claims to divinity (5:17-18), the problem being primarily theological rather than ethical. Jesus cautions the disciples against attributing the blindness of the man born blind to an ethical cause, neutralizing the issue of sin for the purposes of the narrative and clearing the way for an emphasis on faith response. In the FG, Pilate appears on the narrative stage innocent and without the tar and feathers of other information (cf. Luke 13:1) or historical hindsight, a leader whose genuine but abortive progress toward Jesus later descends into condemnation of an innocent man with all its theological and ethical implications. Peter's denials result from a failed theological response to Jesus, and Judas commits a betrayal that is as much theological as it is ethical.

By classifying the various characters according to their faith response, the stratification is at once simplified and expanded. It is simplified by centering on one issue, and it is expanded by its exploration of that one issue in all its complexities.[140] The issue is singular rather than simple. Commenting on this element in regard to characterization in the novel, Harvey notes that characters form bits of a central vision. The central vision is fractured into characters, and the characters move around the central vision in a dynamic fashion.[141] He writes,

> Beneath the superstructure of the individualized character, we may sense those depths in which identity is submerged and united within a greater whole. And with the very greatest novels one feels that the individual character is thereby

---

[139] The analogy here with the FG is with the context of "in the beginning" and creation (1:1-4), a state of affairs from which the world has departed into darkness. In the FG, Jesus is the norm, and the world, in darkness and at odds with Jesus, is an aberration.

[140] A similar move is made, for example, by Dickens in *David Copperfield*. Edgar Johnson notes that the dominant theme of the novel is "the discipline of the heart." To a large extent, the characters function as living explorations of this theme from a variety of perspectives. See *David Copperfield* (New York: Penguin, Signet Classic) afterword by Edgar Johnson, 871-79. Similarly, *Martin Chuzzlewit* explores the themes of selfishness/selflessness.

[141] W. J. Harvey, *Character in the Novel* (London: Chatto & Windus, 1965), 123-24.

immeasurably enriched, that he is not obliterated, or dehumanized into allegory or symbol, but filled with an inexhaustible reservoir of meaning so that he becomes, as it were, a shaft of light defining the greater darkness which surrounds him.[142]

In the same way, the trials and tests experienced by the characters in the context of first-century Palestine made universal by the presence of Christ become universal trials and tests of faith and commitment, or, the relation of one's ideals to one's actions and experience. In this way, the characters of the FG are at once universal and particular: universal in that each must respond to Jesus and particular in that each responds differently. Yet universal patterns in particular responses may be discerned: Pilate responds to Jesus tragically, Peter comically, and the Jews and Thomas ironically. And, Jesus responds to the Father and does so obediently and heroically. The FG, then, does not simplify on the basis of good or bad, but simplifies according to the issue of faith response and explores those responses in all their complexities and consequences.

Pilate, Peter, Thomas, and the Jews meet Jesus in all their particularity and universally as various responses to Jesus as defined by the outworking of paradigms of faith and knowledge in particular circumstances. Those who encounter Jesus in the FG function as living explorations of types of response to Jesus in a way analogous to the four soils (souls?) as types of responses in the synoptic Parable of the Sower. These characters are caught in the matrix of the upper world meeting the lower world typical of romance, or in the terms more familiar to FG scholarship, as they attempt to integrate their beliefs and experience, they are caught in the matrix of Johannine dualism. As is typical in the FG, narrative has replaced parable/pericope format of the Synoptics as the dominant form. Recall that the four literary archetypes each display a discernible pattern of a character's actions in relation to that character's beliefs or ideals, and these patterns are marked by the four patterns: of representation (romance), reduction (tragedy), negation (irony), and integration (comedy). Jesus represents an ideal in all its fullness, Pilate the possibility of faith and its reduction of an ideal amid circumstance; the Jews fail to realize the ideal; and Peter fails to properly integrate the ideal with his circumstance.

Described in another way, Pilate is knowledge in excess of faith, the Jews are faith and knowledge separated from each other, and Peter is faith in excess of knowledge. Pilate, like all tragic heroes, exists in a world only precariously like romance, one ready to be plunged into the chaos and disintegration resulting from the separation of the self from one's beliefs caused by the onrush of events. Peter, as archetypal comic figure, struggles to bring his overly ideal vision of the world in line with the kind of tempered realism the world requires. Peter and Pilate, who represent comic and tragic opposites and, significantly, never meet, are dynamic characters in process of development or destruction. The Jews take on the role of representatives of the world of realism, concrete and immoveable rejection of the world of romance in all its fullness, and in this sense are statically integrated in their own way. Some of the Jews, like Nicodemus, respond to inner turmoil and sneak across the battle lines at night to scout out the other side, but most face no internal struggle occasioned by a mixture of faith and

---

[142] Harvey, *Character*, 129.

knowledge; since they are without faith, the only struggle is external, a struggle for power and control.

II. E Conclusion

To attempt to fully distinguish between story, character, and setting in romance is to a great extent to go against its nature. In contrast to other archetypes, romance presents a unified world, an imaginative vision of a world in which story, character, and setting comprise interrelated parts of a unified whole, a whole unified within the terms of the conception, vision, and the beliefs to which it aspires. Because beliefs and ideals are at one with experience, story drifts easily into character, character into setting, setting into story in a free flowing exchange. As such, romance is implicitly confident, simply assuming the values it projects and aspires to in the life and world of the hero. Romance as an archetype presents a world of values and ideals as self-evident, without justification, a kind of enacted ontological argument wherein the premise, or hero, once accepted, leads to a certain conclusion. Reciprocally, in the FG the prologue formally supplies the premise, and the story of Jesus supplies its enactment. To apply an alien frame of reference to the FG or romance is to separate the hero from ideals and identity, inviting and anticipating an inevitable move toward tragedy and irony.[143]

While romance contains departures from its unified vision, these departures, or the lower, fallen world, provide obstacles to be overcome, test the ideal, display the ideal, and concentrate the central vision by contrasting it with a kaleidoscopic display of its opposites. Archetypal journeys to or from the hero serve to highlight and focus the hero and the values the hero represents. As reduction, negation, and integration, respectively, tragedy, irony, and comedy are fundamentally explorations and expressions of various stages of disunity between a set of beliefs or ideals and the world as it is.

---

[143] This is the move made by Wayne Meeks in his seminal article, "The Man from Heaven in Johannine Sectarianism," 44–72. Meeks substitutes a sociological and mechanistic paradigm for a theological one, a tendency extended into irony and deconstruction by Kelber and Moore. See Werner Kelber, "In the Beginning Were the Words: The Apotheosis and Narrative Displacement of the Logos," *JAAR* 58 (1990): 69–98; and "The Birth of a Beginning: John 1:1-18," *Semeia* 52 (1990): 121–44; reprinted in Stibbe, *Anthology*; Stephen Moore, "Are There Impurities in the Living Water that the Johannine Jesus Dispenses? Deconstruction, Feminism, and the Samaritan Woman," *Biblical Interpretation* 1 (1993): 207–27; reprinted in *Poststructuralism and the New Testament: Derrida and Foucault at the Foot of the Cross* (Minneapolis: Fortress, 1994), 43–64; *Literary Criticism and the Gospels: The Theoretical Challenge* (New Haven, CT: Yale University Press, 1989).

3

Tragedy and Pilate

III. A Introduction

For Western civilization, works of tragedy such as *Hamlet, King Lear*, and *Oedipus the King* endure as great works of art and function as key cultural reference points. Yet it seems a bit odd, given that tragedy contains so much pain and suffering, that tragedy continues to exert an ongoing cultural and even philosophical influence. Whatever sociological or psychological explanations emerge, the power and influence of tragedy as an art form resides in its presentation of something true about human life. Falseness of expression in art results in a loss of power,[1] and critics and readers continue to find tragedy a powerful and enduring form of human expression.

Tragedy inevitably raises religious and theological concerns related to human suffering, the moral order, the presence or absence of God, human freedom and responsibility, and other issues. But tragedy never touches on such issues at a distance; tragedy will not tolerate trafficking in unfelt abstractions. Tragic heroes experience the tempests of life like so many lightning rods in a storm.[2] Reading tragedy as an object lesson in the wages of sin misses the point as does seeing tragedy as mere fate in action.[3] Literary criticism greatly enhances our understanding and appreciation of tragedy as an art form through explication of plot, character, and so on, but is not inclined, if it were indeed able, to provide answers to questions raised. Tragedy seems to throw down the gauntlet to theologians.

Theologians often look to tragedy to express something they believe to be true of human existence. Human suffering is real and profound, and tragedy challenges any glib theodicy to take stock of reality.[4] Theologians and preachers, those most practical of theologians, must address a human situation they deeply understand, a situation

---

[1] Dorothy Sayers, *The Mind of the Maker* (London: Methuen and Co., 1941), 74.
[2] Frye, *Anatomy of Criticism*, 207.
[3] Ibid., 209ff.
[4] See Donald Mackinnon, *Borderlands of Theology and Other Essays* (London, 1968); *The Problem of Metaphysics* (Cambridge: Cambridge University Press, 1973); David Ford, "Tragedy and Atonement," in *Christ, Ethics, and Tragedy: Essays in Honor of Donald Mackinnon*, ed. Kenneth Surin (Cambridge: Cambridge University Press, 1989), 117–30.

displayed in all its power in tragedy.[5] For redemption to be truly understood and the comic aspects of the Christian faith to be appreciated, tragedy and what tragedy expresses must be fully taken into account.[6]

A pause here to offer a distinction essential might prevent confusion. Literary critics for the most part see the genre of tragedy as a specific art form, a type of drama that flourished in ancient Greece and Elizabethan England exemplified by works like *Hamlet* and *Oedipus*. Aristotle's *Poetics* provides the basic starting point for any discussion of tragedy and is here employed in that capacity. While tragedy undoubtedly interests theologians on its own terms, many theologians tend to refer to tragedy as something common to human experience[7] and use the designation "tragedy" in a general sense to refer to everything from the death of a child to the holocaust or as a kind of shorthand for the problem of evil. Tragedy in common usage generally means anything crossing an undefined threshold of suffering or something that ends badly. In contrast, tragedy as a genre or archetype follows a general pattern of presentation developed through certain types of plot, character, and theme, and, while tragedy may indeed be a productive place to study the problem of evil, it certainly cannot be reduced to only that. This chapter concerns tragedy as a genre and archetype in and of itself and as an art form in relation to conceptual and theological themes rather than a general and unspecified notion of "tragedy."

A significant work connecting the FG specifically with ancient Greek tragedy is Brant's *Dialogue and Drama: Elements of Greek Tragedy in the Fourth Gospel*.[8] Brant argues that the author of the FG was familiar with Greek tragedy and that the FG employs a number of features derived from these influential Greek works, specifically features of the "so called Johannine anti-language, including wordplays, ambiguity and misunderstanding, dualism, and irony in its interpersonal dimensions."[9] Brant is careful not to read the entirety of the FG as a tragedy; rather, she examines the performative aspects of the FG derived from tragedy, those elements of drama that create a sense where "we are not the readers of the gospel but its audience."[10] Perhaps to clarify her argument amid a sea of commentaries, Brant tends to downplay the theological aspects of the FG in favor of the theatrical: for example, "I am the bread of life" is less of a theological puzzle and more of a "verbal gesture."[11] In general, Brant's work illuminates the dramatic and theatrical aspects of the FG and moves its analysis beyond being narrow and text bound.

---

[5] George Hall, "Tragedy in the Theology of P. T. Forsyth," in *Justice the True and Only Mercy*, ed. Trevor Hart (Edinburgh: T&T Clark, 1995), 77–104. Forsyth encouraged his students to view drama as a way of appreciating human concerns.

[6] Fredrick Buechner, *Telling the Truth: The Gospel as Tragedy, Comedy, and Fairy Tale* (San Francisco: Harper and Row, 1977).

[7] In addition to Beuchner, Ford, Hall, see Donald Mackinnon, "Theology and Tragedy," *Religious Studies* (April 1967): 163–69. Brian Hebblethwaite, "Mackinnon and the Problem of Evil," in *Christ, Ethics, and Tragedy: Essays in Honor of Donald Mackinnon*, ed. Kenneth Surin (Cambridge: Cambridge University Press, 1989), 117–30.

[8] Jo-Ann Brant, *Dialogue and Drama: Elements of Greek Tragedy in the Fourth Gospel* (Peabody, MA: Hendrickson, 2004).

[9] Brant, *Dialogue and Drama*, 3. Brant notes that this list appears in Bruce Malina and Richard Rohrbaugh, *Social Science Commentary on the Gospel of John* (Minneapolis: Fortress Press), 6.

[10] Brant, *Dialogue and Drama*, 3.

[11] Ibid., 8.

Several things may be noted about the relationship of Brant's analysis to the present work. First, Brant establishes a connection between certain aspects of the FG and Greek tragedy, thus adding support to reading Pilate as a tragic figure.[12] Second, Brant's reading of the FG as a kind of drama fits with this work's attempt to read characters in the FG as participants and representative figures in an extended drama that draws readers into the same drama by presenting readers with the same issues as the original participants. Third, an implication of Brant's work and this work is that the notion of the FG's audience needs to be expanded and universalized beyond a particular place and time, defining and creating its own audience.

Yet, important differences remain between Brant's work and this work. Brant generally reads the FG as a genre (drama or Greek tragedy) rather than an archetype.[13] A genre is much more particular whereas an archetype is more general and can appear in different genres; for example, the archetype of tragedy can appear in a stage drama, novel, or movie or opera. Another difference is that Brant focuses mostly on literary influences rather than on theology. In this work, the focus is on archetypal literary characteristics and the possible connections of romance, tragedy, irony, and comedy to Christian theology. In other words, these archetypes are not simply literary genres or conventions: they are universal patterns that reflect Christian theology.

As noted previously, it is problematic to read an entire Gospel as a tragedy or comedy, but it is possible to view a particular character as tragic or comic. Pontius Pilate as he appears primarily in the FG will be the subject of inquiry as he relates to the role of a tragic character. Following some preliminary matters, a narrative analysis of Pilate will be offered, followed by a discussion of structural elements of tragedy in relation to Pilate, and concluding with a discussion of conceptual matters relating to tragedy. Pilate will be interpreted throughout with special emphasis on his archetypal relation to tragedy within the literary and theological *kosmos* of the FG.

III. B Pilate in the Fourth Gospel

III. B. 1 Pilate as a dynamic character

The FG presents Pilate through a series of scenes marked by a change in temporal location. This inside–outside, back-and-forth scheme forms a dramatic, temporal

---

[12] In addition, several things may be noted about reading Pilate (or anyone else) as a tragic character when he appears in a work that is not expressly a tragedy. Beyond those reasons offered in the introduction with respect to archetype, several lines of thought may be suggested here that will be subsequently taken up. Aristotle noted that tragedies may be written about historical characters, an argument that applies to the case of Pilate to a limited degree because, while Pilate is a historical figure, the FG is not a tragedy nor is Pilate the protagonist. Aristotle asserts that plot is primary over character in tragedy, a point I argue as well. If correct, it follows that a sequence of events, such as those relating to Pilate in the FG, following a plot that is similar to plots of recognized tragedies, then the account of Pilate merits consideration as a tragedy. In the end, the examination of Pilate as a tragic character in this work is itself the best defense for treating him as such in a work not regarded as a tragedy. For a discussion of the problems associated with reading an entire Gospel as tragedy, see Richard Walsh, "Tragic Dimensions in Mark," *Biblical Theology Bulletin* 19 (July 1989): 94–98.

[13] This is a description of Brant's work and not a critique.

reinforcement of the choice confronting Pilate: he must choose not simply between Jesus and the crowds on the basis of ethical or political considerations—the stakes are much higher. He must choose his earth bound way of thinking and its temporal realities, or he must choose to adhere to Jesus and accept his status as living embodiment and testimony of the truth. The choice between the Jews and Jesus is the temporal expression of a much greater question between competing interpretations and archetypal paradigms of reality itself.

Fundamental to understanding Pilate in the FG is to follow his progress as a character when confronted with the person of Jesus, a journey that in turn reflects the reader's understanding of Jesus as offered in the FG. Just as Nicodemus, the Samaritan woman, and others in the FG progress in their understanding of Jesus, so does Pilate. The Pilate who steps out to meet the Jews in 18:29 is not the same Pilate who departs muttering "what I have written, I have written." Failure to take the dynamics of the narrative seriously leads to a static Pilate against which the narrative is interpreted, an approach that tends to be utilized by interpreters relying primarily on historical reconstruction. Carson, for example, does this. Early in his discussion of the trial narrative, he notes,

> Both from biblical and extra-biblical sources, historians have come to know him as a morally weak and vacillating man who, like many of the same breed, tried to hide his flaws under shows of stubbornness and brutality. His rule earned him the loathing of the Jewish people, small groups of whom violently protested and were put down with savage ferocity. (cf. Lk. 13:1)[14]

For Carson, this Pilate functions as a hermeneutical anchor. In another version of the static Pilate, Bond (following Rensberger) contests the basic assumption that Pilate was weak and vacillating, offering instead a strong, irony practicing Pilate who maintains control throughout, a clever Pilate who toys with the subject Jews to extract a confession of loyalty to Caesar.[15] Bond's strong Pilate, like Carson's weak version of the same person, remains static and seemingly impenetrable by the text, impossible of development as a person, secure from whatever slings and arrows the outrageous Jesus throws at him.

Yet Pilate is not without his more sympathetic and insightful interpreters. Referring to his ancient counterpart, one contemporary politician, Tony Blair, observes,

> The intriguing thing about Pilate is the degree to which he tried to do the good thing rather than the bad. He commands our moral attention not because he was a

---

[14] D. A. Carson, *The Gospel According to John* (Grand Rapids: Eerdmans, 1991), 590ff.

[15] Helen K. Bond, *Pontius Pilate in History and Interpretation* (Cambridge: Cambridge University); David Rensberger, *Overcoming the World: Politics and Community in the Gospel of John* (London: SPCK, 1989); "The Politics of John: The Trial of Jesus in the Fourth Gospel," *JBL* 103/3 (1984): 395–411. While Pilate is an ironic relationship to Jesus, the Jews, the FG narrative, and the reader, he is most certainly not ironic himself; to read Pilate as ironic is to mistake irony for ignorance. Further, to read Pilate strictly as ironic manipulator ignores the interpretative clue and symbolic reinforcement of a struggling Pilate offered by Pilate's physical movement between Jesus and the Jews. Finally, in the narratives (cf. Jesus's conversations with Nicodemus and the Samaritan woman) and theology of the FG, Jesus is in control throughout, a fact that seriously undermines any attempt to place Pilate on a similar standing.

bad man, but because he was so nearly a good man. . . . It is possible to view Pilate as the archetypal politician, caught on the horns of an age-old dilemma. We know he did wrong, yet his is the struggle between what is right and what is expedient that has occurred throughout history. . . . It is not always clear, even in retrospect, what is, in truth, right. Should we do what appears principled or what is politically expedient? Do you apply a utilitarian test or what is morally absolute?[16]

The basis on which this interpretation operates is important: Pilate must be interpreted as a dynamic rather than a static character, a man trapped in an authentic struggle making a sincere attempt to set Jesus free.[17]

III. B. 2 The trial narrative as interpretative paradigm

On a related point, the notion of "trial" in the FG deserves a closer look. Harvey expands the idea of a trial beyond Jesus's encounter with Pilate to include the whole Gospel.[18] Harvey establishes and explores the influence of the Jewish legal system on the FG and how this affects a reading of it. In contrast to modern practice that seeks to come to a judicial decision by way of establishing the facts in a case and offering an interpretation as best fitting the facts and therefore meriting acceptance, the Jewish system relied on witnesses wherein a particular witness pro or con was weighed in regard to character. Thus, John the Baptist is not so much a witness to the facts but a witness in regard to Jesus's character and public standing as a prophet. Procedures of offering such testimony or witness could be and often were necessarily informal, such as might occur at the gates of a city or in the porticos of the temple area. The precise charges against Jesus usually had to do with breaking of the Sabbath, as is usually the case in the Synoptics, but in the FG the charge is generally blaspheme.

A related matter is the Jewish understanding of an agent, one who acts on behalf of and with the authority of another. Sons were usually the best agents because they could be most relied upon to represent the interests of their fathers. Credentials were often necessary to validate claims to be an agent of a distant landlord. Thus is the case of Jesus, sent from God as a son with the authority of the Father. The signs serve to identify him as being who he says he is. But the nature of Jesus's case is unique: his claims to represent God cannot be verified, only accepted or rejected: he is either a blasphemer or he is not.

Harvey concludes that, whatever the verdict reached by Jesus's contemporaries, readers must still make up their minds as to the person of Jesus. Directed to either or both Jews and Greeks, the FG may therefore be evangelistic, producing an initial verdict, or strengthening believers in the faith they may already possess. The dynamics of the FG are such that readers in general and believers in particular must always be making up their minds.

---

[16] Tony Blair, *Sunday Telegraph*, April 7, 1996. Cited in Ann Wroe, *Pilate: The Biography of an Invented Man* (London: Jonathan Cape, 1999), 208.
[17] See Raymond Brown, *The Gospel According to John*, vol. 2 (New York: Doubleday, 1966–70), 864.
[18] A. E. Harvey, *Jesus on Trial: A Study in the Fourth Gospel* (London: SPCK, 1976).

Harvey's argument is persuasive, but it is an argument that implies much more than he explicitly states and anticipates further expansion. Harvey interprets the trial imagery, loosely defined, primarily as judicial rhetoric employed to render a verdict on a *past* event, when in fact the rhetoric of the FG is primarily deliberative, rhetoric employed to support a course of *future* action (believe in Jesus). Harvey himself would perhaps agree, but does not explicitly say so.

The point gathers importance as it relates to the fundamental nature of 18:28–19:16, usually referred to as "the trial narrative," or "the trial of Jesus before Pilate" or something similar. In a sense this designation is correct because Jesus is on trial with reference to a historical event, but to view this passage primarily as a trial is to view it in a certain way foreign to its primary emphasis. To begin, the FG contains no account of the formal trial of Jesus before Caiaphas, a fact that begins to erode the interpretative foundation of 18:28–19:16 as being strictly or primarily a trial account.[19] Why recount one trial without the other, especially if the FG contains so many other disputes with the Jews? Furthermore, although the "trial" before Pilate opens with legal questions, it soon moves to questions of kingship, truth, and Jesus as the Son of God—hardly strict matters of judicial procedure. When Pilate sits on the judgment seat and offers his "verdict" that Jesus is "your king," the context of the narrative has moved far beyond the need for a judicial verdict. But if the interpretative paradigm of a trial in a *narrow* sense is resolutely maintained and employed, Pilate will be seen as simply rendering his judicial verdict that Jesus is guilty of sedition and Pilate's threefold affirmation of Jesus's innocence will have fallen on deaf ears. Like Jesus, Pilate seems unable to get a fair trial.

At this point in 18:28–19:16 the "trial" paradigm is weighed in the scales and found wanting. Like Pilate, the issues for the reader extend far beyond the judicial. And, like Pilate, the reader cannot close the lid on Pandora's box and read Pilate's actions as if the real question were merely a charge of sedition. The issues have forever become issues of authority, truth, and response to Jesus as the Son of God as any reading of 18:36ff will demonstrate. Red letter editions of the Bible may prove especially useful in this instance. The "trial" functions, not primarily as a trial for its own sake, but first of all as a narrative vehicle for other issues. In keeping with the FG's theme stated in 20:31, the trial of Jesus before Pilate is primarily, though not exclusively, a vehicle to explore the issues of knowledge, belief, commitment, and action; issues characteristic of the tragic archetype. To view Pilate's encounter with Jesus as exclusively or even primarily as a trial is a bit like the Samaritan woman supposing that her conversation with Jesus is really about getting a drink from a well or Nicodemus wondering how to reenter his mother's womb.

Numerous interpreters note the irony of the fact that Pilate is on trial rather than Jesus, but perhaps the real irony is to read the FG's account as if Jesus really were the one on trial. To note that Pilate is on trial rather than Jesus without seriously applying this insight is to grasp the sword of irony by the blade and not the handle. Why not make the paradigm shift grounded in the prologue that the FG as a whole

---

[19] Concerning the Jewish trial in John Barrett notes, "In fact there is really no trial narrative at all." Barrett, *The Gospel According to John*, 523.

and the "trial narrative" so obviously demand?[20] Jesus is not really the one on trial, but Pilate, the world, and the reader are on trial. Once reconstructions of a static Pilate and a narrowly defined "Jesus on trial" as a hermeneutical paradigms are, like Pilate, dethroned from their pretensions of authority, the actual narrative of 18:38–19:16 can speak more for itself.[21]

A literary analysis of Pilate's encounter with Jesus will follow in which particular attention will be given to the shifting conceptual contexts and dynamics of each scene and to the ways in which Jesus, Pilate, and the Jews seek to control or respond to the terms of the debate. As in his encounters with Nicodemus and the Samaritan woman, Jesus controls the conversations and puts obstacles to understanding in the path of his conversation partners, obstacles that, once surmounted, lead to a greater understanding of Jesus more in line with the understanding of Jesus set out in the prologue. Pilate will be seen to be consistently lagging behind in his understanding of Jesus and of events.

III. C Narrative analysis 18:15–19:22

III. C. 1 Preface: The narrative context: 18:15-27

Just as Jesus's trial before Pilate functions primarily but not exclusively as a vehicle for other issues, so does Jesus's appearance before Annas. The scene is quickly set in 18:12-13, and 18:14 recalls Caiaphas's ignorantly knowing advice to the Jews. And, like the Pilate narrative, this section features an inside/outside structure wherein physical location serves to emphasize a dramatic contrast. Peter denies Jesus under relatively innocent questioning from a slave girl and thus descends from a fiery, sword-wielding protector to join the ranks of the shivering mortals huddled around a fire. Inside, Jesus denies nothing and brings attention to the public nature of his ministry and to the fact that others heard him, facts that could prove detrimental if his captors cared to act on his suggestions. Outside again, Peter denies Jesus twice more. Peter's denials, coming from a close friend and longtime follower, provide an ironic contrast to Pilate, who is neither friend nor follower of Jesus, but champions Jesus's cause more so than anyone else when he has no past reasons for doing so and many present reasons not to do so now. Peter's threefold denial contrasts with Pilate's threefold affirmation of Jesus's innocence. Significantly, no interaction takes place between the inside and outside: Peter, the absolute denier, remains outside, while the steadfast Jesus remains inside in symbolic reinforcement of their exclusive positions. Pilate, on the other hand, travels back and forth on his voyage of discovery and change. The following discussion will center on the changing conceptual contexts as they find expression in narrative form.[22]

---

[20] The point here is not so much to disagree with Harvey, but to expand the implications of his argument.
[21] For convenience and ease of reading, the designation "trial" will be retained.
[22] Historically, it may be objected that those living in the New Testament era would not have distinguished between judicial, political, and religious matters as is typical in modern times. While acknowledging their fundamental unity, it is nevertheless possible to see them as slices of the same pie, a pie best not taken in all at once, but served one piece at a time throughout the seven courses of the drama.

III. C. 2 Scene 1: Judicial concerns: 18:28-32[23]

In traditional tragic fashion, the protagonist's encounter with his or her destiny is not actively sought: for Pilate, this encounter more or less happens. The Jews lead Jesus to the palace, Pilate comes out to meet them, and he becomes involved. The Jews want something done and must go through Pilate in order to have it accomplished, setting up a dynamic in which Pilate is not in control but reacting to a situation, as his concession to meet the Jews on their terms indicates.[24]

As far as the dynamics of the narrative are concerned, Pilate is in a state of innocence and ignorance, comfortably and naively at home in the traditional interpretation of reality in terms of political power. He begins his duties by asking about the charges leveled against Jesus, and in doing so, the discussion proceeds on a basis of legal questions. Even as an authority figure, Pilate begins his legal investigation in a state of dramatic irony wherein Pilate's weakness is already clear to the reader: Jesus is the incarnate divine word and seen by the Jews as a religious and political threat. Pilate's ignorance is in ironic relation to the state of knowledge established in the prologue and assumed throughout the FG. On Pilate's thinking, Jesus is on trial, whereas in the reality assumed in the FG, Pilate, like the world itself, is on trial.

Answering Pilate's question, the Jews respond, "If he were not a criminal, we would not have handed him over to you." The "bewildering logic"[25] of this reply assumes the very thing needed to be proven: namely, that Jesus is a criminal. This "if then" statement by the Jews also attempts to displace Pilate as a judge because it implies that a verdict of guilty has been reached and Pilate need only grant their request. Pilate does not wish to become involved and dismisses them by suggesting that they take Jesus themselves and judge him by their own law. This suggestion may be mockery of the Jews in their subject status or it may be a sincere attempt to be rid of a problem that Pilate, like Gallio in Acts 18:14-15, views as insignificant.

The intentions and desires of the Jews become clearer when they object to being dismissed by noting that they have no power to execute anyone. Pilate and the Roman establishment must participate in order for the Jews to get what they want. This point in the trial marks the judicial/political high point for Pilate. The subject Jews are exposed as weak while Pilate as the governor in charge is the one the Jews must obey and the one who holds the keys of life and death. Now that these elements enter the trial, events become much more serious.

The text informs the reader that "this happened" so that the words of Jesus indicating the manner of his death might be fulfilled. This analeptic comment, proleptic from the discourse point of view, brings the guiding hand of God into current events. Pilate of course is at present unaware of this additional factor. But by making note of the fulfillment of the words of Jesus, the FG signals to the reader the weakness of Pilate's authority.

---

[23] The term "scene" is used merely for ease of reference.
[24] Thomas Brodie, *The Gospel According to John: A Literary and Theological Commentary* (New York: Oxford University Press, 1993), 532.
[25] Brodie, *Gospel According to John*, 533.

Like Greek and Shakespearean tragedy, the trial of Jesus does not proceed very far before revealing that something is rotten in the state of Denmark. The dynamics of the trial drama are present in this first scene. The Jews desire a legal/political solution to what is a religious dispute, albeit one with political overtones (11:45-50; 12:18), and they involve Pilate in a dispute he would rather avoid. The final outcome of the trial demonstrates that such issues do not allow easy separation, either by the Jews or Pilate. The divine order, so prominent elsewhere in the FG, is not absent here. While the trial of Jesus before Pilate follows the general pattern of the encounters of Jesus and Nicodemus and the Samaritan woman, in this instance there are key differences. Nicodemus seeks Jesus out to gain a better understanding, and Jesus provides the initiative in the incident at the well. In contrast, events thrust Pilate and Jesus together in a situation not amenable to gradual learning and easy conversation.

III. C. 3 Scene 2: From politics to truth: 18:33-38a

Retaining the outward trappings of power, Pilate returns inside the palace and summons Jesus where he makes his first contact with the man on trial and asks, "Are you the king of the Jews?" (18:33). This statement appears to come from nowhere, having no immediately apparent antecedent cause. It is possible to mine the mountains of historical reconstruction for an explanation, although 12:13 rests close at hand on the surface, but this hermeneutical strategy tends to slow the forward advance and dynamics of the text. A more likely explanation is within the dynamics of the narrative itself: the change of location signals a change of issues. In any case, regarding the origin of Pilate's question, Jesus appears to wonder the same thing as the reader. But Jesus seizes the initiative and challenges Pilate with his own question, "Is that your own idea, or did others talk to you about me?" (18:34). Rather than seeking information, "Jesus deftly turns the trial on Pilate from the outset"[26] and deftly asks Pilate, in so many words, whether Pilate is a leader or a follower.

Now on the defensive, Pilate here begins his infamous habit of evasion. He asks "Am I a Jew?" (18:35), a self-imposed ad hominem circumstantial argument as if his not being a Jew were adequate excuse for not knowing the identity of Jesus. Equipped with knowledge superior to Pilate, the reader must implicitly beware of making the same excuse. Pilate further protests that the proceeding was not his idea at all (18:35). The feebleness of Pilate's remarks at this point renders a reading of Pilate as clever, ironic manipulator scarcely credible.

Betraying his ignorance, Pilate asks "What is it you have done?" (18:35). The proper question in the context of the FG is not "what have you done?" as if such issues were most important; the proper question is one of identity: "who are you?" Pilate's question here in scene 2 attempts to move the discussion back into the more innocent and manageable judicial context of scene 1 while events and the level of discussion have moved inexorably onward. Jesus picks up Pilate's question about his being king of the Jews and transfers it into a new category: a kingdom "not of this world." It is evident from the rest of the FG that what Jesus says is correct, although not in conventional Jewish

---

[26] Duke, *Irony in the Fourth Gospel*, 129.

messianic terms; however, this redefined kingdom is at present not evident to Pilate. The governor responds, "You are a king, then!" (18:37), as if his original question (18:33) were getting a belated answer. What Pilate likely viewed as something of an admission ("You are a king, then!") fails to give Pilate any advantage. In making this statement (asking this question?), Pilate's thinking moves from the judicial context of scene 1 to the political context of scene 2. But like Nicodemus and the Samaritan woman, Pilate fails to understand, falling behind in the discussion because Jesus is not talking about kingship in terms of earthly political and military realities. The comically misguided Peter drew his sword to defend Jesus as an earthly king, but Jesus informs Pilate that his servants will not fight because "my kingdom is from another place" (18:36).

Yet, Jesus offers a limited approval to Pilate's discovery by noting, "You say that I am a king" (18:37). For this very reason Jesus was born and came into this world. Jesus's statement that he "came into this world" is subject to two complimentary interpretations: (1) coming into the world is synonymous with human birth, and (2) coming into the world refers to the divine Word made flesh. Although perhaps invited to do otherwise, no doubt Pilate understood it to be the former. But Jesus does not allow the conversation to rest on this point and moves the discussion from the political sphere to a claim about truth itself. Jesus came "to testify to the truth" and challenges Pilate and everyone else, if they are on the side of truth, to "listen to me."

Pilate then offers his famous question, "What is truth?" This statement is subject to a variety of interpretations, from cynicism to caviler dismissal to sincere inquiry. Confusion on the matter is to be expected because the nature of truth is precisely the issue at stake. For Pilate, truth means something like material and evident facts in the case, whereas for Jesus truth is self-referential and self-evident: he himself is the truth (Jn 14:6). Jesus is at once the supreme material fact in the case and "the eternal reality which is beyond and above the material phenomena of the world."[27] But Pilate is at present unable to comprehend him as such, and Pilate's very definition of truth is in the process of change.

Although the definitive answer to Pilate's intentions will forever elude us, what is clear is that the reader is in a position to see the irony of Pilate's question. Jesus—the incarnate word at one with the Father (10:30) and the way, the truth, and the life (14:6)—reveals the truth because he *is* the truth. However little Pilate may have cared to ask or answer his own question, he is never closer, physically if not spiritually, to the answer than now.

III. C. 4 Scene 3: Return to innocence: 18:38b-40

On leaving Jesus, Pilate asserts to the Jews, "I find no basis for a charge against him" (18:38b). Here Pilate again fails to grasp the context of the issues at hand. By announcing to the Jews his verdict that no legitimate charges can be brought against Jesus, he attempts to move the discussion back into the judicial context of scene 1. His statement here recalls his initial question to the Jews in 18:29, "What charges are you bringing against this man?"

---

[27] Barrett, *John*, 488.

In 18:39, Pilate seems to realize that he is getting nowhere and moves to the Jewish custom of releasing a prisoner at the time of the Passover. He offers, hesitantly, in the form of question, to release "the king of the Jews." In designating Jesus in this manner, Pilate's context of thinking has moved, reluctantly, from the judicial concerns of scene 1 to the political concerns of scene 2, but Pilate's intentions remain elusive. He may be acting out of arrogance, in which case the designation "king of the Jews" amounts to mockery of the Jews in their subject status. On the other hand, releasing Jesus may be a gesture of genuine good will in which Pilate feels free to designate Jesus as "the king of the Jews" because he is convinced of Jesus's innocence and sees no harm in doing so. Ironic readings of Pilate notwithstanding, the latter is preferable because on the basis of the actual narrative here in the FG, Pilate shows himself to be considerably more pliable in the hands of Jesus than in the hands of the Jews. Even though "the king of the Jews" is announced to the Jews, the context of this statement in 18:39 is more properly interpreted as having arisen from the crucible of his conversations with Jesus inside rather than with his interactions with the Jews outside. Jesus's real innocence, Pilate's apparent judgment that Jesus is harmless, and the surprising nature of Pilate's conversation with Jesus may have combined to develop a personal sympathy for Jesus that he was unlikely to have for the Jews.

But in a powerful reversal, the Jews unequivocally prefer Barabbas and thereby expose Pilate and the naiveté of his handling of the situation. For Pilate, Jesus posed no political threat whereas the rebellious Barabbas was precisely the type of person certain to provoke the legitimate concern of any Roman governor. Significantly, the FG does not mention Barabbas's release. By omitting this detail, the dynamic pressure of the narrative continues past the release of Barabbas, whereas in the Synoptics the choice of which prisoner to release forms the critical literary and narrative divide. Pilate misjudges the Jews and the depth of their commitment to be rid of Jesus, unable at present to see beyond the pragmatic issue of disposing with Jesus and pacifying the crowds. Because Jesus outraged the Jews by claiming to be God, the reader, unlike Pilate, knows that the real issues are theological. The Jewish leaders see Jesus as a blasphemer and as a political liability and take steps to get rid of him, a fact that makes the controversy political at some level. Here again, the reader knows that Jesus is a new revelation from God replacing the old, making the issues once again theological. Like Oedipus, Pilate charges ahead unaware of the true state of things, all the while chasing an innocence forever ruined by facts and aspects he does not know or understand.

III. C. 5 Scene 4: Desperate measures: 19:1-3

Jesus has so far escaped any serious trouble at the hands of Pilate. But the neutral and pragmatic offer to release Barabbas fails, so Pilate resorts to a desperate measure. Pilate does not attempt to win sympathy for Jesus, but to humiliate him, hoping that debasing his prisoner will be enough. At first wince, the flogging of Jesus appears to be intended as preparation for crucifixion, but later developments cast doubt on this interpretation as Pilate continues to insist on Jesus's innocence and attempts to release him. The text marks out that although *Pilate* had Jesus flogged, the *soldiers* place the crown of thorns on Jesus and dress him in the purple robe; likewise, the soldiers perform the insults and deliver the beatings, thereby creating some narrative distance between these misdeeds and Pilate himself, however much or little he may have been responsible for them. The narrative thereby creates some space for Pilate to do the right thing; in other words, the FG does not give up on Pilate and wash its hands of him until Pilate publicly washes his hands of Jesus himself.

III. C. 6 Scene 5: Revelation of divinity: 19:4-8

Again Pilate appears before the Jews and offers another attempt at conciliation, and, having failed to exert control over Jesus, he fails to exert control over the Jews. Pilate announces to the Jews that he is bringing Jesus out and offers an interpretation for his own actions: "To let you know that I find no basis for a charge against him" (19:4). Significantly, he prefaces his remark with Ἴδε ("look" or "behold") so as to set a visual stage for the arrival of Jesus who "came out" and moves from not being seen to being clearly visible. Jesus is described in appropriately visual terms: "Jesus came out wearing the crown of thorns and the purple robe" (19:5). Pilate says to them, "Here is the man," perhaps better rendered by the traditional "behold the man," as if to say, "take a look."

In Pilate's characteristic attempts at compromise, he intends this public display to accomplish two goals. The first is to use the event as evidence for his claim that he finds no basis for a charge against Jesus. His ignominious parading of Jesus before Jesus's would-be subjects provides visible and living proof that Pilate is not seriously threatened by the notion of Jesus as king. The second intention is to display Jesus as humiliated, shamed, and beaten, offering them a pathetic and subdued Jesus who has already suffered enough. If events proceed as Pilate hopes, the crowds will be satisfied and disperse.

But Pilate's hopes are soon dashed. On seeing Jesus, the "chief priests and their officials" shout for his crucifixion. Verse 6 opens, "ὅτε οὖν ἔιδον αὐτν" ("as soon as they saw him") and οὖν here connects their reaction with what happened previously while ἔιδον appears early in the sentence for emphasis. As in the Barabbas incident, Pilate seriously misjudges the situation. In exasperation perhaps combined with mockery, Pilate lashes out with his remark, "You take him and crucify him," but the continuing clash with the Jews demonstrates that this statement was not intended as a serious offer.[28] Pilate affirms for the third time (18:38, 19:4, 19:6) that he finds no basis for a charge against Jesus as if once again he would prefer to discuss Jesus on the judicial basis of scene 1.

In 19:7 the Jews lay their final card on the table. At long last, they inform Pilate that by their law he must die because "he claimed to be the Son of God." The judicial and political paradigms by which Pilate sought to resolve the crisis no longer apply.[29] "Behold the man" for Pilate was synonymous with "behold a [mere] man" and stands

---

[28] So Brown, who notes, "The statement is simply an expression of Pilate's exasperation." Brown, *John*, 877.

[29] For Giblin, Pilate at this point "has become seriously afraid when confronted with an accusation of Jesus; asserting divine sonship. This does not fit with his political cast of mind. He could readily cope with ritual requirements or legal restrictions, but seems to be superstitious about matters regarding divinity." Charles Giblin, "John's Narration of the Hearing before Pilate (John 18:28–19:16a)," *Biblia* 67 (1986): 231.

in ironic contrast with the revelation by the Jews that Jesus claimed to be God. Now deeply involved, he begins to learn that he has been ignorantly playing with fire, something Jesus, the Jews, and the reader have known all along. If it is true that Jesus is the Son of God, then Pilate's attempts to manipulate the situation to a satisfactory end appear in retrospect as ignorant as Oedipus's attempts to end the plague on Thebes by solving the murder of Laius.

III. C. 7 Scene 6: Confirmation of divinity: 19:9-11

This new information that Jesus claimed to be God makes Pilate even more afraid.[30] Although the trial narrative thus far shows Pilate reacting to events while he supposes himself to be in control, during this scene his illusions of control vanish.

After the manner of his "what is truth?" statement, Pilate asks Jesus, "Where do you come from?" Unlike Pilate, who is denied an answer and must make inferences from shifting information in unstable circumstances, the reader knows the answer from previous information given in the FG. By refusing to answer, Jesus remains in control. Ignorantly, Pilate declares his power to free or crucify and thereby implicates himself in Jesus's death. But this assertion is increasingly in doubt on purely pragmatic grounds as circumstances threaten to overwhelm his power to control events. Jesus undermines Pilate's pretensions to power completely by informing him, "You would have no power over me if it were not given to you from above" (19:11). This statement could refer to Pilate's power over Jesus in this situation, or it could refer to the divine sanction given to human government of which Pilate is a representative. But these two aspects need not be exclusive. Pilate acts as an individual in his particular circumstances and, unavoidably, as a representative figure for all human government. In the former, Pilate himself must act and make a legal decision, and in the latter, he must exercise the political power of the institution he represents to carry out his legal decision. But in both cases, his power derives from a source above and beyond the Roman establishment.

The context of his decision goes far beyond the Roman establishment as well. Jesus sets the present events in the context of sin and responsibility when he says, "Therefore the one who handed me over to you is guilty of a greater sin" (19:11). Pilate must understand that the issues before him are no longer merely pragmatic, but real in the sense of values and ethics and theology where real responsibility and real guilt obtain. Judas initiated the betrayal of Jesus that resulted in the present situation whereas unwanted events descended upon Pilate, yet guilt and responsibility cannot be avoided. Whereas Pilate previously functioned with information inferior to that of the Jews and ignorant of the real charges against Jesus, having encountering Jesus for himself he now operates with equal or superior knowledge and must attempt to act upon his knowledge in circumstances not amenable to easy solutions.

---

[30] Brown lists various reasons for this fear but neglects the one most obvious and the one most in keeping with the stated purpose of the FG (20:31): that Pilate had some sort of real encounter with Jesus on the basis of who he claimed to be. Brown, *John*, 877–78.

III. C. 8 Scene 7: Capitulation: 19:12-16[31]

Pilate responds in 19:12 by trying to exercise his power and set Jesus free, his first attempt to do so without resort to pragmatic maneuvering.[32] The imperfect (ἐζήτει) may suggest continued attempts to do so, or it may mean simply that Pilate's attempt(s) to release Jesus were merely unsuccessful. In any case, a certain interpretative messiness obtains when judging Pilate's sincerity and motivations as he attempts to release Jesus.

The Jews respond by linking a potential course of action—releasing Jesus—to a real conclusion: that Pilate would demonstrate himself to be no "friend of Caesar." By making this move, the Jews go over Pilate's head and remind him in no uncertain terms that he governs under the authority of someone far greater than himself. But as far as Pilate, the reader, and the narrative dynamics are concerned, bringing in Caesar at this point has the effect of either (1) removing the debate from the context of the supernatural and placing it again in the context of political reality or (2) raising the specter of the divine claims of Caesar. Pilate showed himself to be most vulnerable to Jesus and the most courageous champion of his cause when, however brightly or dimly, he sees events as the FG presents them, as transcendent realities with Jesus superior to Caesar. By noting that "anyone who claims to be a king opposes Caesar" (19:12), the Jews once again place Jesus, insofar as Pilate is concerned, on the same terra firma as Caesar. Or, conversely, the Jews place Caesar on the rather more elevated terra firma of Jesus. By raising the issue, the Jews insure that for Pilate and dueling rulers, Caesar will increase and Jesus will decrease. The divine Jesus commands no self-evident earthly power or pretentions to political power, but Caesar, whatever his pretensions to divinity, certainly has his divisions.

The occupant of the judgment seat—Jesus or Pilate—in 19:13 is open to debate.[33] If the matter is cast in terms of a historical question, then either Pilate or Jesus sat on the judgment seat, in which case the view that Pilate sat on the judgment seat is preferable on historical grounds. Strictly for grammatical reasons, taking ἐκάθισεν intransitively, in which case Pilate sits on the judgment seat, is to be preferred.[34] But given a certain amount of grammatical ambiguity granted legitimacy by (1) the transitive-intransitive debate itself, (2) the FG's acknowledged use of double meanings elsewhere and, as noted earlier, (3) the fact that Pilate is on trial rather than Jesus, a double meaning of ἐκάθισεν in the narrative is certainly allowable if not required.[35] Thus, however much grammar and history favor Pilate sitting on the judgment seat, the wider theological and literary context of the FG as a whole allows the reader ample imaginative room to see Jesus sitting on the judgment seat and Pilate declaring judgment on himself by virtue of his rejection of Jesus (cf. 3:16-19).

---

[31] It is unclear from the text if Pilate is inside or outside at this point. Thus scene 7 could begin at verse 12 or verse 13. The story would favor the former, while the discourse favors the latter. It makes little difference.

[32] At this point even Rensberger is forced to admit this is a sincere attempt to set Jesus free. Rensberger, *Overcoming the World*, 94; "Politics," *JBL* 103/3 (1984): 405.

[33] Giblin views the scene as judicial farce, relying on an insincere Pilate to do so. Giblin, "Narration," 235.

[34] Carson, *John*, 607.

[35] Similarly, Duke, *Irony in the Fourth Gospel*, 134–35.

Departing from the immediate concerns of the narrative, verse 19:14a notes, "It was the day of Preparation of the Passover; it was about noon" and functions as implicit commentary on Jesus's fate as the lamb being made ready for the sacrifice. Whatever Pilate's intentions at this point, the narrative signals that Jesus's fate is all but sealed. Possibly from the judge's seat, Pilate renders an opinion, "Here is your king," and in doing so Pilate indicates his own movement from the divine to the political to the judicial. This regressive thinking hardly means that he has found Jesus guilty of anything: nothing indicated in the text *before* his presentation of Jesus as king supports this. Rather, this statement means that Pilate may in fact believe that Jesus is king but is in the process of capitulating to the demands of the crowds. Rather than a judicial verdict, "Here is your king" can be taken as some sort of personal statement of Pilate's own opinion uttered in a context of lost innocence and ignominious defeat.

Two options can follow this line of thought. First, Pilate's actions following 19:14b manifest a growing weakness wherein Pilate's conviction to release Jesus melts like ice in the sun. "Here is your king" and "Shall I crucify your king" function merely as the final shots, albeit sincere ones, in a battle that is all but lost. Second, Pilate's conduct from 19:14b onward can be seen as strong and defiant. Pilate presents Jesus as king as something he is inclined to accept, which must be the case if his interactions with Jesus are taken seriously at all, but he also knows that the Jews are winning the political and judicial victory. Pilate offers Jesus as king sincerely as far as he himself is concerned, but offers Jesus to the Jews as a taunt and as an insult. Here Pilate returns to his roots as political manipulator, offering a king to a subject people and leading them into proclaiming themselves loyal to Caesar above all. In doing so, he becomes a kind of Samson who simultaneously destroys his enemies and himself.[36] The crucifixion of the honorable Jesus results only after both sides force each other to sacrifice their integrity.

Thus, Pilate is a divided man, privately knowing that Jesus is innocent and that he is in some sense divine, but publicly as ruler he faces pragmatic realities and begins to move away from Jesus. Pilate sits on the judgment seat and returns to the judicial context of scene 1, but without the relative innocence of the early stages of the trial. Events move Pilate from innocence to experience and knowledge, yet his beliefs as manifested in actions fail to keep pace. Pilate is quintessentially a man at odds with his circumstances, whether theological or political or personal, for in the end he is at odds with himself.[37]

However unclear the pathway between them may be, the Pilate of 19:12 who tries to set Jesus free becomes the Pilate who hands Jesus over to be crucified in 19:16. What is clear is that, like Nicodemus and the Samaritan woman, Pilate interacts significantly

---

[36] Allowing for a complex of motivations perhaps too readily simplified, this interpretation offers the advantage of reconciling elements of Rensberger and Bond's strong, ironic Pilate with the sincere but failed Pilate offered here.

[37] Giblin notes, "Pilate's apparent political victory in the last scene of the hearing and in writing the title on the cross will have to be considered by the reader as a personal tragedy. Pilate has missed the moment of truth, especially in cutting off the witness as soon as he himself has raised the opposite question." Giblin, "Narration," 226. But by failing to accept Pilate's encounter with Jesus as authentic, Giblin cannot extend the notion of tragedy to Pilate's assessment of himself and must confine it to the perception of the reader. Assessing himself, Pilate may have preferred the victory of Pyrrhus to his own.

with Jesus and his understanding about Jesus increases significantly as a result. Circumstances combine with personal weakness in Pilate's case to fatally prevent his movement from knowledge to enacted faith.

III. C. 9 Epilogue: 19:22

Pilate places a notice above the cross reading, "Jesus of Nazareth, the King of the Jews." The chief priests protest and urge Pilate to change and state that this man claimed to be king of the Jews. Although compromised and defeated, Pilate refuses, as if to make a last stand of some kind, one that likely includes bitterness at being out maneuvered, shows defiance in the face of defeat, and displays publicly something of his final reflections on Jesus of Nazareth. However contracted the circle of his authority, Pilate holds his ground on this point and in doing so gets in the last word.

Typical of tragedy, Pilate confronts a world of shifting interpretation and circumstance, where, however much beliefs and interpretation may have adequately accounted for past conditions, they prove inadequate and even dangerous in confrontation with unknown and changing circumstances.

III. D Tragedy and Pilate

Following the previous analysis of the Pilate narrative, Pilate will now be examined as an archetypal tragic figure in order to explore ways in which his character may be illuminated. Consideration of Pilate as a tragic character will occur in conjunction with a discussion of tragedy as an archetype and its relation to theological concerns.

The study of tragedy may be usefully divided into three stages. The first stage centers on tragedy's effect on the audience. The emphasis centers on common elements derived from the audience's reaction to tragedy rather than on the work of tragedy itself. The second stage focuses on common elements within the play itself. Various works widely recognized as tragedies, usually the products of ancient Greece and Elizabethan England, contain reoccurring elements and themes structured in a similar way. Because these form a body of literature known as "tragedy," they can be analyzed for similar properties or archetypal patterns. These properties can be analyzed and compared. The third stage is concerned with the deep structural patterns that provide the ground without which tragedy could not exist. Rather than focus on the audience reaction or common elements within the works themselves, this third emphasis goes deeper, exploring the conceptual foundations that make tragedy possible. The common elements of the second approach serve as vehicles to exhibit the underlying foundations of the third approach, often producing a common reaction in an audience characteristic of the first approach.

As might be expected, a particular writer will often include elements of more than one approach, perhaps using elements from all three. For example, Aristotle's notions of catharsis and fear and pity belong to the first, while his ideas regarding the tragic hero as being neither too good nor too bad and possessing some tragic flaw belong to the second. In spite of a particular writer on tragedy perhaps never fitting neatly into one category, this threefold approach remains valid as a useful way of dealing with the material written on the subject. In this way apples and oranges may be kept in their separate baskets.

III. D. 1 Elements of audience reaction

III. D. 1. a Fear and pity

Fear and pity comprise two commonly recognized elements of tragedy.[38] First isolated by Aristotle, they form essential elements of audience reaction. Aristotle sought to find the source of pleasure in tragedy and believed it rested in a combination of these elements. The action of the tragic hero generates fear as we distance ourselves from it, yet the corresponding sense of pity prevents us from creating too much distance through an identification with the tragic hero as a representative of the human race. Debate continues as to the precise meaning of Aristotle's terms *"phobos"* and *"eleos"* and presents a road best not taken here.[39] A discussion of *phobos* and *eleos* in relation to tragedy offers more potential than a discussion of these terms in relation to Aristotle.[40]

Questions inevitably arise regarding *phobos* and *eleos*. After all, these terms represent Aristotle's attempt to clarify the source of pleasure in tragedy. Because pleasure derived from tragedy is a subjective quality, any attempt at objective clarification will certainly be disputed. Kaufmann notes that the transitive nature of pity implies an object,[41] although, as in Sophocles's *Agamemnon*, several characters may be legitimate objects of pity. In the case of *eleos*, Kaufmann prefers the stronger and less localized term *ruth*. For *phobos*, he follows a similar path and prefers the stronger but more general term *terror* over the usual *fear*, which like pity implies an object. But moving away from identification with elements within a tragic work itself implies a corresponding movement toward abstraction and experiential response. Viewing fear and pity, or ruth and terror as primarily experiential phenomenon produced by tragedy, locates significance with the reader or object. Tragedy becomes something like a dramatic thrill ride, lighter on meaning and heavier on experience.

On the other hand, tragedy can never be divorced from experience. The experience of tragedy happens in a certain way, significantly through personal identification. Pity is experienced through personal imaginative identification with a character or characters as they are caught in and contribute to a situation, an identification that occurs by means of a shared humanity. Othello functions as an object of pity through our feeling for him as a person, not through identification with him as a military leader. Fear obtains through an imaginative identification with a situation as it impacts the life of the character involved. We do not fear Oedipus himself or his particular situation as if we could fall prey to the same mistake; rather, fear results from the

---

[38] Clifford Leech, "The Implications of Tragedy," in *Tragedy: Modern Essays in Criticism*, eds. Laurence Michel and Richard Sewall (Westport, CT: Greenwood Press, 1963), 163.
[39] For a careful exegetical study see Gerald Else, *Aristotle's Poetics: The Argument* (Cambridge, MA: Harvard University Press, 1957).
[40] Walter Kaufmann, *Tragedy and Philosophy* (Princeton: Princeton University Press, 1968), 43–52. Kaufmann takes this approach in his discussion of fear and pity.
[41] Kaufmann, *Tragedy and Philosophy*, 44–45.

mere possibility of ignorantly doing the very thing we most want to avoid. Ignorance as expressed in Oedipus provides the common element between his circumstances and ours. Fear, then, primarily concerns identification with circumstances, while pity occurs through identification with a common humanity as expressed in character as both are manifested in the twists and turns of a particular plot.

James Joyce offers the following treatment of terror and pity through the character of Stephen Dedalus in his novel *Portrait of the Artist as Young Man*.

> Pity is the feeling which arrests the mind in the presence of whatsoever is grave and constant in human suffering and unites it with the human sufferer. Terror is the feeling which arrests the mind in the presence of whatsoever is grave and constant in human sufferings and unites it with the secret cause.[42]

Here human suffering is connected with the experience of pity through the agency of the human sufferer. In tragedy this would be a character in the drama, one who becomes a representative symbol of human suffering. Human suffering is connected with the experience of terror through the agency of "the secret cause," taken here to mean the situation, setting, or plot. The events and characters combine to produce fear and pity in a work of tragedy.

Aristotle's *The Art of Rhetoric* includes a detailed analysis of fear and pity by which Pilate can be examined. For Aristotle, fear is "a pain or disturbance due to imagining some destructive or painful evil in the future."[43] Fear depends on the proximity of the frightening. Pilate has much to fear in his situation: unjust power, in the form of the chief priests who threaten to report him to Caesar; insulted virtue with power, in the form of Jesus the creator of the world; those who have been wronged in the form of the Jews mistreated by Pilate in the past; rivals for advantages that both parties cannot simultaneously enjoy in the form of the power-hungry high priests; superiors in the form of Caesar himself; fearsome things made the more fearsome by not being able to rectify the error in the form of Pilate's too late discovery of the Jews' true motive; the level of hatred of the Jewish leaders against Jesus and the true identity of Jesus; having no assistance, seen in the fact that Pilate is alone and receives no help from anyone including his wife, Herod, or Jesus. Pilate also generates fear by being caught between justice and personal integrity on the one hand and expediency and political survival on the other.

Yet these fears remain remote and harmless as long as they belong to Pilate alone. The reader experiences the fears of Pilate by means of identification with Pilate's situation as he functions as a representative figure for problems inherent in the human condition. While Pilate's role as the Roman governor confronted with the decision of whether or not to execute the incarnate Son of God is unique, some elements

---

[42] James Joyce, *A Portrait of the Artist as a Young Man*, ed. R. B. Kershner (Boston: Bedford Books of St. Martin's Press, 1993), 178. While it is possible that Stephen Dedalus is making a pompous pronouncement and that this statement is therefore ironic, it will be taken here in straightforward fashion. Joyce is notoriously difficult to interpret on such matters.

[43] Aristotle, *Rhetoric*, book II Section 5 in *The Complete Works of Aristotle* v. II, The Revised Oxford Translation, ed. Jonathan Barnes (Princeton: Princeton University Press, 1984), 2202.

of his predicament transcend time and circumstance: conflicting loyalties, public pressure, lack of timely information, unwanted and unavoidable situations, irreversible circumstances, implacable opponents, fear of superiors, concern for career, knowledge of past wrongs, isolation, lack of assistance, and violating one's own conscience—these common experiences of life provide a bridge to Pilate and his situation.

For Pilate, the most fearful of his circumstances is confrontation with Jesus, creator and ruler of the universe. The identity of Jesus extends the consequences of his actions beyond this life as the demands of the temporal clash with the demands of the eternal. While argued above that Pilate was aware of Jesus being divine in some sense, the state of his knowledge is ultimately of lesser importance. In the FG, the state of the reader's knowledge is all important.[44] Just as the reader or playgoer, both ancient and modern, commands superior knowledge about the circumstances of Oedipus's life than Oedipus does as a character, by means of the prologue and preceding narrative the reader of the FG likewise knows more about Jesus than Pilate. The irony of the situation makes the reader unwittingly more identified with Pilate than perhaps desired. Like Pilate, the reader's awareness of being involved in the same choice as Pilate comes too late for escape. The reader, aware of the FG's claims to Jesus's divinity and further disarmed by the knowledge of Jesus's resurrection, confronts the crucified king of the Jews with less protection than Pilate. Loathing of Pilate in his weakness becomes self-incrimination.

But given his presentation in the FG, Pilate is difficult to dismiss through simple loathing for other reasons. Returning to the *Rhetoric* for his analysis of pity, Aristotle defines pity as

> a feeling of pain at an apparent evil, destructive or painful, which befalls one who does not deserve it, and which we might expect to befall ourselves or some friend of ours.[45]

The objection naturally arises that Pilate is guilty and that, therefore, he deserved his suffering, which is of course true. But seeing Pilate only as one deserving of suffering requires a blindness to other positive aspects of his character and circumstances. On the other hand, a too positive reading of Pilate avoids the question of real guilt. Unlike the greedy, initiative-taking traitor Judas, circumstances catch Pilate in a situation he would desperately rather avoid. Pilate escapes the charge of calculated malice that hangs about the Jews, who implacably oppose Jesus in spite of his teaching and miracles. Operating with far less knowledge, Pilate makes a sincere but futile attempt to set Jesus free. Whatever knowledge Pilate gains of Jesus comes too late to take prudent action and avoid the plunge of current events.[46] As if to highlight the desperate plight of friendless Jesus, Peter disowns Jesus immediately prior to the Roman trial whereupon

---

[44] R. Allan Culpepper, *Anatomy of the Fourth Gospel: A Study in Literary Design* (Philadelphia: Fortress Press, 1983), 89.

[45] Aristotle, *Rhetoric*, book II Section 8, 2207.

[46] Steiner observes, "The tragic personage is broken by the forces which can neither be fully understood nor overcome by rational prudence. This again is crucial. Where the causes of disaster are temporal, where the conflict can be resolved through technical or social means, we may have serious drama, but not tragedy." George Steiner, *The Death of Tragedy* (London: Faber and Faber, 1961), 8.

Pilate emerges as one of the few people to defend Jesus. Although forever vilified in the Apostle's Creed, ironically, Pilate takes sides with Jesus and champions his cause more than anyone else and suffers most for doing so. Paradoxically, Pilate might appear weak only because he stood up for Jesus at all. A simple approval of the Jewish request might have preserved his obscurity. Pilate's positive actions, coupled with the terror induced by identification with Pilate's situation, deter any attempt by readers to pass Pilate by on the other side of the road.

Significantly, Aristotle devotes much of his attention to a discussion of the situation of the one who pities rather than to the object of pity. Aristotle writes, "For it is clear that a man must think that he is such as to suffer something bad either in himself or in one of his friends."[47] Those too miserable do not pity because they expect no more suffering, and the exceedingly happy or arrogant do not pity because they consider suffering impossible for themselves. As applied to Pilate, the miserable might consider the consequences of Pilate's actions while the arrogant might consider Pilate and the NT witness of the risen Christ. Most readers fit neither of these categories. Most have suffered and consider its reoccurrence a possibility, or through reflection know that suffering is possible.

Considering objects of pity, Aristotle observes that one pities people close to one's self, such as acquaintances or friends. But if too close, as is the case with children, terror soon overwhelms pity. Pilate's position as a ruler and the circumstances he encounters provide the basis for taking him as a serious character, yet his all too human responses ensure that he remains an object of pity. Common humanity and the universal claims of Jesus inevitably link Pilate and the reader together in a common predicament. Unlike Barabbas, there is no escape by fiat. With fear and pity we recognize in ourselves the potential to act in a similar fashion. However much Pilate arouses terror, the corresponding tendency to pity prevents the reader from washing the hands of him completely.

Terror and pity together form a kind of tragic equilibrium.[48] I. A. Richards notes, "Pity, the impulse to approach, and Terror, the impulse to retreat, are brought in Tragedy to a reconciliation which they find nowhere else."[49] In a similar way, Joyce's Dedalus observes,

> The tragic emotion, in fact, is a face looking two ways, towards terror and towards pity, both of which are phases of it. You see I use the word *arrest*. I mean that the tragic emotion is static. Or rather the dramatic emotion is. The feelings excited by improper art are kinetic, desire or loathing. Desire urges us to possess, to go to something; loathing urges us to abandon, to go from something. The arts which excite them, pornographical or didactic, are therefore improper arts. The esthetic

---

[47] Aristotle, *Poetics*, ii.8, 163–65.
[48] Leech, "Implications," 164ff. Leech finds that "the equilibrium of tragedy consists in a balancing of Terror with Pride," 171.
[49] I. A. Richards, *Principles of Literary Criticism* (London: Routledge & Kegan Paul, 1924), 245. On the combination of fear and pity Richards observes, "Their union in an ordered single response is the *catharsis* by which Tragedy is recognized, whether Aristotle meant anything of this kind or not."

emotion (I use the general term) is therefore static. The mind is arrested and raised above desire and loathing.[50]

If correct, all proper art produces or demands serious thought rather than producing action by itself. Tragedy leads to contemplation or deep feeling rather than action. *Othello*, for example, is more than an object lesson in serpents and doves. Of course, the mind's being "arrested" may result in prudent action, but this is a secondary effect.

With regard to fear and pity, the FG presents a complex portrait of Pilate that prevents this Roman governor from being dismissed out of hand as a bad example. As 20:31 indicates, the FG clearly possesses a rhetorical purpose, a purpose given greater depth and power through the character of Pilate; the FG does not demean itself or its message by creating a straw man out of Pilate and setting him alight. The full dignity, gravity, and awfulness of the human situation as confronted by the person of Jesus are laid bare in Pilate.

III. D. 1. b *Catharsis*

Aristotle connects terror and pity with catharsis.[51] Else remarks concerning catharsis: "'Catharsis' has come, for reasons that are not entirely clear, to be one of the biggest of the 'big' ideas in the field of aesthetics and criticism, the Mt. Everest or Kilimanjaro that looms on all literary horizons."[52] In spite of Else's concern to reconnect the catharsis debate to Aristotle, his remark shows that the debate has forever escaped. The debate about catharsis presents a mountain best not climbed here, while a gaze is certainly in order.[53] "Catharsis" in Aristotle is usually taken to mean something like "purgation" or "purification," often thought to be dependent on a medical use of the term.[54] Nuttall offers a defense of this view and believes that Aristotle followed Plato in holding the emotions in low regard.[55] On this view, tragedy does not then purge something out of the emotions, but purges the emotions themselves. Relying primarily on a linguistic argument, Else sees Aristotle's "catharsis" in relation to fear and pity, which Else mistakenly takes to be structural elements of the drama itself and confuses them with the dramatic effects.[56] Lucas doubts that catharsis needs to be taken in the sense of purification or purgation and notes that Aristotle wrote the *Poetics* in the shadow of Plato's negative remarks on poetry and drama.[57] If this is the case and catharsis can be shown to have a positive social effect, tragedy in Aristotle's day becomes much safer from a Plato-style attack. Leaving Aristotle behind, Lucas

---

[50] Joyce, *Portrait*, 178–79.
[51] Aristotle, *Poetics*, vi.2, 61.
[52] Else, *Argument*, 443.
[53] A. D. Nuttall, *Why Does Tragedy Give Pleasure?* (Oxford: Clarendon Press, 1996). See also, F. L. Lucas, *Tragedy: Serious Drama in Relation to Aristotle's Poetics* (London: Chatto and Windus, 1928). For a cogent survey of representative views, see Mark Packer, "Dissolving the Paradox of Tragedy," *The Journal of Aesthetics and Art Criticism* 47 (Summer, 1989): 211–19.
[54] Geoffrey Brereton, *Principles of Tragedy: A Rational Examination of the Tragic Concept in Life and Literature* (Coral Gables, FL: University of Miami Press, 1968), 28.
[55] Nuttall, *Tragedy*, 8.
[56] Else, *Argument*, 230. The relevant sections in Aristotle's *Poetics* are ix. p. 70; xiii.2, p. 75.
[57] Lucas, *Tragedy*, 50.

himself thinks the phenomenon known to us by the label "catharsis" relates to an intensification of feeling or reawakening of slumbering emotions. For Lucas, catharsis purges nothing but apathy.

Parts of these views may be constructively combined. If Nuttall's reading of Aristotle is followed, fear and pity or other emotions remain important only through their absence. This seems implausible in theory and impossible to accomplish in reality. Yet tragedy drains the emotions in some way. It seems better to see tragedy as purging certain elements of the emotions, more particularly certain types of fear and pity. Pity easily degenerates into sentimentality, a self-centered emotional reaction disproportionate to the events involved. Likewise, fear often occurs out of proportion to the object, either too much or too little. Tragedy purges the sentimentality from pity and strips away insignificant fears by presenting an exceedingly fearful situation in which fear and pity are directed to objects and situations of real fear and real pity. The emotions undergo catharsis and are thereby refined through a furnace of reality and experience rather than through esoteric contemplation. Jaspers takes this view of catharsis a step further and sees tragedy as a "catharsis of the soul." He writes,

> It [tragedy] makes him more deeply receptive to reality, not merely as a spectator, but a man who is personally involved. It makes truth a part of us by cleansing us of all that in our everyday experience is petty, bewildering, and trivial—all that narrows us and makes us blind.[58]

Incorporating Lucas's idea of emotional reawakening, the ultimate effect of catharsis is purification resulting in emotional and aesthetic vivification.

While remaining a real historical figure, Pilate becomes symbolic for the difficult circumstances of the human race. Like Oedipus, events relentlessly move him to an untenable position, one not possible to relieve by means of practical skill. Yet Pilate's desperate weakness does not allow us to forget that he is human. Through terror and pity characteristic of tragedy, Pilate attracts and terrifies, producing catharsis characteristic of tragedy.

III. D. 2 Structural elements of tragedy

In spite of the enduring influence of Aristotle, tragedy generally lacks a set structure. Neoclassical French tragedy tended to follow Aristotle as a kind of literary Ten Commandments, but Shakespeare, to the consternation of many, featured tragedies with flexible structures. Nevertheless, certain elements identified by Aristotle appear in tragedy often and strongly enough to merit their designation as elements of tragedy. In this sense, the discussion has moved from effects on the audience to an analysis of the primary structural elements: plot and character. The discussion will proceed with

---

[58] Karl Jaspers, "The Tragic: Awareness; Basic Characteristics: Fundamental Interpretations," in *Tragedy: Modern essays in Criticism*, eds. Laurence Michel and Richard Sewall (Westport, CT: Greenwood Press, 1963), 12.

III. D. 2. a Plot

Most of the *Poetics* may be safely viewed as an analysis of elements of tragedy rather than a metaphysical analysis of what tragedy says about human life.[59] Aristotle believed that every tragedy consisted of six qualities: plot, character, thought, diction, spectacle, and song.[60] Aristotle's remarks on fear, pity, catharsis, the nature of the tragic hero (neither wholly good nor wholly bad) remain important in contemporary discussions of tragedy as do the additional plot-related elements of recognition, the tragic error, and action more important than character.[61] Aristotle held plot to be the most important. He offers three reasons for the supremacy of plot over character.

> But most important of all is the structure of the incidents. For Tragedy is an imitation, not of men, but of an action and of life, and life consists in action, and its end is a mode of action, not a quality.[62]
>
> Again, if you string together a set of speeches expressive of character, and well finished in point of diction and thought, you will not produce the essential tragic effect nearly so well as with a play which, however deficient in these respects, yet has a plot and artistically constructed incidents. Besides which, the most powerful elements of emotional interest in tragedy—*peripeteia* or reversal of the situation, and recognition scenes—are parts of the plot.[63]
>
> The Plot, then, is the first principle, and, as it were, the soul of a tragedy: Character holds the second place. A similar fact is seen in painting. The most beautiful colors, laid on confusedly, will not give as much pleasure as the chalk outline of a portrait. Thus Tragedy is the imitation of an action, and of the agents mainly with a view to the action.[64]

Defending Aristotle, Cornford states, "That action is primary, character secondary, seems to be true of any drama, ancient or modern, that can be called tragedy."[65] Plot must be connected in some way with the personalities of the characters to be tragic; the driving force of personality serves only to move the action down a certain path.[66] The Greeks emphasized plot over character more so than Shakespeare, who breathes into his characters a pervasive vitality.[67] The looseness of Shakespeare's plots as compared to the Greek writers is a common observation, but even in Shakespeare plot is primary. Separation of character from plot transforms the character into a separate personality

---

[59] Kaufmann, *Tragedy*, 31ff.
[60] Aristotle, *Poetics*, vi.7, 62.
[61] Brereton, *Principles*, 27.
[62] Aristotle, *Poetics*, vi.9, 62.
[63] Aristotle, *Poetics*, vi.13–14, 63.
[64] Aristotle, *Poetics*, vi.15, 63.
[65] Francis Cornford, *The Origin of Attic Comedy* (London: Edward Arnold, 1914), 196.
[66] Brereton, *Principles*, 46, notes the indissoluble connection between plot and character.
[67] George Hegel, *Aesthetics: Lectures on Fine Art*, vol. II. trans. T. M. Knox (Oxford: Claredon Press, 1975), 1176–77.

abstracted from the confines and purposes of the tragedy itself. If one cared to follow this path and imagine Hamlet strolling about Elsinore Castle arm in arm with his wife Ophelia, this fairyland Prince of Denmark ceases to be tragic altogether.[68] Like Hamlet, Oedipus can scarcely be imagined apart from the events of the play's plot.

Although differing in their precise formulations, both Hegel and Scheler see tragedy in terms of a clash of values or powers.[69] Any clash must necessarily occur within a relationship of events brought to life by means of plot. For Hegel, the inner qualities of an individual spring to life as "the actual execution of inner intentions and aims."[70] Drama occurs during a clash of two such parties so that "the action has to encounter hindrances from other agents and fall into complications and oppositions where both sides struggle for success and control."[71] Scheler notes, "It [i.e., tragedy] appears in the realm of changing values and circumstances. Something must happen for it to appear. There must be a period of time in which something is lost or destroyed."[72] Brereton argues that tragedy is an exploration of the question of power by means of the tragic hero as exploratory agent.[73] Tragedy necessarily takes the form of narrative sequence of events occurring through a period of time.

The importance of plot over character may be seen in the fact that some works of tragedy lack a clear central character. Leech wonders, "whether, or to what extent, tragedy needs a tragic hero" and notes that "the tragic burden can be shared."[74] For example, in *Antigone*, Creon rivals Antigone for our attention while *Agamemnon* offers Clytemnestra, Cassandra, and Agamemnon as tragic characters. In both cases, these works are clearly tragic because the situation and turn of events—the plot—require it.

The ascendancy of plot over character, to whatever degree, is of no small importance when interpreting Pilate. The FG presents Pilate in a carefully structured way as if to emphasize the importance of plot and events. The outside/inside, back-and-forth scheme carefully marks the discourse development and controls character development. Some interpretation of Pilate appear similar to Bradley's treatment of Shakespeare's characters in abstracting Pilate from a structured order of events as presented in the FG.[75] Seen from the end result of his conduct alone, especially when viewed through the safety of time, Pilate appears weak and reprehensible. The

---

[68] Largely ridiculed today, this type of criticism gained influence through the work of A. C. Bradley. See A. C. Bradley, *Shakespearean Tragedy: Lectures on Hamlet, Othello, King Lear, and Macbeth* (London: Penguin Books, 1904). L. C. Knight offers a famous attack on Bradley in *How Many Children Had Lady Macbeth* (Cambridge: The Minority Press, 1933). For a balanced discussion of the Bradley/anti-Bradley debate, see Dorthea Krook, *Elements of Tragedy* (New Haven and London: Yale University Press, 1969), 21ff. Other aspects of Bradley's work remain important and influential. See A. C. Bradley, "Hegel's Theory of Tragedy," in *Oxford Lectures on Poetry* (London: Macmillan, 1919), 70–95.

[69] Hegel, *Aesthetics*, 1153–58. Kaufmann disputes Hegel's notion of tragedy as a "collision of equally justified powers," *Tragedy*, 200–210. Max Scheler, "On the Tragic," in *Tragedy: Modern Essays in Criticism*, eds. Laurence Michel and Richard Sewall (Westport, CT: Greenwood, 1963), 27–44. Hegel and Scheler will be discussed in more detail below.

[70] Hegel, *Aesthetics*, 1161.

[71] Ibid., 1162.

[72] Scheler, "Tragic," 30.

[73] Brereton, *Principles*, 116ff.

[74] Leech, *Tragedy*, 43, 46.

[75] See note on Bradley above.

sequence of events revealed in the plot functions to both expose Pilate's weakness and vulnerability in the face of powers he neither knows nor understands, and to reveal his strength as he grows in knowledge and understanding of these very forces as they threaten to destroy him. Unlike the hero of romance who commands events through strength of character, events for Pilate reveal his naked self and drive him to ruin. Had Pilate been completely weak, he would have been defeated by his circumstances immediately. If character were more important than plot in Pilate's case, his character qualities would have driven the movement of events, and this is manifestly not the case.

Aristotle notes that a tragedy must be complete and whole, by which he means having a beginning, a middle, and an end.[76] Noting that a tragedy needs a beginning, a middle, and an end may not seem like a profound observation, but Aristotle has his finger on an essential point: a tragedy must be a concentrated, definite story that begins and ends at particular points. He writes, "A beginning is that which does not itself follow anything by causal necessity, but after which something naturally is or comes to be."[77] In the case of Pilate, the reader needs to know nothing about him until events arrive at his palace. The story of Pilate is in this respect self-contained, yet the story in which Pilate finds himself begins much earlier. On the terms of Jn 1:1 the story began in eternity past.[78] Information available then and now about the Pilate of history further complicates the question of a beginning point.

Any work of literature assumes a certain body of knowledge and this is particularly true in the case of tragedy. Greek tragedies often used familiar materials, usually drawn from the Greek epics, with each author shaping the material for his own purposes. Shakespeare explicitly relied on familiar historical material for many of his plays, for example *Julius Caesar* and *Antony and Cleopatra*, and made general use in other cases, for example in *Macbeth*. However helpful, the mere fact of historical or literary precedents need not demand that readers be aware of them: for example, a thorough knowledge of the real Macbeth adds little to an appreciation of *Macbeth* the tragedy. As noted above, knowledge of Pilate derived from historical reconstruction can distort or even crush an appreciation of the FG's presentation of that same figure. At the same time, knowledge of the FG's claims about Jesus is essential. If the rest of the FG, or even the canon of scripture as a whole, is taken as analogous to the background the epics of Homer supplied for Greek tragedy, the tragedy of Pilate may be said to begin with his encounter with Jesus at his trial. For, as Hegel notes, every action may have numerous presuppositions, but the real action begins when the conflict actually breaks out.[79] In terms of dramatic structure and the FG's presentation of Pilate, the story begins at the trial.

Continuing his discussion of plot, Aristotle writes, "An end, on the contrary, is that which itself naturally follows some other thing, either by necessity, or as a rule, but has nothing following it. A middle is that which follows something as some other thing

---

[76] Aristotle, *Poetics*, vii, 65–66.
[77] Aristotle, *Poetics*, 65.
[78] Culpepper notes "historical analepses in John enrich the narrative by extending it back to the beginning of time and by tying it to the central events in the larger biblical story." Culpepper, *Anatomy*, 58.
[79] Hegel, *Aesthetics*, 1169.

follows it."[80] The determination of an ending point in the story of Pilate in the FG is more problematic. The end in the drama of Pilate is best located in 19:22 where Pilate peevishly responds to the Jewish leaders' request to change the sign on the cross with, "what I have written, I have written." Beyond this, Pilate ceases to be the center of any dramatic action. Although dramatic on its own terms, the crucifixion is in a sense anticlimactic because, after the trial (or after Gethsemane) nothing remains to be decided. Pilate is mentioned later in connection with the request of the Jews to remove the crucified bodies before the Sabbath and in connection with Joseph of Arimathea's request for the body itself. In both cases he appears removed from the action and says nothing, merely the locus of perfunctory bureaucratic authority.

Although comprising only thirty-five verses and thus relatively brief, the FG presents Pilate with an economy, structure, and precision that demands thoughtful reflection. Aristotle notes that a tragedy should be neither too brief nor too long; if too brief, the events will seem to never gather their power; if too long, the events will lose a sense of unity.[81] But these requirements have more to do with the concentration of emotional effect rather than with the nature of tragedy itself. The account of Pilate with its definite inside/outside structure and sequence of events certainly has the potential for a play. As noted, Shakespeare made frequent use of historical material. Aristotle observes, "And even if he [the poet] chances to take an historical subject, he is none the less a poet; for there is no reason why some events that have actually happened should not conform to the law of the probable and possible."[82] It does no violence to the FG if its presentation of Pilate happens to be material readily suited for tragedy.

Concerning sequence, Aristotle wrote, "I call a plot 'episodic' in which the episodes or acts succeed one another without probable or necessary sequence."[83] For all its structure, the FG's account of Pilate cannot be said to be merely episodic as might be said of Homer or a sequence of pericopes characteristic of the Synoptics. Unlike romance, event produces event within a definite cause-and-effect relationship until the action reaches completion when Pilate capitulates.

Aristotle also noted the importance of reversal and recognition in a tragic plot. For Aristotle, the best plots are those wherein the reversal and recognition happen at exactly the same time. He observes,

> Reversal of the situation is a change by which the action veers round to its opposite.... Recognition is ... a change from ignorance to knowledge.... The best form of recognition is coincident with a reversal of the situation, as in *Oedipus*.[84]

Like *Oedipus*, the events of the trial unfold in such a way so as to effect a simultaneous reversal and recognition. In a reversal similar to Oedipus, Pilate begins as the person in charge; he is Caesar's appointed agent ruling with all the authority of Rome. From him

---

[80] Aristotle, *Poetics*, vii.3, 65.
[81] Aristotle, *Poetics*, vii.4–7, 66. Kaufmann in his definition of tragedy calls for tragedy to be about two to four hours long and the experience to be "highly concentrated." Kaufmann, *Tragedy*, 85.
[82] Aristotle, *Poetics*, ix.9, 69.
[83] Ibid.
[84] Ibid., xi.1–2, 72.

the Jews seek permission to punish one of their own in regard to a religious dispute. However well-intentioned and innocent his action, Pilate's fall from power begins as soon as he agrees to the Jews' request to meet them on their turf. Here he makes initial contact with the web of circumstance that will be his doom. As he investigates the charges against Jesus, Pilate, like Oedipus, begins an ignorant quest for the truth. As events proceed, Pilate unwittingly moves from investigating the truth of what he thinks is something else (the charges against Jesus) to an investigation of which he himself is the subject.[85] Like Pilate, Oedipus begins by searching for the source of the curse on the city only to have himself and his life's circumstances revealed. By raising questions about Jesus's status as a king, Pilate exposes himself as one who is not really the ruler in charge. Beuchner writes, "And what Jesus hits Pilate over the head with is Pilate himself. Jesus just stands there in silence in a way that throws Pilate back on his own silence, the truth of himself."[86] The situation is precisely the reverse of what Pilate supposed. As events press the matter further, Pilate finds himself unable to cope, not only with the truth itself but also with questions about the truth. However comforting and enabling they may have been, the past paradigms by which Oedipus and Pilate lived their lives no longer function as adequate.

Worst of all, Pilate recognizes too late that the man upon whom he must pass judgment is in some sense divine, entitled by birth and divine right to be "king of the Jews." No doubt Aristotle would have delighted in this element of surprise and reversal being simultaneously bound up in the recognition of a character's true identity. Pilate's recognition of Jesus and the impossible nature of his own situation occur at the same time, too late to extricate himself from the circumstances. The Roman ruler who began in a position of authority is undermined from below through the manipulations of the subject Jews, undermined from above by the divine authority of the one who gave him his authority, and undermined from within by his own ignorance and failure to manage the situation to a satisfactory conclusion. More terrible than Oedipus, whose actions are past and therefore irrevocable, Pilate confronts future participation in the death of his own "Father," God himself come in the flesh. Pilate's reversal is complete.[87]

In a similar way, the trial sequence brings about the reversal of the Jews. The Jews, presumably, begin in a position of opposition to Pilate and Roman rule. As heirs of the OT law, they recognize the ascendancy of God alone and enjoy a special relationship with him as a "kingdom of priests." As adherents and zealous practitioners of the law, they wish to avoid ceremonial impurity during the Passover and request Pilate to meet them on their own ground. But in their desire to prosecute claims against Jesus, they implicate themselves. They reject Pilate's offer of the true king of the Jews and choose in his place the infamous Barabbas. Having chosen poorly once, Pilate offers them a second choice, Christ or Caesar, a choice that events have forced an unwilling Pilate to

---

[85] Culpepper, *Anatomy*, 95. Larry Bouchard, *Tragic Method and Tragic Theology: Evil in Contemporary Drama and Religious Thought* (University Park and London: The Pennsylvania State University Press, 1989), 35.
[86] Buechner, *Telling the Truth*, 17.
[87] Commenting on *peripeteia*, or tragic reversal, Lucas notes that it is "the tragic effect of human effort producing exactly the opposite result to its intentions, this irony of human blindness." Lucas, *Tragedy*, 113.

make for himself. In presenting the Jews with their leader as he invites them to "behold your king," Pilate is fully aware of his actions and offers their king in part as a taunt.[88] The Jews respond with enthusiastic self-implication, "we have no king but Caesar," in effect claiming to be more loyal to Caesar than Pilate. The patriarch Abraham initiated a long history of Jewish conflicts with the secular gentile rulers; ironically, his descendants proclaim loyalty to the very king who dominates them while disowning the long promised Messiah.

The position of the Jews is completely reversed but no recognition occurs. Unlike Pilate, the Jews never waver and fail to realize the irony of their declaration of loyalty to Caesar. Pilate begins in ignorance and ends in knowledge, while the Jews, who should have begun in knowledge, persevere in ignorance to the end. Pilate begins in power and ends in weakness, while the Jews begin in weakness and end in power. Yet Pilate appears somewhat noble in defeat, having offered some display of integrity, justice, and appropriate fear, while the Jews achieve a victory that the reader knows to be ashes in their hands.

Having seen how the story of Pilate fits with an Aristotelian conception of tragedy and plot, Pilate may be seen as similar to Shakespearean patterns of tragedy as well. Frye notes three pervading patterns of Shakespearean tragedy, patterns that may usefully be applied to the present discussion of plot and will serve to illustrate the complexity of Pilate's situation.[89] In the first pattern, tragedies of order, an authority figure is killed by a rebel figure who is then pursued by a nemesis figure. The central figure of the tragedy may vary among categories. For example, Hamlet is a nemesis while Macbeth is a rebel. Pilate fits this pattern if events are viewed as potential or future with Jesus being the authority figure, the Jews being the rebels, and Pilate the nemesis. Like Hamlet, Pilate proves inadequate as a nemesis: the rush of events overwhelms both and erodes their untenable neutrality. Neither finds the rush of events a convenient time to explore questions of philosophy or theology.

Frye's second pattern, tragedies of passion, features a conflict between the world of passion and the world of order. For example, *Antony and Cleopatra* depicts Antony's struggle between the order of Rome and the passion of Egypt. If a romantic interest is set aside, Pilate fits this category in that he is caught between the passion of the crowds outside and the inside order controlled by Jesus. Antony and Pilate are both real Roman rulers governing subject countries who physically move between two worlds: Antony moves between Rome and Egypt and Pilate moves between the Jews and Jesus. Both toil under the ever-present gaze of Caesar. Each tries to have it both ways: Antony attempts to ease his situation by marrying Caesar's sister yet continues in his desire for his "Egyptian dish." Pilate attempts to ease his situation through the release of Barabbas and the flogging of Jesus yet persists in his desire to placate the Jews. Perhaps against their training and better judgment the Dionysian defeats the Apollonian.[90] For both men, the world of order refuses to go away. Jesus, like Caesar, demands ultimate loyalty.

---

[88] Duke, *Irony in the Fourth Gospel*, 135.
[89] Northrop Frye, *Fools of Time: Studies in Shakespearean Tragedy* (Toronto: University of Toronto Press, 1967).
[90] Frederick, Nietzsche, *The Birth of Tragedy*, trans. Shaun Whitside (London: Penguin Books, 1993). Nietzsche saw tragedy as the fusion of the Dionysian world of passion with the Apollonian world of order.

The third pattern in Frye's scheme, tragedies of isolation, presents the central figure as misunderstanding the inner workings of the world, resulting in isolation and destruction. For example, Lear reaps the consequences of bestowing his kingdom on his treacherous daughters and Timon of Athens manifests the consequences of unguarded generosity. Timon, Lear, and Pilate display inadequate knowledge of the true inner workings of the world. Consequently, the world passes them by and crushes them in the process. A profoundly theological world confronts Pilate who employs futile pragmatic means to manage events.[91] Awareness of the past, planning for the future, and ad hoc management of current human events comprise critical skills for the management of one's own life and for civilization itself. When confronted with real, transcendent realities, these skills prove useless for Pilate and, by implication, for others who would employ them for similar ends.

III. D. 2. b Character

While difficult to remove entirely from a treatment of plot, character merits its own separate discussion. Although it is true, as noted above, that a tragedy need not focus on only one tragic figure, most tragedies do in fact have one central figure who commands most of the attention. Aristotle believed that the tragic hero to be of a certain type, neither too good nor too bad and discusses the suitability of four types for tragedy based on their conformity to a certain type of plot.[92] First, a virtuous man whose fortune changes from prosperity to adversity is unsuitable because this plot "merely shocks us."[93] Job is probably such a character. Second, a bad man passing from adversity to prosperity possesses no quality of tragedy because "it neither satisfies the moral sense nor calls fourth pity or fear." Third, the destruction of a villain is unsuitable for tragedy because it would "satisfy the moral sense, but it would inspire neither pity nor fear." Judas Iscariot is an example of the third type: his actions are terrible but inspire little or no pity. Regarding the fourth type, Aristotle notes that "there remains, then, the character between these two extremes—that of a man who is not eminently good and just, yet whose misfortune is brought about not by vice or depravity, but by some error or frailty."[94] Given these criteria, Jesus can hardly be considered tragic.

The first three character types fail as tragic heroes because they all express a certain one-dimensional view of human existence. The first two express a character who retains all essential elements of his or her character and moves through a progression of circumstances wherein the inner of qualities of the character need not be expressed at all. For example, a good and just farmer might be ruined by drought, while a

---

[91] MacRae observes, "In any case Pilate plays the role of an ironical figure. Here I do not refer primarily to his famous question, 'What is truth?' (18.38), which may or may not be sarcastic. Indeed if one sees in Pilate a symbol of the power of the state, it might be better understood as not sarcastic at all but as reflecting the incapability of the state to deal with issues involving the truth as Jesus reveals it from the Father." G. MacRae, "Theology and Irony in the Fourth Gospel," in *The Gospel of John as Literature: An Anthology of Twentieth-Century Perspectives*, NT tools and studies 17, ed. Mark Stibbe (Leiden: E. J. Brill, 1993), 110.
[92] Aristotle, *Poetics*, xii, 75–77.
[93] Lucas quips, "The objection to perfect characters is not that their misfortunes are unbearable; it is rather that they tend to be unbearable themselves." Lucas, *Tragedy*, 30.
[94] Aristotle, *Poetics*, xii.3, 76.

corrupt and dishonest one might be blessed with abundance. The inner qualities of the individuals remain divorced from their own involvement in external circumstances. In other words, character remains aloof from plot, and these characters, therefore, do not make suitable tragic heroes. The villain, the third type, is rightfully blamed for his or her own conduct. Characters of the fourth type, neither too good nor too bad, cannot be easily dismissed by being entirely responsible for their own actions nor be merely victims or beneficiaries of circumstances beyond their control. Aristotle believed plot to be more important than character in tragedy, yet in stressing that a tragic character be neither too good nor too bad he ensures that the character will be somehow involved with the plot through inner generation of the character's own actions. Indeed, Aristotle offers his comments on character in the context of a discussion of plot. The tragic hero must respond to and be in some degree responsible for a situation and its development.

Given Aristotle's character types, Pilate certainly does not fit the first two: he is certainly not a virtuous man moving from prosperity to adversity, nor is he a bad man moving in the other direction. And it is difficult to see Pilate as a villain alone, for villains do not make sincere attempts to free an innocent man and do so contrary to their own earthly self-interest. While much could be said about the degree to which he does so, Pilate clearly fits the fourth category best. The Roman governor can neither be entirely blamed nor exonerated for his actions. The more clearly blame can be traced to its definitive source, the more fleeting is the presence of tragedy.[95] Character and plot mix in Pilate's case as he finds himself caught in a situation, yet he moves the plot forward as his character is expressed and revealed.

The tragic hero is usually a person of high degree, one who in Aristotle's words is "highly renowned and prosperous."[96] Given their increased responsibility, authority, and potential consequences of their actions, kings and rulers provide more appropriate subjects for tragedy than persons of lower status in society.[97] Frye observes that all tragedies display the presence of a heroic quality in the central figure or figures, a great capacity for doing and action. This heroic action "is above the normal limits of experience" and "suggests the infinite imprisoned in the finite."[98] Elsewhere Frye notes,

> If superior in degree to other men but not to his natural environment, the hero is a leader. He has authority, passions, and powers of expression far greater than ours, but what he does is subject both to social criticism and to the order of nature. This is the hero of the *high mimetic* mode, of most epic and tragedy, and is primarily the kind of hero that Aristotle had in mind.[99]

Frye's assessment reflects widely held assumptions about tragedy. And herein lies the greatest obstacle to Pilate's status as a tragic character. Pilate may be seen to

---

[95] Scheler notes that to the extent a clear and definite answer exists to the question "Who is guilty?," corresponds to the sense of the tragic being absent. Scheler, "Tragic," 38.
[96] Aristotle, *Poetics*, xii.3, 76.
[97] Arthur Miller wrote *Death of a Salesman* with a view toward making the common man an appropriate subject for tragedy. My own view is that Miller wrote a dramatic masterpiece, but not necessarily a great tragedy.
[98] Frye, *Fools*, 5.
[99] Frye, *Anatomy*, 33–34.

lack adequate power of action, lack power of authority, and lack adequate powers of expression. For someone in a position of authority and at least potentially above and beyond the ordinary, Pilate seems all too human, a man unsure of his authority, unsure of his real power, unsure of himself.

This assessment of Pilate is at least partly due to the nature of the plot in which he is featured. The action has already begun (as seen in the FG and the Synoptics and the fact that the Jews bring Jesus to Pilate) and Pilate is swept away by events. However firmly or weakly he holds them, Pilate's pretensions to power and authority stand ready to be torn from his hands. Pilate appears weak only when no consideration is given to how others might have fared when facing similar challenges. Pilate finds himself *in medias res* as do Oedipus and Hamlet. In consequence, events destroy Pilate and expose his weakness without the mediating effect of character revelation expressed in previous action. In addition, the concentrated plot of the trial episode in the FG allows little room for extended soliloquies in the manner of Hamlet. And, Pilate appears without benefit of sympathetic glimpses into his personal life wherein we might have witnessed discussions with his wife regarding her propensity to dream or his personal anguish over the intractability of Herod.

Additionally, character ambiguities manifest in Pilate are precisely the stuff that tragedy is made of. The mixed nature of the tragic hero allows for the tragic expression of the ambiguities, paradoxes, and contradictions inherent in human life. Characters with no such ambiguities are either nearly or completely good or bad and therefore inappropriate for tragedy. In this respect, Pilate is no different than the hesitating Hamlet or the faltering Macbeth. Pilate confronts Jesus and his accusers with inadequate knowledge, a growing knowledge to be sure, but his knowledge grows at a rate behind that demanded by his circumstances. Pilate might well have profited from Nietzsche's dictum that "understanding kills action, action depends on a veil of illusion."[100] Instead, he fails to act in the meantime wherein ignorance might have been a blessing. Like Hamlet and Oedipus, Pilate is a mixed character, neither wholly good nor wholly bad, caught in the twilight zone of knowing both too much and too little and is all the more human and all the more tragic for being so.

III. D. 2. c Hamartia

Aristotle mentions the much discussed notion of the tragic flaw or *hamartia* in a context primarily treating plot but also dealing significantly with character as well.[101] In this respect, the discussion of *hamartia* offers another appropriate transitional link between plot and character. *Hamartia* is generally taken to be some sort of moral failing or an error with no explicitly moral connotations. The fact that the NT uses *hamartia* to designate "sin" has complicated discussions of Aristotle as many have sought to flood the Greeks with Christianity via that lexical porthole. Else notes that most moderns prefer the interpretation of *hamartia* as error when used in a Greek context.[102] He begins by noting that Aristotle's mention of *hamartia* occurs in a discussion of plot,

---

[100] Nietzsche, *Birth of Tragedy*, 39.
[101] Aristotle, *Poetics*, xiii.
[102] Else, *Argument*, 378.

although, as mentioned above, character is significant here as well.[103] Arguing on the basis of Aristotle's *Ethics*, Else believes that Aristotle had in mind actions resulting from ignorance, in particular actions stemming from ignorance of details rather than ignorance of general principles.[104] For Else, then, *hamartia* is a detail of plot.

Like the debate about catharsis, debate about *hamartia* rages in flagrant disproportion to what Aristotle actually wrote about it. Perhaps Kaufmann's approach is best. He writes,

> And his [Aristotle's] main point probably was that the suffering that evokes our *phobos* and *eleos* should neither be patently deserved nor totally unconnected with anything that those stricken have done; the great tragic figures are active men and women who perform some memorable deeds that bring disaster down upon them; they are not passive and, in that sense, innocent bystanders. But they are more good than bad and hence stir our sympathies.[105]

Likewise, Lucas sees *hamartia* as more of a "false step taken in blindness."[106] Taking *hamartia* in this manner allows it to be thought of as something within or done by the tragic hero that allows the plot to proceed. Without something being amiss somewhere in the character or the history of his or her actions, nothing remains to be tested or exposed, and the doom of the hero is made to appear arbitrary and capricious. Ultimately, tragedy does not depend on the moral status of the tragic hero.[107]

Pilate's *hamartia* may be seen as his ignorance of the true identity of Jesus rather than ignorance of general principles or blatant immoral behavior. The Jews strategically allow Pilate to continue in ignorance of Jesus's claims of divinity. Only when well into the encounter do they announce, "We have a law, and according to that law he must die, because he claimed to be the Son of God" (19:7). The fact that Pilate proceeds in ignorance is not to say that he escapes blame; Pilate is ultimately responsible for his own actions. Rather, as the trial of Jesus as presented in the FG begins, Pilate enters this situation in a state of relative ignorance and innocence. As a gentile ruler, Pilate may be excused for not being thoroughly familiar with what he considers a Jewish religious dispute. Speculations about what Pilate may or may not have known about Jesus are inconclusive and foreign to the literary purposes of the FG.

But as Pilate grows in knowledge, the more responsible he becomes. As noted, the basis of his involvement moves from initial questions of a political/judicial nature (ruling on simple guilt or innocence; 18:29-32) to questions regarding authority (the fact and nature of Jesus's kingship and authority; 18:33-37a) to philosophical (questions about truth with Jesus claiming to be on the side of truth; 18:37b) to metaphysical and theological (the source of power and the true divine nature of Jesus Christ; 19:7-11). Although the Jews control the demands on the outside, Jesus controls the conversation

---

[103] Aristotle, *Poetics*, xiii.4-6, 76.
[104] Else, *Argument*, 383. For example, Othello is ignorant of Iago's treachery and his wife's innocence and not ignorant of general principles, laws, or social customs prohibiting the killing of his wife.
[105] Kaufmann, *Tragedy*, 68-69.
[106] Lucas, *Tragedy*, 130.
[107] Frye, *Anatomy*, 38.

on the inside, all the while moving Pilate along in his understanding. As Pilate's knowledge and involvement increases, his level of desperation likewise increases as he attempts to be rid of Jesus and avoid a real choice. He begins by rejecting responsibility for Jesus altogether ("Take him yourselves and judge him by your own law," 18:31); then in a serious misreading of the situation he offers the Jews the choice of Jesus or Barabbas (18:38-40); and finally in pathetic desperation he has Jesus flogged and permits his mocking (19:1-5). Pilate's growth in knowledge moves him from the Greek sense of *hamartia* as ignorance or "false step taken in blindness" to more of a Christian sense of *hamartia* as sin or moral choice.

III. D. 3 Tragedy in Greek and Christian perspective

In his treatment of Greek tragedy in general, Hesla seeks to compare and contrast some of the important elements of Greek and Christian tragedy.[108] He notes that in Greek tragedy, the hero inhabits a *moira*, a sphere of influence governed by a set of laws, or *dike*. The frequently reckless pursuit of *arete*, or excellence, often leads one to commit a *hamartia*, an error. The plot commences when a clash occurs between various *moirai*. Hesla notes, "Being finite and ignorant, mortals cannot know in advance the limits that *dike* has set to their *moirai*."[109] One can probe the limits of life and answer its questions only through experience and thereby gain wisdom. Ignorance can be exposed through action and result in shame. In contrast, Hesla notes that Christian tragedy presents the hero with a fairly well-defined choice between good and evil, a circumstance seen most clearly in Macbeth's decision to murder Duncan. Pilate spans Hesla's conceptions of both Greek and Christian tragedy. The Roman governor's *hamartia* occurs when he exceeds his *moira* during his unavoidable and ignorant foray into a world where God becomes all too real. And having once entered this world, he confronts moral and metaphysical choices that cannot be divorced from the world he left behind.

Developing a thesis similar to Hesla's, W. H. Auden offers his own comparison of Greek and Christian tragedy.[110] For Auden, Greek tragedy is the tragedy of necessity while Christian tragedy is the tragedy of possibility. Thus, *Oedipus* stirs the response "What a pity it had to be this way," while *Macbeth* prompts the question "What a pity it was this way when it might have been otherwise."[111] In the case of Pilate, the Greek sense that "it had to be this way" stems from the fact that Pilate held the reins of human power while the Jews brought Jesus his way to be crucified. And because his decision lies in the future in the terms of the story itself, Pilate's ultimate betrayal of Jesus provokes Auden's Christian response to tragedy by making one ponder that "it might have been otherwise." Given Auden's analysis, Pilate is tragic in both a Greek and Christian sense.

---

[108] David Hesla, "Greek and Christian Tragedy: Notes Toward a Theology of Literary History," ed. Robert Detweiler (JAAR Thematic Studies XLIX, 1983), 71–87.

[109] Hesla, "Greek and Christian Tragedy," 75.

[110] W. H. Auden, "The Christian Tragic Hero: Contrasting Captain Ahab's Doom and its Classic Greek Prototype," in *Tragedy: Modern Essays in Criticism*, eds. Laurence Michel and Richard Sewall (Westport, CT: Greenwood Press, 1963), 234–38.

[111] Auden, "Christian Tragic Hero," 234.

Auden also compares and contrasts the differing Greek and Christian conceptions of *hubris* or the tragic flaw. He writes,

> The hubris which is the flaw in the Greek hero's character is the illusion of a man who knows himself strong and believes that nothing can shake that strength, while the corresponding Christian sin of Pride is the illusion of a man who knows himself weak but believes he can by his own efforts transcend that weakness and become strong.[112]

Thus, Oedipus's secure position as ruler of the city and husband to Jocasta is destroyed while Macbeth's attempt at worldly advancement betrays the weakness inherent in his character. Pilate is somewhere in the middle. As the Roman ruler, he begins in a position of strength, but given his later display of weakness, questions arise regarding how secure Pilate believed himself to be. Yet he does begin as the man in charge even though events expose the depth of his weakness. Rather than trying to transcend his weakness and become strong, Pilate wishes to maintain the illusion of strength to the Jews, Romans, Jesus, and to himself.

Although doubtless, more could be said in regard to Pilate and elements of tragedy, the preceding discussion is sufficient to show that Pilate may be rightfully called a tragic character. The very nature of his situation—moving from ignorance to having to condemn or release the incarnate God—certainly commands attention as offering great potential for tragedy. Beyond the general facts of the situation, Pilate possesses a tragic flaw and undergoes a tragic recognition. In addition, as presented in the FG, Pilate has many similarities to Oedipus. Tragedy has a certain effect on the audience and achieves this through elements of structure common with tragedy.

III. E Conceptual elements of tragedy

III. E .1 Introduction

Thus far, elements of audience reaction have been considered followed by a discussion of the elements of tragic drama itself. This section moves to an examination of the conceptual elements of tragedy. If tragedy is to be more than simply an art form that follows a general format to achieve a certain effect, it must express something true about the world. This discussion of the conceptual elements in tragedy attempts to make explicit through criticism and analysis what is implicit in most works of tragedy.[113]

Beginning a conceptual study tragedy, something needs to be said about procedure. In her book *Elements of Tragedy*, Krook offers some helpful preliminary remarks on method.[114] She notes the common criticism that any attempt to find the common

---

[112] Auden, "Christian Tragic Hero," 235.
[113] Preston Roberts, "A Christian Theory of Dramatic Tragedy," *The Journal of Religion* 31 (January 1951): 1–20. Roberts notes that tragedy makes the implicit explicit and the explicit implicit.
[114] Krook, *Elements*, 1–7.

elements of tragedy results in clumsy, trivial, or false generalizations.[115] Circularity of knowledge, that recurring problem, raises another obstacle, concerning which Krook observes: "For we cannot come to our search for the universal elements of tragedy without some notion, however imperfectly grasped and analyzed, of what tragedy is; and we cannot make our selection except in the light of this notion."[116] This same limitation affects many other areas of study. In response Krook notes the following:

> [A distinction] derived from Plato, between "knowledge" ("science") and "opinion," where opinion is a body of intuitive, unanalyzed perception and judgment which is transformed into knowledge when and only when it has been fully articulated, analyzed and systematized.... It [Krook's study] attempts to articulate more fully, precisely, and systematically the elements we *in practice* (as opinion) recognize as the universal elements of tragedy; and insofar as it succeeds in doing so, it renders explicit the implicit criteria we employ in judging this or that work to be tragic.[117]

Thus, any study beyond a mere empirical list must at some point make a connection between two or more relevant facts in such a way as to be illuminating beyond the brute facts themselves. At the same time the integrity of each discrete unit must be maintained.

But merely studying and classifying the phenomena of tragedy is inadequate in the sense of being incomplete. This approach typically sees tragedy as simply the display of human suffering or discussion of the mechanics of drama. Kaufmann may be taken as broadly representative of this kind of approach. Writing in *Tragedy and Philosophy*, Kaufmann stresses an empirical approach, one that analyzes many individual works of tragedy and arrives at limited conclusions verified by their applicability. Kaufmann's definition of tragedy is as follows:

> Tragedy is (1) that form of literature that (2) presents a symbolic action as performed by actors and (3) moves into center immense human suffering, (4) in such a way that it brings to our minds our own forgotten and repressed sorrows as well as those of our kin and humanity, (5) releasing us with some sense (a) that suffering is universal—not a mere accident in our experience, (b) that courage and endurance in suffering or nobility in despair are admirable—not ridiculous—and usually also (c) that fates worse than our own can be experienced as exhilarating. (6) In length, performances range from a little under two hours to about four, and the experience is highly concentrated.[118]

Kaufmann's definition features an empirical description coupled with existential concerns. Reflecting an ongoing concern for emotional aspects of life, elsewhere he writes of his suspicion of theology as a whole and philosophy removed from personal

---

[115] Raymond Williams makes this claim, (discussed below), in *Modern Tragedy* (London: the Hogarth Press, 1966, 1992).
[116] Krook, *Elements*, 5.
[117] Ibid., 6.
[118] Kaufmann, *Tragedy*, 85.

experience.[119] Consequently, Kaufmann offers no ideas derived from tragedies that may, in his opinion, divorce tragedy from experience. At the same time, he offers no theory that may illuminate the tragedies themselves. While Kaufmann carefully supports his definition, it tends toward mere description. Kaufmann's definition lacks the penetration and illumination characteristic of a good theory and displays the weakness of too great a stress on experience. Elsewhere he offers, for example, a cogent interpretation of *Oedipus* that moves beyond the empirical and phenomenological while his definition itself remains restricted and limited.[120]

Nevertheless, the existential aspects and audience response aspects of tragedy remain important, especially regarding evil and suffering. But at what stage do they become important and why are they significant? A critical divide in the study of tragedy may be expressed by the following two questions: does tragedy merely express the brute facts of evil, suffering, human nature, and the human condition and thereby make us more existentially aware of them? Or, does tragedy express something about the way things are in and of themselves that cause events to result in evil and suffering?[121] More comprehensive, the second approach sees the concern for audience response as derived rather than divorced from the conceptual and will be the approach taken here.

The attempt to analyze tragedy in a conceptual way meets with other problems and objections. Writing from a Marxist point of view, Williams opposes any attempt to abstract tragedy from the particular circumstances that produced it. He writes,

> Tragedy is then not a single and kind of fact, but a series of experiences and conventions and institutions. It is not a case of interpreting this series by reference to a permanent and unchanging human nature. Rather, the varieties of tragic experience are to be interpreted by reference to the changing conventions and institutions. The universalist character of most tragic theory is then at the opposite pole from our necessary interest.[122]

For Williams, tragedy is not something that can be abstracted from a particular time, place, and intellectual milieu. To isolate tragedy and say "this is tragedy" reflects the ideological stance of the person and age making that claim. Rather, tragedy and its interpretation displays a developing, organic quality bound up in its times, a reflection of a changing cultural and intellectual climate. By connecting tragedy with its context, Williams sees tragedy itself and the fluctuations of the interpretation of tragedy as reflecting ideological and social concerns of the age that produced them. Any attempt

---

[119] Walter Kaufmann, *Critique of Religion and Philosophy* (London: Faber and Faber, 1958); *Religions in Four Dimensions: Existential, Aesthetic, Historical, Comparative* (New York: Reader's Digest Press). Commenting on his *Critique* he writes that he argued "the importance of beliefs was widely overestimated, that theology was one of the worst aspects of religion, and that it was wrong to dissociate religion from experience." *Four Dimensions*, 14.

[120] Kaufmann, *Tragedy*, 102–33.

[121] Reflecting this division in approaches to tragedy, Palmer separates critical approaches to tragedy into three groups; those emphasizing audience response, those emphasizing some sort of dualistic chasm, and those that see tragedy as the flowering of the human spirit. See *Tragedy and Tragic Theory: An Analytical Guide* (Westport, CT: Greenwood Press, 1992).

[122] Williams, *Modern Tragedy*, 45–46.

to isolate "the tragic" reduces tragedy to an assertion of ideology reflecting concerns of that particular age.[123]

In response, it must be noted that Williams's own assertions are inevitably ideological and reflect his own Marxist concerns, thereby falling prey to his own criticism. If Williams's thinking is taken to its logical conclusion, any assertion about tragedy falls under a cloud of suspicion. In order to discuss tragedy the category of "tragedy" must be recognizable, an ideological claim in itself. This issue is further complicated by asserting that some particular element occurs in a significant way in two or more tragedies.[124] Raising the red flag of ideology in treatments of tragedy unproductively moves the discussion from the explanatory powers of particular assertions to an analysis of the writer and the concerns of a particular age that writer might reflect.

Nevertheless, Williams's emphasis on the historically particular nature of tragedy is well taken, but cannot be made absolute in a way that his own writing contradicts. The value of any theory of tragedy cannot be reduced to an expression of particular concerns and instead rests on its own comprehensiveness, internal coherence, and explanatory powers, as does any theory in any other discipline. A Christian point of view, as is adopted in this study, offers the potential to demonstrate these three elements because Christianity claims a comprehensive framework for interpreting all of history. One need not adhere to Christianity to accept that Christianity, given its own terms, offers a potential framework for a treatment of tragedy in the same way that one need not be a Marxist to appreciate Williams's otherwise compelling analysis.

III. E. 2 The tragic clash

A few basic conceptions of tragedy may be helpfully analyzed relative to the tragic clash. Harold Watts seeks to explore the perennial question of the relationship between religion and drama, although our particular concern here is tragedy.[125] Watts argues for two kinds of religious myths or narratives: the cyclical and the linear. Humans find comfort in the cycles of life such as planting and harvest. But a more profound insight is that, however comforting the natural patterns of life, individual humans are linear beings. Each will be born and each will die. Watts identifies these contradictory patterns as the comic and the tragic, the cyclical and linear, respectively.[126] In comedy, however much humans are at odds with life in a particular situation, the comforting cycles of life will reassert themselves and human beings will be reconciled to their

---

[123] Ibid., 62.
[124] Williams makes this claim when he states, "The ages of comparatively stable belief, and of comparatively close correspondence between beliefs and actual experience, do not seem to produce tragedy of any intensity, though of course they enact the ordinary separations and tensions and the socially sanctioned ways of resolving these. The intensification of this common procedure, and the possibility of its permanent interest, seem to depend more on an extreme tension between belief and experience than on an extreme correspondence. Important tragedy seems to occur, neither in periods of real stability, nor in periods of open and decisive conflict." *Modern Tragedy*, 54.
[125] Harold H. Watts, "Myth and Drama," in *Tragedy: Modern Essays in Criticism*, eds. Laurence Michel and Richard Sewall (Westport, CT: Greenwood Press, 1963), 83–105.
[126] Frye notes a similar pattern in his distinction between the pattern of increasing isolation from society in tragedy and the pattern of integration into society in comedy. Frye, *Anatomy*, 35.

circumstances. In contrast, tragedy is profoundly linear. Each individual will die regardless of the existence and reassurance of cyclical patterns. A linear worldview implies real choices, unalterable decisions that must sometimes be enjoyed and sometimes endured. These real choices offer no hope of asserting imaginative control over the world as is possible in comedy.

Aside from his dubious assumptions about the history and development of religions on which his analysis is based,[127] Watts offers an analysis of tragedy and comedy and their relationship to religion that is at once simple and profound. The linear nature of tragedy may be seen in the inevitability of destruction as events plunge toward a conclusion. Although tragedies may perhaps end happily, something is lost or destroyed in the crush of events and the linear aspect dominates the circular. For Pilate the rush of events moves him unwillingly downstream. Pilate's assertion of Jesus's innocence, presentation of the choice of Barabbas, and his efforts to set Jesus free, all represent his attempts to reassert the given cycles of life as he knows them (as political realities) through ad hoc management of events. But by the time Pilate symbolically and literally steps out of his palace to meet the Jews, events have already started toward their inevitable conclusion. The Jews have rejected the teaching, claims, and miracles of Jesus while Jesus himself, the "sent one" from God who has overcome whatever human struggles with his mission in the Garden of Gethsemane, remains ultimately in control and informs Pilate of this very fact (19:11). Jesus seems somehow at home in the governor's palace while Pilate seems a stranger. Pilate faces a situation of the profoundest kind: the incarnate Son of God offering himself as a sacrifice on behalf of sinful humanity that will not respond to political solutions. Events are irrevocably linear and beyond the understanding and control of the Jews, Caesar, and Pilate himself.

The linear nature of tragedy leads to an inevitable dramatic clash. Usually tragedy leads to the ultimate linear clash: the clash between life and death for Pilate means a clash between spiritual life and spiritual death. All significant drama of any kind, both comedy and tragedy, must include some sort of plot complication as failure to do so leads to reporting a static state of affairs or a mere chronicle of discrete events. The fact of plot complication and dramatic clash are undisputed; precisely what the clash of tragedy is made up of remains to be seen.

---

[127] Watts offers no supporting argumentation. However, Gilbert Murray and others of the Cambridge School of Classical Anthropologists traced the origins of various elements of tragedy to Greek rituals. See Gilbert Murray, "An Excursus on the Ritual Forms Preserved in Greek Tragedy," in *Themis*, ed. Jane Harrison (Cambridge: Cambridge University Press, 1912), 341–63. Francis Ferguson, who generally accepts this account of tragedy's origin, notes that "Professor Murray is interested in the ritual forms in abstraction from all content; Sophocles saw also the spiritual content of the old forms: understood them at a level deeper than the literal, as imitations of an action still 'true' to life in his sophisticated age." See Fergusson, *The Idea of a Theater* (Princeton: Princeton University Press, 1949), 33. Williams criticizes attempts to find the historical origins of tragedy as derived from religion. He writes, "The detailed and complicated argument about the origin of tragedy (made more complicated though not less detailed by the extreme scarcity of evidence) is inevitably specialised." *Modern Tragedy*, 42–43. Critical of Murray, Gerald Else offers a critical interaction and review of representative views of the origin of tragedy in *The Origin and Early Form of Greek Tragedy* (Cambridge, MA: Harvard University Press, 1965).

A few examples are in order. In Pilate's case, there is a clash between knowledge and ignorance and between the kingdom of God and the kingdom of fallen humanity. The clash between ignorance and knowledge likewise presents itself in *Oedipus*. *Hamlet* displays the struggle between action and inaction delicately nuanced with questions of being or nonbeing and knowledge and ignorance. *Antigone* shows the ongoing struggle between private and public duties as represented by Antigone's love for her brother Polynices and Creon's obligation to treat him as a rebel. Macbeth wrestles with loyalty and duty, qualities he had previously excelled at, and personal ambition. Othello wavers between love and jealousy. *The Bacche* contrasts the Apollonian formalism and restraint with Dionysian pleasure and experience. *Timon of Athens* moves between open generosity and vengeful cynicism.

The opposing sides in these dramatic clashes, whether between individuals or within individuals,[128] may be legitimately justified in some way. However imperfectly manifested, each side carries some moral capital. Of these examples, perhaps Macbeth is most clearly in the wrong, but Shakespeare balances his murder of Duncan with other factors: demonstrated loyalty, the unsolicited prophecies of the wicked sisters, the urging of his resolute wife, the genuine desirability of being king, a certain weakness of character—all combine with easy opportunity to lend Macbeth a certain understandability and sympathy in his actions within the terms of the drama itself. Iago, Judas Iscariot, Polynices, and Hamlet's uncle Claudius, each causally significant in the initiation or development of the dramatic action, receive little or no such balance in their characters to morally justify their actions. Timon and Lear simply act foolishly but do so with noble intentions. *Agamemnon* chronicles a series of ills with each being at least partially justified by some preceding action.

Hegel broke new ground in the study of tragedy by positing a dramatic clash and explaining it in terms of a clash between two equally justified powers, a theory that largely follows his familiar scheme of thesis, antithesis, synthesis. For Hegel, drama has "developed into the most perfect totality of content and form . . . the highest stage of poetry and art generally."[129] This "highest stage" is because speech is the only "element worthy of the expression of spirit."[130] Drama itself works in a particular way. Unlike epic with its all-encompassing qualities and leisurely presentation of external circumstances, drama concentrates the activities of the individual in specific and limited circumstances.[131] And rather than a purely "lyrical emotional situation" in which deeds are described without participation in them, drama displays the individual and the individual's inner life through concrete activity.[132] Hegel observes, "For a drama does not fall apart into a lyrical inner life and an external sphere as

---

[128] Sutherland notes that in tragedy, the individual often "becomes the battleground of two competing patterns of thought, understanding, and action." Stewart Sutherland, "Christianity and Tragedy," *Journal of Literature and Theology* (July 1990): 162.

[129] G. W. F. Hegel, *Aesthetics: Lectures on Fine Art*, trans. T. M. Knox (Oxford: Clarendon Press, 1975), 1158.

[130] Hegel, *Aesthetics*, 1158ff.

[131] See also Aldous Huxley, "Tragedy and the Whole Truth," reprinted in *Tragedy: Developments in Criticism*, ed. R. P. Draper (London: MacMillan, 1980), 151–57.

[132] Hegel, *Aesthetics*, 1161.

its opposite, but displays an inner life and *its* realization."[133] Drama combines—and concentrates—the action of the epic with the interior reflection of the lyric and forms a middle ground between them.

Hegel thus inseparably links plot and character as the inner life of the character is revealed in action. He writes, "In drama a specific attitude of mind passes over into an impulse, next into its willed actualization, and then into an action."[134] The action proceeds from the character and has "its repercussion on his character and circumstances . . . and now his whole being must take responsibility for that the issue is in the external world."[135] The character is responsible for and responds to that character's own works, or, "himself picks the fruit of his own deeds."[136]

Hegel's discussion of character and its relationship to action is preliminary to a discussion of the nature of action within the drama as a whole. The actions and aims of the individual become drama only when "it calls up in other individuals different and opposed aims and passions."[137] The inner qualities and motivations of characters or both sides displayed in action involve dramatic collisions "so that the action has to encounter hindrances from other agents and fall into complications and oppositions where both sides struggle for success and control."[138] This comment highlights drama as it relates to human motivations.

Drama also contains a metaphysical element. Hegel connects the dramatic opposition with the display of external powers, or what is "essentially moral" or "divine or true." The divine does not appear as removed and tranquil, but appears in community where collisions and drama take place.[139] Thus, the divine is made immanent in the action. As the unity of the divine forces its way into real situations, it is particularized and expressed through individual agents who command "reciprocal independence" and oppose each other in a justifiable way. If taken alone, each side can justify itself, for, as Hegel notes, "each can establish the true and positive content of its own aim and character only by denying and infringing the equally justified power of the other."[140] Because each side infringes on the other, each is involved with guilt and blame and must answer for it.[141]

Whatever the concrete collisions, for Hegel the drama ultimately stems from the divine. In consequence, no ultimate collision is possible and everything must be resolved. He writes, "Therefore the drama, no matter in what way, must display to us the vital working of a necessity which, itself self-reposing, resolves every conflict and contradiction."[142] The opposing interests of each opposing side ultimately dissolve into a unity in the tragic conclusion as each side adapts to working together harmoniously. For Hegel, the appearance of Fortinbras at the end of *Hamlet* hints at such a resolution.

---

[133] Ibid., 1160.
[134] Ibid., 1161.
[135] Ibid.
[136] Ibid.
[137] Hegel, *Aesthetics*, 1162.
[138] Ibid.
[139] Ibid., 1196.
[140] Hegel, *Aesthetics*, 1196.
[141] Ibid., 1198.
[142] Hegel, *Aesthetics*, 1197.

Hegel's view entails that the divine be present in a presumably pure state in individual characters who each manifest the divine within temporal circumstances. This state of affairs results in a dramatic clash in which each side opposes the other. Thus, a clash of opposites derives from problems associated with temporality itself, not from any particular state of affairs within the temporal world. Presumably, any intrusion of the divine into the world is doomed to produce opposing forces. Hegel does not take into account the mixed nature of human existence, both in the world itself and within individuals, manifested in drama as setting and character set in motion by plot. For Hegel, the divine retains its ultimate unity even though expressed in opposing actions as if a house divided against itself stands firm. On this view, Pilate faces no conflict extending beyond his temporal circumstances, the various oppositions being ultimately reconciled in the divine.

The metaphysical nature of Hegel's theory renders it untestable by any appeal to examples, so it can be critiqued only on the basis of a theological or conceptual analysis. The mixed nature of human existence (and human nature) is better understood as derived from conditions inherent within the world and within human beings themselves rather than the presence of the divine at odds with itself within a temporal context. In Christian terms, Hegel is wrong on two major points. First, the presence of the divine (setting aside for the moment the obvious differences between Hegel and Christianity on this issue) in the world does not inevitably lead to conflict. Temporality by itself is not the issue. Genesis presents God and human beings in harmonious relationship within the temporal world. The problem extends beyond temporality to include the will, something not inevitably a problem as seen in the harmonious relationships of the Trinitarian God. Second, Hegel fails to acknowledge or take into account the effects of the fall. On a Christian understanding, the mixed nature of human existence with its inherent conflicts reflects vestiges of a once harmonious relationship tainted by the ongoing effects of human sin. But whatever his flawed metaphysics, Hegel offers many insights into the tragic clash.

Scheler offers a theory of the tragic collision broadly similar to Hegel's but with key differences, the most important being the absence of an appeal to the divine. Tragedy for Scheler, rather than being merely an art product, is "an essential element of the universe itself"[143] and thus intimately connected with the temporal. Scheler purposely avoids what he deems surface concerns such as speculations on why tragedy gives pleasure. Instead, he offers an analysis of basic elements that make tragedy possible. He thinks the experience of tragedy varies greatly with historical context but the essence of tragedy does not. Scheler stresses the importance of defining the tragic before proceeding with any significant discussion of it. He writes, "But to know where the tragic has its source, whether in the basic structure of existence or in human passions and unrest, is to know already what the tragic is."[144] This need not preclude a discussion of "the basic structure of human existence," but requires that the tragic be made explicit if it is to be related to such a structure.

---

[143] Max Scheler, "On the Tragic," 27.
[144] Scheler, "Tragic," 29.

For Scheler, tragedy exists only in the area of values and their relationships.[145] Tragedy itself is not a value: it appears only through the interplay of values within a framework of time. Values inevitably conflict, which in tragedy results in the destruction of a positive value of less significance.[146] The values in conflict must be of "high positive value" such that a high positive value destroys another high positive value rather than a conflict between inherent opposites like good and evil or beautiful and ugly. The more evenly balanced the conflict, the greater the tragedy. Such balance leads to a certain sense of grief, one in which neither side of the conflict is clearly to blame. This tragic balance advocated by Scheler matches the position of tragedy as existing somewhere between romance and irony in Frye's archetypal criticism. Scheler notes, "The great art of the tragedian is to set each value of the conflicting elements in its fullest light, to develop completely the intrinsic rights of each party."[147] The greater the sense that one side of the conflict is clearly to blame, the lesser the tragic effect.

The destruction of a high positive value by another combines with a sense of inevitability to produce what Scheler terms "the tragic knot." By this he means the way in which positive values conflict and are destroyed. The tragic knot occurs when the expression of a high positive value produces its own destruction. He writes,

> If we are observing a certain action which is realizing a high value, and then see in that same action that it is working towards the undermining of the very existence of the being it is helping, we receive the most complete and the clearest of tragic impressions.[148]

For Scheler, the tragic knot needs to be pulled tighter yet. The destruction of one positive value, which often includes the person holding that value, by another positive value must be done in such a way that the destruction seems at once absolutely necessary and completely unpredictable, inevitable yet subject to contingent circumstances. In this way *the value relationships combine with causal relationships*. The tragic occurs only when "in one glance we embrace both the causality of things and the exigencies of their immanent values."[149] The causality of things and the expression of values are often not aligned in ordinary affairs, such as when the rain falls on the just and unjust. But in tragedy, values and circumstance are at once independent and absolutely combined.

---

[145] Scheler, "Tragic," 29ff.
[146] This contrasts with Hegel's idea that the tragic clash be between two equally justified powers.
[147] Scheler, "Tragic," 31.
[148] Scheler, "Tragic," 34. This relates to the nature of the tragic reversal. Henn remarks "The reversal arises when the action which we take to safeguard ourselves betrays us and brings about our downfall. The recognition comes when we realize how we have been deluded (this is the mental kind); or when in a physical demonstration, we recognize by a material evidence that a thing is so. In the one case there is an awakening from the 'strong delusion' that has brought us to belief in the lie; in the second, a physical event produces a specific kind of knowledge." T. R. Henn, *The Harvest of Tragedy* (London: Methuen & Co., 1956), 18. While noting their close connection, Muecke notes that Scheler is viewing what is generally taken to be irony as tragic. As will be seen, this is not the key element in Scheler's theory. D. C. Muecke, *The Compass of Irony* (London: Methuen & Co., 1969), 48.
[149] Scheler, "Tragic," 35.

Scheler notes, "The tragic comes into sight only when this independence of the two elements becomes embodied in a concrete event."[150]

Scheler himself offers only limited examples of his theory as it applies to actual tragedies. A few more extensive examples may be supplied to illustrate and to test the viability of Scheler's ideas expressed so far. In Hamlet's case, the conflicting positive values of action and thoughtful reflection combine with the initially unrelated events of his father's murder and his mother's "o'er hasty marriage" to his murderous uncle. Depending on one's point of view, Hamlet's clumsy attempts at action destroy his detached reflection on a messy situation, or conversely, his propensity to philosophize destroys his ability to act decisively. Antigone's private loyalty to her brother clashes with Creon's public duty to protect his city and punish wrongdoers during the chance event of Antigone's brother attacking Creon's city. The positive value of Creon's rulership remains intact while his private world is destroyed as is Antigone herself. The values of love and honor collide as the wicked Iago, by chance Othello's trusted advisor, enflames his leader's jealousy and sense of being wronged so that Othello smothers Desdemona with a pillow. In Pilate's case, the contingent events of history provoke a clash between worldly survival and political power on the one hand and personal integrity and eternal divine values on the other. Given these interpretations of these particular works, Scheler's theory offers a compelling interpretation of tragedy.

Continuing, Scheler sees "tragic guilt" as something other than moral or ethical blame. Tragic guilt does not occur as the result of a moral choice wherein one chooses between a clearly recognized good and evil. For guilt to be tragic, everyone must be seen as having done his or her duty. The tragic misdeed is that which "silences all possible moral and legal powers of judgment" whereas the untragic is where "by moral and legal lights it is seen to be obvious and simple."[151] The tragic hero moves above non-tragic guilt because the rest of the world possesses an inadequate view of things. For Scheler, Jesus is tragic because he acted according to his own knowledge and obligations and suffered accordingly. He observes, "Moral or 'guilty guilt' is based on the act of choice; 'tragic' or 'unguilty guilt' is rather based on the sphere of choice . . . and so the tragic hero 'becomes guilty' while doing a guiltless thing."[152] Scheler believes that tragic guilt occurs because tragedy has "its ultimate roots in the essential makeup of the world itself. It is this which clears away all sense of culpability or responsibility."[153]

Here Scheler's ideas become murkier and more problematic. As noted above, the dramatist may balance the competing sides in a dramatic balance, such as when Shakespeare connects Iago's hatred of Othello to Othello's choice of the book smart Michael Cassio over the battle experienced Iago and to Iago's unfounded suspicion that his wife has been "twixt my sheets" with Othello. Yet it remains doubtful that moral and ethical judgments may be entirely suspended, however difficult they are to make. Scheler takes his ideas too far in suggesting that one may be free from moral guilt and yet experience tragic guilt. This implies that one may be guiltless

---

[150] Ibid.
[151] Scheler, "Tragic," 39.
[152] Scheler, "Tragic," 43.
[153] Scheler, "Tragic," 33. Scheler's statement here is correct by itself; tragedy is related to the essential makeup of the world. But in context, Scheler is incorrect, as discussed below.

or completely good and yet tragic, a notion at odds with Aristotle and with the overwhelming majority of centuries of writers and critics. Scheler connects the tragic only with setting, or "the essential makeup of the world" to the exclusion of character, insofar as the ideal of tragedy is concerned. Scheler offers Jesus as the paradigmatic tragic figure, the one the world destroys and whose goodness becomes apparent at a later time. The crucial mistake here is to confuse the tragic with romance and suppose that Jesus is in fact tragic. Lacking crucial ambiguities resulting from being a mixture of the good and bad, Jesus is heroic, aware of his destiny, in full control of events, and selflessly proceeding to the cross. However much the tragic hero may or may not enjoy a point of view superior to others, the tragic hero shares the common condition of humanity in having a view of things that is ultimately and necessarily inadequate.

The strength of Scheler's theory is its ability to combine the values held and expressed by a character, and the values and circumstances of the surrounding world through a causal nexus expressed in plot in a way that Scheler himself does not explore. Scheler seems content to place his emphasis on values as expressed in setting to the detriment of values inherent in a given character, meaning that something amiss in a character may exacerbate something amiss it a given situation. Moving beyond Scheler, the events of a plot expose qualities and values latent in setting *and* character.[154] Here again Aristotle's contention of plot being superior to character in tragedy comes into importance because plot unites character (and values represented by that character) and setting (primarily values latent in that setting) in a causal series of events. The ambiguities, ironies, and inconsistencies of a given situation combine in a plot with the ambiguities, ironies, and inconsistencies of a particular character or characters to produce what we call tragedy. Tragedy is, therefore, not rooted only in character but also in the setting. By extension, the roots of tragedy penetrate to the soil of humanity in general as expressed in individual characters and penetrate also into the soil of world itself, the way things are.

Approaches to tragedy centering on character to the exclusion of setting or situation and vice versa are inadequate. In critiquing Scheler's position, it has been shown that Jesus can never be tragic because he lacked the ambiguity within his character to be reasonably blamed for his death even though the situation around him is one filled with ambiguity and relative values. The Romantics proposed an optimistic secular version of this tendency in seeking to exalt the intrinsic potential of human beings and de-emphasize humanity's inherent flaws and limitations. Responsibility for evil lies with society, reform of which would allow for full development of the individual. In this way, blame is transferred from character to setting with a corresponding emphasis on

---

[154] Chatman notes, "Unlike events, traits [referring to traits that make up a character] are not in the temporal chain, but coexist with the whole or a large portion of it. Events travel as vectors, 'horizontally' from earlier to later. Traits, on the other hand, extend over the time spans staked out by the events." Chatman, *Story and Discourse*, 129. Chatman's statement regarding the atemporality of character traits may be extended to those traits (values, ideals, etc.) found in a particular cultural or ideological setting. Plot, then, does not determine character or setting (as these are already explicit or implicit in character and setting), but rather forms the temporal pathway on which character and setting are expressed.

the self.[155] On the other hand, Adam fails to be tragic because blame is not transferrable to the past and his surroundings.[156] The fracturing of values in both character and setting are necessary for tragedy. Lacking these requirements, the fanatic makes a poor candidate for tragedy[157] because the fanatic irrationally commits to a cause without adequate appreciation of shortcomings inherent in the self or in the way things are.

Uniting character and setting with the ambiguities and contradictions inherent to both in a causal nexus as expressed in plot allows a plausible explanation of the ambiguous nature of assigning responsibility to a character or a set of circumstances. To the extent that the blame for a certain course of events can be transferred from problems inherent in a setting to a particular character or group of characters, the characters are responsible. At the same time, responsibility can be transferred from a character to a situation because of difficulties and incongruencies inherent in the situation itself. This balance can only be convincingly accomplished in a situation where the value relationships are united with the causal relationships by means of plot. A properly formed tragic plot forms an open-ended conduit of exchange between character and setting and between necessity and contingency.[158] Oedipus, Hamlet, and Pilate can be seen as villains or victims and neither interpretation is really convincing insofar as it excludes the other contradictory interpretation. Fear and pity as classic elements of audience response also depend upon this two-way ambiguity: fear arises by an imaginative identification with the situation and the consequent transfer of blame to the person; pity arises by an imaginative identification with the person and the consequent transfer of blame to the situation.[159] Neither side merits complete or exclusive justification, so an unresolved dynamic tension obtains between fear and pity, attraction and revulsion, guilt and innocence.[160] The particular value clashes exhibited in tragedy occur in such a way that renders both sides a measure of justification and vilification, a situation that can only exist in a world beset by relative values and fractured by the fall. Tragedy, then, explores the difficulties of relating beliefs to experience and exposes a world where even positive values can legitimately conflict

---

[155] Steiner, *Tragedy*, 116ff. Steiner notes, "If the romantic movement inherited from Rousseau his presumption of natural goodness and his belief in the social rather than metaphysical origins of evil, it inherited also his obsession with the self." *Tragedy*, 136.

[156] Frye notes in a discussion of irony that "tragedy is intelligible because its catastrophe is plausibly related to its situation." He sees Adam as "inevitably ironic" and Jesus as "incongruously ironic" and the tragic hero, in this case Prometheus, as about halfway between. *Anatomy*, 41.

[157] Oscar Mandel notes, "And it is incontestably true that fanatics do not make tragic figures." Mandel, "Tragic Reality," in *Tragedy: Modern Essays in Criticism*, eds. Laurence Michel and Richard Sewall (Westport, CT: Greenwood Press, 1963), 63.

[158] This helps explain the similarities and differences between the Greeks and Shakespeare regarding the tension between fate and free will. Notions of fate emphasize the power of a situation to compel certain actions, a Greek tendency, while the dynamics of free will emphasize the power of an individual to make free moral choices and thereby control events, more characteristic of Shakespeare and his Christian milieu. These generalities, albeit useful ones, indicate tendencies rather than dichotomies. The connection in a causal nexus expressed in plot as argued here helps explain the inviolable connection between the two.

[159] See "Elements of Audience Reaction," above.

[160] Myers argues that good and evil achieve an aesthetic balance in tragedy, but does not argue why or in what way this is achieved. Henry A. Myers, "The Tragic Attitude toward Value," in *Tragedy: Modern Essays in Criticism*, eds. Laurence Michel and Richard Sewall (Westport, CT: Greenwood Press, 1963), 45–59.

with each other. In doing so, tragedy imaginatively, experientially, and theologically recalls and references the fall. Tragedy endures as an art form in no small measure because it reaches into this most basic fact of human existence.

III. E. 3 Relative values: Knowledge and ignorance in tragedy

Much of the previous discussion assumes that values can and do exist in relative relationship to each other, a situation prima facie true. Presumably, a state of affairs might exist wherein values do not conflict. For example, on a Trinitarian understanding of the Christian God, each of the three separate persons of the Godhead possess equally and fully the attributes of God within a fully united single being. Within a temporal framework a possible state of affairs that includes free contingent beings in which positive values do not conflict is, at best, precarious.

If one positive value conflicts with another, ignorance and its consequent ambiguities and contradictions become crucial for tragedy. These elements exhibited in tragedy provide key factors that make tragedy itself possible. Ignorance in tragedy can take the forms of ignorance of fact and ignorance of value implementation. In the first, Oedipus lives in ignorance of a set of true and significant facts about his own life and these circumstances make the drama possible. Elsewhere, as in Sophocles's *Women of Trachis*, strategic ignorance on the part of the central characters moves the plot along and precipitates the tragic conclusion. But rather than being merely plot devices, the character's ignorance of particular facts says something about life itself: that humans can never know or grasp things adequately and that such a situation is filled with dangerous possibilities.

In Sophocles's *Electra*, certain characters operate in ignorance of potentially important information. But here the significant ignorance displayed is collective ignorance regarding the ignorance of all characters—and, by extension all humanity as well—as to the proper implementation of a value, in this case justice. The carefully balanced claims of each competing party prevent any one character from occupying the undisputed moral high ground. The rival claims to justice in *Electra* seem at once a bizarre combination of intractable self-centeredness and a plausible appeal to a larger principle. In Shakespeare, Lear's relatively dove-like innocence manifests ignorance of snake-like values realized in the world in his daughters. Macbeth shows an adequate grasp of the value clash entailed by his murder of Duncan but displays ignorance of what the future may actually be like once the murder is committed and one value is set against the other.[161] In *Romeo and Juliet* and *Antony and Cleopatra*, the major characters ignorantly underestimate the danger of the value clash between the public position and personal passion. Hamlet combines ignorance of facts with ignorance of value implementation as he walks a delicate line of ignorance/knowledge linked with action/contemplation. Pilate combines ignorance of facts with ignorance of implementing values that he assumes to be entirely relative. Ignorance of value clashes, potential or actual, makes the world a dangerous place.

---

[161] The wicked sisters' predictions further Macbeth's delusions about the future in precisely this way.

Ignorance of the type generally found in tragedy is of a particularly insidious kind. Factual omniscience would of course be useful, but remains impossible for mortals. In *Agamemnon* and *Electra* factual omniscience would prevent this or that death but would not solve the problem of the implementation of values in a world where positive values inevitably conflict. While important to Hamlet's uncertainty, an open question remains as to whether or not more information would solve Hamlet's "to be or not to be" dilemma, an impasse bound up in a quandary about whether and when to act or refrain from doing so. An omniscient wisdom directing the implementation of values might provide help regarding the choice of one course of action as compared to another, but in the end this provides only part of the answer. Oedipus and Pilate are both at heart men of action and each would rather solve problems through material means, but their particular dilemmas do not allow them to do so. Hamlet differs in that he is not a man of action but attempts to find his way through his predicament with careful reflection.

Ignorance in an inert state presents few difficulties. But the progress of time in tragedy renders the easy comfort of ignorance as precarious as dawn before the advance of the sun. Events force the condition of ignorance into the open where the complexities of life result in a tragic collision. The particularly maddening quality of ignorance is that such a condition can never be fully alleviated. The dilemma is such that Oedipus, Hamlet, and Pilate, compelled by inner and/or outer forces with the need to know, face a situation in which their increase of knowledge results in a situation, from their perspective, arguably worse than the one in which they began. Given present realities, ignorance is a necessary part of the human condition and events will force potential clashes into reality.

The condition of partial ignorance gives rise to several other qualities important to tragedy such as ambiguity, paradox, contradiction, and irony.[162] These elements operate only in circumstances where given states of knowledge contain elements somehow at odds with each other. Ambiguity results from incomplete or incorrect knowledge; paradox operates when two states of affairs or ideas conflict in a way not resolvable within a given framework of knowledge; irony obtains only when a given state of knowledge, intentions, or point of view is at odds with another superior or inferior to itself.[163] Contradiction differs from the other three in that two items may contradict within a unified and complete state of knowledge: for example, 2 + 2 = 4 necessarily contradicts all other possibilities. The contradiction in view here may be referred to under the more general term of ambiguity, the type that obtains when two sides appear to be equally justified and yet contradict in the assertion of their separate interests. The ambiguities, paradoxes, ironies, and contradictions derived from ignorance allow the

---

[162] Richard Sewall notes that "basic to the tragic form is its recognition of the inevitability of paradox, of unresolved tensions and ambiguities, of opposites in precarious balance." See Richard B. Sewall, "The Tragic Form," in *Tragedy: Modern Essays in Criticism*, eds. Laurence Michel and Richard Sewall (Westport, CT: Greenwood Press, 1963), 120.

[163] Norman Knox observes "the structure of irony always contains a deceptive conflict between two points of view." Knox, "On the Classification of Ironies," *Modern Philology* 70 (1972): 58. See also Norman Knox, "Irony," in *The Dictionary of the History of Ideas*, vol. II (New York: Charles Scribner's Sons, 1973), 626–34; Booth, *A Rhetoric of Irony*; Muecke, *Compass*, especially 14–39, 151–58; Duke, *Irony in the Fourth Gospel*, 13–18. The point is discussed in chapter three below.

tragic artist the very means by which two opposing sides can appear justified in their implicit or explicit assertion of values. Only in a fractured world can one positive value be set over against another. Tragedy as an art form uses the ignorance inevitable in a fractured world to function as a drama, and in doing so tragedy says something about the world itself.

The ignorance important for contingent human beings that is most commonly found in tragedy is inevitably connected to the past. Persons may be excused from blame if the future turns out to be otherwise than what might reasonably be expected. Blame may also be lessened if present events lie beyond the scope of what someone might reasonably be expected to know. The past presents another situation in that the range of what someone might reasonably be expected to know is considerably larger than what might be known about the present. And, given that the present necessarily finds its roots in the past, the need to know about the past is much greater. A thorough knowledge of the past may lead one to alter or continue various actions in a positive way. Yet a comprehensive knowledge of the past and its collective wisdom serves only to heighten the scope of the problem: more is known all the time and tragic collisions will still occur. Furthermore, given the time difference between past and present, the past is subject to a greater variety of convincing interpretations than the present or the future. Tragedy casts doubt on the assertion that "the one who is ignorant of history is condemned to repeat it."

Tragedy happens when the past comes roaring to life into the present in a particular way.[164] Like a rock thrown from the past shattering the tranquility of the present, a chance event can place positive, harmonious values in opposition to each other in ways not easily anticipated, or if anticipated, not easily managed. Ignorance and the qualities derived from ignorance comprise key elements of a world where positive values may be found in opposition to each other.

III. E. 4 Absolute values: Moral order in tragedy

Given the difficulty of adequately knowing and responding to the past, much less to the present and future, it does not follow that a tragic protagonist or any human being is without responsibility for particular actions. Whatever conflicts may arise from ignorance and the fractured state of knowledge and the consequent fracturing of values, judgments between one course of action and another must nevertheless be made. Courts of law attempt to establish the relevant facts in a particular case and offer competing interpretations based on an appeal to established values embodied in law. An appeal to ignorance of the law exonerates no one completely because, presumably, a law is a particular embodiment of a larger principle generally accepted as valid.

But morality in tragedy is not inherently fluid; rather, it is difficult to implement. In tragedy, the careful balancing of opposing forces does not imply the absence of standards by which actions may be judged. On the contrary, the very fact that

---

[164] Although he does not connect the past with ignorance as here, T. R. Henn sees the past as a net closing in on the present. See Henn, *Harvest*, 35–42.

certain actions may be legitimately justified in some sense implies the existence of a moral order against which opposing actions may be both opposed or defended. The legitimacy of a point of view inevitably involves an appeal to a larger principle either directly through an accepted formulation of a particular value or indirectly through a principle formulated for the common good. Although the source of the moral order, whether in divine command, natural law, or social convention, might be disputed, the present discussion requires only the simple acknowledgment that two opposing sides or forces may command roughly equal moral justification within the moral order itself, while at the same time acknowledging that not all actions approximate moral parity.

As Krook shows, a tragic work inevitably contains some violation of the moral order.[165] For Krook, the existence of a moral order provides the basic framework for her analysis of tragedy.[166] The four elements in Krook's understanding of tragedy will be treated below, the first and fourth being the most important for the present discussion. First, a character commits an act of shame wherein an objective, real act, universal in significance, precipitates the action of the tragedy. This violation of the moral order need not be committed by the main tragic character, as when Macbeth murders Duncan, and may be committed by someone else as, for example, when Claudius murders Hamlet's father.[167] The violation of the moral order must arise "out of the fundamental human condition" and be "necessarily universal," usually acts of betrayal and rejection.[168] In Pilate's case, the act of shame and violation of the moral order is the betrayal of Jesus by Judas Iscariot, a single act that sets in final motion the larger clash between the Jews and Jesus. Krook's notion of the "act of shame" is precisely the same kind of event that in Scheler's analysis links the value relationships into a set of contingent circumstances and sets them at odds with each other.[169] In tragedy, separate positive values move from being in latent potential conflict to actual conflict by means of a violation of the moral order.

In the second element of Krook's analysis, intense, deeply felt, real suffering occurs that is related to and commensurate with its cause. The suffering must be conscious and felt to be undermining and destructive of the human vessel, often resulting in death. For Pilate, loss of his personal integrity and his pretentions to power result in suffering and spiritual destruction, but not in physical death. Third, according to Krook, knowledge must be gained regarding some aspect of the human condition, not by the characters in the play, but by the audience. Ultimately this point coincides with purpose of the FG: to initiate and strengthen belief in the risen Jesus on the part of the reader by means of knowledge of and response to certain facts. Pilate's state

---

[165] Krook, *Elements of Tragedy*, 8–34. Henn presents a view broadly similar to Krook. Henn uses the imagery of the spring and the trigger, the spring being a potential conflict and the trigger being the event that brings about the conflict. Henn, *Harvest*, 59–64.

[166] Krook, *Elements*, 15, 17.

[167] A violation of the moral order must be distinguished from a *hamartia*. The former is an intentional act committed by someone, while the latter is 'false step taken in blindness' (Lucas) usually consequent on a flaw latent within the main character ready to be exposed through challenges within the plot.

[168] Krook, *Elements of Tragedy*, 10–11.

[169] Note the examples given to test Scheler's theory wherein a contingent event unites the opposing values in a plot relationship. See above.

of understanding and belief, although it progresses, must be judged as incomplete and therefore a negative example. The reader gains the knowledge about the human condition, learning that temporal solutions may conflict with theological realities in a way that forces a choice between them.

Fourth, building on Aristotle's idea of catharsis, Krook believes that tragedy results in an affirmation of "the objective moral order which at once incorporates the human and transcends it."[170] The stature of the tragic hero is such that suffering expiates the violation of the moral order and in doing so restores its integrity. For Krook,

> The final "affirmation" of tragedy springs from our reconciliation to, or acceptance of, the necessity of the suffering rendered intelligible by the knowledge; by illuminating the necessity of the suffering, the knowledge reconciles us to it; by being reconciled to ("accepting") the suffering as necessary, we reaffirm the supremacy of the universal moral order; and by this act of recognition of and submission to the universal moral order, which the reaffirmation of its supremacy implies, we express and affirm the dignity of man and the value of human life.[171]

The presence of the moral order ultimately reaffirms human dignity rather than human dignity being derived from some other source. The greatness inherent in the tragic hero may be connected to the hero's worthiness as a sacrifice expiating the moral order as a representative figure for the human race. But, like all tragic heroes, Oedipus, Hamlet, Lear, and Pilate are clearly inadequate for the task of expiating the moral order. Instead, they are foils who highlight the worthiness of Jesus as the one who does in fact expiate humanity's collective violation of the moral order. If tragedy looks back to the fall, it also points forward to the cross.

The presence of the moral order in the world is connected to the presence of some sort of divine or supernatural element to human life. H. D. F. Kitto asserts that tragedy contains a necessary religious element regardless of the ability of the individual or age to see it properly.[172] The religious dimension in tragedy is that the moral order of the universe—the fact that one exists being a religious concern—is reaffirmed in tragedy. However much an individual or group may find itself in confusion and be destroyed, in tragedy the moral order of the world is intact. The gods or moral order need not be present in a particular work for this to be true; the order is everywhere implicitly present. As evidence, Kitto asserts that however well drawn and interesting a character may be, that character "never absorbs all our attention,"[173] meaning that a drama raises issues and questions beyond itself. Furthermore, "only when the human drama is seen against the background of divine action is the structure and significance of the play truly seen."[174] In so doing, the tragic artist combines seeming

---

[170] Krook, *Elements of Tragedy*, 15.
[171] Krook, *Elements*, 17.
[172] H. D. F. Kitto, *Form and Meaning in Drama* (London: Methuen & Co., 1956). See esp. Chapter 8, "Religious Drama and its Interpretation," 231–45. Reprinted in *Tragedy: Modern Essays in Criticism*, eds. Laurence Michel and Richard Sewall (Westport, CT: Greenwood Press, 1963), 147–60.
[173] Kitto, *Form and Meaning*, 238.
[174] Ibid.

contraries, "sharpness of detail and the greatest possible generality" that allow the characters in tragedy to become concretely realized representative exemplars of the human condition.[175]

Richard Sewall cautiously attempts to say something about the tragic form and the moral order by noting three areas of discussion: first, the cosmos and humanity's relation to it; second, the nature of the individual and the individual's relation to the self; third, the individual in society. In the first, Sewall notes that humans are a part of this world and that tragedy is humanistic by virtue of being focused on an event in this world. Yet tragedy "assumes man's supersensory or supernatural, or metaphysical being or principle."[176] The tragic view is never purely naturalistic or mechanical. The tragic cosmos is one preoccupied with evil, not evil in isolation, but in relation to and in tension with the good, a tension that insures that humans are not the measure of all things and that the universe remains a mystery.

In the second, on the tragic individual, Sewall lists some of the various ambiguities and paradoxes inherent to the human condition: not divine nor fully of the earth, neither fated nor free, both creature and creator, guilty and innocent. In this confusion, the tragic individual is animated by pride and suffers on a high level, more so than the immature, the brutish, or the extreme optimist or pessimist. Suffering is part of the human condition, and in suffering the tragic hero comes to be identified with humanity at large.

Third, the tragic individual in relation to society chooses to rebel, question, and act, rather than quit, be silent, or be cynical. This puts the tragic hero in "a head on collision with the forces that would oppress or frustrate. Conscious of the ambiguities within and without, which are the source of his peculiar suffering, tragic man accepts the conflict."[177] By proceeding, the tragic hero learns and is transformed and in being transformed, transforms those around, leading to a higher vision, yet the old paradoxes and ambiguities remain.

In *The Death of Tragedy*, George Steiner brings a historical and theological element to the issue of relative and absolute values in tragedy as he surveys tragedy through its history. Steiner offers a simple argument: tragedy and tragic poets need an intellectual climate infused with known beliefs and assumptions about life—a moral order— that includes a strong sense of the theological or transcendent, a sense that allows and indeed compels the issues to transcend the temporal. Steiner writes, "Tragedy is that form of art that requires the intolerable burden of God's presence. It is now dead because His shadow no longer falls upon us as it fell on Agamemnon or Macbeth or Athalie."[178] For Steiner, the intellectual and theological milieus present in ancient Greece and Elizabethan England caused tragedy to flourish. Steiner argues that the

---

[175] Sternberg argues the same thing in relation to Biblical (Old Testament) characters. He notes, "Each biblical character is *sui generis*, a unique combination of universals and idiosyncrasies." Meir Sternberg, *The Poetics of Biblical Narrative: Ideological Literature and the Drama of Reading* (Bloomington, IN: Indiana University Press, 1985), 253.
[176] Sewall, "Tragic Form," 121.
[177] Sewall, "Tragic Form," 126–27.
[178] Steiner, *Death of Tragedy*, 192.

lack of a transcendent order in more recent times accounts for the decline in tragedy as an art form.[179]

For Kitto, Sewall, and Steiner, the presence of the divine or a moral order forms a key part of each writer's analysis. Kitto's argument is the most one sided in that it lacks a clear presentation and account of the evil in the world. Steiner and Sewall make the presence of evil and the incongruities of life very much part of their analysis. Sewall is perhaps more optimistic than Steiner in that he believes that the tragic hero marshals an inherent pride and stands against "the slings and arrows of outrageous fortune."

For other critics, the moral order, by whatever term it is known, need not necessarily be connected to the divine. For Williams, the moral order may be connected to the divine in particular historical situations, but its source is ultimately fluid and changes with the progress of history.[180] Thus Shakespeare drew upon a Christian worldview, while later dramatists like Ibsen relied on society itself, and in modern times the order is viewed to be individuals themselves. Increasingly, however, tragedy in modern times—if possible—is restricted in scope such that it becomes experience set against experience. The works of Ibsen and Miller, while significant, do not reach the same heights and depths as *Oedipus* and *Hamlet*.

The fractured state of the world and the ignorance consequent upon it seem at once to converge and diverge with the presence of a moral order. The moral order functions as a reference point that prevents arbitrary acts resulting from the fractured state of knowledge and values from simply being relative; at the same time, the fractured state of the world of experience and knowledge can prevent humans from adequately grasping or implementing the ethical norms suggested by the moral order. The tragic hero is obligated by the presence of the moral order to grasp and/or implement the moral order in a situation divided by ambiguities and contradictions.[181] This condition does not entail ethical nihilism, nor does it entail that nothing ethical can be accomplished or even attempted: it only means that the potential exists that two positive moral values can be moved from an inert state into open conflict by some violation of the moral order. In this sense tragedy is a consequence of the fall, which created a state of affairs that is the fertile ground for tragedy. Thus, tragedy endures not simply because it is a historically significant art form: it endures because it implicitly reflects a profound theological truth about human existence.

It may be noted as a historical fact, as Steiner does, that artists produced the greatest tragedies in times when the presence of the divine remained deeply felt as a moral order at the same time the moral order was beginning to unravel. The Middle Ages, when the moral order tended to be absolute, was the age of romance and produced very little if anything normally designated tragedy. In comparison, the late modern and postmodern worlds present values relativized to such an extent that appeals to an absolute moral

---

[179] Steiner notes, "When the new world picture of reason usurped the place of the old tradition in the course of the seventeenth century, the English theatre entered its long decline." *Death of Tragedy*, 23. Kaufmann disputes Steiner's analysis by noting, "Are there not millions of believers today?" *Tragedy and Philosophy*, 192. But Kaufmann confuses the particular and the universal. However many believers exist today is irrelevant to the fact that a comprehensive theological worldview no longer commands adherence as it did in the time of Sophocles or Shakespeare.

[180] Williams, *Tragedy*.

[181] Myers observes, "Tragedy represents supplementary elements of relativity and absoluteness in values." Myers, "Tragic Attitude," 49.

order seem strangely out of place. Postmodernism in particular seems to prefer and even celebrate the ironic. In such conditions, conflicts of positive value, such as there are, typically emerge from an assertion of the personal rights of an individual or group, as opposed to an implicit or explicit appeal to moral order ordained by God. Neither the tendency toward absolute values of the Middle Ages nor the tendency to relative values of recent times has proved to be a productive environment for tragedy. The ages most productive of tragedy are those when the absolute values of one age are in transition and in open conflict with the relative values of the next.[182] Sophocles wrote in a time of philosophical and theological transition and this secular/religious tension is reflected in Oedipus himself. Likewise, Shakespeare took advantage of the imaginative and theological wealth of the Middle Ages at the same time he anticipated the modern world. Indeed, Hamlet can be viewed as being caught between the Medieval past and the modern future. To the extent that Christianity provided coherence to beliefs and experience to Shakespeare's world, Pilate stands at the dawn of this age while *Hamlet* and *Dr. Faustus* anticipate its decline.

Perhaps nowhere does the clash between relative and absolute values appear in sharper focus than in the case of Pilate. Human government, sanctioned in the Bible by God as a way to implement order and good upon the earth, functions to implement positive values and restrain negative values. Any government's ability to achieve this stability is inevitably relative. In the particular time and place of Jesus, Pilate stood as the one empowered to implement this role. As a ruler in his or any other era, Pilate's position inevitably required mastery of the relative values of political intrigue and ad hoc management of current events. Pilate's confrontation with Jesus, through whom "all things were made" (1:3), highlights the inevitable limitations of any system or any person employing relative values. In contrast to Pilate ("What is truth?"), Jesus ("I am the way, the truth, and the life") represents and embodies absolute adherence to absolute values. In doing so, Jesus is at once true to the absolute moral order ultimately derived from God himself, and, as a member of the Godhead, true to himself; Pilate belongs to an order of relativized values that defies anyone to be true to it.

III. F Conclusion

In tragedy, the coherence of romance gives way to a world in fundamental conflict with itself and anticipates the arrival of irony wherein the disjunction between beliefs and experience is most fully realized. Sharing many of the characteristics of other tragic characters, Pilate may likewise be viewed as an archetypal tragic character. Moreover, to a great extent tragedy as an archetype is concerned with a widening disjunction between humans and their environment, between absolute values and their enactment in experience, and between humans and God. However concentrated and brief, the matrix of theological and structural variables that make up tragedy occur profoundly in the FG's portrayal of Pilate.

---

[182] For an illuminating analysis of the progress of intellectual history with respect to transcendent and "sensate" values and their expression in art and science, see Pitirim Sorokin, *The Crisis of Our Age* (Oxford: One World, 1941, 1992).

4

Irony, Thomas, and the Jews

IV. A Introduction

Irony in the FG has been the focus of much attention in recent years. But rather than simply identifying and classifying examples of irony in the FG according to standard categories, the present work will explore irony in the FG as embodied in the characters of Thomas and the Jews. In this way, variations of irony may be explored in a more dynamic fashion than has otherwise been done and thus complement the tendency of the FG to utilize characters to explore different relationships to Jesus. Additionally, irony will be explored in relation to values and beliefs inherent in its use and in the perception of its use rather than in relation to classification of specific types of use as is normally done. In relation to the values and beliefs employed in its use and perception, irony may be classified as positive, equivocal, and negative irony, classifications that will be discussed below. By combining the two aspects of irony as seen in relation to values and beliefs together with its embodiment in character, irony may be explored as a mode of perception and thinking. Separate literary readings of Thomas and the Jews will be offered.

Thomas, it will be argued, embodies a kind of equivocal irony (to be explained in detail later) wherein the application of beliefs to specific circumstances renders those beliefs problematic. This famous disciple is "the personification of an attitude,"[1] an ambiguous, Erasmian character whose very ambiguity mirrors the perspective of the perceptive yet ambiguous ironic reader. Additionally, because he is a disciple, Thomas is an exploration of irony from within.

The Jews will be seen as representative of negative irony, a perspective characterized by the collapse of perception into a two-dimensional view of reality. The Jews are the polar opposite of Jesus and the character (collectively) most frequently ironized. While no doubt of paramount historical importance to the story of Jesus, the fact that they are so frequently Jesus's conversation partners and so frequently ironized within the

---

[1] Brown, *The Gospel According to John*, 1031. Brown's comment refers to Thomas in 20:24–29.

FG establishes their status as representative of and vehicles for a certain point of view.[2] The Jews in the FG, it will be argued, embody the perspective of negative irony with its characteristic negation of beliefs or ideals, in this case the vertical action of God in Jesus in favor of the demands and perspective of present experience. In this sense, the Jews represent a perennial perspective, one that transcends charges of anti-Semitism by virtue of the fact that the same perspective with respect to the perception of Jesus haunts much of Christendom as well. This does not mean that the Jews are successful ironists in their own right, merely that they manifest an attitude of mind characteristic of one dominated by negative irony. With reference to the four archetypes as defined in the present work, in the FG, Thomas and the Jews are characters in which irony is itself ironized.

IV. B Thomas and the Jews in the Fourth Gospel: Variations on the ironization of irony

IV. B. 1 Thomas and the ironization of the ironist: Seeing and not seeing and seeing

Interpretation of Thomas naturally centers on his post-resurrection encounter with Jesus in 20:24-29. The length of the narrative alone—six verses in comparison with two isolated comments in 11:16 and 14:3—coupled with the fact that Thomas is here the primary character serves to direct attention on Thomas in his last appearance in the NT. And Thomas's actions within this narrative, namely, his steadfast refusal to believe in the risen Lord on the basis of the testimony of his fellow disciples, naturally dominate interpretation of his character. Given the post-resurrection importance of Thomas in the FG, several things about this passage may be noted that will be of assistance for an ironic interpretation of Thomas in 11:16 and in gaining a better grasp on the character of Thomas as a whole.

The first is that "doubt" is not an accurate description of Thomas's actions. If doubt is taken to mean "uncertainty," then doubt itself does not accurately describe Thomas's actions in the resurrection narrative. Certain in his unbelief, doubt is precisely the thing Thomas never does. Jesus's admonition to "stop doubting and believe" is probably better understood as "stop being faithless or unbelieving (ἄπιστος), but instead be faithful or believing (πιστός)." A definite contrast is indicated. "Doubt" can of course mean "faithless" in English, but this is not its normal meaning. Translation aside, the narrative itself indicates something of the nature of Thomas's unbelief when he rejects the enthusiastic testimony of the disciples out of hand (20:25) and places

---

[2] In one sense this is a kind of stereotyping, but in another, more accurate sense, it simply reflects a certain level of historical reporting. For example, the combatants of the English civil war, whatever the nuances and complexities of their respective positions, are known today simply as the roundheads and cavaliers. The extent to which "the Jews" are stereotyped in the FG is in direct proportion to the possibility that historical reconstructions of the Jewish milieu of the NT era may actually obscure their simplified meaning and function within the FG itself. The issue of the Jews' representative status is treated at greater length below.

fixed conditions necessary for him to believe in Jesus's resurrection. Significantly, a week passes between Thomas's rejection of the disciples' testimony and his beholding of the risen Lord. No doubt during this week the disciples continued to insist on the reality of the resurrection and that Thomas with equal fervor continued to deny it. The disciples' exasperation might well have been matched or exceeded by Thomas's displeasure at suffering a choir of fools. The context is one of absolute intractability rather than skeptical debate.

The second thing to be noted is that Thomas is both included as one of the disciples and distinguished from the rest. Even the expression "one of the Twelve" (20:24) shows elements of inclusion and exclusion, although this in itself may not mean much.[3] Thomas is notably absent from the other disciples and does not witness the risen Lord.[4] He is thus physically distinguished from the rest, a fact that very likely indicates that he is to be distinguished in other matters as well. The other disciples are in a locked room "for fear of the Jews" while Thomas is elsewhere and, by virtue of simply being elsewhere, perhaps roaming the streets in public, he is not to be painted with the same brush. Thomas's demonstrated idiosyncratic individuality over the rejection of the disciples' testimony when combined with the fearfulness of the disciples may well indicate a certain distance and disdain for their hiding away. The appearance of Jesus to the disciples emphasizes the relief of these fears. Jesus first tells them "Peace be with you" and then invites them to examine the evidence. Fear is nowhere directly associated with Thomas, for whom evidence is of primary concern. When Jesus appears to Thomas and the other disciples a week later, the doors are again locked, but inclusion of this detail calls attention to the fact that Jesus passed through walls with no mention being made, as previously, of fear of the Jews. While the primary purpose of the Thomas incident within the context of the narrative itself is to emphasize the importance and validity of believing without having seen (20:29), to one extent or another, Thomas is distinguished from the other disciples.

Having established that doubt is not part of Thomas's character and that Thomas is distinguished from the other disciples on the basis of temporal location and lack of fear, his other appearances in the FG can be analyzed with these factors in mind. Thomas first appears in the FG in the early stages of the Lazarus narrative of chapter 11, where his comment "Let us also go, that we may die with him" (11:16) is of central importance for seeing Thomas in all his ironic glory and interpreting his character as a whole. On receiving word that Lazarus is sick, Jesus, who had promised that "This sickness will not end in death" (11:4) and who "loved Martha and her sister and Lazarus" (11:5), inexplicably tarries two more days. Manifesting the same fear of the Jews as in 20:19, the disciples greet Jesus's intention to return to Judea with alarm by noting "A short while ago the Jews there tried to stone you, and yet you are going

---

[3] However, Brodie observes that "one of the twelve" is used elsewhere in the FG only in relation to Judas (6:71). Brodie, *The Gospel According to John*, 570.
[4] Dorothy Lee argues that the absence of Thomas here is only a literary device and that Thomas is no more doubtful than the other disciples. Both assessments are disputed here. Lee reads Thomas in isolation from his other appearances and allegorically with reference to the "Johannine Community." See Lee, "Partnership in Easter Faith: The Role of Mary Magdalene and Thomas in John 20," *JSNT* 58 (1995): 37–49.

back?" (11:8). After some confusion over the status of Lazarus, Jesus tells them plainly, "Lazarus is dead, and for your sake I am glad I was not there, so that you may believe. But let us go to him" (11:14).

Thomas enters the narrative immediately following: "Then Thomas (called Didymus) said to the rest of the disciples, 'Let us also go, that we may die with him.'" Again the pattern of 20:24-29 appears: fear of the Jews on the disciples' part, Thomas distinguished from the rest of the disciples by a show of courage. Normally Thomas's remark is interpreted with reference to the dangers of returning to Judea voiced previously in 11:8. Carson's comments are representative of critical opinion:

> On this occasion Thomas reflects not doubt but raw devotion and courage, even though it was courage shot through with misunderstanding and incomprehension: misunderstanding, in that he had not grasped the assurance implicit in vv. 9-10, and incomprehension, in that the death Jesus had to face as the Lamb of God (1:29,36) could not possibly be shared by his disciples. Yet there is another sense in which Thomas, like others in this Gospel, spoke better than he knew: his words have become a clarion call to would-be disciples, after the resurrection, to take up their cross daily and follow Jesus.[5]

On this basis, Thomas is interpreted in straightforward fashion "heroically" as someone willing to follow Jesus to death after the manner of Peter, naive perhaps, but no less dedicated.

But there is another possible interpretation of this statement. Rather than being interpreted as heroically naive, it is possible to interpret "Let us also go, that we may die with him" as a kind of pessimism with overtones of fatalism or as a kind of mature courage. It remains a statement of dedication, but one tempered by realism, facing the full force of the difficulties ahead with no illusions, like a hardened soldier ready for battle. Context offers little help in adjudicating between these conflicting interpretations.[6]

And there is yet another possible interpretation, one more like the latter, but derived from a different exegetical base. The issue concerns the antecedent of the pronoun "him" (αὐτοῦ) in Thomas's statement "Let us also go, that we may die with him." The two above interpretations both make the straightforward assumption that "him" refers to Jesus, but is this necessarily the case? The other possibility is that "him" refers to Lazarus. The two possibilities are illustrated as follows by supplying the antecedent:

A- "Let us also go, that we may die with *Jesus*."
B- "Let us also go, that we may die with *Lazarus*."

---

[5] Carson, *The Gospel According to John*, 410. Similarly, Barrett, *The Gospel According to John*, 394; G. R. Beasley-Murray, *John* (Waco: Word Books, 1987), 189.

[6] In discussing this verse, a fellow doctoral student noted that the naive or heroic interpretation had never occurred to him and that he had always read it in terms of mature, if pessimistic, courage. Since perceiving the different interpretations of this verse as a teenager, I have never accepted the "naive" Thomas.

The former is assumed without question by virtually all commentators, the latter almost never mentioned. Bultmann mentions it but rejects it out of hand, while Michaels confines his remarks to an admission that the latter is grammatically possible.[7] And yet the Lazarus merits consideration as the antecedent of αὐτοῦ simply by virtue of its immediate proximity to a possible antecedent of someone whose identity, if conceptually unpalatable, is unmistakable—Lazarus. Jesus ends his statement in 11:15 with "But let us go to him" and "him" (αὐτόν) here without question refers to Lazarus. In contrast, six verses separate Thomas's remark from mention of returning to Judea wherein going "to die with Jesus" would be an appropriate interpretation. Additionally, both Jesus and Thomas use similar language ("Let us go" and "Let us also go") when referring to the intended journey of returning to Lazarus. Rejecting Lazarus as the antecedent of αὐτοῦ in 11:16 has far less to do with careful exegesis and much more to do with its simply being an unknown or unpalatable interpretation and/or one without an adequate frame of reference in which such an interpretation seems acceptable or reasonable.

An ironic Thomas offers a better option. Unlike his fellow disciples who suppose "if he sleeps he will get better," Thomas sees the real problem and offers a more perceptive commentary. The deconstructionist Thomas cleverly detects an aporia in the logic of Jesus being the Messiah apparently missed by the other disciples. The sickness that "will not end in death" (11:4) has done exactly that, and a vast gulf exists between Jesus's promises and his performance. Thomas might well have thought, "What good are all these miracles and healings and all this commotion if he can't help his friend? And where does that leave us?" Potential trouble in Judea—the Jews with their sticks and stones—so important to the other disciples, is incidental to the story in comparison with the fact that Lazarus is dead. If Thomas is being ironical, the other disciples may well be the victims of it. And Thomas's recognition of the difficulty posed for Jesus by the death of Lazarus undercuts his own position as a disciple and renders it ironic and equivocal.[8] Thomas remains, yet in doing so he can to a significant degree only pretend to go along. "Doubting Thomas" might well describe him at this point. Thomas, now as later, clearly perceives the difficulty missed by the other disciples but fails to see the possibility of resurrection and in doing so fails to allow for the possibility of the direct action of God.

An analysis of other comments on Jesus's tardiness within the narrative of chapter 11 offers additional support for reading Thomas's comment in 11:16 and his character as ironic. Rather than reflecting the fears of the disciples expressed in previous verses (recall the separation of Thomas from the other disciples and their fears in chapter 20), Thomas's comment instead anticipates similar comments to come. With slight differences in Greek, Martha and Mary both tell Jesus, "Lord, if you had been here, my

---

[7] Bultmann offers his comment in reference to Zahn, who held this position. Bultmann, *The Gospel of John*, 400, note; J. Ramsey Michaels, *John* (Peabody, MA: Hendrickson, 1984), 189.

[8] Muecke comments, "The ironic attitude of a 'General Ironist' is complicated by his own equivocal position. On the one hand his sense of irony implies detachment, and since the irony he perceives is General Irony, as I have defined it, he will be detached from life itself or at least for that general aspect of life in which he perceives a fundamental contradiction. On the other hand, the picture he sees of an ironic world must show himself as a victim." Muecke, *The Compass of Irony*, 122.

brother would not have died" (11:21, 32). Unlike Thomas, Martha affirms the reality of resurrection but only as something to be realized in the future. Although uttered with understandable pathos and expressing greater faith, the sisters make the same point as Thomas: Jesus could have prevented the death of Lazarus but did not. Running the emotional gamut from oversentimentality to cold detachment, the conflicting currents of opinion among the Jews express the same dilemma: "Then the Jews said, 'See how he loved him!' But some of them said, 'Could not he who opened the eyes of the blind man have kept this man from dying?'" (11:36-37). Whatever their position relative to Jesus in a hierarchy of faith (perhaps, in descending order Martha, Mary, Thomas, the Jews), all express substantially the same thing. Only Thomas, however, does so from a mixed perspective, as someone firmly on the inside, loyal (he remains a disciple) but ironic, equivocal, believing yet unbelieving, perceptive to the same extent that he is blind.

Given this reading of Thomas, Carson's comments bear repeating and highlight the altered interpretative context.

> On this occasion Thomas reflects not doubt but raw devotion and courage, even though it was courage shot through with misunderstanding and incomprehension: misunderstanding, in that he had not grasped the assurance implicit in vv. 9-10, and incomprehension, in that the death Jesus had to face as the Lamb of God (1:29, 36) could not possibly be shared by his disciples. Yet there is another sense in which Thomas, like others in this Gospel, spoke better than he knew: his words have become a clarion call to would-be disciples, after the resurrection, to take up their cross daily and follow Jesus.[9]

If read in light of the ironic Thomas, Carson's comments are seen to be themselves "shot through with misunderstanding and incomprehension" because Thomas did indeed grasp "the assurance implicit in vv. 9-10" and astutely applied this insight. Thomas, it appears, knew better than he spoke. The clarion call is perhaps muted or sounding the wrong note.

The point illustrated here is important because it suggests that the mode of thought inherently related to archetype is very much related to proper interpretation: to read Thomas as naively heroic or to read Pilate ironically is to fundamentally misinterpret both characters. To adopt an ironic frame of reference for Thomas, at least provisionally, allows the reader to enter into and explore his world and allows the theology and worldview of the FG to interact with and evaluate this point of view from within this point of view itself. Additionally, the interpretation of Thomas being advanced here provides an overall coherence to Thomas's character within the FG narrative and theology otherwise lacking.

The naive heroic Thomas has come half circle. The naiveté of the disciples, the reader, and commentators has been skewered and Thomas, at least for now, is having the last laugh. The altered interpretative context offered for Carson's analysis illustrates the

---

[9] Carson, *John*, 410. Lindars, likewise referring to future discipleship, designates Thomas's remark as "unwitting irony." Lindars, *John*, 392.

importance of point of view with respect to irony; by interpreting Thomas ironically, this "heroic" interpretation has likewise been subjected to an ironic deconstruction or negation. Yet, to the same degree that this interpretation is adopted (or relished), the reader likewise identifies with Thomas as practicing ironist and runs the risk of participating in Thomas's blindness and folly. In the FG's conception of things, sharing insights with Thomas is, like irony, risky business. Self-exposure is as possible as insight. In this way, equivocal irony as seen in Thomas becomes a kind of trap in its double-mindedness. Thomas might well be known as "Didymus" (or the twin) for reasons having little or nothing to do with his sibling status and much more to do with his ironic—or twinned—double-mindedness.[10] For Thomas, perception of Jesus's failure to act in the life of Lazarus both prefigures and precipitates a failure to accept even the possibility of God acting in human affairs to raise Jesus from the dead. Despite his insight, "Let us also go, that we may die with him" marks a perceptive descent into blindness.

Thomas next appears in 14:3 in the context of the beginning of Jesus's farewell discourse. Jesus tells the disciples, "You know the way to the place where I am going" (14:4). Thomas replies, "Lord, we don't know where you are going, so how can we know the way?" (14:5). As elsewhere, the comment is at once perceptive and blind, perceptive in that it asks an obvious question related to realistic circumstances, blind in that the answer to both parts of the question has been provided in the preceding verses. Alternatively, descending into that slime of irony again, Jesus is being ironic and knows that they don't know, or Thomas is being ironic and calling into question Jesus's connection with anything beyond houses, rooms, coming and going. Recalling such interpretative conundrums as "destroy this temple," "born again," and "living water," the fact that everything in 14:1-3 can be taken as literal reference to physical objects complicates the issue. Is this figurative language or not? What is he talking about? What narrative is to be employed? While Jesus's words as normally understood within the larger context of the FG certainly refer to heaven, in Thomas's context or frame of reference, this heavenly dimension is not self-evident. Notably, Thomas's question forms a counterpart to Jesus's final words to his disciples in chapter 16 where Jesus states, "I came from the Father and entered the world; now I am leaving the world and going back to the Father." The disciples, relieved, reply, "Now you are speaking clearly and without figures of speech" (16:28-29). Characteristically, Thomas in 14:5 is the first to perceive the difficulty and may not be so thick after all. Or he may be the thickest of all. Here, as in the Lazarus narrative and indeed much of the FG as a whole, the present and future connection between heaven and earth, the action of God in the life of Jesus, and the person of Jesus with respect to the Father, combine to form a complex set of issues related to the frame of reference occupied by both character and reader. If there is no connection, then Thomas has put his finger on the problem; if there is a connection, and 14:6 states that there is, then Thomas is in the dark. Thomas in 14:5 may be very perceptive, or he may have descended from the sophistication of irony into pedestrian misunderstanding. Thomas and Jesus are at a draw but destined for a showdown.

---

[10] Barrett mentions this possibility. "It is conceivable, though not probable, that Thomas appears as the doubting disciple on account of his name. Δίδυμος, a natural rendering of ('Thoma,' a 'twin'), means primarily 'double,' 'twofold'" Barrett, *John*, 571. The fact that only the FG includes "Didymus" (twice) strengthens this possibility.

Given his past performance, Thomas's rejection of the disciples' resurrection testimony in chapter 20 is entirely predictable. If the death of Lazarus casts doubt on Jesus, the death of Jesus himself raises the same problem to an infinitely higher degree. The resurrection of Lazarus may have proved to be a short-lived and ill-founded hope, for the one who raised Lazarus from the dead is now dead himself. How can Jesus be "the way, the truth, and the life" if he is dead? And what of "No one comes to the Father except through me?" A sorry hope indeed. Fear of the Jews, so important to the other disciples here and in the Lazarus narrative, for Thomas is incidental to the fact that circumstances have rendered a fundamental promise impossible of accomplishment. The disciples' report is the braying of fools in the ears of Thomas, who won't get fooled again. Read in this light, Thomas's list of conditions appears entirely reasonable.

Thomas's perception is equally the cause of his blindness. The ironist, so often the first to see, at the same time risks premature closure. Irony rests on differences and oppositions, qualities that threaten to become ends in themselves. Double vision becomes myopia. In the FG, Thomas's irony also prevents him from making a sustained vertical connection between Jesus and the plan of God and between Jesus and his relationship of divinity with the Father. Glitches in the progress of the story threaten the connection between beliefs and experience. Circumstances threaten to negate his theology and his irony. The solution Jesus offers to Thomas is to "put your finger here; see my hands. Reach out your hand and put it into my side. Stop doubting and believe" (20:27). The verse contains two elements: physical reality and belief. Belief, and the escape from irony and misunderstanding, involves placing physical reality into some larger context, in this case, the context of the activity of God in the incarnation and the connection of God and earth and the connection between God and humanity consequent on the incarnation. Thomas is paradigmatic of this move. In the end, ironically and yet predictably, Thomas, that most blind disciple, comes to see most clearly of all.[11]

IV. B. 2 The Jews and the ironization of irony: Seeing without seeing

IV. B. 2. a *The Jews and symbolic narrative*

The various ways in which οἱ Ἰουδαῖοι (hereafter "the Jews") is used is an important issue in the study of the FG. This term has been analyzed by Fuller, who notes that "the Jews" in the FG can be used in five ways.[12] It can be used (1) as a term contrasting to the gentiles; (2) as a term contrasting to the Samaritans; (3) as a term used in relation to explanations of Jewish customs; (4) as a term designating the Jerusalem populace; and, most importantly; (5) as a term referring to a group increasingly and consistently

---

[11] Lee correctly concludes, "The character of Magdalene and Thomas draws the implied reader, through misunderstanding, along the pathway of faith which in this Gospel is the journey to the center of life." Lee, "Partnership," 49.
[12] Reginald Fuller, "The Jews in the Fourth Gospel," *Dialogue* 16 (1977): 31–37. cf. Culpepper, *Anatomy of the Fourth Gospel*, 125–32.

hostile to Jesus and the disciples.[13] The first three concern only clarification of detail and may be set aside here. Fuller lists 5:10, 5:15, 5:16, and 5:18 as referring to the Jerusalem populace, but, because these references occur in a context where "Pharisee" might be expected (cf. 2:18, 20) and because they occur in a context of unbelief (see below), they belong to the last category. Analyzing the last category, Fuller notes a number of occasions where other designations are transposed into "the Jews."[14] For example, the "crowd" of 6:22 and 6:24 becomes the "Jews" in 6:2, 6:41, and 6:52; the "Pharisees" of 9:15 become the "Jews" in 9:18, returning to "Pharisee" in 9:40; and, significantly, in the Pilate narrative, only the term "the Jews" appears. Fuller concludes,

> Thus the "Jews" become for the evangelist the quintessential expression of "unbelief"—by which he means the acceptance of Jesus as the final bearer of God's revelation. Thus, too, for him "the Jews" have the same attributes as the *kosmos* in the distinctive Johannine sense of the word.[15]

Furthermore, Fuller notes that in the FG, Jesus's conflicts with the Jews, rather than being anti-Semitic, are fundamentally Christological.[16] Significantly, in most cases, Fuller links the use of "the Jews" to theological concerns and in doing so provides a basis on which "the Jews" may be viewed as a character in a collective sense representative of a certain point of view. However, Fuller offers no extended narrative analysis.

Dorothy Lee offers another angle on "the Jews" as a collective character when she examines a series of similar narratives termed "symbolic narratives."[17] She identifies six narratives: (1) the story of nicodemus (3:1-36 [2:23–3:36]); (2) the story of the Samaritan woman (4:1-42); (3) the healing at the pool (5:1-47); (4) the feeding of the five thousand (6:1-71);[18] (5) the healing of the man born blind (9:1-41); and (6) the raising of lazarus (11:1–12:11).[19] While each contains unique features, Lee notes a common progression of five stages.

> Stage 1: *Foundational Image or "Sign,"* such as bread, water, or the healing of an individual or feeding of crowd.

---

[13] Fuller, "Jews in the Fourth Gospel," 32.
[14] Ibid., 31–37.
[15] Ibid., 36.
[16] Ibid. Similarly, Culpepper notes, "Through the Jews, John explores the heart and soul of unbelief." Culpepper, *Anatomy*, 129. Brown explains "the Jews" in a more restricted sense: "the Fourth Gospel uses 'the Jews' as almost a technical title for *the religious authorities, particularly those in Jerusalem, who are hostile to Jesus*." Brown, *John*, LXXI (his emphasis). Whether "the Jews" is general or specific and technical, Brown, in any case, agrees with the general point: "'The Jews' belong to 'the world,' that is, they are part of that division of men who are in dualistic opposition to Jesus and refuse to come to him as the light. (John is not anti-Semitic; the evangelist is condemning not race or people but opposition to Jesus.)" Brown, *John*, LXXII.
[17] Dorothy Lee, *The Symbolic Narratives of the Fourth Gospel: The Interplay of Form and Meaning*, JSNTSS 95 (Sheffield: Sheffield Academic Press, 1994).
[18] Paul Anderson offers a similar literary analysis for this passage. Anderson attempts to integrate his reading with specific events in the *Sitz im Leben* of the "Johannine community." Anderson, "The *Sitz im Leben* of Johannine Bread of Life Discourse and its Evolving Context," in *Critical Readings of John 6*, ed. R. Alan Culpepper (Leiden, NY, and Koln: Brill, 1997), 1–59.
[19] Lee, *Symbolic Narratives*, 12–13.

Stage 2: *Misunderstanding*: the central character interprets the sign in relation to material reality. Consequently, Jesus is interpreted the same way.

Stage 3: *Struggle for Understanding*: the struggle usually takes place in dialogue with Jesus.

Stage 4: *Attainment or Rejection of Symbolic Understanding*: attainment of a symbolic understanding representing the attainment of faith, or, the movement away from faith in which the symbol is interpreted on materialistic terms.

Stage 5: *Confession of Faith or Statement of Rejection*: the climax of stage 4 in which a commitment is made, (the Samaritan woman), or Jesus is explicitly rejected.

In each narrative, the sign or symbolic action functions as an interpretative obstacle to be overcome so that "symbol and narrative operate together in a cohesive and integrated way."[20] The key element is whether the sign and Jesus are seen according to the flesh (σαρξ) or according to divine glory (δοξα). Significantly, in each of the four narratives in which the Jews play an important role as a collective character (the healing at the pool, the feeding of the five thousand, the healing of the man born blind, and the raising of Lazarus), they manifest a materialistic understanding that is shown to be inadequate. For Lee, as for Fuller and the present work, the primary emphasis falls on the Jews as a collective character representative of a certain point of view or frame of reference rather than on the Jews as Jews in any national or ethnic sense.[21]

Lee's literary analysis is largely correct and is broadly similar to the one followed here. However, an analysis of the Jews in 4:43–6:71 will be offered with special emphasis on their archetypal relation to negative irony within the literary and theological *kosmos* of the FG. For the Jews at this point in the FG narrative, the possibility of faith offers a dynamic missing from later narratives where a relationship of entrenched opposition to Jesus prevails.

IV. B. 2. b *The Jews in 4:43–6:71: The ironization of irony*

Although they do not begin that way, the Jews become the consistent opponents of Jesus in the FG and the group/character most consistently ironized. The situation of the Jews in the FG abounds in ironies. To the extent that they claim to see most clearly they show themselves to be most blind. They manipulate their Roman rulers into putting their messiah to death by claiming to be more loyal to Caesar than Pilate. And their foray into power politics succeeds only because Jesus willingly places himself into the historical matrix that brings about his death. Their very success unwittingly corresponds to the purposes of God. By establishing the primacy of one point of view in the prologue, the Jews are seen to frequently speak better than they know (e.g., 11:49). But these ironies are established in relation to choices made and actions taken and are not inherent to the situation of the Jews at the beginning of the FG.

---

[20] Ibid., 227.
[21] This is generally the view of Stibbe in his analysis of 8:31-59, which he classifies as satire. Stibbe, *John's Gospel*, 105–31.

As noted, however great their eventual opposition and rejection of Jesus, the Jews begin the FG in a state of relative innocence. The priests and Levites sent from Jerusalem to investigate John the Baptist serve more as neutral enquirers whose question and answer session with John establishes that John is not the Christ and that Jesus is the Christ (1:19ff.). Following the temple cleansing, the mood is more adversarial but of a kind more characterized by incredulity and misunderstanding than anything else. The Jews ask for a sign by which to prove his authority: Jesus replies "Destroy this temple, and I will raise it again in three days" (2:18-19). In a manner prefiguring the major characteristic of the Jewish response to Jesus in the FG, the Jews negate this outrageous statement by interpreting it with reference to realism and concrete experience. Impossible on the terms of what is immediately apparent, "temple" and its associated references form an invitation to move to some other context of interpretation. What is in one context nonsense, in another is at least ambiguous (If he does not mean X, then what is Y?), and in another context, that of the cross and the FG narrative, makes perfect sense. What is called for is a hermeneutic of integration wherein interpretative obstacles are transposed into some other frame of reference. Characteristic of the Jews, lack of comprehension of this type is consistently ironized. Unlike the double-minded and equivocal Thomas, the Jews display misunderstanding most noteworthy for its persistence.

Aside from the private visit from Nicodemus the Pharisee,[22] the Pharisees are mentioned in neutral terms in 4:1 where it is noted, "Now, Jesus learned that the Pharisees had heard that he was gaining and baptizing more disciples than John." The Pharisees, previously interested in John the Baptist (1:24), now have reason to be more interested in Jesus. In response, Jesus returns to Galilee via Samaria, but the issue is not explicitly one of danger. The overall sense of Jesus's ministry from the verses 1:19–4:54 is that it is going pretty well. Culpepper observes,

> These [early] chapters have a powerful "primacy effect," that is, they firmly establish the reader's first impression of Jesus' identity and mission. The reader is led to accept the evangelist's view of Jesus before the antithetical point of view is given more than passing reference.[23]

The healing of the paralytic (5:1-15) and his failure to demonstrate any faith signals a decline from previous good circumstances. The healing of the paralytic and the healing of the man born blind are similar in many respects[24] and form narrative bookends to Jesus's open-ended battles with the Jews that increasingly dominate 5:17–8:59. The similarities end as the paralytic's lack of faith is juxtaposed against the triumphant faith of the man born blind in chapter 9.

---

[22] For Lee, "Nicodemus . . . represents the 'Jewish' leadership, which, at this stage of the Gospel, is still theoretically open to Jesus." Lee, *Symbolic Narratives*, 56.
[23] Culpepper, *Anatomy*, 91. cf., Stibbe, *John's Gospel*, 111.
[24] Raymond Collins notes, "Both the lame man and the blind man are representative figures in the tradition of the Fourth Gospel, but they are antithetically symbolical to the point that one cannot be understood without the other." Collins, "Representative Figures in the Fourth Gospel," 43; cf. Bultmann, *John*, 329; J. Louis Martyn, *History and Theology in the Fourth Gospel* (New York: 1968), 49–50.

Significantly, the paralytic's lack of faith (5:1-15) is also set against the contrasting backdrop of the faith of the royal official immediately preceding (4:43-54). The healing of the royal official must be taken into account for the healing of the paralytic to be seen in its proper narrative context. The official hears of Jesus's presence and seeks him out to come and heal his son. A kind of obstacle or test, Jesus's response is not encouraging: "Unless you people see signs and wonders you will never believe" (4:48). But the man persists. In a step of faith, he departs and his servants meet him on the way to tell him his son is healed. The time corresponds to Jesus's words, and in response he and all his household believe.[25]

The details of the story are worth a closer look, especially with regard to the nature of the inner logic of the events that resulted in faith. In one sense, it is not at all clear that the royal official's response is justified. A doubter might raise the following issues: How did the royal official know the reports about Jesus he had heard from others were true and not simply a rumor? Was his son seriously ill after all? Had his father panicked as parents often do? Was the fever about to break anyway? Was the timing of the healing simply a coincidence? How could they be sure about the coincidence of the time? What of the distance involved? Was there another healer in the area? Did the son's recovery impel the royal official to overreact? Did his joy simply get the best of him? Did his belief have proper warrant? Yet in spite of these aporias worthy of Hume, to his credit the royal official believes. Whereas Jesus's encounters with Nicodemus and the Samaritan woman followed a linear progression of vertical steps toward faith (although the faith of Nicodemus is unclear), in the case of the royal official, an interconnected complex of events confirms, tests, develops, and provides the interpretative basis for triumphant faith. For the royal official, events themselves function as a network of simultaneous invitations and confirmations of faith while they could just as easily function as obstacles, functioning as invitations or obstacles in the same way that "born again," "living water," and "bread of life" do for others elsewhere in the FG.

The subsequent healing of the paralytic and his lack of response contrast in almost every way with the response of royal official. Set in Jerusalem during the time of a feast (5:1), the situation is thoroughly Jewish. The five colonnades and the thirty-eight years of invalidity could mean much (corresponding to the law and the thirty-eight years of wilderness wandering, Deut. 2:14) or little.[26] But given the overwhelmingly Jewish context of 5:1–10:42 and beyond and the paradigmatic function of this incident as introducing this section, much is more likely than little. In any case, being an invalid for thirty-eight years contrasts with the ambiguous illness of the official's son and renders the healing of the paralytic prima facie much more remarkable. Unlike the healing of

---

[25] For Schnackenburg, the fact that the healing confirms the fullness of faith casts a cloud over the royal official in light of 4:48. Rudolf Schnackenburg, *The Gospel According to John.* vol. 1, trans. Kevin Smyth (London and New York: Burns & Oates, Crossroad, 1968–82), 468. But this objection fails to consider perseverance of the official in spite of the potential rebuke of 4:48 and fails to allow for faith to develop as a reciprocal process of challenge, action, and confirmation. Compare the faith dynamics of challenge, action, and confirmation in the account of the man born blind or the Old Testament story of Gideon.

[26] For opposing views see Carson, *John*, 241–42; Lindars, *John*, 213–214 (con); and Brodie, *John*, 238–40 (pro).

the official's son, the healing of the paralytic offers a secure basis of faith because it is immediate in terms of time and location and it establishes the causal connection between Jesus and the healing as virtually certain. But with these advantages, the healed paralytic does not respond with anything beyond physical healing. Jesus's words to the royal official "Unless you people see signs and wonders, you will never believe" (4:48) provide ironic commentary in this context: the paralytic sees but does not believe. The immediate and distant juxtaposition of the royal official and the man born blind with the paralytic form a narrative-based irony that reinforces the overall ironic structure of the FG.

The healing of the paralytic initiates an open conflict with the Jews over the issue of the Sabbath.[27] Responding to their objections, Jesus states, "My Father is always at his work to this very day, and I too am working" (5:17). If the theology on which this statement is based is understood and accepted—that God works on the Sabbath and the fact that Jesus designates God as his Father, which if true, entitles him to work on the Sabbath like the Father—then Jesus offers an adequate explanation. Jesus's working on the Sabbath is an interpretative obstacle to be overcome, an occasion for increased understanding.[28] The Jews understand the theological importance of Jesus claiming God as his Father, which implies Jesus's equality with God, but despite Jesus's acceptance of and elaborations on this assessment (5:19-23), they reject the conclusion that follows. If Jesus's reasons for working on the Sabbath are not considered as anomalies or challenges to their present frame of reference, however skeptically and provisionally, no amount of explanation will improve their understanding. While the Jews might well be forgiven for misunderstanding Jesus's reference to "temple" (2:19), the decisiveness of the paralytic's healing ought to have produced more fruit. Whatever the positive inducements offered by the paralytic's healing and Jesus's provision of an interpretative context, the reaction is one of negation. Double-mindedness at this point might have proved helpful. In Kuhnian terms, the invitation to make a paradigm shift has badly misfired. The Copernican revolution has failed; the earth does not revolve around the Son.[29]

---

[27] Culpepper observes, "The conflict with unbelief escalates in chapter 6. There are no other significant conflicts in John, no conflict with demons or nature, no conflict with himself, and little sustained conflict with the disciples." Culpepper, *Anatomy*, 91.

[28] Lee writes "The second level meaning . . . emerges once the contradiction in the first level meaning is exposed." Lee, *Symbolic*, 112.

[29] Regarding Johannine dualism and paradox in relation to its theology, Barrett notes that, rather than John's dualism being static dualism as found in gnosticism, "the distinguishing feature of John's dualism is its mobility; it is dualism in motion, in becoming. For the keyword is the *egeneto* of 1:14." (Barrett, "Paradox and Dualism," 106) As an example, Barrett observes, "Jesus enters the realm of death and by doing so transfers men out of it into life. Again, the dualism is not static but in motion." (Barret, Paradox, and Dualism, 107) In a truly static dualism, contradiction obtains and paradox is impossible, paradox having a certain living quality of mystery and potential lacking in the dead incoherence of a contradiction, as in, for example, a square circle. Although Barrett's precise concerns lie elsewhere, his insights regarding the dynamic of paradox might be applied to the present instance of the Sabbath healing. The Sabbath healing functions in the same way as statements such as "You must be born again," "whoever drinks the water I give him will never thirst," "I am the bread of life," and "My kingdom is not of this world." Each on its own and in context calls for further exploration and interpretation that can only begin to be achieved in a context beyond surface incongruencies.

The healing of the paralytic and its aftermath inaugurate a new phase in the narrative of Jesus's ministry and represent a missed opportunity of singular importance. Although in the near future at least some interaction occurs, from now on Jesus's relationship with his opponents inexorably deteriorates. From 5:19, Jesus proceeds to insist on the connection between himself and the Father (5:19-31), to insist on the validity of his own testimony (5:31-47), and to denounce the Jews for the first time (5:39-40, 5:45-47). Jesus casts the Jews as seeking eternal life in the wrong place—diligent study of the scriptures (5:39)—rather than in himself. The issue is not simply one of place or activity: it is to locate eternal life, like Jesus, in the wrong sphere of causality.

The next event in the narrative is the feeding of the five thousand, a group gathered, "because they saw the signs he had performed by healing the sick" (6:2). After the feeding, the crowds (destined to be designated "Jews") identify Jesus as "the Prophet who is to come into the world" (6:14), a view that is at once correct and grossly wide of the mark.[30] The crowds understand him horizontally as one somehow related to Moses and Deuteronomy 18:18, but fail to integrate their understanding of Jesus into a proper vertical or theological context. Jesus moves away—physically and theologically—from those who would grasp him in this inadequate manner. Removed from the crowd, the disciples experience the tempest on the lake. In a kind of living parable of faith, the disciples "were willing to take him into the boat" based on Jesus's simple words of self-identity: "It is I; (Ἐγώ εἰμι) don't be afraid" and immediately they reached the salvation of the opposite shore.[31] In contrast, through some diligent empirical detective work amid confusion (6:22-34), the crowds boat across the lake undisturbed and find Jesus physically on the other side of the lake, and that is all. Thus, the FG's account of this event can be seen as a kind of test of understanding and belief, an invitation to move beyond literal event alone and see it as both literal and literary, informed by the prologue and the theology of the FG. To see the narrative as a literal event apart from and without its larger theological and narrative symbolism is to see it as like the crowds, to see it as Nicodemus reentering his mother's womb, to see it as mere water from a well.

Refusing to answer the question as to when he arrived, Jesus instead challenges their reliance on miracles throughout 6:26-33. The crowds ask for manna as if (again) Jesus is another Moses, but they offer a promising link between heaven and earth when they state "it is written: '*He* gave them bread from heaven to eat'" (6:31). In response, Jesus affirms the Father as the source or cause of the manna and not Moses. On the back of this association of the manna with the action of the Father, Jesus transfers these associations to an as yet unspecified "he": "the bread of God is the bread that comes down from heaven" (6:34). The reply, "from now on give us this bread," is neutral

---

[30] The miracle of the feeding, notably more compressed than those in the Synoptics, serves as a parabolic introduction to the discussion that follows. Whatever the actual makeup of the crowds, the content and context of 6:25-59, set in a synagogue (6:59), is thoroughly Jewish.

[31] Commenting on the symbolic qualities of this incident Brodie remarks, "While the disciples were indeed going to Capernaum, they were also going somewhere else—to union with the divine Jesus. He was their 'land,' their ultimate goal, and once they had accepted the theophany, they had, in a sense, already arrived." Brodie, *John*, 265, 290. cf. Lindars, *John*, 248.

as to what constitutes the bread, specifically neither manna nor calling attention to the personification of the bread as "he." Bread at this point is an open invitation to a conception of bread in terms of synecdoche—bread needs to be understood within a broader frame of reference in the same way that "crown" refers to all aspects of kingship. In a sequential way, Jesus associates bread with manna and manna with the action and provision of God in the past. When fully understood, eating bread functions within the context of the FG as a metaphor for belief in Jesus.

The request of 6:34 and Jesus's response in 6:35-40 form the climax of this passage; the give and take of previous verses becomes a torrent of theology in 6:35-40 that fills in the content of "bread of life." Jesus is the bread of life. The "he" or "that which" or "the one who" of 6:33 (ὁ καταβαίνων) has "come down from heaven" (6:38), the one who "does the will of him who sent me," the Son of whom, if looked to and believed, provides eternal life (6:40).[32] As with the case of Jesus healing on the Sabbath, these statements make sense if seen within the proper frame of reference. The resulting misunderstanding is profound: in place of some fuller understanding, for the Jews Jesus is "the son of Joseph, whose father and mother we know" who, on earthly logic, did not come down from heaven but came from a location rather more close by. Significantly, at this point and not before, the crowd is designated "the Jews" (6:41).[33]

In spite of further statements, including Jesus's attempt to reconnect himself with bread and manna (6:48-51) and advance on this basis (eating manna resulted in death; believing in Jesus results in eternal life), the Jews respond without vision: "How can this man give us his flesh to eat?" (6:52). While technically best-designated misunderstanding,[34] the responses of the Jews represent a radical form of ironic negation. Irony relies on a potential or recognized conflict of understanding, while misunderstanding tends more toward simply not understanding. The border between misunderstanding and irony in these and similar cases is blurred if not crossed. In misunderstanding, the two levels of understanding characteristic of irony are rather flattened out into one—and this is exactly the point. The promising association of bread, manna, and the action of God in human affairs with Jesus himself collapses when it is negated through a distinctive preoccupation with material reality.

---

[32] Anderson notes, "Throughout vv. 6-15 and vv. 25-40 the crowd is tested as to whether it will see beyond the bread which Jesus gives to the 'bread' which Jesus is." Anderson, "*Sitz im Leben*," in Culpepper, *Critical Readings of John 6*, 5.

[33] Painter views the change for "the crowds" to "the Jews" in static categories, indicative of "a change of audience and a change of time," rather than an indication of a failed response. John Painter, "Jesus and the Quest for Eternal Life," in Culpepper, *Critical Readings of John 6*, 61-94.

[34] On misunderstanding, see D. A. Carson, "Understanding Misunderstandings in the Fourth Gospel," *Tyndale Bulletin* 33 (1982): 59-91. For Carson, misunderstandings are generally consequent upon temporal sequence in salvation history rather than a historical *Sitz im Leben* of the early church, the latter view being the target of much of the article. Complete understanding of Jesus occurs only after the cross and resurrection have illuminated previous events. Thus, Carson locates the misunderstandings in the context of the story (using Chatman's terms), rather than in the theological and rhetorical context of the discourse. This is to a certain extent correct but neglects a significant point. While a post-resurrection stance is important, a post-resurrection stance in and of itself cannot be sufficient basis for an understanding of Jesus, and, derivative of this, a post-resurrection stance in and of itself cannot fully explain the use of misunderstandings in the FG. The nature of the misunderstandings is often ontological and theological and transcends whatever increase in understanding can be gained from temporal sequence in the Gospel events alone.

On being told that "no one can come to me unless the Father has enabled them" (6:65), a form of radical transcendent causality, many disciples desert Jesus. When Jesus asks the twelve if they wish to leave too, Peter replies, "Lord, to whom shall we go? You have the words of eternal life. We have come to believe and to know that you are the Holy One of God" (6:68-69). Significantly, Peter connects Jesus with eternal life and identifies him in terms that, if less than a full affirmation of deity, affirm that Jesus is greater than a prophet. Unlike the Jews, Peter connects heaven and earth: "eternal life" connects earth with heaven and designating Jesus as "the Holy One of God" connects heaven with earth. Rooted in the incarnation itself, heaven and earth and God and creation, however estranged, are seen as interpenetrating and inseparable. The stairway to heaven, referred to in 1:51, is envisioned as bearing two-way traffic.

The narratives of the paralytic and the feeding of the five thousand and their ensuing discussions follow a similar pattern: a miraculous event giving rise to an exchange ultimately centered on the frame of reference with which it is to be viewed. In both cases, the Jews fail to make the required transition from one frame of reference to another. The materialistic perspective of the Jews prevents them from making the transition to a great theological reality. The issue of heaven (or God) or earth as the source and sphere of causality is of primary importance. The Jews limit causality to only one sphere: the material, or if not material, to the past, whereas for Jesus, the "cause" of his actions is vertical, heavenly, of the Father, whose actions Jesus performs. The vertical causality so important to romance is intolerable to this kind of thinking characteristic of negative irony. The decision to put Jesus to death by making use of the realistic means of political manipulation is the natural outcome of one of two radically different ways of viewing things, an incipient conflict rooted in the early stages of the FG's narrative. "The Jews" in the FG function as archetypal or paradigmatic representatives of an entrenched point of view.

IV. C Conceptual issues in irony

IV. C. 1 Survey and classification of studies of irony in the FG

The presence and use of irony in the FG is a well-established feature of literary analysis of the FG during the last several decades. Irony in the FG is a major concern of MacRae, Wead, Culpepper, Duke, O'Day, and Staley, with Duke's *Irony in the Fourth Gospel* being the standard and best work.[35] While Duke is certainly theological, his primary concern is an applied study of irony as a literary structure and device to which the present work is indebted. Duke's comprehensive classification of irony in the FG need not be repeated here. Like Duke, Culpepper is generally content to explore the presence of irony as a literary phenomenon.

---

[35] Culpepper, *Anatomy*; Duke, *Irony in the Fourth Gospel*; O'Day, *Revelation*; David Wead, *The Literary Devices in John's Gospel* (dissertation, Basel, 1970); MacRae, "Theology and Irony in the Fourth Gospel," in *The Gospel of John as Literature: An Anthology of Twentieth-Century Perspectives*, ed. Mark Stibbe (New York: E. J. Brill, 1993), 103–13; Jeffrey Lloyd Staley, *The Print's First Kiss: A Rhetorical Investigation of the Implied Reader in the Fourth Gospel*, SBL Dissertation Series 82 (Atlanta: Scholars Press, 1988).

With mixed success, O'Day attempts to move beyond the literary and link narrative mode and theological claim. O'Day notes that two states of knowledge in opposition to each other are necessary for irony to function at all. To see the irony of a situation is to see things with a state of knowledge, one believes, superior to that which is immediately apparent. Irony draws the reader in by requiring the reader to make a series of right judgments in regard to the proper state of knowledge. To illustrate, O'Day offers a detailed analysis of this principle at work in Jesus's encounter with the Samaritan woman in chapter 4. For O'Day, revelation in the FG is not to be connected with existential encounter with Jesus as revealer or connected to propositions; rather, revelation occurs in one's encounter with the text and being drawn into it through irony. She observes, "*The locus of revelation is thus seen to lie in the biblical text and in the world created by words of that text.*"[36] Thus, for O'Day, narrative mode is a theological claim.

O'Day correctly draws attention to the interplay of narrative mode and theological claim, but reverses the proper order. Rather than narrative mode, in this case irony, making and establishing a theological claim, the theological claims of the FG work themselves out in a narrative that inevitably makes use of irony.[37] To argue the reverse is a bit like supposing a tennis net supports the posts that hold it up. The eternal divine word coming into the world as flesh and dwelling among us is a new way of thinking at odds with present reality. This is a theological claim. The prologue makes the initial presentation of this claim that is supported and worked out afterward in the narrative. Irony, with its conflicting states of knowledge, may well be the expected result. As will be argued later, while irony rests on values, beliefs, and perceptions and challenges them, it does not establish them.[38]

Wead calls attention to the author's point of view, both in terms of physical position and mental understanding, as it relates to irony and other literary devices.[39] The fact that the author's understanding of the characters and events is superior to those within the Gospel allows irony to work; thus, "The 'godlike' position of the author is one of the key marks of irony."[40] Wead also comments on the need for a "union of thought between the author and his audience" in order for irony to be recognized and employed, a union that finds its foundation in the prologue. He writes,

> John acts upon the assumption that his readers have superior knowledge from his prologue, the information he has given them in the entire gospel, and other traditions known to Christians. This superior knowledge forms the basis for the "reality" upon which irony depends.[41]

---

[36] O'Day, *Revelation*, 47. Her emphasis.
[37] In contrast, O'Day states, "Johannine irony provides the overarching category through which to view Johannine dualism." O'Day, *Revelation*, 8.
[38] O'Day makes an astute distinction by noting that Johannine irony can be approached in two ways: as a literary device (Culpepper, Duke) or with reference to John's theology (O'Day, MacRae). O'Day, *Revelation*, 3–6. Here irony will be approached in a more general manner related to questions of value and belief, which inevitably involve questions of theology.
[39] Wead, *Literary Devices*, 1–12.
[40] Ibid., 50.
[41] Ibid., 67–68.

Wead rightly connects irony with the superior point of view and understanding of the author, one who wishes to put forth a transcendent theological reality and bases his irony upon it.

Staley offers a variation on irony in the FG in his contention that the implied reader is victimized. He comments, "In the prologue, the implied author establishes the implied reader's sense of control over rudimentary aspects of the story, only to undermine the implied reader's superior position through victimization in chapters 4, 7, 11, 13, and 21."[42] The incidents Staley refers to are (1) the Samaritan woman (4:1-42), where the reader is led astray by supposing this parody of a type scene will turn out other than it does; (2) Jesus's declining his brothers' suggestion that he attend the feast only to attend anyway (7:1-10); (3) the Lazarus incident, including the two Bethanys (10:40–11:18); (4) the introduction of the heretofore unmentioned beloved disciple (13:1-30); and (5) the continuation of the book following its assumed ending in 20:31. Assuming Staley is correct, however much the implied reader is led astray from an insider's position set out initially in the prologue, the irony in the FG remains generally stable so that the implied reader's victimization is limited.[43] It may be noted, however, that what Staley sees as dead ends are perhaps better taken as rough spots and detours. Staley's reader response methodology is notably horizontal and linear in its emphasis. Thomas as a character embodies the kind of equivocal irony analogous to that outlined in Staley's narrative analysis. To use E. M. Forster's categories in this instance, Staley's reading is notably a "flat" reading, whereas Thomas provides a "round" exposition of this type of irony.

Moore and Kelber challenge the stability of Johannine irony by arguing that the FG's irony collapses into paradox as Jesus, the source of living water to the Samaritan woman, on the cross becomes the one who thirsts.[44] Culpepper frames the issue as follows:

> The issue in dispute between those who read John's irony as stable and those who read it as unstable hinges on whether the narrative context and intertextuality of John 19:28 collapses the distinction between the physical and figurative senses of thirst. Does the text allow the reader to find a vantage point from which the figurative sense is stable or does the text defy such interpretations?[45]

---

[42] Staley, *First Kiss*, 116. See also Tom Thatcher, "The Sabbath Trick: Unstable Irony in the Fourth Gospel," *JSNT* 76 (1999): 53–77.

[43] Culpepper reads Staley as holding to a Johannine irony that, however provisionally unstable, is stable in the end. See R. Alan Culpepper, "Reading Johannine Irony," in *Exploring the Gospel of John: In Honor of D. Moody Smith*, eds. R. Alam Culpepper and C. Clifton Black (Louisville: Westminster John Knox Press, 1996), 198–99. See Staley, *First Kiss*, 95–118. Charles Giblin offers an alternative reading of the incidents of Jesus's brothers and the death of Lazarus. Namely, these pericopes, together with the changing of the water into wine (2:1-11) and the healing of the official's son (4:43-54), show that Jesus will act on his own terms and not in response to the merely human concerns of others. See Giblin, "Suggestion, Negative Response, and Positive Action in St. John's Portrayal of Jesus," *NTS* 26, 197–211.

[44] Moore, *Literacy Criticism and the Gospels*, 159–63; "Are There Impurities in the Living Water that the Johannine Jesus Dispenses? Deconstruction, Feminism, and the Samaritan Woman," *Biblical Interpretation* 1 (1993): 207–27; reprinted in *Poststructuralism and the New Testament: Derrida and Foucault at the Foot of the Cross* (Minneapolis: Fortress, 1994), 43–64. Werner H. Kelber, "In the Beginning Were the Words: The Apotheosis and Narrative Displacement of the Logos," *JAAR* (1990), and "The Birth of a Beginning: John 1:1-18," *Semeia* 52 (1990): 121–44, reprinted in *The Gospel of John as Literature: An Anthology of Twentieth-Century Perspectives*, ed. Mark Stibbe (New York: E. J. Brill, 1993), 209–30.

[45] Culpepper, "Reading Johannine Irony," 203–04.

Culpepper defends the stability of irony in this instance by noting that (1) the reader is prepared for the "I thirst" by Jesus's statement, "Shall I not to drink the cup the Father has given me?" (18:11); (2) Jesus fulfills what the Father has given him, hungering and thirsting for this fulfillment (4:34); (3) "I thirst" fulfills scripture and figuratively announces his own death; and (4) Jesus the dying man might reasonably be expected to be thirsty. Well worth a closer look, Culpepper's defensive strategy is to nuance the senses in which living water and thirst might be used and in doing so must inevitably move beyond the confines of the narrative itself; Moore and Kelber, on the other hand, in effect base their argument for the collapse of irony on what is in reality a collapse of the various uses of water into one sense. Theological collapse is narrative collapse, and narrative collapse is theological collapse. Culpepper interprets the text with all its intertextual and prophetic hills and historical valleys; Moore and Kelber see only water in all its flatness.[46] Interpretation seemingly becomes a matter of perspective to a significant degree and in this sense one is forced to make clear the paradigm one wishes to employ or, alternatively, one's interpretative paradigm is exposed. However imposing the theology of the FG may be, Moore and Kelber prefer the two-dimensional flatland of deconstruction. Even Culpepper's defense is notably nontheological.

From this survey of treatments of irony in the FG, the broad outlines of classifications of irony begin to emerge, classifications of irony based on values and beliefs and applicable to any context. For Duke, Culpepper, Wead, and O'Day, irony in the FG operates from a stable narrative and theological position. For Staley, the irony is stable, but this stability does not prevent the reader from being taken for a bit of a ride. For Moore and Kelber, the irony of the FG is radically unstable if not completely collapsed. Indicated on the chart below, these three conceptual variations on irony will be, respectively, termed positive, equivocal, and negative irony.

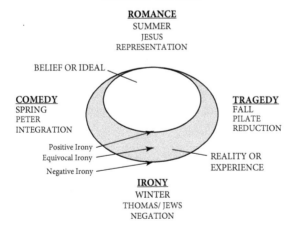

---

[46] Moore might well agree and say this is precisely his point. Regarding the attempt to clearly differentiate between the figural and literal in the Samaritan woman narrative, he notes, "To draw a clear line between them, as Jesus attempts to do, is about as effective as drawing a line on water." Moore, 62.

The content and nature of each type of irony will be developed in detail below. For now it is enough to note the difference in perspectives and observe that in these interpretations of treatments of irony in the FG manifest distinct perspectives. But first, irony will be defined more precisely and its use and perception of irony in whatever form will be seen as related to beliefs, values, and worldview.

IV. C. 2 Values and beliefs in irony

Irony is a slippery concept, difficult or impossible to grasp fully and yet an important aspect of any sophisticated discourse. While it is beyond the purpose and scope of this work to provide a comprehensive classification and definitions of the various types of ironies, a basic framework and definition of irony will be offered as a starting point for further discussion. Muecke's delineation of the three elements of irony (followed by Duke) will be used,[47] however much it must be admitted that any definition of irony is pregnant of a thousand qualifications.

The first is that irony is double layered. For irony to be present, two levels of understanding must be possible, for "Irony . . . needs and looks for contradictions and dualities."[48] In a famous example, when Shakespeare's Mark Antony states, "Brutus is an honorable man," his seemingly straightforward statement when repeated is intended to be taken ironically and mean precisely the opposite. Thus, irony is often defined as "saying one thing and meaning another," often, but not always true. This ambiguity relates to the second element: that irony presents opposition. There must be some perception of at least some degree of opposition between two or more possible meanings. Irony cannot be merely double layered, for many statements may be double layered without being in opposition, as, for example, in allegory. In stable irony, the opposition between layers will result in one of the layers being negated in favor of the other. The third element is that irony *usually* contains an element of unawareness giving rise to someone being victimized. The victim varies according to context and according to the perceptions of the reader. The victim may even be the author.

These three elements of irony suggest that irony is not simply a literary device, but is also absolutely related to values, beliefs, and perceptions. Several things may be observed. Minimally, the presence of irony intended or not indicates other ways of perceiving and/or calls something into question and, maximally, irony clearly negates one meaning in favor of another. The difference relates to Booth's familiar designations

---

[47] Duke, *Irony in the Fourth Gospel*, 14–18. Muecke, *The Compass of Irony*, 19–21. Stibbe notes, "Irony itself is an oppositional structure which thrives on two orders of meaning contrasting with one another. For a word, a phrase or a sentence to be ironic, it must be possible to imagine someone or some group interpreting something superficially and missing completely the deeper dimension of truth." Stibbe, *Storyteller*, 120. Norman Knox offers a similar definition; "Irony may be defined as the conflict of two meanings which has a dramatic structure peculiar to itself: initially, one meaning, the *appearance*, presents itself as the obvious truth, but when the context of this meaning unfolds, in-depth or in time, it surprisingly discloses a conflicting meaning, the *reality*, measured against which the first meaning now seems false or limited and, in its self-assurance, blind to its own situation," (his emphasis) Norman Knox, "Irony." For an incisive evaluation of Muecke, see Knox, "On the Classification of Ironies," *Modern Philology* 70 (1972): 53–62.

[48] Muecke, *Compass*, 129.

stable and unstable irony,[49] or irony characterized by negation and questioning, respectively. The stability or instability of irony is bound up with the perceptions of its use and perception, which, again, relates to values and beliefs.

When considered abstractly as a literary structure, device, or methodology, irony is value neutral. But to confine irony to the status of literary device is to confuse its particular form and manifestation with its relationship to values and beliefs. The actual use of irony and perceptions of its use are absolutely bound up with values, beliefs, and ideals.[50] "Double layered" is a useful conception of irony, but misleading insofar as it casts irony as a neutral two-layered structure after the manner of a cake or a house. While irony is double layered with opposition between the two layers and is in this sense trans-ideological, both the content of each layer and the position of each layer relative to each other rest on perceptions and beliefs of the ironist and those of the audience. According to Hutcheon, "Irony is always (whatever else it might be) a modality of perception—or, better, of attribution—or both meaning and evaluative attitude."[51] Referring to irony as "double layered" provides a convenient way of referring to something inherent in irony, but irony can never be only that.

On encountering irony, the actual choice of one layer over another inevitably involves questions of value or belief. The "superior" position implied by the ironist may not be shared or accepted by an audience. In terms of its perception, Mark Antony's designation of Brutus as an honorable man affirms, questions, and then negates the notion of Brutus actually being an honorable man. But Brutus might just as easily have made the same speech about Mark Antony. Or, with regard to values and beliefs, to the extent one perceives Brutus to actually be an honorable man, the irony may perhaps be missed or taken as a self-indictment on the part of Mark Antony. However strong the tendency to do so, perception of irony does not imply acceptance of the values implied in its use. On values in irony and its perception Booth observes,

> Even if an author presents no argument or position, claiming strict objectivity, indifference to the reader, or aesthetic impassivity, the reader will find himself choosing, perhaps unconsciously, to accept or reject the pose, or stand, or tone, or claim to poetic craft. But irony dramatizes this choice, forces us into hierarchical participation, and hence makes the results more actively our own.[52]

But it is also clear by now why irony causes so much trouble. An aggressively intellectual exercise that fuses *fact and value* [my emphasis], requiring us to construct alternative hierarchies and choose among them; demands that we look down on other men's follies or sins; floods us with emotion-charged value judgments which claim to be backed by the mind; accuses other men not only of wrong beliefs but of being wrong at their very foundations and blind to what

---

[49] Booth, *The Rhetoric of Irony*.
[50] This is the major argument of Linda Hutcheon, *Irony's Edge: The Theory and Politics of Irony* (London and New York: Routledge, 1994), and figures prominently in Booth. Hutcheon observes "Irony can and does function tactically in the service of a wide variety of political positions, legitimating or undercutting a wide variety of interests." Hutcheon, *Irony's Edge*, 10.
[51] Hutcheon, *Irony's Edge*, 122.
[52] Booth, *A Rhetoric of Irony*, 41. Booth offers the example of Mark Antony but does not mention that perception of the irony does not entail an alignment with Mark Antony's assessment of Brutus.

these foundations imply—all of this coupled with a kind of subtlety that cannot be deciphered or "proved" simply by looking closely at the words; no wonder that "failure to communicate" and resulting quarrels are often found where irony dwells.[53]

Booth argues that decisions about irony inevitably rest on "knowledge of value" and faults Frye over his eschewal of such judgments in literary criticism.[54] Even simple understatement or overstatement involves a value judgment. The ironist takes a risk in being perceived correctly, at least to the extent that being perceived correctly is a desired intention. Irony also opens up and exposes the beliefs and values of the reader or perceiver, who may or may not make the same interpretative moves as the ironist.

Given the value-laden nature of irony and the many forms in which irony appears, the classification of irony as positive, equivocal, or negative, follows naturally. The reference to irony as double layered suggests as much. The terms "positive" and "negative" are of course hardly neutral and imply some kind of content and values; the conceptual foundations of irony are guided in the present work by both a Christian perspective and how these terms might be traditionally conceived.

IV. C. 3 Positive, equivocal, and negative irony[55]

IV. C. 3. a Positive irony

In positive irony, a known, accepted, or offered belief or standard is assumed or affirmed by which departures from it are ironized or negated. Positive irony is manifestly present in the overall theological structure of the FG and is the primary type of irony employed. Supremely logocentric, the FG has a definite theology and point of view to which it aspires to cultivate belief (20:31) and negate unbelief (3:18). Introduced and grounded theologically in the prologue, Jesus is the ideal of the FG and the center of its function as romance; it is on the basis of who Jesus is as "the Word made flesh" that most of the irony in the FG operates. Because he is God and because he is human, Jesus ironizes this heretofore unbridged dichotomy between ideal and experience, between God and a fallen world. The treatments of FG irony by Duke, O'Day, and Wead assume the position of positive irony. In addition to positive irony, the FG contains equivocal irony, represented by Thomas, and negative irony, represented by "the Jews."

The theological basis on which irony in the FG operates as positive irony very much relates to its familiar "dualism." The dualism of the FG has less to do with an upper world meeting a lower world as much as it has to do with a proper understanding of Jesus, earthly life included, in light of who he claimed to be. While irony in the FG is a matter of perceiving it in its various literary forms such as those identified by Duke, it is much more an issue related to perception, faith and belief, and theological understanding of Jesus. In the FG, perception of Jesus as the Word, the "Holy One of God," or as "My Lord and my God" is a matter of faith and belief; yet belief and faith

---

[53] Booth, *A Rhetoric of Irony*, 44.
[54] Ibid., 193.
[55] Positive, equivocal, and negative irony are my terms.

consist of a proper perception and understanding of Jesus as the Word, the "Holy One of God," or as "My Lord and My God." The dualism suggested by darkness and light, blindness and sight, and so on forms the basis for an analogy with irony. The dualism of the FG relates to the frequent use of irony and relates to conflicting interpretation of the same data. The advantage offered by the prologue is a two-edged sword: to perceive the irony yet remain without belief is a radical form of self-indictment.

Exhibiting positive irony in another form, Swift's *A Modest Proposal* offers the ostensibly serious proposal for solving the problem of poverty and hunger among the Irish by using surplus Irish children as table delicacies for rich English aristocrats. The problem of "What can we do to relieve the poor?" is transposed into "What can we do to be relieved of the poor?"[56] The true value Swift assumes when writing *A Modest Proposal* is based on the sanctity and value of human life and is employed ironically to expose and negate its opposite: mistreatment of the Irish. The value structure of *A Modest Proposal* is polarized and much of its power stems from feigning the exact opposite of what it proposes, hiding its satire behind the straight face of irony. The greater the tone of militancy and invective, or the greater emotional element, the more irony moves toward satire.[57] Although it works by negation characteristic of irony, the irony Swift employs is positive irony in that it assumes a recognized value or belief, one whose value remains in whatever particular circumstance in order to negate its opposite. Swift's *Modest Proposal* bridges the gap between the eternal and present by employing an enduring principle and directing the application of this universal principle to a specific circumstance.

IV. C. 2. b Equivocal irony

Irony in other works is not so straightforward and occupies the swampy middle ground of equivocal or unstable, or paradoxical irony. For example, in Erasmus's *In Praise of Folly*, Folly is the name given to a personification of a certain kind of wisdom on which the world operates. No one gets married or attempts anything without Folly working her spell. While the work is ironic in that it contains irony, the extent of its irony is difficult to determine. Affirmation and negation, principle and experience, are mixed like iron and clay, presented as a kind of wisdom and offered to the reader for evaluation. Folly deserves a measure of respect, but to adopt Folly as a comprehensive explanation of things would be folly of an ill-informed kind. In a similar vein, Thackery's *Vanity Fair*, an ambiguous but value-affirming ironic novel, one without heroes, also affirms and negates: Becky Sharp is at once subject to criticism and sympathy, responsible for her actions yet an indictment of her society and times.[58] Irony of this type relies on recognition and appreciation of opposites.

The book of Esther displays equivocal irony of another sort. Whereas *In Praise of Folly* can be said to be intended to occupy a middle ground, Esther presents a case where an interpretative dilemma obtains. While Esther does not explicitly mention

---

[56] Muecke, *The Compass of Irony*, 74.
[57] Frye, *Anatomy*, 223.
[58] A. E. Dyson, *The Crazy Fabric: Essays in Irony* (London: Macmillan and Co., 1965), 72–95, esp. 90–91.

God, an implicit theology seems to affirm the sovereignty of God over human affairs.[59] What is not clear is the relationship of Mordecai and Esther to the plans and actions of God of which they, presumably, are a part. Or are they? Is their attempt to save themselves and their people one of heroic, courageous, and principled action or are they unwitting secular instruments of the sovereignty of God? The issue is, therefore, not of a middle ground, but of polar opposites with each interpretation vying for control. One interpretation negates the other, but which one is correct? The matter is further complicated by whether or not this interpretative oscillation was intended by the author. Is this the clever strategy of a genius to draw in the reader, mitigate opposites, or simple authorial bungling? Credit or blame is equally plausible. And, once recognized, the reader is inevitably sucked into a debate involving judgments of value and belief. The ironic-heroic dilemma also affects interpretation of Shakespeare's *Henry V*, Marlowe's *Dr. Faustus*, Flannery O'Connor's *Wise Blood*, the FG's treatment of Pilate, and countless others. Even *Don Quixote*, ironic and satirical yet sympathetic to its famous protagonist, may be read as a satire of a misguided knight and/or it can be read as an indictment of a society that has lost its ideals. The mixed reception of Esther by both Jews and Christians no doubt reflects something of these interpretative difficulties. Esther and *In Praise of Folly* may be classed as equivocal, although their ambiguity is of a radically different kind.

Equivocal irony can also be expressed by means of a naive speaker uttering ironies unawares. Commenting favorably on the life of Uncle Silas Phelps and his preaching in particular, Huckleberry Finn observes, "He never charged nothin' for his preaching, and it was worth it, too." Near the conclusion of *The Tempest* Miranda observes, "O brave new world that has such people in it." Miranda refers to "beauteous mankind," but her words can be taken ironically, as Aldous Huxley did for the title of his negative utopia. Recalling the tendency of the FG toward double meaning, Thomas's statement to go that "we may die with him" may be of the same cloth, a statement presented in the narrative as ostensibly naive, as it is usually taken to be, but one that on further examination means something entirely different, functioning as a trap laid out for the clever. On this reading, Thomas is presented, like Socrates, as something of an *eiron*, as one only pretending to be naive or presented as such, but one who, unlike Socrates, in the end is ironized in his irony.

In Jane Austen's *Pride and Prejudice*, a work, like the FG, of shifting perceptions and judgments explored through character, Mr. Bennet is similar to Thomas in that both are archetypal ironized ironists. From the detachment of his library, Mr. Bennet presides over his silly wife and five daughters, some of whom are silly and some not. The absurdities of life and wife supply a feast of irony. The arrival of his cousin, Mr. Collins, becomes an event of particular enjoyment. Prompted by Mr. Bennet to comment on his "talent of flattering with delicacy," Mr. Collins offers suitably inane remarks. We then read,

---

[59] See Frederic Bush, *Ruth, Esther* (Dallas: Word Books, 1996), 325–26. For a survey of issues related to irony and theology in Ruth, see K. Larkin, *Ruth and Esther* (Sheffield: Sheffield Academic Press, 1996), 58–69. Stan Goldman, "Narrative and Ethical Ironies in Esther," *JSOT* 47 (1990): 15–31.

Mr. Bennet's expectations were fully answered. His cousin was as absurd as he had hoped, and he listened to him with the keenest enjoyment, maintaining at the same time the most resolute composure of countenance, and except in the occasional glance at Elizabeth, requiring no partner in his pleasure.[60]

Whether or not Elizabeth shares his pleasure, the narrative presents the reader with an invitation to do so. Unlike Thomas, whose irony is easily passed over, the effect of this interchange is to establish Mr. Bennet as someone on the inside, someone in the know with whom sophisticated readers might well identify. But to exchange glances with Mr. Bennet is to run the risk of (not) seeing as he does.

Mr. Bennet's irony and detachment fall under scrutiny on the scandalous departure of his daughter Lydia with the unscrupulous Mr. Wickham. Concluding an unsuccessful search for them in London, Mr. Bennet returns home, saying nothing of the affair. But prompted by Elizabeth, who cautions him "not to be too severe on himself," he remarks, "No, Lizzy, let me once in my life feel how much I have been to blame. I am not afraid of being overpowered by the impression. It will pass away soon enough." The remark is at once sincere and an escape, the irony being that the impression does "pass away soon enough," perhaps too soon. Mr. Bennet regains something of his resolute composure of countenance and, turning his wit on his daughter Kitty, threatens to lock her away from society:

Kitty, who took all these threats in a serious light, began to cry.
"Well, well," said he, "do not make yourself unhappy. If you are a good girl for the next ten years, I will take you to a review at the end of them."[61]

To the extent that the reader has earlier feasted at the table of irony with Mr. Bennet, this series of exchanges is perhaps lighthearted and funny, propelling the reader over the real irony when Mr. Bennet's irony and wit are perhaps wearing a bit thin. At the very least, Mr. Bennet at this point is an equivocal figure, the human qualities and sensitivity the situation demands having been exchanged like a birthright for the pottage of irony's detachment and superior perspective. To exchange glances with him at this point is to risk seeing one's self in the mirror.

Mr. Bennet's descent into blindness reaches its nadir during the events immediately preceding Darcy's engagement with Elizabeth. He has no knowledge at all of Darcy's efforts in patching up Lydia's marriage to Wickham and no knowledge of Darcy and Elizabeth's past involvement or their growing affection, recalling only his daughter's past explicit dislike. Lady Catherine, Darcy's aunt, calls on the Bennets to denounce the match, but being detached, the meaning of this event passes him by. Mr. Bennet reads Mr. Collins's letter denouncing the marriage of Elizabeth to Mr. Darcy ironically and satirically and with exquisite delight, painfully inflicting his wit on his daughter. For Elizabeth, "It was necessary to laugh, when she would rather have cried. Her father

---

[60] Jane Austen, *Pride and Prejudice*, Norton Critical Edition, 3rd ed., ed. Donald Gray (New York and London, W. W. Norton, 2001), 47.
[61] Austen, *Pride and Prejudice*, 195.

had most cruelly mortified her . . . she could do nothing but wonder at such a want of penetration." In so doing, he fails, like Thomas, to perceive or accept the obvious clues to the wonder-full nature of present events, in his case that particularly social phenomenon of love and marriage. The scene is one of extended irony, an irony made more effective by Mr. Bennet having traded places with Mr. Collins as ironic victim and being equally or less perceptive than his silly wife. Yet through Elizabeth's reactions, the reader is cautioned against ironizing with indelicacy because of its social effects.

A number of parallels between Mr. Bennet and Thomas may be noted. Paradigmatic of an equivocally ironic point of view, both make astute observations on their respective situations from a position of superior insight and both remain within their social context with relative ambiguity and detachment. From this position, both descend through positions of equivocal interpretation into misunderstanding and blindness at which point both fail to perceive events as they really are. Further, both fail to accept evidence to the contrary, no matter how obvious or compelling. But, within the respective works in which they appear, both Mr. Bennet and Thomas are redeemable and experience a reversal of circumstances through the efforts of others. The difference between them concerns the nature and content of the worlds in which they operate: in the FG, the world is one dominated by theological concerns related to present experience; in *Pride and Prejudice*, the world is profoundly social. Thomas and Mr. Bennet must operate within their respective worlds. For Thomas, his ironic perspective has theological consequences whereas social consequences obtain for Mr. Bennet. Yet it is worth noting that both function as social misfits, each to a certain degree a stranger in his own world. For Thomas though, deliverance happens as theology is reintegrated with experience. For Mr. Bennet, deliverance occurs on social terms through his daughter's marriage to Darcy and through it the restoration of the family fortunes. However different the contexts or narratives in which they occur, both are experiments in equivocal irony in character form. And through a similar process, both Mr. Bennet and Thomas present the same thing: the ironization of the ironist.

Thomas sees too early; his observations, like Austen's Mr. Bennet, also paradigmatic of an equivocally ironic point of view, are astute and premature. Undershooting the mark, Thomas is an ironic character with comic tendencies who fails to anticipate the glory to follow. In contrast, Peter overshoots the mark and fails to anticipate the sorrows and defeats consequent on circumstance and experience. Thomas is to some degree an ironized *eiron*, while Peter is analogous to the *alazon*, or braggart. For Thomas the resurrection delivers hope while for Peter the cross brings restoration and temperance.

IV. C. 3. c *Negative irony*

With respect to values and beliefs, another type of irony exists that may be characterized as negative irony. In this type of irony, a known, accepted, or offered belief or standard is negated or rendered absurd by applying it to a difficult circumstance. Present experience proves decisive over any assertion of transcendent beliefs, as, for example, in Voltaire's *Candide* and its reaction against the providence of God undermined by the horrors of the Lisbon earthquake or similar reactions to the evils of the twentieth century. The statement "God was certainly at Auschwitz" can be taken as employing negative irony to highlight the absence of God. White comments,

The archetypal theme of Satire [or irony] is the precise opposite of this Romantic drama of redemption; it is, in fact, a drama of diremption, a drama dominated by the apprehension that man is ultimately a captive of the world rather than its master, and by the recognition that, in the final analysis, human consciousness and will are always inadequate to the task of overcoming definitively the dark force of death, which is man's unremitting enemy.[62]

Negative irony tends to be parasitic: without some belief or value, even if held only by a few, it has no two levels to set against each other and hence nothing to ironize.[63] In its negation of some belief or ideal without offering some other in its place, negative irony is a form of deconstruction, a radical negation of any pretensions of two levels of meaning. If two levels of meaning are allowed, they cannot be integrated in any meaningful way. Irony of this kind is the archetype of the antihero in which persons holding a belief or ideal worthy of acting upon are viewed as naive, phony, dangerous, or any combination thereof. Booth comments,

> A good deal of literary controversy [exists] today in which critics, unable to believe that an author could really contradict their own beliefs, conclude that he is being ironic. Pious authors cannot possibly have meant their piety, defenders of authority must have been kidding . . . . Jane Austen must have been ironic in her treatment of Fanny Price in *Mansfield Park* because—well, because the Crawfords whom she takes to be so deficient morally are really—to us—so much more interesting.[64]

The preference for the morally deficient Crawfords sheds more light on the views of the interpreter than the novel itself. In American politics, this hero-antihero polarity goes a long way toward explaining the admiration of some for either Ronald Reagan or Bill Clinton wherein admiration for one usually corresponds to loathing for the other.

Negation functions in these simple verbal ironies. Job comments, "No doubt you are the people and wisdom will die with you" and negates the conventional wisdom of his friends, "wisdom" and "friends" being ironic notions in themselves in this case. A entertainment magazine in Great Britain offered a cover story entitled "Party Politics," a title referring to scandal of a certain type that resulted in the fall of Harold Macmillan's government. A British opinion page article entitled "America: Always a Class Act" highlighted the existence of a class system in America. In both cases, a standard or natural meaning assumed from the context of wider use and on which the irony rests is negated, effecting a reversal as the original meanings of "party" and "class" are transposed into ironic commentary.

---

[62] White, *Metahistory*, 9. n.b. "diremption" means "forcible separation."
[63] Gans notes "By its very expression, irony resentfully affirms the authority of the form it has denied. The ironic deconstruction of the hierarchy between words and things pays homage to this hierarchy by implying that it presides over its own deconstruction." Eric Gans, *Signs of Paradox: Irony, Resentment, and Other Mimetic Structures* (Stanford: Stanford University Press, 1997), 68.
[64] Booth, *A Rhetoric of Irony*, 82. It is worth noting in passing the main characters of *Mansfield Park* generally correspond to the four archetypal patterns: Fanny Price as romance or hero, Mariah Bertram as tragic, the Crawfords as ironic, and Edmund Bertram as comic.

On a larger scale, James Joyce's *Ulysses* offers an ironic transposition of the Homeric epic. The lengthy homecoming of Odysseus the hero becomes one day in the life of ordinary Dublin in all its glory, the unfaithful Molly replaces the steadfast Penelope, and the stylistic performance of language becomes an end in itself. Certainly aware of what he is doing, Joyce also speaks for the isolation and disillusion of his times. On this kind of ironic disenchantment, Muecke observes,

> For most "serious" writers, whether poets, novelists, or dramatists, irony is now much less often a rhetorical or dramatic strategy which they may or may not decide to employ, and much more often a mode of thought silently imposed upon them by the general tendency of the times.[65]

When fully realized, negative irony and negation become part of a habit of thinking and worldview characterized by concern for the contradictions and problems of the immediate here and now within a context of isolation, frustration, and limitation. What Steiner calls "the wager on transcendence" is seen a bet not worth making.[66] The metaphysics of absence banishes the metaphysics of presence. The ubiquitous ambiguities of life and language become decisive, creating a context in which the presence of God and the transcendent becomes unrecognizable.

A seminal example of this kind of perspective and negative irony is Beckett's *Waiting for Godot*. In contrast to the hero of romance who acts upon and displays an ideal, for Estragon there is "Nothing to be done." Stasis supplants the quest. Whatever "happens" in the play shows that nothing happens. The situation is static and sterile.[67] Typical of irony, there is no plot and only the barest story. The hero, Godot, whoever or whatever he is, never arrives so as to render the lives of Estragon and Vladimir meaningful, nor is he at all likely to arrive, rendering mere reference to his arrival absurd and meaningless. Waiting is absurd, but so is travel. Williams remarks, "Pozzo and Lucky belong to the world of effort and action; Vladimir and Estragon to the world of resignation and waiting. Neither response is more significant than the other, in any ultimate way: the travelers fall and the tramps wait in disappointment."[68]

Beckett forever seeks to keep the present radically in front of the audience or reader to enforce the "directly communicated experience" of waiting.[69] Whenever the dialogue threatens to "mean" something and transcend circumstance, it is negated by some means, prolonging and intensifying the sense of waiting, if indeed boredom and waiting can be intensified. Estragon's incomprehension and indifference negates Vladimir's attempt to talk of the two thieves or the savior. Contrary to expectation, Godot is never identified, let alone arrives, focusing attention on his ever-present non-

---

[65] Muecke, *Compass of Irony*, 10.
[66] George Steiner, *Real Presences: Is There Anything in What We Say?* (London and Boston: Faber and Faber, 1989), 214.
[67] Chatman notes, "Joyce, Woolf, Ingmar Bergman, and other modern artists do not treat plot as an intricate puzzle to be solved. It is not a change in the state of affairs, but simply the state of affairs itself." Seymour Chatman, *Story and Discourse: Narrative Structure in Fiction and Film* (Ithaca, NY: Cornell University Press, 1978), 92.
[68] Raymond Williams, *Modern Tragedy* (London: The Hogarth Press, 1992), 154.
[69] Raymond Williams, *Drama from Ibsen to Brecht* (London: The Hogarth Press, 1993), 303.

arrival. Near the end, the building desire to leave and wander in the Pyrenees, idyllic and hopeful, is deflated with a scatological remark, stifling hope within the bounds of present reality.[70] Even suicide, that most final of all commentaries on life, to some degree sublime in its sadness, is impossible of accomplishment. Estragon removes his belt to hang himself and his trousers fall down. Dialogue does not always follow or flow, interrupted with silence, frustrating expectations. Even the instances of comic dialogue and repartee serve to ground the action radically in the present, counterbalancing any attempt to consider any other situation or frame of reference wherein one might search for meaning. The play is focused in the here and now, even to the point of calling attention to the stage and the performance as performance as a means to accomplish this. After one interchange, Vladimir and Estragon also comment on themselves,

Estragon: "That wasn't such a bad little canter."
Vladimir: "Yes, but now we'll have to find something else."[71]

At one point Estragon leaves the stage to relieve himself. Lucky, perhaps the most philosophical character, is weighted with baggage and roped by his neck, jerked, as the audience is, held fast by this constant reminder of present experience.

The central emphasis of ironic, frustrated waiting in *Godot* has a strong literary parallel in the waiting of the man at the pool in chapter 5 of the FG. The pool itself, a potential but sterile source of hope, functions as ironic commentary analogous to the tree in *Godot*. Jn 5:3 describes the scene, "Here a great number of disabled people used to lie—the blind, the lame, the paralyzed." None can move well and some not at all. In any case, and unlike the royal official, they do not move but lie about in a scene of static hopelessness. Perhaps the addition of 5:4 was an attempt to insert some hope into this dismal scene and make sense of it. Estragon and Vladimir wait—as does the paralytic who waits, and has waited, for a Godot-like deliverance from some ill-defined healing not available at the pool. In a Catch-22, because he is lame, the paralytic cannot enter the pool, yet to enter the pool is his only hope of being cured, his hopes and waiting endlessly frustrated. Yet, because the dubious healing cannot be accessed, its effectiveness can never be tested and proved false or true. Waiting of this kind renders life at once meaningful and absurd. For the tramps and the paralytic alike, deliverance on the terms they live by is impossible of accomplishment. They can only pretend. Both continue in a condition of unstated negative irony. When Jesus asks, "Do you want to get well?" (5:6), the disjointed answer supplied by the paralytic does not really apply to the question. Because he fails to integrate his healing into the metanarrative of the FG, for the paralytic the healing, however fortunate, is meaningless. The reader is implicitly cautioned: without faith in the Messiah the offer "to get well" may result in nothing more than blindness, or, as Jesus cautions the paralytic (5:14), something worse.

Whereas the FG demands that its characters and readers take into account the transcendent world and its claims to render this word meaningful, *Godot* is equally

---

[70] Samuel Beckett, *Waiting for Godot: A Tragicomedy in Two Acts* (London: Faber and Faber, 1965), 81.
[71] Beckett, *Godot*, 65.

relentless in terminating these moves. In *Godot*, the fallen world or radical experience continues its triumph over the world of wonder and grace. In the FG, the cross achieves something whereas in *Godot* it is a means of ironic commentary. Representation, in the sense of "this means this *and* that" characteristic of romance, in *Godot* has broken down; in *Godot*, this is all there is. In such an environment, metaphor itself survives as a tenacious and unwanted weed and then only precariously. The hero is banished because there is nothing to stand for. The arrival of the Messiah in the FG both contrasts and coincides with the non-arrival of Godot; for some, the arrival of the Messiah is seen to the extent that he is placed into the proper meta-narrative, the Messiah and his meta-narrative being inseparable; for others, failure of the meta-narrative coincides with his rejection. For the latter, life is reduced to *Godot*-like waiting.

By its combination of temporal waiting and negation of the transcendent, *Godot* reduces life to a kind of one-dimensional view of reality. This can be interpreted with reference to the end of modernity, with its angst over the (non)arrival of meaning, or the incipient arrival of postmodernity with its acceptance and unconcern that Godot will never arrive. Nealon offers an insightful interpretation of *Godot* as transitional between modernism and postmodernism.[72] On Lucky's think he comments,

> The text of Lucky's speech is akin to the product of taking all the great works of Western thought, putting them through a paper shredder, and pasting them back together at random . . . . Lucky's think . . . is a narrative that disrupts and deconstructs all notions of universal, ahistorical, consistent meta-narrative—all Godots.[73]

For Nealon, *Godot* is the tyranny of meta-narrative. Citing the following dialogue, Nealon argues that Vladimir and Estragon are "on the verge of a deconstructive breakthrough, but their dependence on the meta-discourse of Godot holds them back."[74]

> **Estragon:** . . . Let's go far away from here.
> **Vladimir:** We can't.
> **Estragon:** Why not?
> **Vladimir:** We have to come back to-morrow
> **Estragon:** What for?
> **Vladimir:** To wait for Godot . . .
> **Estragon:** . . . And if we dropped him? (*Pause*) If we dropped him?
> **Vladimir:** He'd punish us.[75]

For Nealon, *Godot* implies or anticipates the move toward postmodernism and the rejection of meta-narrative. The breakthrough Nealon argues for, the one separating the modern from the postmodern, is the rejection of grand narratives in favor of the

---

[72] Jeffrey Nealon, "Samuel Beckett and the Postmodern: Language Games, Play and 'Waiting for Gadot,'" in *Waiting for Godot and Endgame*, ed. Steven Connor (London: Macmillan, 1992), 44–53.
[73] Nealon, "Beckett and the Postmodern," 47.
[74] Ibid., 50.
[75] Beckett, *Godot*, 93.

celebration and freedom of language games.[76] Thus, in some of their playful exchanges, Vladimir and Estragon anticipate the emphasis on language itself characteristic of postmodernism.

In such contexts, however, the meaning-fullness of language tends to decline. For Jesus and the Jews, because they do not share the same meta-narrative or frame of reference, the conversation tends to move away from any sort of serious dialogue and more toward a talking past each other. At one point Jesus admits as much, saying "Why is my language not clear to you?" (8:43). In such situations of antithetical paradigms, the only recourse is to satire and a radical denunciation of the opposing side.[77] The healing of the paralytic and its immediate aftermath cast a long shadow over succeeding chapters wherein the ensuing narratives are narratives of frustration. To fail to enter the meta-narrative or frame of reference of the FG is to participate in the blindness of the Pharisees and ultimately to place one's self by the pool.

Irony, whether positive, neutral, or negative, because it rests fundamentally on values and beliefs and not narrative structure is characterized by the possibility of narrative disembodiment and narrative stagnation. While irony may be embodied in and carried by a character, as is the case with Thomas and Mr. Bennet, there is no necessary reason why this must be so. Irony may be found in situations requiring a narrative progression, as for example in tragic irony, but this need not be so for irony to be present. In this sense, irony tends to be more of a state of mind or perception more easily removed from narrative progression than the other archetypes, or, looked at another way, any narrative progression in irony tends to be borrowed from tragedy or comedy. Romance, tragedy, and comedy require embodiment in a character and some form of narrative progress whereas irony does not.[78] A tragedy without character where nothing happens remains unthinkable whereas the same thing cannot be said about irony. In this way, the characteristics of irony as an archetype requiring neither character nor movement correspond to associations of negative irony with isolation, detachment, and sterility.

IV. D Conclusion

In summary, whatever the actual form irony takes, be it verbal, dramatic, or situational, (the classifications are endless), irony necessarily involves issues of belief or value at some level of perception. With this in mind, irony may be characterized as positive, equivocal, or negative with reference to the values and beliefs on which it operates.

---

[76] Nealon, "Beckett and the Postmodern," 51.
[77] Answering charges of anti-Semitism, Stibbe correctly casts the FG's polarized polemic at this point (8:31-59) in terms of satire. Stibbe, *John's Gospel*, 107–131. Significantly, Stibbe notes a number of binary oppositions: truth/error, freedom/slavery, divine/demonic, hearing/not hearing, obeying/not obeying, life/death, honor/shame, and knowledge/ignorance. Stibbe, *John's Gospel*, 124–25.
[78] In comedy this is true to a lesser but nonetheless significant degree. For comedy to be "transitive" rather than "intransitive" (see chapter 5) embodiment in a narrative progression is required.

Insofar as their respective value structures are accepted, both positive and negative ironies are stable whereas equivocal irony is unstable or ambiguous.

In romance, the world of experience is integrated into some system of belief and affirmation and is therefore meaningful in terms of and beyond present experience. In positive irony, the belief or ideal remains constant but it is recognized that experience has departed from it. The stable belief or ideal forms a basis on which to evaluate present experience through irony and satire as, for example, when the mercy of God forms the position against which Jonah is satirized. Negative irony forms the opposite of romance and two are virtually incompatible. Tragedy and comedy may each contain irony, but of a kind that tends to be based on a situation and tends to resist polarization over questions of value and ideology. The actions of Agamemnon, Oedipus, and Hamlet tend to be ambiguous because these tragic heroes experience the tension between ideals and circumstance. Characteristic of tragic heroes, Hamlet waivers between irony and romance, inaction and action, and philosophic detachment and social involvement. Likewise, Pilate waivers between Jesus and the Jews. In romance and also in positive irony, an ideal or belief is assumed by which experience is to be governed or interpreted; in negative irony, any such value or belief is negated by its inability to govern or interpret present experience or render it meaningful. In romance, the concern is for the transcendent and eternal; for tragedy, the past, while in irony the concern lies in the temporal and present. With its emphasis on possibility and hope, comedy is the archetype of the future.

5

Comedy and Peter

V. A Introduction

A literary analysis of Peter's series of encounters with Jesus follows wherein particular attention will be given to the dynamics of each scene, the growth of Peter's understanding of Jesus, and the dynamics of their relationship with a view to laying the groundwork for the study of Peter as an archetypal comic character. Like all characters in the FG, Peter must be understood in relation to Jesus. The story of Peter is less about his encounter with Jesus and his initial faith response, as is the case with Nicodemus, the Samaritan woman, or Pilate, and more about the subsequent perils and possibilities of that faith in action. The growth of Peter's understanding of Jesus will be traced in relation to his knowledge as compared to the knowledge outlined in the prologue and in its application to concrete reality as taught and exemplified by Jesus himself. Peter exhibits the archetypal comic pattern of moving—uneasily—toward an integration of beliefs and reality.

V. B Peter in the Fourth Gospel

V. B. 1 Peter as follower

The prologue tells us that "the Word became flesh and made his dwelling among us" (1:14) and that this Word was testified to by John the Baptist (1:6-7, 14-18). Jesus in the FG appears in maturity without benefit of birth accounts that mark him out as different and specifically designate him in any way, yet we are told that "he was in the world" (1:10). In 1:19-25, the task of John the Baptist is to resist being identified as the Christ, Elijah, or the Prophet. Then in 1:26-28 the Baptist makes known to those in his hearing the fact that this special person is among you, "One you do not know." If the logic of the prologue is allowed to play out in the text, the question is not that Jesus of Nazareth is the Messiah, as is emphasized in Matthew and Luke, but that this "Word made flesh," this one who "comes after me [who] has surpassed me because he was before me," this mystery man is Jesus.[1] The Baptist, we are twice informed (1:31, 33), "did not know

---

[1] Carson discusses this issue more widely in D. A. Carson, "The Purpose of the Fourth Gospel: John 20:30-31 Reconsidered," *JBL* 108 (1987): 639–51.

him." The Baptist's lack of recognition, a telling fact in its own right, is overcome by Jesus being designated by the Spirit through the Spirit's descending and remaining upon him in 1:32, an event linked to the testimony of the Father, "the one who sent me to baptize with water" (1:33). In the FG, the historical witness of the Baptist merges with the witness of the text that the "Word made flesh" is Jesus, simultaneously the "lamb of God" and "Son of God."

Jn 1:35-51 narrates the decrease of the Baptist and the increase of Jesus as the former's disciples becomes followers of the latter as they move from the Baptist's own witness to encountering Jesus for themselves. Two of John's disciples hear John speak and follow Jesus (1:37). Filling out the story narrated in 1:38-39 a bit by combining the details of the separate verses, it may be surmised that these two disciples spent a significant amount of time with Jesus and that Jesus taught them. One of these two, Andrew, finds his brother Simon Peter and informs him, "We have found the Messiah" (1:41). They might have found the Messiah by looking for him on the basis of the witness of the Baptist, or in general terms from the OT itself, or, most likely a combination of both.[2] Thus, Andrew, the Baptist's disciple and instructed by him, is in turn instructed by Jesus himself and designates the Messiah as Jesus to his brother Peter. The point here is that on the terms of both story and discourse Jesus is presented to Peter by his twice taught brother Andrew as the Messiah. Whatever the precise content of Peter's understanding of Jesus at this point, the fact remains that in the FG it may be reasonably inferred that Peter begins with significantly developed knowledge of Jesus and that Peter is more or less aligned with the identification of the Messiah as Jesus right from the start. Significantly, Peter in this passage is passive, the initiative coming from Andrew and, more importantly, Jesus himself.[3] Like his call, Peter is to learn that his mission must be defined and directed by Jesus himself.

A final confession of faith from Peter's own lips does not occur until 6:68-69, where Peter's confession is in many ways equivalent to his confessions in Mt. 16:16, Mk 8:28, and Lk. 9:20.[4] The differences, however, are more striking than the similarities, beginning with the differing narrative contexts of the Synoptics and the FG. The Synoptics present Peter's confession as a high point, the culmination of previous events that leads to a new level of understanding. The situation in John 6 is quite different. Following the feeding of the five thousand and the walking on water, Jesus confronts the crowds with his teaching that he is the bread from heaven, words that the crowds find hard to swallow and give rise to numerous misunderstandings. To those who grumble or find the teaching difficult to understand or accept, Jesus offers further challenges culminating in his statement that "this is why I told you that no one can come to me unless the Father has enabled them" (6:65). Jesus's statement is deliberately

---

[2] The term *Messiah* is found in the NT only here and 4:25. Bruce notes that, while the term in the OT referred to the roles of prophet, priest, and king, at the dawn of the Christian era messianic expectation term took on a predominately royal form. See F. F. Bruce, *The Gospel of John* (Basingstoke, UK: Pickering Paperbacks, 1983), 57. As will be seen, Peter very much displays this understanding.

[3] Brodie observes, ". . . the call of Peter . . . is like the call of David, the outsider who, by sheer choice on the Lord's part, was brought in and given a position of leadership." Thomas Brodie, *The Gospel According to John: A Literary and Theological Commentary* (New York: Oxford University Press, 1993), 161–62.

[4] See Raymond Brown, *The Gospel According to John*, vol. 1 (New York: Doubleday, 1966–70), 302.

provocative and accomplishes its intended effect of separating the committed wheat from the uncommitted chaff (6:66). As many leave, Jesus asks, "You do not want to leave too, do you?" (6:67) and Peter's reply follows. As compared to the Synoptics, Peter's statement comes as the result of a challenge, as the passing of a test by the denial of a negative course of action and remaining loyal when others turn away.[5] Indeed, the notion of testing might be extended back to everything that has happened since the disciples' calling and extended forward to future events as well.

In addition, the content of Peter's statement in the FG differs significantly from the Synoptics. Peter's rhetorical question, "Lord, to whom shall we go?" (6:68) excludes other possibilities. The designation "Lord" can mean much or little, but in this context probably means much.[6] Jesus offers "words of eternal life," implying that all other words are of a different and lesser category. In the FG, Peter does not say that Jesus is the Christ, or Messiah, or a teacher sent from God, as does Nicodemus, but that he is "the Holy One of God." The designation "Messiah" has already been connected to Peter, albeit indirectly, and the designation "Holy One of God" likely includes and advances these concepts.[7] By naming Jesus in this manner, Peter places Jesus alongside God himself as over against those who saw Jesus as a second Moses and would make him king earlier in chapter 6.

In line with the theology and rhetoric of the FG discussed earlier, 6:69 presents a FG epistemology in miniature. Peter says, "And we have believed and have come to know that you are the Holy One of God" (NASB). Significantly, both verbs appear in the perfect tense. On the terms of the FG, belief, however mature or immature, cannot be separated from knowledge and vice versa.[8] Peter's belief allows him to come to know certain things about Jesus even though parts of his belief will later prove to be in excess of his knowledge. Pilate, on the other hand, illustrates the dangers of knowledge in excess of belief and of attempting to isolate the two.

These accounts of Peter in 1:41-42 and 6:68-69 together place Peter firmly on the inside, as one with a significant and developed understanding of Jesus coupled with a tested devotion to him. As if to emphasize the point, Peter's statement of belief is juxtaposed against the mention of Judas as betrayer immediately following (6:71). At the same time, the separating out of Judas as betrayer offers a corrective postscript to Peter's all too inclusive "we" of 6:69.

---

[5] Rudolph Schnackenburg, *The Gospel According to John*, vol. 1, trans. Kevin Smyth (London and New York: Burns & Oates, Crossroad, 1968–82), 75.
[6] Leon Morris, *The Gospel According to John* (Grand Rapids: Eerdmans, 1971), 389.
[7] Moloney states, "For the first time in the narrative a character has expressed faith in Jesus for the right reason: *His origins*. The holiness of Jesus comes from the fact that he is *of God*." (his emphasis) Moloney's specific point is debatable, but is in line with the more general point argued here. Francis Moloney, *The Gospel of John* (Collegeville, MN: The Liturgical Press, 1998), 229.
[8] Carson notes, "Knowledge in the Fourth Gospel is frequently personal (it is knowledge of God and of Jesus Christ that constitutes eternal life, 17:3), but it is no less frequently propositional (as here: the disciples know *that* Jesus is such and such." See D. A. Carson, *The Gospel According to John* (Grand Rapids: Eerdmans, 1991), 303, his emphasis. Carson (303) and Barrett (81ff) note that knowledge and belief are virtually synonymous. C. K. Barrett, *The Gospel According to John: An Introduction with Commentary and Notes on the Greek Text* (London: SPCK, 1978).

V. B. 2 Peter as leader

V. B. 2. a Peter in chapter 13

Chapter 13 signals a change in emphasis in the FG. Tovey notes: "the focus shifts from the public arena of proclamation, where the foremost questions have to do with Jesus' identity and status and response to him, to the inner circle of the believer, where the issues are discipleship and bearing witness."[9] But at least one participant in the story fails to make this same move from public proclamation to discipleship. In this context, Peter reappears and figures prominently in the narratives of the footwashing and predictions of denials. While the incidents overlap, with respect to Peter, the narrative moves from one emphasis to another. Peter begins the chapter as a firmly committed follower of Jesus, one who has persevered through some trials with his faith and commitment intact. But in chapter 13, a rift appears between the kind of discipleship Jesus has in mind for himself in relation to the Father and for his followers as over against the kind of mission and discipleship Peter himself has in mind—for himself and for Jesus. Peter plans a mission of triumph while Jesus intends one of service leading to death. Peter is firmly a follower of Jesus insofar as his understanding of Jesus is concerned, but is mistaken in his conception of how being a follower of Jesus works itself out in time and space, representing, as Lindars puts it, "faith without understanding."[10]

Having concluded the narration of Jesus's public ministry, the FG now turns its attention to Jesus's concern for his followers. Jesus knows that his hour is at hand (13:1) and seeks by the symbolic action of washing the disciples' feet to demonstrate the kind of self-giving love they should have for one another. Peter makes the obvious conclusion implied by Jesus's action even before Jesus later explains it (13:13-17): namely, that if Peter is to be a follower of this Lord and master and if this Lord and master performs acts of menial service to others, then this act of service implies (1) that this Lord and master is demeaning himself in the eyes of his followers and/or (2) that if Peter is to follow this Lord and master, he himself is expected to perform similar acts. Neither prospect appeals to him.

Incredulous, Peter asks Jesus, "Lord, are you going to wash my feet?" (13:6). Jesus's reply is instructive: "You do not realize now what I am doing, but later you will understand" (13:7). Understanding or the lack of it is an important theme in the FG, but the lack of understanding Jesus informs Peter of is not one of theological identity, which Peter seems to understand, but of the nature and object of his mission—sacrificial love and death. Jesus's statement functions as a warning to Peter not to persist with this course of action. But Peter persists. Jesus tells him that "unless I wash you, you have no part with me" (13:8). Because he desires to have a part with Jesus, Peter displays the opposite response of making the task more difficult by asking that his hands and head be bathed as well.

With iron logic, Jesus explains his actions in 13:12-17. He asks if they understand (13:12), then tells them that they themselves call him "teacher and Lord," thereby

---

[9] Derek Tovey, *Narrative Art and Act in the Fourth Gospel* (JSNTS 151, Sheffield: Sheffield Academic Press, 1997), 107.

[10] Barnabas Lindars, *The Gospel of John* (London: Oliphants, 1972), 450.

aligning the disciples themselves with Jesus by their own admission. Jesus also designates himself as "teacher and Lord" (13:13). And, if Jesus is their teacher and Lord, then they ought to follow his example and do likewise (13:14-15). Jesus offers an aphorism to reinforce this message by adding that "no servant is greater than his master, nor is a messenger greater than the one who sent him" (13:16). Jesus concludes by adding that "you will be blessed if you do them [his teachings]" (13:17). These teachings, then, establish the conditions on which a disciple is to follow Jesus. Just as Jesus offers "words of eternal life" (6:68) and is the only way to the Father (14:6), following Jesus necessarily entails service, and this service to others after the manner of Jesus is a necessary part of being on the inside.

Yet Peter continues to misunderstand. A backward glance over the pages of the FG may suggest why he does so. His persistence can be viewed as stubborn blindness or even willful disobedience. But whatever warnings Jesus puts in Peter's way, it is nevertheless true that Peter's actions are justified to a significant degree. Jesus's miracles of turning the water into wine, healing the official's son, healing the invalid at the pool, feeding the five thousand, walking on the water, healing the man born blind, and triumphantly raising Lazarus from the dead may be taken as having occurred before the eyes of Peter. The raising of the dead on the last day, which Martha affirms, is brought forward into the present in the raising of Lazarus. Jesus claimed to exist before Abraham, to be sent from God, to have God as his Father, to be at one with the Father—claims, or similar claims, that repeatedly fell upon the ears of Peter. The raising of Lazarus followed by the triumphal entry combine for a grandiose experience of the first order. In such an environment, the opposition to Jesus and threats of death might well be ignored or taken as a challenge waiting to be met by one inclined to do so. Peter well understood Jesus's own predictions of death as contingent on the actions of others (i.e., Judas's betrayal) and therefore preventable. In any case, Jesus's predictions of his own death and his symbolic footwashing seem to have fallen on deaf ears and blind eyes.

The scene in chapter 13 continues with the issue of betrayal rising to prominence. The context of eating a meal with a familiar group suggests intimacy, but this mood is broken when Jesus declares that, "Very truly I tell you, one of you is going to betray me" (13:21). Peter, notably designated here as Simon Peter (cf. 13:6), asks "this disciple" to inquire which one he means (13:24). On being asked, Jesus dips the piece of bread and gives it to Judas Iscariot, notably designated here as "son of Simon" (13:26, cf. 13:6). Beyond these references to the common name lies a larger point: in this passage, Peter and Judas are at once linked together and distinguished, each departing from the Lord but each in his own way. For Judas, the reception of the bread from the hand of Jesus marks him out as the betrayer and initiates his departure into the night. Peter will practice his own style of betrayal.

Keeping with the FG's concern to portray the crucifixion as glorification rather than humiliation, in 13:31-33, Jesus certainly refers to the cross, but not everyone understands it that way. The speaker and one of his hearers have in mind two very different scenarios. Observe Jesus's words in 13:31-32: "Now the Son of Man is glorified and God is glorified in him. If God is glorified in him, God will glorify the Son in himself, and will glorify him at once." By all indications, events are moving to the climax of Jesus's final glorification. Jesus says this glorification of the Son of Man will occur "now" and "at once" (νυν, εὐθυς). Variations of the verb glorify (δοξαζω) occur four times.[11] Whatever the precise meaning of "Son of Man" as used by Jesus in the FG, in this context this term would certainly call to Peter's mind Dan. 7:13-14 with all of its triumph and glory.[12] God figures prominently in this glorification, for now the Son of Man is glorified and God is glorified in him. And if God is glorified in him, a given fact, God will glorify the Son in himself. Unlike the better informed reader, Peter's attitude may be construed as, "If God is for us, who can be against us," and God is unquestionably involved in this instance. Whatever the danger, the situation is certain to end in triumph, and Peter wants to be a part of it even though Jesus indicates that what he has to do he must do alone, a lonely series of events summed up by "Where I am going, you cannot come" (13:33).

Having made his point about himself, Jesus changes the focus to the disciples in 13:34-35. As if to reinforce the message of the footwashing, Jesus stresses that love is essential: it stems from Jesus himself (13:34a), governs relations with one another (13:34b), and testifies to their being Jesus's disciples (13:35). Peter pays little attention to these instructions. Rather, Peter replies, "Lord, where are you going" (13:36) and in doing so moves the discussion back into the context of glorification and going away found in 13:31-33. Jesus replies, "Where I am going, you cannot follow now, but you will follow later" (13:36). The emphasis falls not so much on the fact of glorification as on its timing and its content. A glorification of the type Peter has in mind will occur, but not now, and the glorification Jesus has in mind at present, death on the cross, will certainly happen to Peter. Persisting in his misunderstanding and yet being blindly correct in his assertion, Peter asks, "Lord, why can't I follow you now? I will lay down my life for you" (13:37). As Jesus has explained, the specific conditions of being a disciple involve service to others and love (13:13-17, 31-33); in contrast, Peter would rather "follow you right now" and promises to lay down his life. Responding, Jesus predicts that Peter will deny him three times and thereby moves the discussion yet further back to the context of Judas and denial. Thus, rather than moving ahead with Jesus, Peter will regress toward Judas.[13] Peter, this strutting rooster, is destined to have his wings clipped.

The thrust of chapter 13 precludes any reduction of Peter's defense of Jesus in the garden to the mere spontaneous defense of a friend. Peter carried a sword and intended to use it. While Peter is a committed and loyal disciple, Peter and Jesus depart for the garden with very different ideas of what should take place.[14] The reader

---

[11] Although its manuscript evidence is given a "C" rating, the phrase in question (ει ο θεος εδοξασθη εν αυτω) receives a positive endorsement by Metzger. Bruce Metzger, *A Textual Commentary on the Greek New Testament* (London: United Bible Societies, 1975), 242. Even if omitted, three repetitions of "glorify" provides nearly the same effect as four.

[12] The debate about the meaning of "Son of Man" only proves the point; it is an equivocal term understood differently in this single example.

[13] Brodie observes, "... within chap. 13 as a whole, his [Peter's] darkness of mind is cast in the context of the Satanic darkness of Judas (13:2, 21-38). Here too [18:10-11] he shows shades of Judas." Brodie, *John*, 527.

[14] Francis Moloney observes, "But such love flows from a radical following of Jesus and never from an imposition of one's own worldview on God's designs." Moloney, *John*, 386.

may with justification wonder how Peter is to be blamed for his mistake, given that many of Jesus's statements are riddled with mystery. But this perception only serves to underscore the responsibility of the reader not to do likewise.

V. B. 2. b *Peter in chapter 18*

Chapters 11–13 display a sense of the historical, event-like quality being very much in the foreground, insofar as the narrative itself is concerned. This quality of narrated events fades into the background in chapters 14–17 as the teaching element becomes primary. Events return suddenly in 18:1, a verse that informs the reader of Jesus leaving with his disciples, crossing the Kidron Valley, and entering the garden. Into this previously safe and intimate temporal and spatial setting, one analogous to places of innocence in romance, Judas enters as betrayer and brings to a head the ongoing conflict between Jesus and his opponents. Lurking trouble becomes active danger as the mob of soldiers and others arrive bearing torches, lanterns, and weapons, the trappings of those who walk in darkness and temporal earthly power, pathetic in comparison to the light and power of Jesus.[15] In spite of the threat, Jesus appears in full control. Jesus knows "all that was going to happen to him" (18:4) and yet offers up himself. In addition, Jesus's position of ultimate control is reinforced as his utterance of "I am he" (Ἐγώ εἰμι, 18:5-6) compels his hearers to draw back and fall to the ground. Soldiers and weapons pose little threat as compared to the power and words of Jesus. Seeking to bring closure to the scene, Jesus tells his pursuers to "let these men go" (18:8). The narrative likewise moves toward closure, noting, "This happened so that the words he had spoken would be fulfilled: 'I have not lost one of those you gave me'" (18:9).

But the scene is not over. As an unwanted addendum, Peter draws his sword and cuts off the ear of Malchus, the servant of the high priest. The act is at once brave and foolhardy, daring yet pathetically ineffective as Peter succeeds only in separating a servant from his ear. In wielding the sword, Peter hopelessly opposes the collective temporal power of the mob, opposes Jesus, and opposes the purposes of God the Father himself. While ostensibly intending otherwise, Peter is thus aligned with the methods and purposes of the very enemies he seeks to combat. Consequently, Peter is placed at some narrative distance from Jesus. The sword is an offensive instrument held in the hand for use on others; in contrast, the cup is a handheld container for something one voluntarily gives to one's self. Ironically, Peter, the friend of Jesus, seeks to thwart the plans of God while Judas, the betrayer, assists their accomplishment.

The openness and confusion of the garden give way to confinement and order of the high priest's courtyard. Having given himself up, Jesus is in the hands of those who will unknowingly execute the plan of God. Peter continues as an outsider, well-meaning but opposed to the plans of God, an assumption given symbolic reinforcement here by Peter's exclusion from the center of the action. The other disciple, twice mentioned as being known to the high priest (18:15, 18:16), acts to bring Peter into the high priest's courtyard. The fact that Peter is brought in by the other disciple, known by the high priest most likely as a disciple of Jesus, and that this other disciple speaks to the girl at

---

[15] See Brown, *John*, 809, 817; Brodie, *John*, 524.

the door on behalf of Peter, makes it obvious that Peter is a disciple of Jesus.[16] Yet when asked by the girl at the door, presumably the same person who gave him entrance, Peter denies being a disciple, a rejection made more disgraceful because no one is likely to believe it. As the scene ends, Peter joins the officials and servants around the fire, fades from prominence as an individual, and becomes closely identified with the group and his surroundings. Jesus, the true light of the world, is replaced by the natural but false light of the world.[17]

The scene shifts to the inside where Jesus is questioned about "his disciples and his teaching" (18:19). Jesus denies nothing. On the contrary, he states that he has "spoken openly to the world.... I always taught in the synagogues or at the temple, where all the Jews come together" (18:20). Jesus "said nothing in secret" and thereby makes all his hearers potential witnesses against him. Carrying this line of thought to its conclusion, Jesus asks, "Why question Me? Ask those who heard me. Surely they know what I said" (18:21). The scene ends inconclusively with Jesus being taken to Caiaphas.

Meanwhile, outside, there is one follower, one of "those who heard me" and one who surely knows what Jesus said, still warming himself by the fire. But when asked if he is "one of his disciples," Peter denies it, negating the key feature of Jesus's statements before the high priests. The narrative juxtaposition of Peter's denials with the steadfastness of Jesus highlights the primacy of the theme of denial versus standing firm.

Peter's final denial differs from the other two. Although asked in historically specific situations, the first two questions focus on Peter's denial that he is a disciple of Jesus, a general and wide-ranging question. In contrast, note the specific historical details of 18:26: "One of the high priest's servants, a relative of the man whose ear Peter had cut off, challenged him, 'Didn't I see you with him in the garden?'" Peter is hereby linked by a specific person (both a fellow servant to the high priest and a relative to Malchus) to a specific time and place (the garden where Peter cut off the ear of Malchus). By implication, if Peter is to deny this query, he must not only deny Jesus, as he has twice done before, he must deny his own actions on Jesus's behalf. To deny Jesus this time entails denying himself as well. In blindness or not, Peter plunges ahead and the rooster crows.

The difference between the sword-wielding Peter of the garden and the shivering Peter of the high priest's courtyard deserves some attention. The usual explanation for this change is that Peter's courage evaporates with Jesus's arrest. But it is much more probable, given his desire to go with Jesus and see the triumphant glory of God (13:31-33), that Peter does not so much become a coward as he sheathes his courage in bewilderment or perhaps even disgust. In retrospect, as the mob approaches the garden, Peter is quite willing to fight for a triumphant Christ, but he is unwilling to offer a show of loyalty for a man whose condemnation is virtually certain. In a reversal of roles, Peter may not see himself so much as denying Jesus as much as he sees Jesus denying Peter, denying the cause of Israel, and possibly denying the cause of God himself by abandoning the garden revolution. It is time for Peter and Jesus to carve their names

---

[16] Brodie makes the plausible and interesting suggestion that the other disciple is Judas. Brodie, *John*, 529. cf. Brown, *John*, 822.
[17] Brodie, *John*, 530.

in the pages of Israel's history just as Moses, Joshua, Ehud, Gideon, Samson, David, and Judas Maccabeus had done. The fact that Peter is perceptive but consistently misinterprets the situation and ignores warnings to the contrary renders the misguided-hero interpretation of Peter more convincing than Peter as braggart turned coward.

If the crowing rooster may be allowed to be part of the hermeneutical milieu of this passage and seen as an image of Peter himself, Peter's denials might be taken not strictly as a sheepish and cowardly response to danger but also as an expression of real denial of Jesus over the shame of Jesus's conduct. Thus, when Peter says, "I am not [a disciple]" he is not a coward but more of a disgruntled leader. Jesus denied Peter by denying Peter's cause. In either case, Peter is courageous in defending his own version of Jesus, and Peter is most vulnerable to denial when he must confront those who question *his* connection to Jesus rather than Jesus's connection to him. In any case, Peter's threefold denial separates Peter from Jesus such that if the relationship is to be reestablished, it must be founded on a different basis than before.

As in the Synoptics, Peter's denials end with the crowing of the rooster (Mt. 27:74-75; Mk 14:72; Lk. 22:61). The Synoptics record a recognition on Peter's part followed by weeping. Significantly, the FG omits this; the rooster crows and that is all. The hard reality of the denial remains unmitigated by contrition. Recall that Peter in the FG, although carefully distinguished, is very much paired with Judas. The fact that bitter weeping does not follow Peter's denial underscores the seriousness of this denial and the danger of misguided discipleship that Peter represents. Personal sorrow is not enough; a radical reorientation in thinking is in order. Although this phase of Peter's appearance in the FG ends on a decidedly negative note, the rooster's call announces the morning and the first glimmer of new light to come.

V. B. 2. c Peter in chapter 20

It is first necessary to retreat into chapter 19 to properly focus Peter's role in the resurrection appearances of chapter 20. Much has been made of 20:30-31 with its editorial comments as the natural end of the FG and chapter 21 forming an appendix. But the same thing might be said for 19:35-37 with its testimony and summary as forming a natural end to the story of Jesus, an ending soon to be shown premature. The end comes as Jesus dies and the scripture is fulfilled. The concern over the correspondence of the details of Jesus's death to the fulfillment of scripture fades into the background as Joseph of Arimathea asks Pilate for the body of Jesus in 18:38. The movement from (a) history and its relationship to scripture to (b) history by itself emphasizes the brute fact of Jesus's death. The account details two phases of the burial process: first, wrapping of Jesus's body and its anointing by the seventy-five pounds of spices supplied by Nicodemus, according to Jewish burial customs albeit to a lavish degree, and, second, the placing of the prepared body into the new garden tomb supplied by Joseph. If Jesus is dead, he must be buried can also mean, when viewed from another perspective, that if Jesus was buried, he must have been dead. Like Dickens's emphasis on Marley being "dead as a doornail," care is taken to show that Jesus is likewise dead as that piece of ironmongery.

Chapter 20:1-9 builds on the certainty of the death of Jesus. The narration of the resurrection of Jesus must undo what has been done. Mary and the two disciples function transitionally as witnesses to the death of Jesus in their expectation of an occupied tomb and as witnesses to the empty tomb on finding it so. The account opens with Mary Magdalene's discovery that the stone had been removed from the entrance, news that she hurriedly reports to Simon Peter and the other disciple. Mary's report, "They have taken the Lord out of the tomb, and we don't know where they have put him!" (20:2), does not admit the possibility that Jesus has risen from the dead. Peter and the other disciple arrive at the tomb and likewise discover it empty. With characteristic eagerness, Peter enters the tomb first, and, presumably with the other disciple, sees the grave clothes. Thus the placing of Jesus in the tomb in 19:41-42 is reversed and his burial preparations narrated in 19:39-40 are reversed as well.

Concerning Peter, 20:1-9 must be taken primarily as foregrounding Peter's role as historical witness rather than any kind of symbolic function wherein Peter and the other disciple are played against one another. Along these lines Quast observes,

> Contrary to what might be expected, the capacity in which Peter performs is actually heightened by *not* being linked to any response of faith on the part of Peter pertaining to the significance of what he saw. Peter did not immediately understand the significance of what he saw; therefore his witness can be regarded as an objective report of the actual physical situation.[18]

This, coupled with the fact that neither Peter nor the other disciple says anything, allows for little character development. Yet the other disciple "saw and believed," and this condition of faith is not indicated of Peter, but here it most likely refers only to the fact of Jesus's unexpected resurrection. It is noted that "they still did not understand from Scripture that Jesus had to rise from the dead" (20:9). Despite Peter's denial, the fact that Mary reported to Peter and that he ran to the tomb indicates that he remains an important figure and subtly begins the process of reestablishing his relationship with Jesus.

V. B. 3 Peter as follower and leader

V. B. 3. a Peter in chapter 21

Chapter 20 closes with the status of Jesus being resolved: Jesus is worthy of belief because he has been raised from the dead. In contrast, the position of Peter with respect to Jesus remains unresolved, his threefold denial lacking any kind of narrative mitigation. Chapter 21 opens by setting the scene on the Sea of Tiberias where Jesus appears again to his disciples. Peter, named first in 21:2, functions as leader of the group, announcing "I'm going out to fish." The others follow. This nighttime fishing expedition may represent a lapse into quotidian existence, but more importantly it represents the failure of Peter's leadership. They catch nothing. Peter fails as leader in two contexts: disciple and fisherman. Jesus appears early in the morning and suggests a more successful way of fishing. Jesus is master over the grave and over fishing, Peter's erstwhile area of expertise. Yet by offering Peter's spectacular success at fishing, albeit

---

[18] Kevin Quast, *Peter and the Beloved Disciple: Figures for a Community in Crisis* (JSNTSS 32, Sheffield: Sheffield Academic Press, 1989), 117.

on Jesus's terms, the negative effects of Peter's occupational failure are forgotten as is indeed fishing itself.

Peter's plunge into the water recalls his characteristic impetuous plunges into other activities but with a difference: in this case Peter returns to Jesus. The narrative movement of 21:1-14 suggests several themes: want to plenty, night to day, separation to union, cold to warm, work to worship, ignorance to knowledge, sea to land, and Peter to Jesus. The burning coals recall the fire in the high priest's courtyard, but this time the fire is prepared by a friend, while the provision of fish served by the hand of Jesus recalls the meal in chapter 13, this time given to the true disciples. The comment that "None of the disciples dared ask him, 'Who are you?'" coupled with the absence of any two-way conversations in vv. 7-14 builds into the scene a quality of wonder and reverence typical of romance. Jesus the risen Lord is firmly in charge yet continues his example of humility by serving the meal. The actions and tone of 21:1-14 place the final abasement of Peter and the beginnings of his reinstatement on the gentlest of terms. Verse 14 offers a summary and draws this phase of the narrative to a close.

For the first time in this scene, Jesus engages in a significant and personal conversation (21:15ff.). Jesus thrice refers to Peter as "Simon son of John" (21:15, 21:16, 21:17) and recalls Peter's first contact with his Lord (1:42). If John is the name of the beloved disciple, either the son of Zebedee or the Elder as well may be the case (and any reader of the FG cannot help but speculate on this person's identity), then Jesus's reference to "Simon son of John" is significant if read over against Simon Peter's connection with Judas son of Simon in 13:24-26. The respective narrative contexts of these name associations would indicate this to be so. In both cases, Peter is moving from being allied with the traitorous Judas to being allied with something altogether more positive.

The focus changes in 21:15 as Jesus engages Peter in a sustained personal conversation, and, in a limited way, follows the familiar FG pattern of event (fishing and meal) followed by discourse. Jesus first asks Peter, "Do you love me more than these?" (21:15). "These" may refer to either the other disciples or to the fishing gear and the ordinary life it represents. The former is to be preferred,[19] but the meaning is ambiguous enough to accommodate both. Peter's reply is instructive in that it makes no comparisons, differing significantly from the form of the question and showing something of a new found maturity of thought (compare Mk 14:29). Jesus's second question to Peter is perhaps more difficult. Jesus asks, "Do you love me?" The element of comparison having been dropped, the issue becomes Peter's love for Jesus in and of itself without reference to others. The scene as a whole is deeply personal, as Jesus's posing of the question a third time evokes an emotional response in Peter. Peter's appeal to Jesus, "Lord, you know all things; you know that I love you" (21:17), affirms the omniscience of Jesus and implicitly testifies to the truthfulness of Peter's assertions. Peter, whatever his mistakes, truly does love Jesus.

Quite the opposite of flashing a sword to prove his love, Jesus instructs Peter to "feed my lambs." Herding sheep calls to mind images of pastoral activity rather than grandiose achievement. The references to tending sheep recall Jesus's teaching that he is the good shepherd (10:1-21). On the terms of that previous passage, Peter is a

---

[19] Barrett, *John*, 584.

hireling who runs away and abandons the sheep to the wolves. Jesus's instruction to Peter to feed his sheep gives to Peter the role of shepherd. Peter's earlier question to Jesus, "To whom shall we go?" (6:68), referred to Jesus in that context, but might be expanded upon here to include other issues as understanding moves into action and doing. The flock will hereafter hear his voice and respond, the implicit assumption being that Peter will not "run away because he is a hired hand and cares nothing for the sheep" (10:13). Peter's association with sheep also recalls Jesus's teaching that "the good shepherd lays down his life for the sheep" (10:11). It also anticipates Jesus's words to Peter concerning the death he would die.

Peter's designation as shepherd by Jesus entails following Jesus, a course of action that will lead to being led "where you do not want to go" (21:18-19). Peter's desire to "follow you now" (13:37) means, contrary to Peter's previous attempts at following, that he will not be master of his own fate. Jesus challenges Peter to "Follow me" (21:19) may be read as "follow me now" and do so with the knowledge gained from Jesus himself (20:18-19) that following Jesus means giving up control of his life. The sword of self-will must be forever put away. If Peter is to shepherd the sheep of Jesus, Peter must likewise follow the voice of the Good Shepherd.

If this were a Western movie, we could well imagine that Peter and Jesus would saddle up and ride off into the sunset together. But this ending is not to be. Peter seems to accept the role Jesus outlined for him, but "turned and saw" the beloved disciple following as well. Peter's query "What about him?" seeks to locate Peter's own following of Jesus with reference to others rather than simply following Jesus with reference to Jesus alone. For Peter, and other would-be followers, being a disciple of Jesus cannot mean pursuing one's own vainglorious visions of discipleship, nor can it mean following the way of the cross on any terms but its own.

V. B. 3. b *Peter and the status of chapter 21*

Chapter 21 is often thought of as comprising an appendix to the rest of the FG, with 20:30-31 forming the natural ending as it offers a statement of purpose for the whole Gospel. The arguments for and against the unity of the FG and the related questions of divergent traditions and redactions in themselves lie outside the scope and object of the present work.[20] The question of the unity of the FG is of concern as it relates to Peter and will be explored on a limited basis with this in mind.

Some hold that chapter 21 forms an integral part of the Gospel as a whole. Minear offers an excellent case for including chapter 21 with the rest of the Gospel, but probably errs in restricting the concluding verses of chapter 20 to chapter 20 itself.[21] Brodie argues that 19:35-37, 20:30-31, and 21:24-25 fit a larger pattern of conclusions with separate emphasis on witness, writing, and witness and writing, respectively.[22] Tovey offers a broader argument based on the thematic unity of chapter 21 with previous themes in the book, a unity that he regards as decisive for including chapter 21 in the original

---

[20] For a survey of the issues, Brown argues unity (*John*, vol. 2, 1077–82) and Carson argues for it (*John*, 665–68).
[21] Paul S. Minear, "The Original Functions of John 21," *JBL* 102/1 (1983): 85–98.
[22] Brodie, *John*, 574–82.

Gospel.[23] For Tovey, the FG displays two great themes or movements. The first has to do with the public proclamation where the issues concern Jesus's identity and response to him and culminates temporarily in 12:44-50. The second theme begins in 13:1, a widely acknowledged division point, and concerns the inner circle of believers where the issues are discipleship, bearing witness, and remaining in Jesus. The first theme reaches its climax in chapter 20 with Jesus's encounter with Thomas whereas chapter 21 completes the second theme of discipleship and witness as it centers on Peter's rehabilitation and commission.[24] The treatment of Peter offered in the present work—that Peter displays this twofold movement in himself—corresponds to Tovey's overall argument.

Additionally, the false ending of 20:30-31 could be a bit of staged misdirection, a misunderstanding handed to the unwary for the purpose of breaking up stock response. Staley writes,

> But just like the disciples who, at the story level, make wonderful confessions (1:41-51) only to discover later on that following Jesus entails much more than knowing the proper words (6:60-71; 16:28-33), so too the implied reader, at the discourse level, is forced to realize through his victimization (20:30-21:1) that there is more to his journey of faith than mere confession.[25]

To see the FG as ending in 20:31 runs the risk of seeing Jesus as Peter saw him at the height of his folly: as the Holy One of God abstracted from duties and responsibilities and failing to account for the necessity of discipleship within the confines of earthly life. Chapter 21, then, is not extricable from the very heart of the FG itself. The Synoptics echo the discipleship theme: each account of the confession of Peter is followed by a section predicting Jesus's death that is in turn followed by a section detailing the cost of discipleship (Mt. 16:13-26; Mk 8:27-38; Lk. 9:18-27). Whereas the Synoptics connect Jesus's identity with the theme of death and discipleship by simple narrative proximity, in the FG, Peter embodies the perils of not connecting Jesus as Lord and God with a more sober and enlightened view of what that understanding means in practice.

V. C The comic and Peter

V. C. 1 Introduction

Comedy forms a natural conversation partner to tragedy, a mirror image in many respects. At their most basic level, comedies end happily and tragedies end badly. Both comedy and tragedy endure as significant forms of cultural expression yet there are

---

[23] Derek Tovey, *Art and Act*, 106–15. See also B. R. Gaventa, "The Archive of Excess: John 21 and the Problem of Narrative Closure," in *Exploring the Gospel of John*, eds. R. A. Culpepper and C. C. Black (Louisville: Westminster John Knox Press, 1996), 240–52.

[24] Tovey notes, "Peter is a representative type of discipleship and belief in Jesus . . ." and, "Suffice to say that the rehabilitation of Peter resonates with teaching found in the farewell discourse and elsewhere." Tovey, *Art and Act*, 112, 113.

[25] See Jeffrey Lloyd Staley, *The Print's First Kiss: A Rhetorical Investigation of the Implied Reader in the Fourth Gospel*, SBL Dissertation Series 82 (Atlanta: Scholars Press, 1988), 112.

important differences. Comedy seems more at home in the present world and appears in numerous forms of expressions in everything from newspapers to TV and film. Tragedy, on the other hand, has fallen on hard times. Yet certain tragedies of the past, notably *Oedipus the King, Prometheus, Hamlet, King Lear*, and perhaps *Antigone*, provide widely influential cultural reference points in a way that individual works of comedy do not. Even Shakespeare's best known comedies, perhaps *A Midsummer Night's Dream* and *Twelfth Night*, fail to command as much attention as certain tragedies. Aristophanes languishes in relative obscurity compared to Aeschylus, Sophocles, and Euripides. Comedy in life and art is ubiquitous, while individual comedies with the cultural authority of *Oedipus* and *Hamlet* are not. Tragedies are perhaps more like mountains while comedies are more like the plains, not as spectacular or commanding, but all the more livable for being so.

Tragedy attracts more widespread critical attention than comedy as seen in the number of attempts to give a theory of tragedy. No doubt the critical attention given to tragedy stems from the influence of Aristotle's *Poetics,* a seminal work of literary criticism that provided the starting point for any discussion of tragedy and remains influential today. Critical discussion of tragedy has thus had a standard conversation partner through the ages that comedy has always lacked. It is possible that Aristotle wrote a similar critical work on comedy no longer extant. Lane Cooper sought to correct this in his book *An Aristotelian Theory of Comedy*[26] in which he attempts to give what Aristotle might have said based on a synthesis of what he did say in other sources, making some educated guesses, and mirroring the issues and format of the *Poetics*.

The lack of a standard critical work on comedy is a fact of history. But what is not clear is whether or not that contingent historical fact should be taken, as the primary reason critical theory of comedy appears less developed than tragedy, however diverse theories of tragedy may be. A more compelling explanation lies in the very nature of comedy itself and its subject matter. Comedy includes much that is unexpected, thereby breaking the link of expected causal relationships and rendering a theory of comedy in many respects more difficult to create. Although widespread in life, comedy often appears to be mysterious and just beyond our grasp.

Comedy requires a fundamentally different kind of theory than tragedy. For the present, the differences can be summarized by stating that tragedy concentrates and destroys while comedy creates and integrates. Tragedy concentrates certain forces so as to bring about the reduction and/or destruction, physical or otherwise, of individuals. Thus, tragedy requires a theory that clarifies how this thematic and dramatic concentration takes place, precisely the kind of explanation offered in Aristotle's *Poetics*. The exposition of tragedy offered above follows the same approach. Comedy, on the other hand, is a more general phenomenon, and is expansive in the sense of moving toward a new and integrated arrangement of things, one perhaps not immediately apparent at the start. And, discussions of comedy inevitably involve discussion of jokes, humor, wit, and related issues. A theory of comedy, therefore, needs to be more general in nature, yet still be specific enough to yield some explanatory value, a theory that this work hopes to provide.

---

[26] Lane Cooper, *An Aristotelian Theory of Comedy* (Oxford: Blackwell, 1924).

V. C. 2 Elements of audience reaction

V. C. 2. a Comic emotions: *Sympathy and ridicule*

Sympathy and ridicule, the dominant emotions in comedy, function the same way that fear and pity do in tragedy: they provide a balance between closeness and distance in the reader's emotional relationship to a character. Ridicule proceeds only where there is little or no emotional involvement with a given character, whereas too much sympathy for a character tends to prevent any sort of objective evaluation of a character. The amount of sympathy and ridicule obviously varies, but these elements must have some sense of balance if a comic tone is to be maintained. For example, in *A Comedy of Errors*, the mix-up caused by having two sets of identical twins causes all sorts of ridiculous complications, but we never see the characters as objects of ridicule because they are acting in accordance with what they might reasonably believe to be true, and we feel a corresponding amount of sympathy with them. The tendency toward ridicule is not too pronounced, so the need for sympathy is not very strong either.

Peter is different altogether in that the tendency toward sympathy and ridicule are both very strong, although the tendency toward ridicule is often missed by readers so inclined for confessional reasons or out of reverence for the Bible. Additionally, the FG presents Peter as a sympathetic, developed character with little tendency toward caricature. Yet, Peter's actions and statements consequent on his understanding of Jesus coupled with the pre-crucifixion events *taken by themselves and seen in a certain light* hold Peter up to severe ridicule, a feature especially notable in the contrast of Peter's sword-wielding defense of Jesus set against his threefold denial. Peter's pretensions far outstrip reality to the point where the divergence between them moves beyond the ridiculous toward something poignant and perhaps even painful. The Synoptics mitigate the effects of Peter's denial by immediately narrating the fact of Peter's bitter remorse (Mt. 26:75; Mk 15:72; Lk. 22:62). In addition to contrasting Peter to himself, the FG makes Peter's denial all the more painful by contrasting it with the steadfastness of Jesus before Annas (sandwiched between Peter's denials) and Pilate's threefold declaration of Jesus's innocence. In the FG, Peter's restoration comes not through tearful repentance, but through reinstatement and commissioning by Jesus himself.

In both the Synoptics and in the FG, the tendency to sympathy balances the ridiculous quality of Peter's actions. Peter is real, well-intentioned, and transparent, someone with endearing qualities sufficient to even cover over his Quixotic mistakes. Unlike the dark and thieving Judas, Peter is someone with some moral capital to spend. The betrayal by Judas is inherent to his character; Peter is merely blind to himself. At the same time, Peter's denial is painful, but its very painfulness shortens the emotional distance and prevents Peter from being held up for ridicule alone. Had Peter been merely naive, his denial would have been too close emotionally, unexpected and shocking in the wrong way, malicious on the part of those who might have prevented it. On the other hand, Peter's comic excess, most apparent in his uneven encounter with Malchus, is behavior that needs to be brought under control if Peter is to be useful. The reader, like Jesus, can almost predict Peter's actions yet sees Peter's actions as being justified in some way, however distressing the arrival of those actions may be. Without pathos, Peter veers toward farce; without being slightly foolish, Peter careens toward tragedy, a theme to be explored later. Only by steering a middle course can an emotional tone suitable for comedy be maintained. And only through both sympathy and ridicule does the FG's account of Peter achieve the emotional depth characteristic of serious comedy.

V. C. 2. b Laughter

Laughter is the most obvious element of audience reaction in comedy and may be viewed as the comic counterpart to catharsis in tragedy. But, as noted above in reference to sympathy and ridicule, laughter, although associated with the comic, is not a necessary requirement of it. Yet, laughter is common enough so that it transcends the borders between jokes, wit, satire, humor, and the comic.[27]

Although catharsis in tragedy may well manifest itself physically, laughter has an obvious biological aspect that is physically apparent in a way that catharsis in tragedy is not. Laughter produces actions that, on reflection, seem a bit strange. Hauser describes laughter as follows:

> Laughter is produced through a complex interplay of anatomical structures and physiological processes, and these are brought into operation by culturally conditioned behavioral and emotional stimuli in normal, healthy individuals.[28]

Hauser also offers a technical description of laughter that explains, among other things, differences between smiling and laughing. Significantly, she notes that laughter, whatever its biological manifestations, is brought into operation by certain conceptual and emotional stimuli.

Bergson examines the conditions under which laughter occurs. He observes,

> ... the *absence of feeling* ... usually accompanies laughter. It seems as though the comic could not produce its disturbing effect unless it fell, so to say, on the surface of a soul that is thoroughly calm and unruffled. Indifference is its natural environment, for laughter has no greater foe than emotion.[29]

For example, Peter is a comic character, yet we do not laugh at him precisely because the reader is emotionally engaged and is not "thoroughly calm and unruffled." There is generally too much sympathy for Peter to laugh, 13:9 being an exception. In a similar way, works of comedy in which the characters themselves face too much emotional

---

[27] Henri Bergson, *Laughter: An Essay on the Meaning of the Comic*, trans. Cloudesley Brereton (London: Macmillan, 1911). Bergson's treatment is a case in point. His work is wide ranging and moves naturally between relevant topics. Koestler begins his treatment of creation with a discussion of laughter. Arthur Koestler, *The Act of Creation* (London: Hutchinson, 1964), 27–49.

[28] Gertrud Hauser, et al., "The Biology of Laughter. Medical, Functional, and Anthropological-Human Ethnological Aspects," in *Laughter Down the Centuries* vol. III, eds. Siegfried Jakel, Asko Timonen, and Veli-Matti Rissanen (Turku, Finland: Turun Yliopisto, 1997), 9.

[29] Bergson, *Laughter*, 4. In his famous definition of the comic, W. H. Auden makes a similar observation: "A contradiction in the relation of the individual or the personal to the universal or the impersonal which does not involve the spectator or hearer in suffering or pity, which in practice means that it must not involve the actor in real suffering." Auden, "Notes on the Comic," in *Comedy: Meaning and Form*, ed. Robert Corrigan (Scranton, Pennsylvania: Chandler, 1965), 61.

turmoil do so at the expense of laughter. Some comedies simply cease to be funny. For Bergson, laughter must originate in some aspect of our humanity that is relatively calm and stable. He writes,

> To produce the whole of its effect, then, the comic demands something like a momentary anesthesia of the heart. Its appeal is to intelligence, pure and simple.[30]

Bergson does not mean that the comic resulting in laughter involves a conscious mental process. Bergson correctly regards laughter as an appeal to intelligence, while the mental processes involved are often sudden and unconscious. Like good food, a joke is better experienced than explained.

Attempting to integrate the physical and biological, Freud regards the process of joke formation as a kind of "psychic compression" or economy of expression wherein the psychic energy needed to express something is compressed into the form of a joke.[31] This basic idea of compression can take several forms, such as condensation, multiple use of the same material, or double meaning.[32] Compression into a joke often allows psychic or social barriers to be overcome. On reception, this compressed psychic energy is released and laughter results. The psychic release manifest in laughter corresponds roughly to the amount of psychic energy conserved during the joke's formation, working as a kind of thermodynamic law of laughter. Laughter, then, is something like a psychic safety valve.

These three examples take three different approaches to laughter, approaches that will be dealt with below in relation to theories of the comic. The basic point is that laughter contains a connection between the abstract or cognitive aspects and the concrete and material expressions of it. Comedy is in this respect like tragedy, which connects the abstract and material through suffering and death whereas irony differs from both by being primarily cognitive with no analogous physical expression. Comedy tinged with irony may well evoke a physical response, but pure irony is no laughing matter. Detached from experience, irony is cognitive, disembodied in a way unlike romance, tragedy, and comedy. The connection between the cognitive and concrete—the mental and the physical—so important to laughter, will be seen to be central to comic itself. But whatever their connections, comedy or humor as a cause or stimulus must not be confused with laughter as an effect.

V. C. 3 Structural elements of comedy

V. C. 3. a Character

Like tragedy, plot and character form the two most basic elements of comedy. Following Aristotle, it was argued here that plot is more important than character in tragedy. Following this same line of reasoning, Cooper simply assumes a close correspondence between comedy and tragedy so that whatever is not obviously different in comedy

---

[30] Bergson, *Laughter*, 5.
[31] Sigmund Freud, *Jokes and their Relation to the Unconscious*, trans. and ed. James Strachey (London: Routledge & Kegan Paul, 1960), 42–44.
[32] Freud, *Jokes*, 41–42. Freud offers a detailed analysis of jokes.

and tragedy must be the same in both. The following statement from Cooper may be compared to Aristotle's statement on tragedy by substituting "tragedy" for "comedy." Cooper writes,

> (1) The Plot, then, is the first principle, and, as it were, the very soul, of comedy. (2) And the characters of the agents come next in Elements in the order of importance. –There is a parallel in the art of painting: the most striking colors laid on with no order will not be so effective as the simplest caricature done in outline. –Comedy is the imitation of an action: mainly on this account does it become, in the second place, an imitation of personal agents.[33]

Thus, for Cooper, in comedy, plot is primary and character as secondary. Cooper, however, is mistaken; in comedy, character is primary and plot is secondary.[34] Whether or not Cooper correctly represents Aristotle here is not the issue. Referring to his own and Aristotle's position that plot is primary over character in tragedy, Cornford remarks, "Nothing of all this applies to comedy."[35] Comedy relies less on a linear sequence typical of Aristotelian thought and more on a holistic emphasis on character. The comic character is comprised of a mixture of beliefs, desires, freedom, and choice, these qualities being hard to separate from each other.

Hegel compares tragedy and comedy and argues for the supremacy of character over plot in comedy. Regarding dramatic poetry (tragedy, comedy, and drama), Hegel states that it "makes central the collisions between characters and between their aims."[36] For Hegel, the difference between genres has to do with the relation of the individuals to the nature and purpose of their aims that manifest themselves in actions. Every true action involves two parts: (1) the *substance* of action, which Hegel traces to some aspect of the divine, the good and great, such as honor, love, duty; and (2) the *subject*, which Hegel defines as "the individual himself in his unfettered self-determination and freedom."[37] For Hegel, tragedy is more closely related to substance, while comedy is more closely related to subject, or character. Hegel observes of comedy, "The mastery of all relations and ends is given as much to the individual in his willing and action, as to external contingency."[38] For Hegel, the resolution of tragedy relates to the substance in that "the eternal substance of things emerges victorious in a reconciling way," whereas in comedy "it is subjectivity, or personality, which in its infinite assurance retains the upper hand."[39] Regardless of the accuracy of Hegel's analysis of the respective

---

[33] Cooper, *Aristotelian Theory*, 184–85.

[34] The Italian Renaissance critic Francesco Robortello offers another attempt to transpose Aristotle's work on tragedy on to comedy in "On Comedy," in *Theories of Comedy*, ed. Paul Lauter (New York: Anchor, 1964), 48–63.

[35] Francis Cornford, *The Origin of Attic Comedy* (London: Edward Arnold, 1914), 197. Cornford argues for the supremacy of character over plot in comedy.

[36] G. W. F. Hegel, *Aesthetics: Lectures on Fine Arts*, trans. T. M. Knox (Oxford: Clarendon Press, 1975), 1193. By "drama" Hegel means a work midway between comedy and tragedy. For a helpful discussion of Hegel, see George McFadden, *Discovering the Comic* (Princeton: Princeton University Press, 1982), 91–96.

[37] Hegel, *Aesthetics*, 1194, his emphasis.

[38] Hegel, *Aesthetics*, 1194.

[39] Ibid., 1199.

resolutions of tragedy and comedy, his emphasis on character in comedy is correct: comedy unmasks a character while tragedy unmasks a situation.

Using Hegel's terms and analysis, in tragedy, a substance restricts a subject's or character's action. For example, in *Antigone*, Creon must act according to duty and punish Polynices, who has attacked the city. Pilate must act to administer justice and/or maintain political control as he confronts God in the flesh. The restrictions on action imposed on a subject result in a collision and the consequent destruction of that character. On the other hand, in comedy, a character chooses in freedom to act according to a substance (love, honor, greed, or whatever) and this choice, usually done in blindness and/or excess, results in complication and folly. Thus, Peter, a subject or character possessed of "infinite assurance," chooses to act according to some substance such as love or honor but does so in blindness.

Further comparing tragedy and comedy, Wylie Sypher notes that tragedy is a "closed" form of art with an emphasis on necessity and law, whereas comedy is less complex and less structured with "a precarious logic that can tolerate every kind of improbability."[40] He observes,

> The coherent plot is vital to tragic theater (Aristotle says that plot is the very soul of tragedy); and a tragic action needs to convey a sense of destiny, inevitability, and foreordination. The tragic plot often implies there are unchanging moral laws behind the falling thunderbolt. The fate of a tragic hero needs to be made "intelligible" as the comic hero's fate does not; or at least tragic fate has the force of "necessity" even if it is not "intelligible." Somehow tragedy shows what "must" happen, even while there comes a shock of unsurmised disaster. As Aristotle said, in tragedy, coincidence must have an air of probability. Then too, tragedy subordinates "character" to the design of the plot; for the purpose of tragedy, says Aristotle, is not to depict "character," but, rather, to show "men in action," so that the "character" of a tragic hero reveals itself in a deed which expresses his moral disposition. Comedy, on the contrary, can freely yield its action to surprise, chance, and all the changes in fortune that fall outside the necessities of tragic myth, and can present "character" for its own sake.[41]

Bergson expresses a similar opinion,

> And so we see why action is essential in drama [tragedy], but only accessory in comedy. In a comedy, we feel any other situation might equally well have been chosen for the purpose of introducing the character; he would still have been the same though the situation were different. But we do not get this impression in drama. Here characters and situations are welded together, or rather, events form part and parcel with the persons, so that were the drama to tell us a different story, even though the actors kept the same names, we should in reality be dealing with other persons.[42]

---

[40] Wylie Sypher, "The Meanings of Comedy," in *Comedy: Meaning and Form*, ed. Robert Corrigan (Scranton, PA: Chandler, 1965), 35–36.
[41] Sypher, "Meanings of Comedy," 35–36.
[42] Bergson, *Laughter*, 145.

Hegel, Sypher, and Bergson make the same essential distinction: tragedy relates to necessity while comedy relates to choice, a distinction inextricably linked with tragedy's emphasis on plot, the vehicle of necessity, and comedy's emphasis on character, the vehicle of choice. Obviously, these qualities will vary with each individual work, but they remain distinctive and defining tendencies of their respective archetypes.

The primacy of character over plot in comedy is clearly seen in Cervantes's *Don Quixote*, one of the great comic figures in all of literature. Having lingered too long over too many books of knights and chivalry, this misguided soul acts on his delusions and embarks on a career of knight errantry. The reality that Don Quixote sees is not usually the same reality seen by everyone else. An inn becomes a castle, the innkeeper becomes the warden of the castle, windmills become giants, flocks of sheep become armies. The fact that Don Quixote mistakes them as such has nothing to do with inns, innkeepers, windmills, or sheep in and of themselves. Rather, perceiving them in this manner has everything to do with Don Quixote and his state of mind. Whatever happens in the book serves to expose this state of affairs by juxtaposing illusion with reality. Had Don Quixote been in his right mind, nothing would have happened; there is no hint of causality or necessity following on from external events alone. Only his false beliefs about reality propel him to act as he does.

Furthermore, because Don Quixote himself generates the action of the story, as in romance, there is no necessary causal relationship between the separate incidents. The fact that tilting at windmills occurs before his encounter with the goatherds is of no consequence and reversing the order would make little difference. This is not to say the book can be read in any order with no effect—the characters of Don Quixote and Sancho Panza and their relationship develop as the book proceeds—but this could have been done irrespective of the order of the content of the incidents themselves. *Don Quixote* is typically comic in that it is fundamentally episodic. In contrast, Aristotle notes, "But most important of all [in tragedy] is the structure of the incidents."[43] In this remark "structure of the incidents" means the incidents as they relate to one another in a causal sequence more so than their individual composition. Unlike comedy, tragedy features a strong causal link between incidents. For example, the public versus private clash in *Antigone* is causally and sequentially linked to the attack on the city, and the action necessarily follows from this incident. Strong causal links between incidents lead to an emphasis on plot. But in *Don Quixote*, the primary link between incidents is Don Quixote himself. In both comedy and romance, character is primary over plot, although in romance, the hero is integrated with his/her surroundings and/or worldview, whereas in comedy, the hero is not.

The example of *Don Quixote* is obvious and illustrates the point. But other examples are to be found as well. It is no accident that Hardy's later novels emphasize plot and tend more toward tragedy, whereas Dickens's works, especially his early works, are generally comic and feature looser plots and generally flatter characters.[44] The fact that comedians perform independently of plot and tragedies are performed as works

---

[43] Aristotle, *Poetics* vi. 9, p. 62.
[44] The distinction of flat and round characters comes from E. M. Forster, who singles out Dickens as a writer whose characters are generally flat and Jane Austen as a writer whose characters are generally round. Forster, *Aspects of the Novel* (London: Edward Arnold, 1927), 65ff.

containing a causal sequence is not due simply to commercial reasons: it is inherent to the nature of comedy to be linked to character and tragedy to be linked to plot. The primacy of character over plot permits sitcoms to continue from week to week as the characters with their strengths and weaknesses to remain intact, ready for new adventures with each new episode. Comic strips rely on the same dynamic. *The Canterbury Tales*, a loose collection of tales connected only by the convention of a trip to Canterbury, relies mostly on character for its comic effect. The plays of Aristophanes (especially *The Birds*) are notable examples of works being driven by character rather than plot.[45]

A more difficult example is a work like *A Comedy of Errors*. Here the confusion caused by the existence of two sets of identical twins is set in motion by an accident of plot. But even here the plot only provides opportunities for expressions of character. Although the play has a strong element of farce, a genre wherein character development tends to be limited, the characters drive the action by acting on their justified but false beliefs about reality. The existence of the two sets of twins, an accident of plot, provides the possibility of comedy, however likely, but not the necessity of it. Comic characters are mistaken in some way, but they do not have to be so.

The example of Peter and the disciples follows the same pattern. Whatever their backgrounds, of which very little is given in the FG, each must respond to Jesus's teaching, person, and ministry. This challenge forms a common ground for all the disciples, yet there is no set pattern of coming to faith. Peter, Thomas, and Pilate all respond to Jesus in different ways at different times. None is particularly constrained by a situation to act in a certain way. Peter's comic actions happen by his own volition, not by what happens to him. Both Peter and Thomas persist in a course of thinking when each has been given a warning or evidence to the contrary, a fact that is best explained by the power of characters to make choices. Jesus's words to Peter serve as intended warnings, but his misunderstandings, propelled by the force of his character, cause him to overwhelm any helpful boundaries on his actions. Because the comic is more about character than about plot, Peter's appearances in the FG need not be linked in any strong causal relationship manifest in tightly structured incidents, as is the case with Pilate, but can be of looser and more informally arranged, linked together by Peter himself. On the same basis, Shakespeare can use Falstaff, that famous "tub of guts," in several plays because character moves the action in comedy rather than plot as in tragedy.

In comedy, the fundamental stress on character rather than plot has to do with the nature of comedy itself. Comedy is primarily driven by beliefs and desires rather than by events and, significantly, beliefs and desires by their very nature reside in character.[46] Only a conscious being can have beliefs and desires. Moreover, beliefs and desires have to do with the future as they relate to the present; they concern what

---

[45] Frye notes, "In Aristophanes there is usually a central figure who constructs his (or her) own society in the teeth of strong opposition, driving off one after another all the people who come to prevent or exploit him, and eventually achieving a heroic triumph . . . ." Northrop Frye, *Anatomy of Criticism* (Princeton: Princeton University Press, 1957), 43.

[46] The substance of this paragraph will be elaborated in detail below as part of a discussion of conceptual elements in comedy.

will or *might* happen. Beliefs and desires are expressed by making choices, and choice concerns the present as it relates to the future. Tragedy, on the other hand, is concerned with what *has* happened, and the past is not subject to choice. Thus, tragedy contains "reversals" while comedy features "unmaskings." While tragedy and comedy are very much concerned with beliefs and their relationship to reality, in tragedy, reality is related to the past and therefore irrevocable. Oedipus has killed his father and married his mother–this is reality. Events of incident and plot ruthlessly expose this reality and destroy previous beliefs as the past crashes into the present, whereas in comedy, the relation to beliefs and reality is open-ended because comedy is about the future rather than about the past. Don Quixote's beliefs motivate him to ride into the future clad in armor and armed with a lance, and like Quixote, Peter's beliefs lead him to stride into the future armed with a sword.

To be comic, a character must intrinsically possess a strong sense of freedom. To be at odds with reality, a comic character must possess freedom to do so. McFadden comments,

> The associations of the comic with spontaneity, liberation from inhibition and constraint, unblocking, vital movement, and ease and grace of behavior all point to freedom as an indispensable component.[47]
>
> We can conclude that the comic is in a special relation to freedom. Other genres of art cannot do without freedom; but comedy is the only genre continually to assert it. Furthermore, although no genre may be adequately defined by a simple quality, comedy is the only one wherein freedom predominantly gives the tone to the complex quality that emerges from the work as a whole.[48]

McFadden relates the principle of freedom to his basic principle of the comic, which he defines as "a characteristic maintenance-as-itself, despite the implicit threat of alteration."[49] Thus, whatever threats reality may pose, the comic character is free to challenge them and remain intact. The onslaughts of plot test and expose but do not destroy. Peter never shows any hint that his denial is predetermined or fixed; it is simply the outgrowth of his character, an outcome that any perceptive person might have seen coming. In the end Peter is still Peter, though chastened and changed.

In a similar way, this quality of self-preservation or self-projection in the face of difficulties, prompts Torrance to argue that, rather than being simply a butt or scapegoat, the comic character is admirable. He writes, "The Comic hero is a contradiction in terms, or at least in perspectives. He is comic because he differs from others and heroic because he is always himself."[50] Although Torrance is largely correct, there is a very real sense where the fact that the comic character "is always himself" or displays "maintenance-as-itself" deserves an important caveat, one separating comedy from romance. Allowing for an enduring dignity in the comic character, note that the comic character's freedom to act is a double-edged sword: freedom to act is freedom

---

[47] McFadden, *Discovering*, 11.
[48] Ibid., 14.
[49] Ibid., 25.
[50] Robert M. Torrance, *The Comic Hero* (Cambridge, MA: Harvard University Press, 1978), 1.

for folly and mistakes. The same is true for self-preservation and always being one's self: the individual remains intact, but not everything is worthy of preservation. The comic character's freedom is best taken as an unconscious, or unexamined freedom, a freedom that may result in examination and modification once exposed to experience and events. The comic character continues as self and displays perhaps the greatest freedom, the freedom to survive, modify one's behavior, and achieve an integration with the surrounding world.

Freedom resulting in mistakes, rather than being an option for a comic character, is intrinsic to the comic itself. The comic character usually displays a mixture of mistaken or exaggerated beliefs or desires, as has been seen, for example, in Don Quixote. Scott notes this feature in his definition of the comic. For Scott,

> the comic is a contradiction in the relation of the human individual to the created orders of existence which arises out of an over-specialization of some instinct or faculty of the self, or out of an inordinate inclination of the self in some special direction, to the neglect of the other avenues through which it ought also to gain expression.[51]

All the while comic characters may be unaware of their folly. For Bergson, "a comic character is generally comic in proportion to his ignorance of himself. The comic person is unconscious."[52] The comic character's freedom is best taken as an unconscious, or unexamined freedom, a freedom that may result in examination and modification once exposed to events. The comic character is a veritable fountain of folly as much as freedom because the comic character has the freedom to do so. To be free or ignorant or unconscious is to be free from everything but one's self. Choices about the future must be made by fallible beings within the blindness of the present.

If the comic stems more from character than from plot and if the comic character is fundamentally about mistaken or exaggerated beliefs or desires freely expressed, then it becomes clear why comedy often features fantastic plots. Comic plots grow out of a character's mistaken beliefs, and the human capacity to be mistaken is almost boundless, especially in regard to the future. Comic characters reflect the human propensity to make unjustified inferences that lead to credible falsehoods about life. Fantastic plots take on an air of plausibility, not because things normally happen that way, but because characters express their beliefs and desires in choices that make them happen that way. One does not normally single-handedly confront a band of armed soldiers, yet doing so seems consistent enough with Peter's character to make his actions inherently plausible.

The supremacy of character over plot in the comic does not mean that comic characters are more fully developed than tragic characters; the reverse is quite often the case. In a comic character, some trait or belief is usually exaggerated such that other aspects of character suffer as a consequence, as Scott notes above. The greater the exaggeration, the more the work tends to move from drama (as Hegel defines it)

---

[51] Nathan Scott, "The Bias of Comedy and the Narrow Escape into Faith," in Corrigan, *Comedy*, 104.
[52] Bergson, *Laughter*, 16.

toward farce with a consequent flattening of character. The characters in *A Midsummer Night's Dream* are less developed than those in *Twelfth Night*, the former having a more fantastic plot than the latter. Dickens's novels can be richly comic, but his characters, Mr. Micawber for example, tend to be relatively flat. The works of Jane Austen are generally comic and feature well-rounded and developed characters coupled with a greater stress on irony and plot. Much of the greatness of Don Quixote and Falstaff lies in the fact that both defy this tendency and combine a roundness of character with strong comic tendencies.

Peter displays the significant qualities of a comic character. His desires and beliefs propel him to make choices and act on those choices within a context of freedom. Jesus can only do so much to curb Peter's excess. Reality will eventually speak with its own voice. For Peter, the very freedom that made him a comic character becomes the very thing that will be restricted. Jesus tells him, "Very truly I tell you, when you were younger you dressed yourself and went where you wanted; but when you are old you will stretch out your hands, and someone else will dress you and lead you where you do not want to go" (21:18). This narrowing of freedom will ultimately deprive him of life itself, yet there is something refreshing about Peter and his next statement, "Lord, what about him?" The Peter we have come to know, although chastened and wiser, is still very much alive.

V. C. 3. b Plot

Like any other type of plot, comic plots must feature a clash of some kind. Rather than the clash being related to the past being manifest in the present as in tragedy, comic plots feature competing versions of the future as they are manifest in the present. Thus, in tragedy, a past action or an action soon to be past catches up to the protagonist, whether or not the protagonist was responsible for it. In comedy, the future is envisioned in a way that impacts the present. The future presents numerous opportunities inevitably tied to beliefs and desires. If character X has belief Y about the future coupled with desire Z, X stands a good chance of acting on that desire. Acting on one's desires with respect to the future contains as many pitfalls as it does possibilities.

The comic action usually grows out of a conflict between two or more visions of what the future should look like. Frye notes, "The action of comedy is not unlike the action of a lawsuit, in which plaintiff and defendant construct different versions of the same situation, one finally being judged as real and the other as illusory."[53] Although Frye's comparison is correct as far as it goes, a better comparison might be made between comedy and deliberative rhetoric rather than judicial rhetoric, the latter being more appropriate for tragedy. In deliberative rhetoric, the rivals each construct competing versions of what *should* take place rather than what *has* taken place, as in judicial rhetoric, which may well be what Frye intended to say. To act, then, is to simultaneously display and test a set of beliefs and one's character.

The comic action, then, features a course of events in relation to the future, or possible futures, plots in which the one action or state of affairs competes with another.

---

[53] Frye, *Anatomy*, 166.

Usually a character's desires are blocked in some manner and the desired future refuses to come easily into the present. Frye observes, "The obstacles to the hero's desire, then, form the action of the comedy, and the overcoming of them the comic resolution."[54] This idea makes no explicit value judgment on the desired future because the comic character could desire an inappropriate reality, as Malvolio does in *Twelfth Night*. In comedy, a social judgment takes place regarding the desirability of a given state of affairs,[55] but this judgment has less to do with the nature of the comic itself than with the values of the society in which it occurs. Comedy often features a note of grace in not having all one's desires fulfilled, as is plainly the case with Peter.

The comic character acts on desires and meets with resistance through what are normally called blocking agents. Blocking agents in comedy may be divided into two types: active and passive. Active opposition takes the form of blocking characters, usually members of the older establishment whose vision of the future is at odds with those who desire change. Frye outlines this process as follows,

> What normally happens is that a young man wants a young woman, that his desire is resisted by some opposition, usually paternal, and that near the end of the play some twist in the plot enables the hero to have his will. In this simple pattern there are several complex elements. In the first place, the movement of comedy is usually a movement from one kind of society to another. At the beginning of the play the obstructing characters are in charge of the play's society, and the audience recognizes that they are usurpers. At the end of the play the device in the plot that brings hero and heroine together causes a new society to crystallize around the hero, and the moment then this crystallization occurs is the point of resolution in the action, the comic discovery, *anagnorisis* or *cognitio*.[56]

A typical example of this pattern is *A Midsummer Night's Dream*, in which Egeus forbids his daughter to marry Lysander in favor of her marrying Demetrius. Several of these elements are apparent in Peter's situation in the FG. The prologue establishes a context wherein darkness has usurped the position of the light. Jesus is aligned with the light and with God and has come into the world to bring light to everyone. Peter understands Jesus to be the Messiah, it is assumed, in 1:40-42, and he understands him further to be "the Holy One of God" in 6:69. Peter and Jesus have this understanding in common; those holding any other view are blocking agents, usurpers, hirelings, and false shepherds.

The most obvious blocking characters in the FG are the Jewish leaders, who oppose Jesus more than anyone else in the FG. Throughout, the Jewish leaders represent the older established order, the insiders who block innovation and change and oppose Jesus. The temple, with its status as the center of Jewish religion, is destined to be replaced by Jesus himself, the true temple who will be thrown down and rebuilt in three days (2:19-22). Nicodemus, a cardinal member of the Jewish establishment, is

---

[54] Ibid., 164.
[55] George Meredith presents the social functions of comedy. See Meredith, *An Essay on Comedy and the Uses of the Comic Spirit* (Constable: London, 1918).
[56] Frye, *Anatomy*, 163.

told he must be "born again." The new society consists of those who are born again, drink of the living water, or receive deliverance from blindness. The Jewish leaders do not simply oppose Jesus, but also oppose those who follow or would follow him and attempt to block the formation of the new society by excommunicating believers from the synagogue. Furthermore, steps are taken to destroy Jesus himself. The disciples have been aware of the danger of following Jesus (11:8). Following the resurrection of Lazarus, the Jewish leaders plot to take his life (11:53). Events move toward their climax during the Passover celebration when the Jewish leaders come to the garden with a detachment of soldiers to arrest Jesus. In the garden, Peter's identity with Jesus is such that he draws a sword and opposes these blocking characters.

Insofar as Peter's view of things is concerned, the major blocking character is Jesus himself. Peter's vision of a glorious future competes with Jesus's own vision of what that glory consists of. In the incident of the footwashing, Peter's understanding of Jesus, the mission of Jesus, and Peter's own role in it conflicts with Jesus's emphasis on service and love. Jesus commands Peter to "put your sword away" and thus blocks Peter's role as participant in this glorious revolution. Peter displays boundless confidence in Jesus's identity, authority, and power, but profoundly misunderstands his specific intentions.

Those standing around the fire with Peter may also be seen as blocking characters who serve a transitional function. Whatever the actual danger lurking behind each question, Peter's denials are certainly out of proportion to the potential threat to his safety, especially when compared with Peter's previous actions. The Peter who commits three denials under verbal challenge stands in contrast to the Peter who wields a sword at physical danger. Compared with the real danger of confronting an armed band, the potential danger posed around the fire seems small indeed. Whatever the disciples thought, nothing in the FG states explicitly that they were in danger and care has been taken to show that Jesus took steps to secure their safety (18:8). Peter's interlocutors provide three opportunities for him to take a stand—three unheeded warnings of perils to come. In this sense, they are blocking characters who perform a potential ministerial function. Their role is not so much to present a destructive threat to Peter as it is to prevent Peter's own self-destruction. Or, given the larger purposes of Jesus, this fireside chat provides the situation that will expose and destroy Peter's pretentious behavior. The story unfolds such that the pretentious side of Peter's behavior dies at his own hand. Both Peter and Judas hang themselves.

The blocking element in the comic plot could be passive and simply be reality itself. This is the case with Don Quixote, whose adventures constantly war with physical reality and society's failure to be anything at all like that portrayed in his many books. In a kind of reversal of Don Quixote, Falstaff (*King Henry IV*, pt. 1) desires honor, but only to a point. Honor usually entails some sort of real encounter with difficulty or danger and this encounter Falstaff cannot bring himself to allow. For Falstaff, discretion as the better part of valor means above all things to avoid bodily harm. Don Quixote is comic because he acts on his beliefs and they are blocked by reality; Falstaff is comic because he sees the potential clash of belief and reality and only pretends to act. Peter's character displays both of these aspects of his confrontations with reality. He is a garden variety Don Quixote in Gethsemane, but more like Falstaff in the high priest's courtyard where erstwhile bravery gives way to denial. The crowing rooster signals the nadir of Peter's mixture of action and pretension and suggests that Peter, in addition to being mistaken about Jesus, is ignorant of himself.[57]

Ironically, in the process of promoting the cause of Jesus on earth, Peter himself becomes a blocking character. Peter's attempt to stop Jesus from washing the disciples' feet means much more than stopping the act itself: Peter fully knows that Jesus's actions define his role as leader and the disciples' role as followers, so tries on this basis to stop it. In the garden, Jesus is willing to die for one reason and Peter for another. Jesus's command to Peter, "Put your sword away! Shall I not drink the cup the Father has given me?" (18:11), shows that Peter stands between the will of the Father and the mission of the Son and highlights the profound implications of Peter's mistake. Peter's role as blocking character must end if he is to participate in the ministry of Jesus.

V. D Conceptual elements of comedy

V. D. 1 Introduction

The fundamental issue of methodology is whether or not a definition can be given that is sufficiently comprehensive to cover an adequate amount of data while at the same time being narrow enough to offer clarification of issues. The same methodological issues and issues related to the validity of any theory arise in a discussion of comedy.[58] Although the details would vary, the arguments employed in defending the formation of a theory of comedy are substantially the same covered in the introduction and in relation to tragedy and need not be repeated here.

Raskin also offers an insightful classification of the theories of humor.[59] The most important type, and the type offered by Raskin himself and the present work, is a theory based on incongruity wherein two or more incongruous elements are juxtaposed against each other. Bergson's famous work on laughter is of this type.[60] The second type of theories is that based on "*hostility, superiority, malice, aggression, derision, or disparagement.*"[61] The third type is the release theories of which Freud is the most famous proponent. Freud argued that creating a joke involved a psychic compression that was released by the recipient and resulted in laughter. Rather than being incompatible, these three approaches are really talking about different yet related elements of the same thing. Raskin observes,

---

[57] Frye observes, "The blocking characters of comedy are nearly always imposters, though it is more frequently a lack of self-knowledge than simple hypocrisy that characterizes them." Frye, *Anatomy*, 172.

[58] For example, L. C. Knights is critical of any theory of comedy and believes that they are useless in terms of actual literary criticism. He mentions the theories of Bergson, Freud, and Meredith and is particularly critical of the Meredith. But Freud and Bergson make no attempt at literary criticism (Knights would probably admit this) and Knights does point out a certain generality in Meredith. Knight's radical dichotomy between literary criticism and theories of comedy and categorical rejection of them is extreme. See L. C. Knights, "Notes on Comedy," in Corrigan, *Comedy*, 181–91.

[59] Raskin, *Semantic Mechanisms of Humor*, 30–41.

[60] Bergson holds that laughter results from the imposition of the mechanical upon the living, the rigid upon the living. But Bergson is only focusing on a narrow aspect of a more general one offered here. See Bergson, *Laughter*.

[61] Raskin, *Humor*, 36. His emphasis.

In our terms, the *incongruity*-based theories make a statement about the *stimulus*; the *superiority* theories characterize the *relations* or *attitudes* between *speaker* and the *hearer*, and the *release/relief* theories comment on the feelings and psychology of the *hearer* only.[62]

Raskin's analysis clarifies a number of issues. For example, superiority theories of the second type are primarily concerned with the ethical aspects of the actual use of humor, not with the nature of humor itself. Setting these concerns aside avoids the confusion generated by the ethical or moral questions in a comic production voiced by Plato, Puritans, and countless others, and avoids the issue of whether or not a comic character is base or good. Release/relief theories focus on issues related to human biology and psychology of the hearer, whereas incongruity theories contain a strong conceptual element, as must be the case if humor is not a physical substance but must be transmitted in some manner that passes through a cognitive process. It may be observed that, depending on one's point of view, most literary criticism either fails to make adequate allowance for these distinctions or that literary criticism is more holistic in its approach and all the better for it.

The conceptual elements of comedy themselves differ from tragedy such that a theory of comedy will look very different from a theory of tragedy. The movement in tragedy is from qualities or values in the abstract with latent potential opposition to their opposition in reality resulting in destruction. Tragedy concentrates its forces by means of plot, the vehicle of necessity. Conversely, comedy moves forward toward integration by means of character, the vehicle of freedom. The comic pattern is toward openness and expansion, from concrete reality with its difficulties toward integration with the imaginative and abstract where a sense of resolution is possible. Sypher's comment illustrates the point,

> Often the comic hero is rescued because Improvisation and Uncertainty are the premises of comic action, and the goddess Fortuna presides over great tracts of the comic scene. But the law of Inevitability or Necessity bears heavily on the tragic hero, who is not eligible for rescue because in tragedy man must somehow take responsibility for the flaws in the nature of things or at least pay a penalty for them.[63]

While tragedy moves from past to present and irony essentially stagnates in the present, comedy moves from present to future, the field of integration, possibility, and hope. Comedy unmasks a character, while tragedy unmasks a situation. The differences between the two archetypes are such that their respective theories take on a substantially different shape. A theory of tragedy tends toward causality, narrowness, and exclusion, while the open nature of the comic fosters a tendency toward freedom, openness, and generality.

---

[62] Raskin, *Humor*, 40. His emphasis.
[63] Sypher, in Corrigan, *Comedy*, 48–49.

V. D. 2 Beliefs and frames of reference[64]

The theory of comedy in the present work largely follows the basic outlines offered by Koestler and paralleled to a great extent by Raskin. Koestler sees comedy as the perceiving of a situation or idea in terms of two self-consistent but habitually incompatible frames of reference.[65] Raskin follows the same line of thinking:

(107) *A text can be characterized as a single-joke-carrying text if both of the conditions in (108) are satisfied.*
(108) (i) *The text is compatible, fully or in part, with two different scripts*
 (ii) *The two scripts with which the text is compatible are opposite*[66]

What Koestler and Raskin mean by this will become clear as this basic framework is expanded below. As indicated by his title, *Semantic Mechanisms of Humor*, Raskin is primarily concerned with two things: (1) semantic mechanisms and (2) as they are applied to humor. But stripped of the jargon and methodology of his academic field, Raskin's theory parallels Koestler's and is at once simple and illuminating, capable of wide application far beyond the confines of its immediate audience and beyond its specific subject matter of humor. Its interpretative potential will become apparent as these basic ideas are expanded and applied to literature and comedy.

In comedy, beliefs about the present are all important because out of these beliefs will flow the future. Beliefs animate actions and these actions shape the future as it is realized in the present. The future is open because the actions that will shape it into the present are influenced by beliefs and combinations of beliefs that are subject to change. The open future inherent to comedy relies on multiple possibilities. Thus, comedy resides to a significant degree in beliefs. Shakespeare, for example, exploits this fully in *Much Ado About Nothing* where everything rests on false beliefs. There is nothing of substance in Benedick and Beatrice's false information about each other or Hero's supposed infidelity and death.[67] The past is subject to various interpretations, interpretations often disputed in tragedy, while the essential facts remain unalterable, or the present is destined to be altered for the worse by mistaken interpretation of the past, as is the case with Othello and his unconcern for the future. In comedy, beliefs will shape and arrange the present and thereby create facts rather than be merely subject to them.

Significant for comedy, few, if any, of the beliefs comprising any frame of reference can be exhaustively investigated and determined with absolute certainty. Uncertainty is part of life, especially in regard to the future. Setting aside debates about epistemology, this is only to say that any frame of reference includes tacit assumptions about reality that may not be adequately justified yet held in innocence. The lack of volition and the innocence in which one sees the world in a particular frame of reference is an important component of comedy. For example, in *Twelfth Night*, Olivia justifiably and

---

[64] Equivalent to Raskin's term *script*, the term *frame of reference* is used by Koestler and will be used here.
[65] Koestler, *Creation*, 35.
[66] Raskin, *Humor*, 99. His emphasis.
[67] Hero is a character's name in the play.

innocently assumes a certain frame of reference about Viola: that Viola is a man. On this (false) assumption, Olivia falls in love with her. If this frame of reference breaks apart, the comedy is over insofar as it concerns Olivia's frame of reference. Or, a character may be in large measure responsible for holding a patently false belief. For example, again in *Twelfth Night*, Malvolio's own vanity and the manipulations of others lead him to mistakenly believe that Olivia is in love with him. However achieved, Malvolio's frame of reference, once in place, governs his actions in a kind of innocent tranquility. Malvolio's frame of reference with its false beliefs about Olivia endures beyond the point where actual contact with Olivia might have more wisely been taken as a source of doubt.

V. D. 3 Frames of reference in conflict

Individual frames of reference do not in themselves produce comedy. According to Koestler, "It is the clash of the two mutually incompatible codes, or associative contexts, which explodes the tension."[68] Comedy results from the simultaneous conflict of two or more frames of reference set in motion when a character acts or is acted upon with a view *toward a future integration of some kind*. In irony, the clash of frames of reference is essentially stagnant, disembodied, and concerned with the present and its perception. In comedy, as Richter observes, "an error in and of itself is not ridiculous, any more than ignorance is . . . . But the error must be able to reveal itself through an effort, through an action."[69] A frame of reference acted upon brings ignorance or error into contact with reality, a movement teeming with comic possibilities. Malvolio's infatuation with Olivia when acted upon conflicts with Olivia's innocent view of things. This kind of conflict sets up the incongruity essential for comedy. One way of understanding a given situation must conflict with another way of understanding the same situation. Bergson calls this clash of perspectives a "reciprocal interference of a series." He writes,

> Each of the characters in every stage-made misunderstanding has his setting in an appropriate series of events which he correctly interprets as far as he is concerned, and which give the key-note to his words and actions. Each of the series peculiar to the several characters develops independently, but at a certain moment they meet under such conditions that the actions and words that belong to one might just as well belong to another. Hence arise the misunderstandings and the equivocal nature of the situation. But this latter is not laughable in itself, it is so only because it reveals the coincidence of the two independent series.[70]

---

[68] Koestler, *Creation*, 35.

[69] Jean Paul Richter, *Introduction to Aesthetics*, number 28, "Inquiry into the Ridiculous," in Lauter, 317–18.

[70] Bergson, *Laughter*, 96. This is not Bergson's main theory, which has to do with the difference between the "mechanical" and the vital life force of human existence, laughter occurring when the former is superimposed upon the latter. See Koestler's discussion of Bergson, *Creation*, 45–49. Koestler notes that Bergson was closer to the heart of the comic here than anywhere else.

For example, in Moliere's *The Miser*, Harpagon (the miser) accuses Valere of stealing his cash box. Valere knows nothing about the cash box, but thinks his own love for Harpagon's daughter Elise has been discovered. Harpagon knows nothing about the love affair. Valere pleads,

> A treasure indeed, no doubt of it, and the most precious you possess; but you will not lose it by letting me keep it. On my knees I beg you for this charming treasure; and if you would do what is right, you must needs let me have it. [act V, scene iii]

Each interprets the present with a frame of reference about the present that each is justified in holding. Valere assumes a frame of reference completely at odds with Harpagon's, and "treasure" here forms a verbal neutral ground over which these two parties duel in blindness. Perhaps the best example of this in the accounts of Peter occurs in Jn 13:31-32, which bears repeating here:

> "When he [Judas] was gone, Jesus said, "Now is the Son of Man glorified and God is glorified in him. If God is glorified in him, then God will glorify the Son in himself, and will glorify him at once."

Although this example differs from the one above in that here only one party is mistaken, the dynamic Bergson calls "mutual interference of a series" is the same. "Now" and "Son of Man" and the nature of God's glorification of the Son provide equivocal issues of interpretation that Peter and Jesus understand within different frames of reference.

The clash of perspectives must be perceived to produce a comic in effect. In Peter's case, the reader perceives that something is amiss in Peter's understanding of the situation. While the conflict must be evident to an observer to achieve its comic effect, observers may be internal and external to the action. In *Twelfth Night*, the realistic frame of reference shared by Sir Toby Belch and the audience allows them to know that Malvolio is deceived and to observe with laughter. Something may strike someone as comic in a way unique to an individual, as is the case when only one person finds a given situation comic or incongruous and thereby laughs alone. It may happen that a participant may view things differently much later and only then see the incongruity in a situation, as is often the case when we grow older and reflect on our past.

A detailed examination of the structure of a joke will illustrate the clash of perspectives inherent in comedy. In a well-executed joke, one frame of reference is established by a narrative or context, and this frame of reference is juxtaposed against another frame of reference at the punch line. The more established a frame of reference and the more suddenly and decisively it is exchanged for another frame of reference, the funnier the joke and the greater the laughter—this is the universal structure of comedy. For example, consider the following joke:

> The leaders of Russia, the United Kingdom and the United States are given an audience with God and allowed to ask one question. The Russian leader asks,

"When will we solve our ethnic conflicts?" God answers "2065" and the Russian leader thinks "I'll be dead by then." The British Prime Minister is next and asks "When will we solve our unemployment problem?" God answers, "2073," and the Prime Minister thinks "I'll be dead by then." Finally, the American President asks, "When will we pay off the national debt?" In response, God answers, "Mr. President, I'll be dead by then."

If this joke is indeed funny, it is so because it establishes a pattern or frame of reference with the first two examples and juxtaposes this frame of reference with the notion of God—normally understood to be eternal—being "dead by then." In another example, a sign in a church nursery reads "We shall not all sleep, but we shall all be changed." Here, "sleep" and "changed" occupy two frames of reference: a church nursery and the scriptural reference to the resurrection in I Corinthians 15:51. But not everyone will get the joke because some may not be familiar with the Biblical reference and the comic juxtaposition will fail as a result. This failure of contexts explains why some humor does not work, as in this joke, for example: "How do you get forty Canadians out of a swimming pool?" Answer: "Tell them to get out." Some may find this joke funny, but others certainly will not because this joke requires understanding something about being Canadian and their frame of reference.[71] Some jokes simply are not very funny because they fail to establish one frame of reference and/or weakly juxtapose it on another, the classic bad joke. Lest readers be deprived of such an example, consider this one: "What do you call a dog cursed by sheep?" Answer: "A baad dog."

This description of humor as the juxtaposition of two frames of reference (Raskin calls them "scripts") applies to all humor: it accounts for all humor by identifying a universal structure and it accounts for the particular instances of humor in that particular frames of reference vary by age, sex, background, occupation, nationality, beliefs, and countless other factors. In other words, the structure is the same, but the circumstances of those structures are infinitely variable.

As in jokes, in extended comedy, the greater the juxtaposition and persistence of two competing perceptions about a given situation, the greater the comic effect. For example, in *A Midsummer Night's Dream*, the fairy queen Titania's spell-induced love for Bottom the weaver would be comic in itself, but Bottom's previous translation into an ass intensifies the comic juxtaposition. Malvolio's advances on Olivia are all the more comic for his cross-gartered attire, a style she detests. Peter's misunderstanding of the situation persists to the point of drawing a sword and beyond. The following are some of the innumerable variations on this basic theme of incongruity or juxtaposition: serious/frivolous, big/little, rich/poor, fast/slow, knowledge/ignorance, fat/thin, insider/outsider, ideal/real, best/worst, country/city, young/old, pretentious/realistic, public/private, divine/human, and male/female, the

---

[71] I first heard this joke in a group of about twelve, and the only people who laughed were the two Canadians and me, my Scandinavian background having enough in common with being Canadian that I laughed with them. I later told this joke during a presentation on comedy to my university faculty colleagues, and, again, the only ones who laughed were the Canadians and others who had lived in Canada.

last pair being perhaps the greatest source of comic juxtaposition.[72] The more these or similar juxtapositions are incorporated into a work of comedy, the better that comedy will be.

In order to be comic, the conflict of ways of understanding must remain open-ended. There must be the possibility of change and discovery so that it is perceived that the frames of reference at odds with each other might be resolved, not merely resolved in perception, but in reality. Comedy operates to a large extent on beliefs and perceptions that are at odds with reality in the present but with reference to the future. These beliefs are not inevitable and necessary as they relate to facts, as is the case with Oedipus who learns the truth of his situation. In comedy, beliefs are merely mistaken. Beliefs and desires of any kind are open to change in a way that past events are not. L. J. Potts comments, "The abnormality of comic characters is not absolute; we should feel that they are capable of behaving normally if they would."[73] For this reason, a juxtaposition of frames of reference caused by insanity or some mental deficiency is not comic because for those in such circumstances, it must be this way. In tragedy, the conflict of frames of reference embodies a sense of necessity and inevitability because unalterable facts drive action. But in comedy, the juxtaposition of two frames of reference is more accidental and unexpected. The comic juxtaposition is tenuous because it relies on false beliefs to produce an incongruity that need not be so, hence the emphasis in comedy on chance, coincidence, and the unexpected. The observer is free to see the conflict of the competing frames of reference and exchange one for the other. This exchange or movement between one frame of reference and another produces laughter. In the FG, the separate frames of reference of Jesus and Peter move apart gradually, thus preventing a sudden, laughter producing exchange of one frame of reference for the other.

The dramatic conflict in comedy remains open-ended because it relies on a conflict arising in the present as it relates to the future and what will happen. At some time in comedy, perhaps at any moment, someone's frame of reference might end at any point when all is seen in a new light, including mistaken beliefs about the past. Conversely, a comic juxtaposition might begin at any moment as when someone misunderstands something. Beliefs about a state of affairs are always subject to change, and, so long as change remains possible, comedy can continue. This is not to say that obstacles to a comic ending reside only in beliefs or desires. The obstacles may indeed be real and dangerous, but comedy can continue so long as the obstacles do not have the last word.

The juxtaposition of two competing frames of reference in comedy can proceed only as long as no *decisive* challenge is presented to a particular interpretation of events. The tenuous nature of a comic juxtaposition, the sense that things do not have to be this way but they are, suggests that each frame of reference will challenge the other, but only to a point. The degree of an individual's adherence to a particular frame of reference determines the point at which a belief is modified by its holder. In Ben

---

[72] For a further treatment, see L. J. Potts, "The Subject Matter of Comedy," in Corrigan, *Comedy*, 198–213.
[73] Potts, "Subject Matter," 199.

Jonson's *The Fox*, Volpone (the Fox) and his clever servant Mosca marvel at the self-deception of the three men who each hope to inherit Volpone's fortune.

> Mosca:
>
> True, thy will not see't
> Too much light blinds them, I think. Each of them
> Is so possest and stuft with his own hopes,
> That any thing unto the contrary,
> Never so true, or never so apparent,
> Never so palpable, they will resist it
>
> Volpone:
>
> Like a temptation of the devil.[74]

Likewise, Don Quixote's delusions of knighthood and chivalry withstand numerous conflicts with reality. In contrast, a comic misunderstanding may last only an instant, as is the case with most jokes and word plays. A decisive challenge to one frame of reference usually happens by means of some assertion of reality. All is cleared up in *A Comedy of Errors* when the revelation of the two sets of identical twins explains the wild misunderstandings. Thomas, who refuses to accept Jesus as risen from the dead for an entire week, changes decisively on viewing the hands of the risen Lord. The comic juxtaposition aspect of comedy ends when a particular frame of reference is no longer at odds with reality, when reality intrudes sufficient to modify beliefs and the multiple possibilities of the future dissolve into the realities of the present.

V. D. 4 Comic reality[75]

However much comedy relies on the incongruence of two competing frames of reference and however much it relies on a resolution of its various frames of reference into reality, the reality that emerges must be of a certain type. A resolution and integration of competing frames of reference into reality does not mean that the reality achieved by that resolution is necessarily pleasant and comic. Unmasking of illusions does not in itself make for a comic resolution. For example, in Moliere's *Tartuffe*, Tartuffe's hypocrisy and parasitism are absolutely clear to everyone but Orgon, yet Orgon persists in believing in Tartuffe's virtue and this persistence drives the comic mixture of illusion and reality. Only when Tartuffe attempts to seduce Orgon's wife Elmire in his hearing does Orgon belatedly see things as they really are. But Tartuffe's unmasking alone will resolve the situation because Orgon has transferred ownership of his property to Tartuffe and faces the very real possibility of being evicted from his own house. The expulsion is only averted through the intervention of the prince, who brings about a truly comic ending wherein the villain is punished and order restored.

---

[74] Ben Jonson, *The Fox*, Act V, Scene I., in *The Complete Plays of Ben Jonson*, vol. 1 (London: J. M. Dent, 1910), 468.

[75] Raskin offers no counterpart to this in his theory of humor.

The *Tartuffe* example illustrates the two most significant phases of comedy. The first is the clash of frames of reference, generally what we refer to as comedy with its tendency to be funny; the second is a resolution into a desired reality, generally what we refer to as comic where the happy ending is achieved. In order to finally be comic, the multiple possibilities of the future characteristic of the comedy phase must dissolve into a *desirable* reality in the present. The relationship of the two phases can vary. In the case of *Tartuffe*, the first ends before the second, but they may coincide. For example, in Ben Jonson's *The Fox*, the final unmasking of Volpone (the Fox) occurs at virtually the same time as the comedy resolves into a new reality wherein the innocents are restored and the villains punished. In another variation, the comedy phase may be essentially missing or de-emphasized, yet the work contains a comic ending that requires the work to be taken in its entirety as comic, as is the case in *The Winter's Tale*. Likewise, the comedy or humorous and incongruent phase is missing from melodrama, which Frye calls "comedy without humor."[76] In another variation of the relationship of the two phases, the second or resolution phase does not occur at all nor is it even hinted what that phase might be. Such is the unpretentious nature of practical jokes, home video shows, slapstick, and related materials that need not be of present concern.

The two phases of the comic emerge separately in Peter's presentation in the FG. The phase of comedy wherein the two frames of reference compete contains humor only if seen in a certain light, the humor of the comedy phase being overshadowed by the seriousness of the situation and by knowledge of the denials to follow. The conflict of frames of reference reaches its climax as Peter draws a sword at almost the very moment when Jesus accepts the cup given him by the Father. Whatever remains of the courageous Peter vanishes like smoke with his denials in the high priest's courtyard. The resolution phase of the comic, to the extent that it occurs at all, awaits further development in chapter 21.

Comedy relies on a course of events that is out of the ordinary and often fantastic. Likewise, the emphasis in a comic resolution is on chance, coincidence, and the unexpected.[77] In comedy, the resolution of the circumstances is usually unlikely, given how mixed up things may appear in the present and ordinarily comes about through the intervention of some outside force. This force may be impersonal and appear as luck or providence, as when chance events reunite parents with children and children with siblings. Or this outside force may be the personal intervention of an outside agent, as when Oberon sorts matters out in *A Midsummer Night's Dream* or Portia pleads the case of Antonio in *The Merchant of Venice*, or both, as in *The Tempest* where Prospero takes up where the storm leaves off. Robertson observes,

> This very arbitrariness is one of the most persistent aspects of comedy. Comic heroes are finally integrated into the society to which they properly belong, not because of their inherent goodness or prowess, but because of events that are

---

[76] Frye, *Anatomy*, 40.
[77] For a discussion of these features, see Frye, *Anatomy*, 170.

unexpected, irrational, sometimes downright miraculous, and often precipitated by a *deus ex machina* who simply decides to act on behalf of the protagonist.[78]

In any case, in comedy, the normal linear flow of life and events is arrested, the iron links of necessity and causality typical of tragedy are broken, and reality and life itself is altered for the better, as if the marvelous world of romance breaks into the confusion of comedy with a touch of restorative grace. In a world governed by causality and necessity, the achievement of the comic ending by some outside intervention will quite naturally seem implausible, extraordinary, and even fantastic. To the extent that one excludes the fantastic, as Thomas the ironic realist does, the comic ending will seem unbelievable, or at least violating aesthetic sensibilities by exchanging what we would like to happen for what is likely to happen.[79]

A pause to reconnoiter the situation of Peter on that crucial week may prove useful. As Jesus dies by crucifixion, any sort of restoration and comic ending appears impossible. With Jesus firmly in the grave, the story of Peter simultaneously flirts with farce and careens toward tragedy on precisely the same evidence. Peter's earlier words "To whom shall we go? We believe and know that you are the Holy One of God" seem ridiculous or painfully mistaken. Jesus's washing of the feet becomes a supreme example of service laden with pathos—or it is an ironic mockery of his friends? Judas, whose death is not mentioned in the FG, becomes either an even greater villain or the only one shrewd enough to switch sides in time. Peter either did not defend Jesus adequately or he was lucky to escape with his life. The sword in the garden turns to ashes in his hands if Peter supposes that all he believed in was utterly without foundation. If his beliefs are true, the failure of Jesus is profound in that it implicates God who failed to act on his behalf, in which case the sword might have been put to best use on Peter himself. The denials become either a series of unmaskings or sickening affirmations of reality. The bitter weeping of the Synoptics becomes anguished personal sorrow or it becomes the remorse of a fool. Time will either heighten regret or cast doubt on the validity of Jesus himself. One does not know whether to laugh or cry.

A comic resolution is possible in Peter's case only through the unlikely and fantastic intervention from the outside, accomplished in this case by God himself. Frye states, "The mythical or primitive basis of comedy is a movement toward the rebirth and renewal of the powers of nature."[80] But this is precisely not the case in the FG because the powers of nature are unable to renew as in the death of Lazarus. "If he sleeps, he will get better" (11:12) will not do. God raises Jesus from the dead and breaks the relentless linear pattern of life that leads inexorably to death. God acting in freedom breaks the iron chain of causality. In so doing he vindicates the words of Jesus, transforms the disciples' understanding of Jesus and the scripture, and establishes the foundation for the transformation of all of reality itself: the resurrection of Jesus is the theological and ontological—the archetypal—basis for all comedy. Jesus breaks linear pattern of

---

[78] David Robertson, "Tragedy, Comedy, and the Bible: A Response," *Semeia* 32 (1984), 102.
[79] Given Aristotle's emphasis on causality, it is perhaps no accident that no Aristotelian theory of comedy exists.
[80] Frye, *A Natural Perspective*, 119, cf. 123.

tragedy and establishes the circular pattern of comedy characterized by restoration and grace.

Nothing happens in comedy, if it is to remain comedy, that is final. Reality can only intrude so far. In this sense, comedy contains a sense of life being cyclical by including things that are not final and excluding thing about life that are final. Setting aside matters like tone and focusing on plot, *Romeo and Juliet* is finally a tragedy only when Romeo mistakes Juliet's sleep for death and kills himself. The tragicomedy format of *The Winter's Tale* relies on "death" not being final after all. Because Malvolio is materially no worse off than before, he is free to laugh with everyone else about his humiliating foray into love but chooses instead to "be revenged on the whole pack of you." In contrast to comedy, reality triumphs in tragedy in a way that excludes all but the most final aspects of life. The forcefulness of the evidence and the finality of the facts force Oedipus to change his mind about the truth when he wishes it were otherwise.

Even the resolution into happiness achieved at the end of a comedy is not final. Unlike tragedy, in comedy, the desired reality is in large measure realized. Imaginative and millennial hopes for an ideal future have come true and grant something like a state of grace. Comedy resolves then into a reality in which realized hopes provide justification for the possibility of further realized hopes. But this resolution is precarious and can be only temporary. Marriage forms the traditional end of comedy rather than married life. The details of exactly how "they lived happily ever after" are not normally included in the story. In *Much Ado About Nothing*, justice on Don John the villain can wait until tomorrow and must not mar the festivities of the wedding day, yet tomorrow with its judgments and quotidian existence must inevitably come. Recalling the four archetypes illustrated on the chart (see introduction), comedy moves into romance where the dynamics and struggles are of a different order, a representation of self-evident and realized values and the struggle for their preservation. The comic resolution satisfies only by drawing a curtain on a particular episode of life.

In a variation of the comic pattern that reflects the need for continuing contact with reality, the comic resolution may be strongly anticipated but not actually occur. The normal pattern of the completed comic wherein the desired reality is realized may be referred to as *transitive* comedy, and its counterpart may be referred to as *intransitive* comedy.[81] In the latter, the hoped-for resolution fails to take place or is modified to a significant degree. Transitive comic must end because any prolonged contact with the broken real world will destroy its imaginative synthesis; only intransitive comic can continue. The intransitive pattern is seen in Shakespeare's *Love's Labour's Lost* where the imaginative synthesis of the anticipated marriage of the four gentlemen to the four women fails to occur, partly through the death of the king of France and partly due to the gentlemen not being ready for it. The traditional transitive comic pattern is notable in the play for its being broken. Significantly, both Peter and the four gentlemen of *Love's Labour's Lost* must move from their separate abstractions and make greater allowances for present mortal life while their hopes await future realization.

But rather than being an occasional exception, the intransitive comic pattern is fundamental to such comic formats as sitcoms, comic strips, and episodic comic works

---

[81] Transitive and intransitive comedies are my terms.

like *Don Quixote*. It must be this way because if the promise of transitive comic is realized, the story must end as there is no conflict to report. Thus, Charlie Brown will never be a winning baseball manager nor will Lucy hold the football in place for him to kick. If the seven castaways on *Gilligan's Island* are rescued, the show is over. Yet there is no necessary reason for it to be this way. The intransitive comic continues to offer hope, however small or great, of becoming transitive.

As intransitive comedy, Peter presents a character where the comic resolution is only partial. On Sunday morning, Jesus rises from the dead, achieving a final victory over that most final of foes and a reconciliation of the believer with God. But the classic comic ending of wrongs being made right and a new order being established in material fact does not occur. Peter's discord with Jesus is over, but the Romans still control Palestine and evil persists in a world as implacably opposed to Jesus as ever and this world will soon turn its opposition on his disciples. Peter's great error consisted not so much in being wrong, but in being premature. The rule of God inaugurated in Jesus will be established in fact in the eschaton when the intransitive will give way to the transitive at the direction of Christ himself and not before.[82] Peter, then, becomes paradigmatic of every Christian: a believer invited to live between the future victory of God inaugurated in Christ and its actual eschatological realization. In the meantime, Peter must readjust his expectation to conform with a life of humility and service. In differing formulations, Jesus instructs Peter to "feed my sheep," shepherding being associated with loyalty, persistence, and circumscribed sacrificial bravery rather than grandiose achievement.

Peter's error consisted of supposing that the moment of comic resolution had arrived or was on the verge of doing so, a future kingdom to be inaugurated at the point of a sword. The rift between Jesus's superior understanding of God's purposes and his own sense of mission as one sent by the Father to submit to and do his will, and Peter's perceptions of them provides the clash of frames of reference necessary for comedy.

V. D. 5 Comedy and Christianity

The general comic pattern of Christianity has long been recognized: moving from the confusion of present circumstances to some kind of unified, joyful future state, as Dante did in his *Divine Comedy*. But other connections between comedy and Christianity exist that might be usefully explored.

The first is the connection between the traditional end of a comedy—marriage and a feast—and their analogs in Christian theology. Revelation 19:7 speaks of the "wedding of the Lamb has come, and his bride has made herself ready" and 19:9 speaks of those who are "invited to the wedding supper of the Lamb." These verses are surrounded by an immediate context of joy and celebration. Wedding imagery also appears in 21:2 and 21:9, again in a context of joy and celebration.

---

[82] This reinforces the connection of chapter 21 with the rest of the book. Had the FG ended at 20:31, the resulting transitive ending would seem premature and out of place with the disciples' need to continue after Jesus's departure.

The second connection between comedy and Christianity to be explored is much less familiar: the connection between laughter and the resurrection. Recall that the structure of comedy is the juxtaposition of one frame of reference with another, the universal structure of jokes. But this mental juxtaposition has a very curious effect—laughter. Laughter is so common that we do not think about it much, but the physical manifestations of laughter are very strange indeed: unexpected movements, peculiar sounds, altered breathing, behavior that can easily be seen as outlandish, even bizarre. These changes from not-laughter to laughter can be summarized as moving from a state of non-animation to animation, from normal behavior to extraordinary behavior, from stasis to joy.

A parallel can easily be drawn to the Christian doctrine of the resurrection wherein one state of affairs—death—is suddenly and decisively transformed in to another state of affairs—life, not simply a return to normal life, but transformed into a kind of super life lived to its fullest in glorified bodies. Thus, the sudden juxtaposition of two frames of reference in a joke that results in the physical transformation of laughter is parallel to the sudden change from one condition or frame of reference to a more animated condition in the resurrection. Both rely on a sudden change of conditions and both result in sudden, decisive physical transformation. If this line of thinking is continued, then jokes and laughter are signs that anticipate that future event where human life will be transformed into something better, an event where the wiping away of tears and the end of suffering are made available now, if only for a moment, in the present experience of laughter.

The third connection between comedy and Christianity concerns the issue of laughter in heaven, for if laughter points to the resurrection, the resurrection also points to the end of laughter. Recall that laughter relies on the juxtaposition of one frame of reference with another, or moving from seeing things in one way to seeing them in another way that is richer and superior, or viewed another way, from ignorance to knowledge. If heaven is about seeing things more fully and clearly and possibly without ignorance, the context for humor is called into question as is even the possibility of humor and laughter based on humor. Laughter based on joy is certainly possible, but laughter based on humor may be a thing of the past.[83] How can laughter exist when it arises from the clash of frames of reference and in heaven God will be the one and only frame of reference?

Unsettling as it may be, this line of thought can be further supported. Even on earth, although humor and laughter are important, we do not normally think of humor as the highest form of human activity. Dinners with friends where everyone laughs are great, but not nearly as satisfying as conversations that move beyond humor. In the movie theater, dramas are inherently more moving and profound than comedies. On earth, the intense closeness of human relationships is analogous to the perichoretic relationship of Father, Son, and Holy Spirit. If heaven is about sharing the intra-Trinitarian life of God, then humor seems suddenly out of place. Heaven is the presence of God and will have greater sources of delight than a stand-up comic, a microphone, and a brick wall.

---

[83] I owe the clarification of laughter based on humor and laughter based on joy to my colleague Jack Painter.

V. E Conclusion

The character of Peter has been shown to follow a recognizable pattern of identification with Jesus, self-induced estrangement with Jesus, and restoration to service. This pattern illustrates the fundamental pattern of comedy: that of being at odds with reality, or a clash of frames of reference, and a movement forward toward a future integration of beliefs with reality. Additionally, comedy has a greater emphasis on character than plot corresponding to greater emphasis on freedom and openness than tragedy. The study of Peter as an archetypal comic character both illumines the character of Peter in its own right, but also supports and casts new light on his role as illustrating a certain path of discipleship. To the degree that Peter displays the discipleship theme and the comic archetype, this pattern lends support to the inclusion of chapter 21 as fundamental to the unity of the FG. Most importantly, the archetypal comic pattern of confusion followed by resolution and joy finds its theological and ontological basis in the act of God in raising Jesus from the dead.

6

Conclusion

VI. A Retrospect

Leland Ryken's remark that "the Bible is an indispensable book for anyone who wishes to understand literature"[1] signals a kind of conclusion, but it might just as easily have marked a beginning. Even if Ryken intended his statement to be confined to the Bible in its importance as a historical and cultural document, its implications in the present work have been extended to the Bible as a work of theology that claims to interpret all of reality of which literature is a part. But, taking into account the Bible as a work of literature, Ryken's statement might well be modified to read, "An understanding of literature is indispensable for anyone who wishes to understand the Bible." Some Biblical scholarship has indeed suffered by neglect of this fact. Conversely, T. S. Eliot noted that "literary Criticism should be completed by criticism from a definite ethical and theological standpoint,"[2] meaning that literature cannot escape the influence of theology. Thus, literature and theology do not merely interact when a given interpreter chooses to do so—they interact, implicitly or explicitly, because it is impossible to do otherwise.

The principle of reciprocity has been applied to literature and theology in the present study in an effort to explore the broad contours where this interaction takes place at a given set of reference points. Archetypal criticism provides the broad outlines of the interaction while Jesus, Pilate, Thomas, the Jews, and Peter provide the specific and living reference points. The present work presents a sustained effort to place theology and literature in dialogue with each other in a way that, it is hoped, is both meaningful and illuminating for both disciplines. Just as the opening words of the FG assert that Jesus is "the Word made flesh," it may be seen that these characters in the FG are words made flesh in their own way according to patterns suggested by archetypal criticism and analogous to patterns they manifest in themselves.

Jesus himself provides the central reference point defining the other characters and indeed all of reality. The conceptual variable defining the differences between each archetype is the relationship between beliefs or values and reality or experience. The differences may be characterized by representation for Jesus and romance; reduction for Pilate and tragedy; negation for Thomas, the Jews and irony; and integration for Peter and comedy.

---

[1] Ryken, *Triumphs of the Imagination*, 199.
[2] Eliot, "Religion and Literature," 388.

VI. B Review

Jesus, as a character typical of romance, is the archetypal hero, the one who simultaneously embodies and displays ideals which are held to be true and worthy of emulation. Emphasizing the marvelous and vertical causality, the story of the hero offers an episodic account of the hero's adventures wherein the hero's identity with an ideal and the maintenance and display of that identity and ideal occurs in a context of challenges and difficulties. The hero is one who exceeds reality or the pressure of circumstances and maintains an ideal or belief worthy of death. The identification of the hero with the ideal is such that maintaining the ideal is synonymous with preservation of the self. The open and episodic nature of the romance allows encounters with a variety of other characters defined by their responses to the hero and the ideals that the hero embodies. Just romance is, for Frye, the structural core of all fiction, in the FG Jesus is the structural core of all reality. Pilate, Thomas, the Jews, and Peter are archetypal responses to Jesus in terms of both theology and literary mode of emplotment.

In tragedy, the unity of beliefs and circumstance assumed in romance comes apart, exemplified in the tragic hero. An analysis of the narrative of Pilate in the FG reveals a series of shifting circumstantial and conceptual contexts, contexts that continually move into the future as the uncomprehending Pilate continually fails to grasp the dynamics of the present. Only when it is too late to extricate himself from the situation according to conventional notions of pragmatic action does Pilate realize his true predicament, effecting a tragic recognition and reversal. Aristotle's *Poetics*, itself the foundational work for tragic criticism, formed the basis of an analysis of Pilate according to Aristotle's notions of fear and pity, catharsis, plot, character, and *hamartia*. As outlined by Hegel and developed by Scheler, tragedy displays a tragic clash between opposites having at least some claim to legitimacy united in a causal nexus between a character and values latent in circumstance. A violation of the moral order, whether committed by the tragic protagonist or not, exposes contradictions in present circumstances and results in the hero's destruction. The power of circumstances, expressed in plot as the vehicle of necessity, causes a fundamental divide between a tragic protagonist and a system of beliefs, yet the moral order contingent on God or transcendent beliefs remains. Given the profoundly theological nature of Pilate's encounter with Jesus coupled with its occurrence within the machinery of concrete reality, Pilate exemplifies tragic themes and characteristics. The separation of beliefs and circumstance inaugurated in tragedy anticipates a realized further separation inherent in irony.

Irony is a key feature of the FG, but can never be taken simply as a literary device and must be taken as derivative of its theology. Irony was explored in relation to its embodiment in the characters of Thomas and the Jews as representative of variations on an ironic point of view. Thomas, distinguished from the other disciples in chapters 20 and 11, comments on the death of Lazarus, "Let us go, that we may die with him," a comment that may be taken as ironic with "him" referring to Lazarus. Perception of this remark as ironic, however, entails identifying with Thomas and participating in his ironic blindness, a blindness resulting in his refusal to believe. The Jews embody a tendency toward philosophical and cultural irony characterized by material reality and disbelief in which they repeatedly interpret Jesus and his remarks in a way dominated by earthly and literalistic concerns. Whatever form irony takes, be it verbal, dramatic, and so on, its perception and use requires a value judgment of some kind, a judgment inevitably bound up with questions of value and belief. In this light, irony may then be divided into positive, equivocal, and negative irony. While irony in the FG is generally positive in that it operates from a stable theological base, Thomas and the Jews function as explorations of equivocal and negative irony, respectively. Equivocal irony features a sense of ambiguity with respect to the relationship of beliefs and circumstance whereas the sense of the triumph of experience over values and beliefs pervades negative irony, one in which the notion of meaning itself tends to become problematic and where detachment and stasis predominate.

Comedy features a movement toward the reintegration of experience with values and beliefs, a movement characteristic of Peter in the FG. By the end of chapter 6, the FG presents Peter as someone on the inside, a committed believer and follower of Jesus commanding a well-developed understanding of who Jesus is. But Peter's understanding of what it means to be obedient to God takes a triumphalist turn at odds with Jesus's example and teaching. The post-resurrection accounts detail Peter's reinstatement and point to a more sober assessment of what it means to be a follower of Jesus. After the manner of comedy, Peter displays mistakes and misunderstandings as his frame of reference for interpreting that his experience collides with reality and then is replaced with another. Unlike tragedy with its emphasis on plot and necessity, in comedy the emphasis falls on contingency, character, and freedom. A character's beliefs, freely chosen but mistaken, move the action toward its conclusion. In tragedy, normality is past but continues as ironic commentary on the present, while in comedy, normality, in which experience is integrated with beliefs, continues as a realistic hope for the future. With its tenuous incongruity between beliefs and reality, comedy continues as long as there is no decisive contact with reality. To be truly comic, the reality achieved must be desirable. Comedy may be divided into transitive and intransitive comedies, the desirable comic reality being achieved in the former where in the latter it is not, however much that desirable reality remains implicit and possible.

VI. C Results

The interaction presented here demonstrates the value of this type of extended, systematic comparisons. While it may be wide of the mark to speak of new discoveries, it is nevertheless possible to point to new or fresh angles of interpretation or clarification of those already present. Exploring and defining romance and tragedy should, it is hoped, establish the case for interpreting Jesus according to romance rather than incorrectly according to tragedy. Employing tragedy to interpret Pilate offers a new perspective and brings to light the shifting interpretative contexts of the trial narrative. Pilate is irreducibly a dynamic character incompatible with reductionist tendencies inherent in either weak or strong ironic readings. Interpreting Thomas according to irony provides the conceptual framework to more accurately interpret certain statements and by which to anticipate other exegetical data, which, taken together, bring out the full depth and coherence of his character and his character's function within the FG as a whole. With regard to the Jews as the collective character displaying unbelief, this accepted interpretation has been more adequately situated within the theology and purpose of the FG. Comedy as an archetype provides an overall coherence to Peter's character and allows for a deeper appreciation of his role in displaying the theme of discipleship in the FG. The coherence of Peter suggested by the discipleship theme and by comedy supports the unity of the FG with respect to the status of chapter 21. Additionally and significantly, archetypal criticism helps to locate all of these particular characters within the literary and theological world of the FG and in doing so offers a way in which each character may be understood in relation to the location of other characters within that same world. Identification with one or more of the characters serves to locate the reader within the world defined by the FG.

To the extent the archetypal criticism illuminates these characters with respect to both the literature and theology of the FG, the validity of archetypal criticism is reinforced and enhanced, both in its own right and also as a means of exchange between literary studies on the one hand and Biblical and theological studies on the other. For example, comparisons of Peter with Don Quixote, however justified on their own without reference to archetypes, receive additional validity by similarity to an archetype of ubiquitous scope. Conversely, an archetype may suggest common themes and also suggest helpful, illuminating comparisons perhaps otherwise overlooked, as, for example, in the comparison between Thomas and the arch-ironist Mr. Bennet and between the paralytic at the pool in John 5 and *Waiting for Godot*. Archetypal criticism places comparisons of the FG with literature outside the FG on a more systematic basis. The present work offers a detailed examination of the form and content of these four major archetypes from and within a Christian worldview and with reference to characters in a specific Biblical text that renders literary analysis according to vague and ill-defined notions of comedy or tragedy or according to the simplistic designations ⌣ and ⌢, if they were ever adequate, no longer acceptable.

In addition, the present work has been so bold as to suggest Christian theology and the Christian meta-narrative as the theological and ontological basis for the overall coherence of archetypal criticism in general and the basis for romance, tragedy, irony, and comedy in particular. The implication is that these archetypes cannot be dismissed as anachronistic tools of contemporary literary criticism; rather, they express something fundamentally timeless and fundamentally true about the world itself.

VI. D Prospects

Two prospects growing out of the present work may be suggested. First with regard to the audience of the FG, the reassessment of Gospel audiences by Bauckham and others questions the assumption that the Gospels were, supposedly, directed to isolated and specific "communities."[3] Expanding the trajectory of this reassessment, to the extent that the presence of universal archetypes within the FG suggested by the present work

---

[3] Richard Bauckham, ed., *The Gospels for All Christians: Rethinking the Gospel Audiences* (Edinburgh: T&T Clark, 1988).

points to and clarifies a wider and more universal reading of the FG, any sort of narrow and restricted reading of the FG and its audience is rendered less and less credible. In terms of both literature and theology, the FG is a work of some sophistication not easily reducible to sectarian concerns.

Second, on a related point, while the present concern has been with the interaction of literature and theology by means of archetypal criticism, such an analysis suggests the inclusion of history within a framework beyond that adopted here. This is not so much to suggest the application of narrative forms to history as has been helpfully explored by White, but to suggest a model of interpretation and hermeneutics based around the three components of history, literature, and theology. As Sternberg notes in relation to OT narrative, "Biblical narrative emerges as a complex, because multifunctional, discourse. Functionally speaking, it is regulated by a set of three principles: ideological, historiographic, and aesthetic. How they cooperate is a tricky question."[4] With respect to the FG or any other Biblical text, these three elements may be readily termed the *theological*, *historical*, and *literary*, respectively. Significantly, Brodie classifies the history of Johannine studies according to an emphasis on the theological, historical, and literary,[5] and this classification may be extended to Biblical studies in general. Given the current challenges in hermeneutics, whatever the appropriate weight given to each factor in particular instances, the way ahead may well include a proper appreciation of each.

---

[4] Meir Sternberg. *The Poetics of Biblical Narrative: Ideological Literature and the Drama of Reading* (Bloomington, IN: Indiana University Press, 1985), 41.

[5] Thomas Brodie, *The Gospel According to John: A Literary and Theological Commentary* (New York: Oxford University Press, 1993), 3–10.

Bibliography

Adam, Andrew. *What is Postmodern Biblical Criticism*. Minneapolis: Fortress Press, 1995.
Allot, Miriam. *Novelists on the Novel*. London: Routledge and Kegan Paul, 1959.
Allyn, Leo. *Greek Tragedy and the Modern World*. London: Methuen, 1964.
Alter, Robert. *The Art of Biblical Narrative*. New York: Basic Books, 1981.
Aristotle. *Aristotle's Poetics*. Translated by S. H. Butcher and introduction by Francis Fergusson. New York: Hill and Wang, 1961.
Aristotle. *The Art of Rhetoric*. Translated by and introduction by H. C. Lawson-Tancred. New York: Penguin, 1991.
Ashton, John. *Studying John: Approaches to the Fourth Gospel*. Oxford: Clarendon, 1994.
Auerbach, Erich. *Mimesis: The Representation of Reality in Western Literature*. Princeton: Princeton University Press, 1953.
Auerbach, Erich. *Scenes from the Drama of European Literature*. Gloucester, MA: Peter Smith, 1973. Includes 'Figura,' translated by Ralph Manheim, 11–76.
Austen, Jane. *Pride and Prejudice*, Norton Critical Edition, 3rd edition. Edited by Donald Gray. New York and London: W.W. Norton, 2001.
Baker, Herschel, ed. *Four Essays on Romance*. Cambridge, MA: Harvard University Press, 1971.
Barrett, C. K. *Essays on John*. London: SPCK, 1982.
Barrett, C. K. *The Gospel According to John: An Introduction with Commentary and Notes on the Greek Text*. London: SPCK, 1978.
Bartholomew, Craig, Colin Greene, and Karl Moller, eds. *Renewing Biblical Interpretation*, the Scripture and Hermeneutics Series volume 1. Carlisle: Paternoster Press, 2000.
Bauckham, Richard. 'Jesus' Demonstration in the Temple,' in *Law and Religion: Essays on the Place of the Law in Israel and Early Christianity*. Edited by Barnabas Lindars. Cambridge: James Clarke, 1988, 72–89.
Bauckham, Richard. 'The Beloved Disciple as Ideal Author,' *JSNT* 49 (1993): 34–39.
Bauckham, Richard, ed. *The Gospels for All Christians: Rethinking the Gospel Audiences*. Edinburgh: T&T Clark, 1998.
Beardslee, William A. *Literary Criticism of the New Testament*. Guides to Biblical Scholarship. Philadelphia: Fortress Press, 1970.
Beasley-Murray, G. R. *John*. Waco: Word Books, 1987.
Beck, David. 'The Narrative Function of Anonymity in Fourth Gospel Characterization,' *Semeia* 63 (1993): 143–55.
Beckett, Samuel. *Waiting for Godot: A Tragicomedy in Two Acts*. London: Faber and Faber, 1956.
Beer, Gillian. *The Romance*. London: Methuen & Co., 1970.
Benoit, P. *The Passion and Resurrection of Jesus*. London: Darton, Longman & Todd, 1969.
Bergson, Henri. *Laughter: An Essay on the Meaning of the Comic*. Translated by Cloudesley Brereton. London: Macmillan, 1911.
Bilstein, Elmer M. *Comedy in Action*. Durham, NC: Duke University Press, 1964.
Blair, Tony. *Sunday Telegraph*, April 7, 1996. Cited in Ann Wroe, *Pilate: The Biography of an Invented Man*. London: Jonathan Cape, 1999, 208.

Boice, James M. *Witness and Revelation in the Gospel of John*. Grand Rapids: Zondervan, 1970.
Bond, Helen K. *Pontius Pilate in History and Interpretation*. Cambridge: Cambridge University Press, 1998.
Booth, Wayne C. *The Rhetoric of Fiction*, 2nd edition. Chicago and London: The University of Chicago Press, 1961.
Booth, Wayne C. *The Rhetoric of Irony*. Chicago: University of Chicago Press, 1974.
Borkland, Elmer, ed. *Contemporary Literary Critics*. London: St. James Press, 1977.
Bouchard, Larry D. *Tragic Method and Tragic Theology: Evil in Contemporary Drama and Religious Thought*. University Park and London: The Pennsylvania State University Press, 1989.
Boulton, Marjorie. *The Anatomy of the Novel*. London: Routledge and Kegan Paul, 1975.
Bradley, A. C. 'Hegel's Theory of Tragedy,' in *Oxford Lectures on Poetry*. London: Macmillan, 1919, 70–95.
Bradley, A. C. *Shakespearean Tragedy: Lectures on Hamlet, Othello, King Lear, and Macbeth*. London: Penguin Books, 1904.
Brant, Jo-Ann A. *Dialogue and Drama: Elements of Greek Tragedy in the Fourth Gospel*. Peabody, MA: Hendrickson, 2004.
Brereton, Geoffrey. *Principles of Tragedy: A Rational Examination of the Tragic Concept in Life and Literature*. London: Routledge & K. Paul, 1968.
Brodie, Thomas. *The Gospel According to John: A Literary and Theological Commentary*. New York: Oxford University Press, 1993.
Brody, Baruch, ed. *Readings in the Philosophy of Religion: An Analytic Approach*, 2nd edition. Englewood Cliffs, NJ: Prentice Hall, 1992.
Brooks, Cleanth, ed. *Tragic Themes in Western Literature*. New Haven: Yale, 1955.
Brown, Raymond. *The Gospel According to John*. 2 vol. New York: Doubleday, 1966–70.
Brown, Raymond, Karl Donfried, and John Reumann, eds. *Peter in the New Testament*. London: Geoffrey Chapman, 1974.
Bruce, F. F. *The Gospel of John*. Basingstoke, UK: Pickering Paperbacks, 1983.
Brunel, Pierre, ed. *Companion to Literary Myths, Heroes and Archetypes*. Translated by Wendy Allatson, Judith Hayward, and Trista Selous. London and New York: Routledge, 1992.
Buechner, Fredrick. *Telling the Truth: The Gospel as Tragedy, Comedy, and Fairy Tale*. San Francisco: Harper and Row, 1977.
Bultmann, R. *The Gospel of John: A Commentary*. Oxford: Blackwell, 1971.
Burridge, Richard. *What are the Gospels? A Comparison with Greco-Roman Biography*. Cambridge: Cambridge University Press, 1992.
Burrow, Colin. *Epic Romance: Homer to Milton*. Oxford: Clarendon Press, 1993.
Bush, Frederic. *Ruth, Esther*. Dallas: Word Books, 1996.
Byrne, Brendan. 'The Faith of the Beloved Disciple and the Community in John 20,' *JSNT* 23 (1985): 83–97.
Cahill, P. J. 'The Johannine *Logos* as Center,' *Catholic Biblical Quarterly* 38 (1976): 54–72.
Caird, G. B. *The Language and Imagery of the Bible*. London: Duckworth, 1980.
Campbell, Joseph. *The Hero with a Thousand Faces*, 2nd edition. Princeton: Princeton University Press, 1968.
Carlyle, Thomas. *Sator Resartus and on Heroes and Hero Worship*. London: Dent, 1965.
Carson, D. A. 'Current Source-Criticism of the Fourth Gospel: Some Methodological Questions,' *JBL* 97 (1978): 411–29.
Carson, D. A. *Divine Sovereignty and Human Responsibility: Biblical Perspectives in Tension*. Atlanta: John Knox Press, 1981.

Carson, D. A. *The Gospel According to John*. Grand Rapids: Eerdmans, 1991.
Carson, D. A. 'The Purpose of the Fourth Gospel: John 30:31 Reconsidered,' *JBL* 106 (1987): 639-51.
Carson, D. A. 'Understanding Misunderstandings in the Fourth Gospel,' *Tyndale Bulletin* 33 (1982): 59-91.
Casey, John. 'A 'Science' of Criticism: Northrop Frye,' chapter VII in *The Language of Criticism*. London: Methuen & Co., 1966, 140-51.
Catron, Louis E. *The Elements of Playwriting*. New York: Collier, 1993.
Charney, Maurice. *Comedy High and Low: An Introduction to the Experience of Comedy*. New York: Oxford University Press, 1978.
Chatman, Seymour. *Story and Discourse: Narrative Structure in Fiction and Film*. Ithaca, NY: Cornell University Press, 1978.
Chesterton, G. K. *Orthodoxy*. London: John Lane, 1909.
Collins, Raymond. 'The Representative Figures of the Fourth Gospel,' *The Downside Review* 94 (1976): 26-46; 95 (1976): 118-32. Reprinted in *These Things Have Been Written: Studies in the Fourth Gospel*. Grand Rapids: Eerdmans, 1990.
Cook, Albert. *The Dark Voyage and the Golden Mean*. Cambridge, MA: Harvard University Press, 1949.
Cooper, Lane. *An Aristotelian Theory of Comedy*. Oxford: Blackwell, 1924.
Cornford, Francis. *The Origin of Attic Comedy*. London: Edward Arnold, 1914.
Corrigan, Robert. *Comedy: Meaning and Form*. San Francisco: Chandler, 1965.
Cullmann, Oscar. *Peter: Disciple, Apostle, Martyr*. Translated by Floyd Filson. London: SCM Press, 1962.
Culpepper, R. Alan. *Anatomy of the Fourth Gospel: A Study in Literary Design*. Philadelphia: Fortress Press, 1983.
Culpepper, R. Alan, ed. *Critical Readings of John 6*. Leiden, New York and Koln: Brill, 1997.
Culpepper, R. Alan. 'The Fourth Gospel from a Literary Perspective,' *Semeia*. Edited by R. Alan Culpepper and Fernando F. Segovia 53 (1991): 1-212.
Culpepper, R. Alan. 'Reading Johannine Irony,' in *Exploring the Gospel of John: In Honor of D. Moody Smith*. Edited by R. Alan Culpepper and C. Clifton Black, Louisville: Westminster John Knox Press, 1996, 193-207.
Davies, Margaret. *Rhetoric and Reference in the Fourth Gospel*. JSNT Supplement Series 69. Sheffield: Sheffield Academic Press, 1992.
Dawana, E. *Which Side of the Line: The Non-Jewish Characters in the Fourth Gospel*. unpublished PhD diss., University of Durham, 1997.
de Troyes, Chretien. *The Complete Romances of Chretien de Troyes*. Translated with an introduction by David Staines. Bloomington and Indianapolis: Indiana University Press, 1990.
Dean, John. *Restless Wanderers: Shakespeare and the Pattern of Romance*. Salzburg: Salzburg Studies in English Literature 86, 1979.
Deil, Paul. *Symbolism in the Gospel of John*. Translated by Nelly Marans. San Francisco: Harper and Row, 1983.
Dickens, Charles. *David Copperfield*. Afterward by Edgar Johnson. London: Signet Classic, 1962.
Dipple, Elizabeth. *Plot*. London: Methuen & Co, 1970.
Docherty, Thomas. *Reading (Absent) Character: Towards a Theory of Characterization in Fiction*. Oxford: Clarendon Press, 1983.
Drakakis, John, ed. *Shakespearean Tragedy*. London and New York: Longman, 1992.
Draper, R. P. *Tragedy: Developments in Criticism*. London: Macmillan, 1980.
Duke, Paul. *Irony in the Fourth Gospel*. Atlanta: John Knox, 1985.

Dyson, A. E. *The Crazy Fabric: Essays in Irony*. London: Macmillan and Co., 1965.
Ehrman, B. D. 'Jesus' Trial before Pilate: John 18:28-19:16,' *BTB* 13 (1983): 124-31.
Eliot, T. S., 'Religion and Literature,' in *Selected Essays*. London: Faber, 1951, 388-401.
Else, Gerald. *Aristotle's Poetics: The Argument*. Cambridge, MA: Harvard University Press, 1957.
Else, Gerald. *The Origin and Form of Greek Tragedy*. Cambridge, MA: Harvard University Press, 1965.
Erasmus, Desiderius. *The Praise of Folly*. Translated by with introduction by Hoyt Hopewell Hudson. Princeton: Princeton University Press, 1941.
Exum, Cheryl J. *Tragedy and Biblical Narrative: Arrows of the Almighty*. Cambridge: Cambridge University Press, 1992.
Exum, J. Cheryl, and J. William Whedbee. 'Isaac, Samson, and Saul: Reflections on the Comic and Tragic Visions,' *Semeia* 32 (1984): 5-37.
Fergusson, Francis. *The Idea of a Theater*. Princeton: Princeton University Press, 1949.
Fish, Stanley. 'Discovery as Form in *Paradise Lost*,' reprinted in *Surprised by Sin: The Reader in Paradise Lost*, 2nd edition. Houndmills, Basingstoke, Hampshire, and London: Macmillan, 1997, 340-56.
Fish, Stanley. *Surprised by Sin: The Reader in Paradise Lost*, 2nd edition. Houndmills, Basingstoke, Hampshire, and London: Macmillan, 1997.
Flack, Colin. *Myth, Truth, and Literature: Towards a True Post-Modernism*, 2nd edition. Cambridge: Cambridge University Press, 1989.
Fletcher, Angus. *Allegory: The Theory of a Symbolic Mode*. Ithaca and London: Cornell University Press, 1964.
Ford, David. 'Tragedy and Atonement,' in *Christ, Ethics, and Tragedy: Essays in Honor of Donald MacKinnon*. Edited by Kenneth Surin, Cambridge: Cambridge University Press, 1989, 117-30.
Ford, Josephine Massyngbaerde. 'Jesus as Sovereign in the Passion According to John,' *BTB* 25 (1995): 110-17.
Forster, E. M. *Aspects of the Novel*. London: Edward Arnold, 1927.
Frei, Hans W. *The Eclipse of Biblical Narrative: A Study in Eighteenth and Nineteenth Century Hermeneutics*. New Haven, CT and London: Yale University Press, 1974.
Frein, Brigid. 'Fundamentalism and Narrative Approaches to the Gospels,' *BTB* 22 (1992): 12-17.
Freud, Sigmund. *Jokes and their Relation to the Unconscious*. Translated and edited by James Strachey. London: Routledge & Kegan Paul, 1960.
Fry, William. *Sweet Madness: A Study of Humor*. Palo Alto, CA: Pacific Books, 1968.
Frye, Northrop. *Anatomy of Criticism: Four Essays*. Princeton, NJ: Princeton University Press, 1957.
Frye, Northrop. *Fables of Identity: Studies in Poetic Mythology*. New York: Harcourt, Brace & World, 1963.
Frye, Northrop. *The Great Code: The Bible and Literature*. London, Melbourne and Henley: Routledge & Kegan Paul, 1982.
Frye, Northrop. *A Natural Perspective: The Development of Shakespearean Comedy and Romance*. San Diego, New York and London: Harcourt Brace Javonovich, 1965.
Frye, Northrop. *The Secular Scripture: A Study of the Structure of Romance*. London: Harvard University Press, 1976.
Frye, Northrop. 'The Story of All Things,' in *The Return of Eden: Five Essays on Milton's Epics*. Toronto: University of Toronto Press, 1965, 3-31. Reprinted in, edited by Scott Elledge. Paradise Lost: An Authoritative Text Backgrounds and Sources Criticism. New York and London: W. W. Norton, 1975, 405-22.

Frye, Northrop. 'Vision and Cosmos,' in *Biblical Patterns in Modern Literature*. Edited by David Hirsch and Nehama Aschkenasy, Chico, CA: Scholars Press, 1984, 5–17.
Fuller, Reginald. 'The Jews in the Fourth Gospel,' *Dialogue* 16 (1977): 31–37.
Gall, Robert. 'Toward a Tragic Theology: The Piety of Thought in Heidegger and Tragedy,' *Journal of Literature and Theology* 7, no. 1 (March 1993): 13–32.
Gans, Eric. *Signs of Paradox: Irony, Resentment, and Other Mimetic Structures*. Stanford: Stanford University Press, 1997.
Gerhart, Mary, and Anthony C. Yu. *Morphologies of Faith: Essays in Religion and Culture in Honor of Nathan A. Scott, Jr*. Atlanta: Scholars, 1990.
Giblin, C. H. 'John's Narration of the Hearing Before Pilate (John 18:28-19:16a),' *Biblica* 67 (1986): 221–39.
Giblin, C. H. 'Suggestion, Negative Response, and Positive Action in St. John's Portrayal of Jesus (2:1-11; 4:46-54; 7:2-14; 11:1-44),' *NTS* (January 26, 1980): 197–211.
Goffman, Erving. *Frame Analysis: An Essay on the Organization of Experience*. Cambridge, MA: Harvard University Press, 1974.
Goldman, Stan. 'Narrative and Ethical Ironies in Esther,' *JSOT* 47 (1990): 15–31.
Good, Edwin. 'Apocalyptic as Comedy: The Book of Daniel,' *Semeia: Tragedy and Comedy in the Bible* 32 (1984): 41–70.
Good, Edwin. *Irony in the Old Testament*. Philadelphia: The Westminster Press, 1965.
Gurewitch, Morton. *Comedy: The Irrational Vision*. Ithaca, NY: Cornell University Press, 1975.
Gutwirth, Marcel. *Laughing Matter: An Essay on the Comic*. Ithaca and London: Cornell University Press, 1993.
Hägerland, Tobias. 'John's Gospel: A Two-Level Drama?' *JSNT* 25, no. 3 (2003): 309–22.
Hall, George. 'Tragedy in the Theology of P. T. Forsyth,' in *Justice the True and Only Mercy*. Edited by Trevor Hart, Edinburgh: T&T Clark, 1995, 77–104.
Halliwell, Stephen. 'Human Limits and the Religion of Greek Tragedy,' *Journal of Literature and Theology* 4 (July 1990): 169–80.
Harris, Elizabeth. *Prologue and Gospel: The Theology of the Fourth Evangelist*. JSNTSS 107. Sheffield: Sheffield Academic Press, 1994.
Hart, Trevor, ed. *Justice: The True and Only Mercy: Essays on the Life and Theology of Peter Taylor Forsyth*. Edinburgh: T&T Clark, 1995.
Hart, Trevor. *Regarding Karl Barth: Essays Toward an Understanding of his Theology*. Carlisle: Paternoster, 1999.
Hartman, Geoffrey. 'Ghostlier Demarcations: The Sweet Science of Northrop Frye,' in *Beyond Formalism: Literary Essays 1958-1970*. New Haven and London: Yale University Press, 1970, 24–41.
Harvey, A. E. *Jesus on Trial: A Study in the Fourth Gospel*. London: SPCK, 1976.
Harvey, W. J. *Character in the Novel*. London: Chatto & Windus, 1965.
Hauser, Gertrud, Carlo Aldo, Cappellini, Guidotti Assunta, Rothganger Hartmut and Vienna Alessandro.'The Biology of Laughter. Medical, Functional, and Anthropological-Human Ethological Aspects,' in *Laughter Down the Centuries vol. III*. Edited by Siegfried Jakel, Asko Timonen, and Veli-Matti Rissanen, Turku, Finland: Turun Yliopisto, 1997.
Hebblethwaite, Brian. 'Mackinnon and the Problem of Evil,' in *Christ, Ethics, and Tragedy: Essays in Honor of Donald Mackinnon*. Edited by Kenneth Surin, Cambridge: Cambridge University Press, 1989, 117–30.
Hegel, G. W. F. *Aesthetics: Lectures on Fine Art*. Translated by T. M. Knox. Oxford: Clarendon Press, 1975.

Heliodorus. *Ethiopian Story*. Translated by Sir Walter Lamb. London: J. M. Dent and Sons, 1961.
Henn, T. R. *The Bible as Literature*. London: Lutterworth Press, 1970.
Henn, T. R. *The Harvest of Tragedy*. London: Methuen, 1956.
Hesla, David. 'Greek and Christian Tragedy: Notes Toward a Theology of Literary History,' *JAAR Thematic Studies*, XLIX, no. 2 (1983): 71–87.
Hick, John. *The Metaphor of God Incarnate*. London: SCM Press, 1993.
Hitchcock, F. R. M. 'Is the Fourth Gospel a Drama?' *Theology* 7 (1923): 307–17. Reprinted in Mark Stibbe ed. *The Gospel of John as Literature: An Anthology of Twentieth-Century Perspectives*. NT tools and studies 17. Leiden, New York, Koln: E. J. Brill, 1993, 15–24.
Hoehner, H. W. 'Pilate,' in *Dictionary of Jesus and the Gospels*. Edited by Joel B. Green, Scot McKnight, and I. Howard Marshall, Downers Grove: InterVarsity, 1992, 615–17.
Holman, C. Hugh. *A Handbook to Literature*, 4th edition. Indianapolis: Bobbs-Merrill Educational Publishing, 1980.
Hoskyns, E. C. *The Fourth Gospel*. Edited by F. N. Davey, London: Faber and Faber, 1947.
Hume, David. 'Of Tragedy,' in *Essays: Moral, Political, and Literary*. Oxford: Oxford University Press, 1963, 216–25.
Hutcheon, Linda. *Irony's Edge: The Theory and Politics of Irony*. London and New York: Routledge, 1994.
Jameson, Fredric. 'Magical Narratives: Romance as Genre,' *New Literary History* 7 (1975): 135–63.
Jasper, David. *The Study of Literature and Religion: An Introduction*. Basingstoke, Hampshire, and London: Macmillan Press, 1989.
Jasper, David and Stephen Prickett, eds. *The Bible and Literature: A Reader*. Malden, MA: Blackwell, 1999.
Jemielity, Thomas. 'The Prophetic Character: Good, Heroic, and Naive,' *Literature and Theology* 5, no. 1 (March 1991): 37–48.
Jonson, Ben. *The Complete Plays of Ben Jonson*, vol. I. London: J. M. Dent, 1910.
Josephus. *The Complete Works*. Translated by William Whiston. London and Glasgow: Pickering & Inglis, 1960.
Joyce, James. *A Portrait of the Artist as a Young Man*. Edited by R. B. Kershner, Boston: Bedford Books of St. Martin's Press, 1993.
Jung, Carl. *Contributions to Analytical Psychology*. Translated by H. G. Baynes and C. F. Baynes. London: Kegan Paul, 1928.
Kaufmann, Walter. *Critique of Religion and Philosophy*. London: Faber and Faber, 1958.
Kaufmann, Walter. *Religions in Four Dimensions: Existential, Aesthetic, Historical, Comparative*. New York: Reader's Digest Press, 1976.
Kaufmann, Walter. *Tragedy and Philosophy*. Princeton: Princeton University Press, 1968.
Kelber, Werner. 'In the Beginning Were the Words: The Apotheosis and Narrative Displacement of the Logos,' *JAAR* 58 (1990): 69–98.
Kelber, Werner. 'The Birth of a Beginning: John 1:1-18,' *Semeia* 52 (1990): 121–44. Reprinted in *The Gospel of John as Literature: An Anthology of Twentieth-Century Perspectives*, ed. Mark Stibbe. New York: E. J. Brill, 1993. 209–30.
Kennedy, George. *New Testament Interpretation Through Rhetorical Criticism*. Chapel Hill: The University of North Carolina Press, 1984.
Ker, W. P. *Epic and Romance: Essays on Medieval Literature*. London: Macmillan and Co., 1926.
Kermode, Frank. *The Genesis of Secrecy: On the Interpretation of Narrative*. The Charles Eliot Norton Lectures, 1977-78. Cambridge, MA: Harvard University Press, 1979.

Kermode, Frank, ed. *The Tempest*, Arden Edition of the Works of William Shakespeare. London: Methuen & Co, 1954.
Kitto, H. D. F. *Form and Meaning in Drama*. London: Methuen, 1956.
Kitto, H. D. F. *Greek Tragedy: A Literary Study*. London: Methuen, 1939.
Knight, G. Wilson. *The Imperial Theme: Further Interpretations of Shakespeare's Tragedies Including the Roman Plays*, 3rd edition. London: Methuen, 1965.
Knight, G. Wilson. *The Wheel of Fire: Interpretations of Shakespearean Tragedy with Three New Essays*, 4th edition. London and New York: Routledge, 1949.
Knights, L. C. *How Many Children Had Lady Macbeth?* Cambridge: The Minority Press, 1933.
Knox, Norman. 'Irony,' in *Dictionary of the History of Ideas*, vol. II. Edited by Maryanne Cline Horowitz. New York: Charles Scribner's Sons, 1973, 626-34.
Knox, Norman. 'On the Classification of Ironies,' *Modern Philology* 70 (1972): 53-62.
Koester, Craig R. 'The Savior of the World: John 4:42,' *JBL* 109 (1990): 665-80.
Koester, Craig R. *Symbolism in the Fourth Gospel: Meaning, Mystery, Community*. Minneapolis: Fortress Press, 1995.
Koestler, Arthur. *The Act of Creation*. London: Hutchinson, 1964.
Koestler, Arthur. *Insight and Outlook*. New York: The Macmillan Company, 1949.
Krieger, Murray. *The Tragic Vision: The Confrontation of Extremity*. Baltimore: The Johns Hopkins University Press, 1960.
Krook, Dorthea. *Elements of Tragedy*. New Haven and London: Yale University Press, 1969.
Kuhn, Thomas *The Essential Tension: Selected Studies in Scientific Tradition and Change*. Chicago and London: The University of Chicago Press, 1977.
Kuhn, Thomas. *The Structure of Scientific Revolutions*, 2nd edition. Chicago: The University of Chicago Press, 1970.
Kuhns, Richard. *Tragedy: Contradiction and Repression*. Chicago and London: The University of Chicago Press, 1991.
Kysar, Robert. *The Fourth Evangelist and His Gospel: An Examination of Contemporary Scholarship*. Minneapolis: Augsburg Publishing House, 1975.
Kysar, Robert. *John's Story of Jesus*. Philadelphia: Fortress Press, 1984.
Langenhorst, Georg. 'The Rediscovery of Jesus as a Literary Figure,' *Literature and Theology* 9, no. 1 (March 1995): 85-98.
Langer, Susan. *Feeling and Form*. New York: Scribner, 1953.
Larkin, K. *Ruth and Esther*. Sheffield: Sheffield Academic Press, 1996.
Lauter, Paul. *Theories of Comedy*. Garden City, NY: Doubleday, Anchor Press, 1964.
Lee, Dorothy. 'Partnership in Easter Faith: The Role of Mary Magdalene and Thomas in John 20,' *JSNT* 58 (1995): 37-49.
Lee, Dorothy. *The Symbolic Narratives of the Fourth Gospel: The Interplay of Form and Meaning*. JSNTSup 95. Sheffield: JSOT, 1994.
Lee, Alvin. 'Archetypal Criticism,' in *Encyclopedia of Contemporary Literary Theory*. Edited by Irena Makaryk. Toronto, Buffalo, and London: University of Toronto Press, 1993: 3-5.
Lee, Alvin. 'Northrop Frye,' in *Encyclopedia of Contemporary Literary Theory*. Edited by Irena Makaryk. Toronto, Buffalo, and London: University of Toronto Press, 1993, 324-25.
Lewis, C. S. *The Allegory of Love: A Study in Medieval Tradition*. Oxford: Oxford University Press, 1936.
Lewis, C. S. *The Discarded Image: An Introduction to Medieval and Renaissance Literature*. Cambridge: Cambridge University Press, 1964.

Liebler, Naomi Conn. *Shakespeare's Festive Tragedy: The Ritual Foundations of Genre*. London and New York: Routledge, 1995.

Lindars, Barnabas. *The Gospel of John*. London: Oliphants, 1972.

Lucas, F. L. *Tragedy: Serious Drama in Relation to Aristotle's Poetics*. New York: Collier Books, 1957.

Mackinnon, Donald. *Borderlands of Theology and Other Essays*. London: Lutterworth Press, 1968.

Maclean, Hugh, ed. *Edmund Spenser's Poetry: Authoritative Texts and Criticism*. New York: W. W. Norton, 1968.

MacRae, George W. 'Theology and Irony in the Fourth Gospel,' in *The Word in the World: Essays in Honor of Frederick L. Moriarity, S.J.* Edited by R. J. Clifford and G. W. MacRae. Cambridge, MA: Weston College Press, 1973. Reprinted in Mark Stibbe, ed. *The Gospel of John as Literature: An Anthology of Twentieth-Century Perspectives*. NT tools and studies 17. Leiden, New York, Koln: E. J. Brill, 1993, 103–13.

Malbon, E. S. *Narrative Space and Mythic Meaning in Mark*. Sheffield: JSOT, 1991.

Marin, Louis. 'Jesus Before Pilate: A Structural Analysis Essay,' in *The New Testament and Structuralism*. Edited and translated by Alfred Johnson. Pittsburg: The Pickwick Press, 1976, 97–143.

Martin, Wallace. *Recent Theories of Narrative*. Ithaca and London: Cornell University Press, 1986.

Maynard, A. H. 'The Role of Peter in the Fourth Gospel,' *NTS* 30 (1984): 531–48.

McFadden, George. *Discovering the Comic*. Princeton: Princeton University Press, 1982.

McFague, Sallie. *Metaphorical Theology: Models of God in Religious Language*. London: SCM Press, 1983.

Meeks, Wayne. 'The Man from Heaven in Johannine Sectarianism,' *JBL* 91 (1972): 44–72.

Merchant, Paul. *The Epic*. London: Methuen & Co., 1971.

Merchant, W. Moelwyn. *Comedy*. London: Methuen & Co., 1972.

Meredith, George. *An Essay on Comedy and the Uses of the Comic Spirit*. London: Constable, 1918.

Metzger, Bruce. *A Textual Commentary on the Greek New Testament*. London: United Bible Societies, 1975.

Michel, Laurence and Richard Sewall, eds. *Tragedy: Modern Essays in Criticism*. Westport, CT: Greenwood, 1963.

Michaels, J. Ramsey. *John*. Peabody, MA: Hendrickson, 1984.

Mincoff, Marco. *Things Supernatural and Causeless: Shakespearean Romance*. London and Toronto: Associated University Presses, 1992.

Minear, Paul S. 'The Original functions of John 21,' *JBL* 102 (1983): 85–98.

Moloney, F. J. *Belief in the Word: Reading John 1-4*. Minneapolis: Fortress Press, 1993.

Moloney, F. J. *The Gospel of John*. Collegeville, MN: The Liturgical Press, 1998.

Moloney, F. J. *Signs and Shadows: Reading John 5-12*. Minneapolis: Fortress Press, 1996.

Moore, Stephen D. 'Are There Impurities in the Living Water that the Johannine Jesus Dispenses? Deconstruction, Feminism, and the Samaritan Woman,' *Biblical Interpretation* 1 (1993): 207–27. Reprinted in *Poststructuralism and the New Testament: Derrida and Foucault at the Foot of the Cross*. Minneapolis: Fortress, 1994, 43–64.

Moore, Stephen D. *Literary Criticism and the Gospels: The Theoretical Challenge*. New Haven, CT: Yale University Press, 1989.

Morris, Leon. *The Gospel According to John*. Grand Rapids: Eerdmans, 1971.

Muecke, D. C. *The Compass of Irony*. London: Methuen & Co., 1969.

Muecke, D. C. *Irony*. London: Methuen & Co., 1970.

Murphy, Francesca Aran. *The Comedy of Revelation: Paradise Lost and Regained in Biblical Narrative*. Edinburgh: T&T Clark, 2000.

Murray, Gilbert. 'An Excursus on the Ritual Forms Preserved in Greek Tragedy,' in *Themis*. Edited by Jane Harrison. Cambridge: Cambridge University Press, 1912, 241–363.

Nealon, Jeffrey, 'The Postmodern and *Waiting for Godot*,' in *Waiting for Godot and Endgame*. Edited by Steven Connor. London: Macmillan, 1992, 44–53.

Neyrey, Jerome. 'Despising the Shame of the Cross: Honor and Shame in the Johannine Passion Narrative,' *Semeia* 68 (1994): 113–37.

Nicol, Iain. 'Schweitzer's Jesus: A Psychology of the Heroic Will,' *The Expository Times* 86 (1974): 52–55.

Niebuhr, Reinhold. *Beyond Tragedy: Essays on the Christian Interpretation of History*. New York: Charles Scribner's Sons, 1937.

Nietzsche, Frederick. *The Birth of Tragedy*. Translated by Shaun Whitside. London: Penguin Books, 1993.

Nussbaum, Martha. 'Aristotle on Emotions and Rational Persuasion,' in *Essays on Aristotle's Rhetoric*. Edited by Ameilie Oksenberg Rorty. London: University of California Press, 1996, 303–23.

Nuttall, A. D. *Why Does Tragedy Give Pleasure?* Oxford: Clarendon Press, 1996.

O'Connor, Flannery. *Mystery and Manners*. Edited by Sally Fitzgerald and Robert Fitzgerald. New York: Farrar, Straus, and Giroux, 1957.

O'Day, Gail R. *Revelation in the Fourth Gospel: Narrative Mode and Theological Claim*. Philadelphia: Fortress, 1986.

Packer, Mark. 'Dissolving the Paradox of Tragedy,' *The Journal of Aesthetics and Art Criticism* 47, no. 3 (summer 1989): 211–19.

Painter, John. *John: Witness and Theologian*. London: SPCK, 1975.

Painter, John. *The Quest for the Messiah: The History, Literature and Theology of the Johannine Community*, 2nd edition. Edinburgh: T&T Clark, 1993.

Paolucci, Anne and Henry Paolucci, eds. *Hegel on Tragedy*. New York: Harper and Row, 1962.

Poland, Lynn. *Literary Criticism and Biblical Hermeneutics: A Critique of Formalist Approaches*. AARAS #48. Chico, CA: Scholars Press, 1985.

Polanyi, Michael. *Personal Knowledge: Towards a Post-Critical Philosophy*. London: Routledge & Kegan Paul, 1958.

Polanyi, Michael, and Harry Prosch. *Meaning*. Chicago and London: The University of Chicago Press, 1975.

Porter, Stanley E, ed. *Handbook of Classical Rhetoric in the Hellenistic Period 330 B.C.–A.D. 400*. New York: Brill, 1997.

Porter, Stanley E. *Rhetoric and the New Testament: Essays from the 1992 Heidelberg Conference*. JSNTSup 90. JSOT. Sheffield: Sheffield Academic Press, 1993.

Powell, Mark Allen. *What is Narrative Criticism?* Minneapolis: Fortress, 1990.

Quast, Kevin. *Peter and the Beloved Disciple: Figures for a Community in Crisis*. Sheffield: JSOT Sheffield Academic Press, 1989.

Raskin, Victor. *Semantic Mechanisms of Humor*. Lancaster: D. Reidel Publishing Company, 1985.

Reardon, B. P. *The Form of Greek Romance*. Princeton: Princeton University Press, 1991.

Reeve, Clara. *The Progress of Romance*. Colchester edition of 1785. New York: The Facsimile Text Society, 1930.

Rensberger, David. *Overcoming the World: Politics and Community in the Gospel of John*. London: SPCK, 1989.

Rensberger, David. 'The Politics of John: The Trial of Jesus in the Fourth Gospel,' *JBL* 103, no. 3 (1984): 395–411.
Rhoads, David and Donald Michie. *Mark as Story: An Introduction to the Narrative of a Gospel*. Philadelphia: Fortress Press, 1982.
Richards, I. A., *Principles of Literary Criticism*. London: Routledge & Kegan Paul, 1926.
Roberts, Preston. 'A Christian Theory of Dramatic Tragedy,' *The Journal of Religion* 31 (January 1951): 1–20.
Robertson, David. 'Tragedy, Comedy, and the Bible: A Response,' *Semeia* 32 (1984): 99–106.
Russ, Daniel. 'The Bible as the Genesis of Comedy,' in *The Terrain of Comedy*. Edited by Louise Cowan. Dallas: The Institute of Humanities and Culture, 1984, 40–59.
Ryken, Leland, ed. *The New Testament in Literary Criticism*. New York: Frederick Ungar, 1994.
Ryken, Leland. *Triumphs of the Imagination: Literature in Christian Perspective*. Downers Grove, IL: InterVarsity Press, 1979.
Ryken, Leland. *Words of Delight: A Literary Introduction to the Bible*, 2nd edition. Grand Rapids: Baker, 1992.
Sayers, Dorothy. *The Mind of the Maker*. London: Methuen and Co., 1941.
Scheler, Max. 'On the Tragic,' in *Tragedy: Modern Essays in Criticism*. Edited by Laurence Michel and Richard Sewall. Westport, CT: Greenwood, 1963: 27–44.
Schnackenburg, R. *The Gospel According to John*. 3 vol. Translated by Kevin Smyth. London and New York: Burns & Oates, Crossroad, 1968–82.
Scholes, Robert Kellogg. *The Nature of Narrative*. Oxford: Oxford University Press, 1966.
Scott, Nathan. *The Climate of Faith in Modern Literature*. New York: Seabury Press, 1964.
Segovia, Fernando. 'The Journey(s) of the Word of God: A Reading of the Plot of the Fourth Gospel,' *Semeia* 53 (1991): 23–54.
Sewall, Richard B. *The Vision of Tragedy*, 3rd edition. New York: Paragon House, 1990.
Smith, D. Moody. 'The Presentation of Jesus in the Fourth Gospel,' *Interpretation* 31 (1977): 367–78.
Sorokin, Pitirim. *The Crisis of Our Age*. Oxford: One World, 1941, 1992.
Staley, Jeffrey Lloyd. *The Print's First Kiss: A Rhetorical Investigation of the Implied Reader in the Fourth Gospel*. SBL Dissertation Series 82. Atlanta: Scholars Press, 1988.
Steiner, George. *The Death of Tragedy*. London: Faber and Faber, 1961.
Steiner, George. 'A Note on Absolute Tragedy,' *Journal of Literature and Theology* 4, no. 2 (July 1990): 147–56.
Steiner, George. *No Passion Spent: Essays 1978-1996*. London and Boston: Faber and Faber, 1996.
Steiner, George. *Real Presences: Is There Anything in What We Say?* London and Boston: Faber and Faber, 1989.
Sternberg, Meir. *The Poetics of Biblical Narrative: Ideological Literature and the Drama of Reading*. Bloomington, IN: Indiana University Press, 1985.
Stibbe, M. W. G, ed. *The Gospel of John as Literature: An Anthology of Twentieth-Century Perspectives*. NT tools and studies 17. Leiden, New York and Koln: E. J. Brill, 1993.
Stibbe, M. W. G. *John as Storyteller: Narrative Criticism and the Fourth Gospel*. SNTSMS 73. Cambridge: Cambridge University Press, 1992.
Stibbe, M. W. G. *John's Gospel*. London and New York: Routledge, 1994.
Stingle, Richard. 'Northrop Frye,' in *The Johns Hopkins Guide to Literary Theory and Criticism*. Edited by Michael Groden and Martin Kreiswirth. Baltimore and London: The Johns Hopkins University Press, 1994, 317–21.

Sutherland, Stewart. 'Christianity and Tragedy,' *Journal of Literature and Theology* 4, no. 2 (July 1990): 157-68.
Talbert, C. H. *Reading John: A Literary and Theological Commentary on the Fourth Gospel and the Johannine Epistles.* London: SPCK, 1992.
The Quest of the Holy Grail. Translated with an introduction by P. M. Matarasso. Harmondsworth, England: Penguin, 1969.
The Song of Roland. Translated with an introduction and notes by Glyn Burgess. London: Penguin, 1990.
Thatcher, Tom. 'The Sabbath Trick: Unstable Irony in the Fourth Gospel,' *Journal for the Study of the New Testament* 76 (1999): 53-77.
Tinsley, John. 'Tragedy and Christian Beliefs,' *Theology* 85 (March 1982): 98-105.
Torrance, Robert. *The Comic Hero.* Cambridge, MA: Harvard University Press, 1978.
Tovey, Derek. *Narrative Art and Act in the Fourth Gospel.* JSNTS 151. Sheffield: Sheffield Academic Press, 1997.
Vanhoozer, Kevin. *Is There a Meaning in This Text? The Bible, the Reader, and the Morality of Literary Knowledge.* Grand Rapids: Zondervan, 1998.
Via, Dan O. *Kerygma and Comedy in the New Testament: A Structuralist Approach to Hermeneutic.* Philadelphia: Fortress Press, 1975.
Vinaver, Eugene. *The Rise of Romance.* Oxford: The Clarendon Press, 1971.
Walsh, Richard. 'Tragic Dimensions in Mark,' *BTB* 19 (July 1989): 94-99.
Watson, Francis. *Text and Truth: Redefining Biblical Theology.* Edinburgh: T&T Clark, 1997.
Wead, David. 'The Johannine Double Meaning,' *Restoration Quarterly* 13 (1970): 106-20.
Wead, David. *The Literary Devices in John's Gospel,* dissertation. Basel: Friedrich Reinhardt 1970.
Whedbee, J. William. *The Bible and the Comic Vision.* Cambridge: Cambridge University Press, 1998.
White, Hayden. *Metahistory: The Historical Imagination in Nineteenth-Century Europe.* Baltimore and London: The Johns Hopkins University Press, 1973.
White, Hayden. 'The Value of Narrativity in the Representation of Reality,' *Critical Inquiry* 7 (Autumn 1980): 5-27.
Williams, Raymond. *Drama from Ibsen to Brecht.* London: The Hogarth Press, 1993.
Williams, Raymond. *Modern Tragedy.* London: The Hogarth Press, 1992.
Wimsatt, W. K. *The Idea of Comedy: Ben Jonson to George Meredith.* Englewood Cliffs, NJ: Prentice Hall, 1969.
Wimsatt, W. K., Monroe Beardsley. *The Verbal Icon.* Lexington, KY: University of Kentucky Press, 1954.
Wright, T. R. *Theology and Literature.* Oxford: Blackwell, 1988.
Wroe, Ann. *Pilate: The Biography of an Invented Man.* London: Jonathan Cape, 1999.
Zakovitch, Yair. '∪ and ∩ in the Bible,' *Semeia* 32 (1984): 107-14.

Index

Abraham (patriarch)   94
active blocking agents   177
Adam and Eve   40, 43
Aeneid (Virgil)   28
Aeschylus   166
Agamemnon (Sophocles)   83, 90, 105
agon (conflict)   4, 27. *See also* romance
All's Well That Ends Well
    (Lafeu)   54 n.108
anagnorisis (recognition)   4, 25, 27.
    See also comedy
Anatomy of Criticism (Frye)   3, 6–8
The Anatomy of the Fourth Gospel
    (Culpepper)   18
Anderson, Paul   129 n.18, 135 n.32
Antigone (play)   90, 105, 166, 171–2
anti-Semitism   122, 151 n.77
Antony, Mark   140
Antony and Cleopatra (play)   91, 94
Apostle's Creed   86
"Archetypal Criticism: Theory of Myths"
    (essay)   3
archetypal literary criticism   2–3, 5–10,
    16, 18–21, 29, 66–7, 108, 142, 166,
    179 n.58, 180, 193, 196–7
archetypes
    and conceptual prefiguration   11–17
    definition   2
    and genre   5
    and human experience   2–10
    objectives and qualifications   20–1
    overview   1–2
arete   99
Aristophanes   166, 173
An Aristotelian Theory of Comedy
    (Cooper)   166
Aristotle   25, 30, 46, 68, 69 n.12,
    82–9, 91–2, 94–8, 110, 166, 170,
    188 n.78, 194
The Art of Rhetoric (Aristotle)   84–5

Auden, W. H.   99–100
Auerbach, Eric   6, 36, 41, 45, 52, 61–2
Austen, Jane   5 n.16, 48, 144

Bacchae (Euripides)   24–5
Barabbas   77, 93, 104
Barrett, C. K.   17 n.58, 39 n.47, 72 n.19,
    127 n.10, 133 n.29
Bauckham, Richard   40 n.51, 196
Beckett, Samuel   148
Beer, Gillian   42, 46
Belch, Toby   183
beliefs
    and frames of reference   181–2
    in irony   140–2
Bergson, Henri   168–9, 171–2, 175,
    179, 182–3
bioi (biography)   24
Blair, Tony   70
blessings, and sorrows   35–6
blocking agents   177–8
Bond, Helen K.   70, 81 n.36
Booth, Wayne C.   7, 140–2, 141 n.52,
    146 n.64, 147
Borkland, Elmer   7
Bradley, A. C.   90
Brant, Jo-Ann A.   68–9
Brereton, Geoffrey   90
Brodie, Thomas   123 n.3, 134 n.31,
    154 n.3, 158 n.13, 160 n.16,
    164, 197
Brown, Raymond   78 n.28, 79 n.30,
    129 n.16, 164 n.20
Bultmann, Rudolf   59, 125 n.7
Burridge, Richard   24 n.6

Cahill, P. J.   13 n.49
Caiaphas   72–3, 160
Candide (Voltaire)   146
The Canterbury Tales   173

Index

capitulation 80–2
Carlyle, Thomas 54–5
Carson, D. A. 70, 124, 126, 135 n.34, 153 n.1, 155 n.8, 164 n.20
catharsis 87–8, 168
causality 48–9, 52, 188 n.78
Cervantes, Miguel de 42, 172
character
  comedy 169–76
  tragedy 95–7
Chatman, Seymour 61, 110 n.154, 148 n.67
Chesterton, G. K. 49–50
Christianity, and comedy 190–1
Christian theology 2, 9–10, 20, 51, 58, 69, 190, 196
Christian tragedy 99–100. *See also* tragedy
Clara, Reeve 28
Cliges (de Troyes) 45, 46 n.74
Clinton, Bill 147
coherentist system 7–8, 8 n.29, 21
Collins, Raymond 59–60, 131 n.24
comedy. *See also* Peter
  beliefs and frames of reference 181–2
  and character 169–76
  and Christianity 190–1
  in conflict 182–6
  intransitive 151 n.78, 189–90
  laughter 168–9
  overview 153, 165–6
  plots 176–9
  reality 186–90
  sympathy and ridicule 167–8
  transitive 151 n.78, 189–90
A Comedy of Errors (Shakespeare) 167, 173, 186
comic action 173, 176, 180
comic character 13, 21, 153, 168, 170, 173–7, 174–5, 180, 185, 192
comic juxtaposition 184–6
comic plots 176–9
comic strips 173, 189
A Connecticut Yankee in King Arthur's Court (Twain) 42
Cooper, Lane 166, 169–70
Cornford, Francis 89, 170
crucifixion 10, 36–8, 51, 77–8, 81, 92, 157, 167, 188

Culpepper, Robert 17–18, 24, 26–7, 48 n.87, 91 n.78, 129 n.16, 131, 133 n.27, 136, 138–9

Dante, Alighieri 61, 190
Daphnis and Chloe 29
David Copperfield (Dickens) 56, 64 n.140
Davies, Margaret 26 n.16, 49
Dean, John 30, 31 n.37, 32, 38
Death of a Salesman (Miller) 96 n.97
The Death of Tragedy (Steiner) 117
Dedalus, Stephen 84 n.42
de Troyes, Chretien 45, 56
diachronic approach 6
Dialogue and Drama: Elements of Greek Tragedy in the Fourth Gospel (Brant) 68
Dickens, Charles 64 n.140, 161, 172, 176
dike 99
Dionysus 25
divine, and tragedy 106–7
The Divine Comedy (Dante) 61, 190
Don Quixote (Cervantes) 42, 144, 172, 190
double layered irony 140
double-mindedness 127, 131, 133
doubt, and irony 122–3
Dr. Faustus (Marlowe) 144
dramatic clash 105–6
dramatis personae 61
dualism 65, 68, 133 n.29, 142–3
Duke, Paul 136, 139, 140 n.47, 142

The Eclipse of Biblical Narrative: A Study in Eighteenth and Nineteenth Century Hermeneutics (Frei) 13 n.50
Electra (Sophocles) 112
Elements of Tragedy (Krook) 100
Eliot, T. S. 98, 193
Else, Gerald 87, 97, 104 n.127
epic romance 28–31
equivocal irony 143–6
Erasmus, Desiderius 143
Ethics (Aristotle) 98
Euripides 24, 166

The Faerie Queene (Spenser) 26, 43
fear, and pity 83–7, 111

Feast of Dedication   34
Ferguson, Francis   104 n.127
figural interpretation   61–2
final reunion scenes   38
Finn, Huckleberry   144
Fish, Stanley   50 n.99
Flack, Colin   6–7
Fletcher, Angus   31
Forster, E. M.   44–5, 46 n.79, 138, 172 n.44
Fourth Evangelist   44
The Fox (Jonson)   186–7
frames of reference
   and beliefs   181–2
   in conflict   182–6
Frazer, James   3
Frei, Hans   13 n.50
Freud, Sigmund   169, 179 n.58
Frye, Northrop   3–10, 13, 15–16, 15 n.53, 18–20, 23, 27, 29 n.30, 40, 48, 51, 53, 56, 59 n.117, 63, 94–6, 103 n.126, 108, 111 n.156, 142, 173 n.45, 176–7, 179 n.57, 187–8
Fuller, Reginald   128–30

Gans, Eric   146 n.63
Garden of Gethsemane   104
generation differences   33
Genesis   43
genre, and archetypes   5
Giblin, C. H.   78 n.29, 80 n.33, 81 n.37, 138 n.43
Gilligan's Island (TV show)   190
The Golden Bough (Frasier)   3
The Gospel of John as Literature: An Anthology of Twentieth-Century Perspectives (Stibbe)   18
The Great Code (Frye)   48–9
Greek tragedy   99–100. *See also* tragedy

hamartia/tragic flaw   25, 97–9, 115 n.167, 194
Hamlet (play)   67–8, 105, 119, 166
Hardy, Thomas   5, 47, 172
Harris, Elizabeth   17
Hartman, Geoffrey   8
Harvey, W. J.   64, 71–2, 73 n.20
Hauser, Gertrud   168
Hegel, G. W. F.   90–1, 105–7, 170–2

Hellenistic Christian church   59
Henn, T. R.   108 n.148, 114 n.164, 115 n.165
Henry V (Shakespeare)   144
Herod   97
hero/protagonist   26–31, 35, 51–6, 176
Hesla, David   99
Hick, John   57
Hitchcock, F. R. M.   46
"Holy One of God"   136, 142–3, 155, 165, 177, 188
Holy Spirit   34, 38, 154, 191
Homer   30, 45, 91–2
hubris   100
human existence   58, 67, 95, 107, 112, 118, 182 n.69
human experience   1–3, 9–11, 61, 68
human suffering   84–5
Hutcheon, Linda   141 n.50
Huxley, Aldous   144

Ibsen, Henrik   118
identity, and self-determination   51–5
ignorance, in tragedy   83–4, 105, 112–14
Iliad (Homer)   30
imaginative identification   57
incongruity-based theories   180
In Praise of Folly (Erasmus)   143–4
interpretative paradigm   138–9
intransitive comedy   151 n.78, 189–90
intra-Trinitarian fellowship,   58
irony   11–15. *See also* Thomas, and Jews
   equivocal   143–6
   ironization of   122–8
   negative   146–51
   overview   121–2
   positive   142–3
   survey and classification of studies   136–40
   values and beliefs in   140–2
Irony in the Fourth Gospel (Duke)   136
Iscariot, Judas   95
The Italian Renaissance   170 n.34

Jameson, Fredric   9 n.34, 59 n.117, 63
Jesus   *passim*
Jesus's piety   34–5
Jews. *See* Thomas, and Jews
Johannine anti-language   68

Johannine community 8 n.29
Johannine dualism 65, 133 n.29
John as Storyteller (Stibbe) 18–19
John's Gospel (Stibbe) 18
Johnson, Edgar 64 n.140
John the Baptist 38, 71, 131, 153
Jonson, Ben 185–7
Joseph of Arimathea 92, 161
Joyce, James 84, 86, 148
Judas Iscariot 36–7, 52, 64, 79, 85, 95, 105, 115, 155, 157–9, 161, 163, 167, 178, 183, 188
Julius Caesar (play) 91
Jung, Carl 2–3

Karl, Jaspers 88
Kaufmann, Walter 83, 90 n.69, 92 n.81, 98, 101–2
Kelber, Werner 66 n.143, 138–9
Ker, W. P. 28, 30
King Lear 166
Kitto, H. D. F. 116, 118
Knight, L. C. 90 n.68, 179 n.58
Knox, John 54, 113 n.163
Knox, Norman 140 n.47
Koestler, Arthur 60 n.127, 168 n.27, 181, 182
kosmos 69, 129–30
Krook, Dorthea 100–1, 115
Kuhn, Thomas 7, 8 n.29, 16, 50, 133

laughter, and comedy 168–9, 191
Lazarus 33–7, 123–30, 138, 157, 178, 188, 194
Lee, Alvin 3
Lee, Dorothy 20, 123 n.4, 128 n.11, 129–30, 131 n.22, 133 n.28
Leech, Clifford 86 n.48, 90
Lindars, Barnabas 35 n.43
literary criticism 2–3, 5–10, 16, 18–21, 29, 66–7, 108, 142, 166, 179 n.58, 180, 193, 196–7
Love's Labour's Lost (Shakespeare) 189
Lucas, F. L. 87–8, 93 n.87, 95 n.93, 98

Macbeth (play) 91, 94, 97, 99–100, 105, 112, 115, 117
McFadden, George 174
Macmillan, Harold 147

MacRae, G. 95 n.91
magical wonders 37
male-female relationships 35
Mandel, Oscar 111 n.157
Mansfield Park (novel) 56, 146 n.64
Marlowe, Christopher 144
marvelous, and risk 32–3, 48, 55
Mary Magdalene 35, 61, 162
Meeks, Wayne 34 n.40, 47 n.86, 66 n.143
mental agility, of hero 35
The Merchant of Venice 187
Meredith, George 177 n.55, 179 n.58
Messiah 60, 94, 125, 130, 149–50, 153–5, 177
Metahistory (White) 11
metaphor 11–12, 14–15, 41, 55–7, 135, 150
metonymy 11–12, 14–15
Michaels, J. Ramsey 125
A Midsummer Night's Dream (play) 166, 176–7, 184, 187
Miller, Arthur 96 n.97, 118
Mimesis (Auerbach) 6
Mincoff, Marco 54, 54 n.108
The Miser (Moliere) 183
Moby Dick (Melville) 45
A Modest Proposal (Swift) 143
Mohammed 54
moira 99
Molière, Jean-Baptiste Poquelin 183, 186
Moloney, Francis 155 n.7, 158 n.14
Moore, Stephen 10 n.40, 66 n.143, 138–9
moral guilt 109
moral order 118–19
Moses 50, 134, 155, 161
Much Ado about Nothing (Shakespeare) 181, 189
Muecke, D. C. 108 n.148, 125 n.8, 140, 148
Murphy, Francesca 18
Murray, Gilbert 104 n.127
Myers, Henry A. 111 n.160, 118 n.181
"My Lord and my God' " 142–3
mythoi (generic plots). *See* comedy; irony; romance; tragedy

narrative emphasis 37–8
Nathanael 39
Nazareth 39, 82, 153

Nealon, Jeffrey   150
negative irony   146–51
New Testament (NT)   10, 48, 59, 73 n.22, 97
Nicodemus   33, 35, 36, 60, 62, 65, 70, 72–3, 76, 81, 131–2, 134, 155, 161, 177
Nietzsche, Frederick   94 n.90, 97
NT. *See* New Testament (NT)
Nuttall, A. D.   87–8

O'Connor, Flannery   61, 144
O'Day, Gail   20 n.74, 136–7, 139, 142
Odysseus   31, 34–7, 54–5, 148
Odyssey (Homer)   30, 32, 45
Oedipus   21, 77, 83–5, 88, 90, 92–3, 97, 100, 112, 119, 174, 189
Oedipus   38, 52, 92, 99, 102, 105
Oedipus the King   166
Old Testament (OT)   35, 41–2, 93
Orthodoxy (Chesterton)   49
OT. *See* Old Testament (OT)
Othello (play)   83, 87, 105, 109, 181

pageantry   33–4
Painter, Jack   191 n.82
Painter, John   135 n.33
Paradise Lost   43
paralytic, healing of   132–4, 136
"Party Politics"   147
passive blocking agents   177
Passover festival   33–4, 40, 77, 178
pathos (catastrophe)   4, 27. *See also* tragedy
Pericles (Shakespeare)   45, 47, 53
peripeteia (tragic reversal)   93 n.87
Peter. *See also* comedy
   in chapter 13   156–9
   in chapter 18   159–61
   in chapter 20   161–2
   in chapter 21   162–5
   as follower   153–5
Pharisees   129, 131
Pilate, Pontius. *See also* tragedy
   18:33-38a (from politics to truth)   75–6
   18:38b-40 (return to innocence)   76–7
   19:12-16 (capitulation)   80–2

catharsis   87–8
19:9-11 (confirmation of divinity)   79–80
19:1-3 (desperate measures)   77–8
as dynamic character   69–71
19:22 (epilogue)   82
fear and pity reaction of audience   83–7
18:28-32 (judicial concerns)   74–5
18:15-27 (narrative context)   73
19:4-8 (revelation of divinity)   78–9
trial narrative   71–3
pity, and fear   83–7, 111
Plato   2
plot and story
   in comedy   176–9
   in romance   44–51
   in tragedy   89–95
Poetics (Aristotle)   25, 46, 68, 89, 166, 194
Polanyi, Michael   7
Portrait of the Artist as Young Man (Joyce)   84
positive irony   142–3
Potts, L. J.   185
Pride and Prejudice (Austen)   144, 146
The Progress of Romance (Reeve)   28
Prometheus   166
psychic compression   169

Quast, Kevin   162

Raskin, Victor   16, 179–81, 186 n.74
Reagan, Ronald   147
realism, and romance   38–44
Reardon, B. P.   5 n.15, 10 n.38, 63 n.138
Reeve, Clara   29 n.28
release/relief theories   180
Rensberger, David   80 n.32, 81 n.36
representation, and romance   55–8
Restless Wanderers: Shakespeare and the Pattern of Romance (Dean)   32
resurrection, of Christ   10, 26–7, 33–4, 36–8, 41, 48, 85, 122–6, 128, 135 n.34, 146, 161–2, 178, 184, 188, 191, 195
The Return of the Native (Hardy)   5
revelation of divinity   78–9

Revolutions (Kuhn) 8 n.29
Richards, I. A. 55, 86
Richter, Jean Paul 182
ridicule, and sympathy 167–8
risk, and marvelous 32–3
Robertson, David 187
Robortello, Francesco 170 n.34
romance
    basic elements of 26–32
    blessings and sorrows 35–6
    in critical opinion 24–6
    distinguishing token/scar 36–7
    final reunion scenes 38
    generation differences 33
    historical relevancy 34
    identity and self-determination 51–5
    influence of supernatural higher power 36
    and interlacing narrative 37–8
    Jesus's piety 34–5
    and journey of Jesus 34
    magical wonders 37
    and male-female relationships 35
    marvel, risk, and triumphant adventure 32–3
    and mental agility 35
    overview 23
    pageantry 33–4
    personal and theological encounters 58–66
    plot and story in 44–51
    and realism 38–44
    and representation 55–8
    shipwreck/apparent loss 37
Romeo and Juliet (play) 189
royal official, healing of 132–3
Ryken, Leland 41, 193

Sabbath 33, 71, 92, 133, 135
Samaritan woman 15, 19, 35–6, 47 n.82, 60, 70, 72–3, 75–6, 81, 129, 132, 137–8, 139 n.46, 153
scars/tokens 36–7
Scheler, Max 90, 96 n.95, 107–10, 108 n.148, 109 n.153, 115 n.169
Schnackenburg, Rudolf 132 n.25
scientific basis 6, 8
Scott, Nathan 175
Scott, Walter 44, 45 n.73

secular scripture 5 n.15
self-determination, and identity 51–5
self-preservation 174–5
Semantic Mechanisms of Humor (Raskin) 181
Sewall, Richard 113 n.162, 117–18
Shakespeare, William 10, 18 n.64, 32, 44–5, 47, 53–4, 89, 91–2, 94, 109, 111 n.158, 118–19, 140, 144, 166, 189
shipwreck/apparent loss 37
Simon Peter. *See* Peter
Sitz im Leben 59
Smith, D. Moody 44
Socrates 144
The Song of Roland 29, 46 n.74, 52
Son of God 36, 39, 72, 78–9, 84, 98, 104, 154
the Son of Man 39, 157–8, 183
Sophocles 10, 83, 104 n.127, 112, 119, 166
sorrows, and blessings 35–6
Sparagmos 4. *See also* irony
stable irony 140
Staley, Jeffrey Lloyd 136, 138–9, 165
static dualism 133 n.29
Steiner, George 85 n.46, 117–18
Sternberg, Meir 117 n.175
Stibbe, Mark 18–20, 24–6, 31 n.35, 40 n.49, 46, 47 n.83, 130 n.21, 140 n.47, 151 n.77
story and plot, in romance 44–51
sui generis (human and divine) 56
superiority theories 180
supernatural higher power 36
Sutherland, Stewart 105 n.128
Swift, Jonathan 143
Swinburne, Richard 50 n.95
symbolic narrative, and Jews 128–30
The Symbolic Narratives of the Fourth Gospel (Lee) 20
sympathy, and ridicule 167–8
synchronic methods 6
synecdoche 11–12, 14–15, 135
Synoptics 35, 49 n.90, 58–9, 64–5, 71, 77, 92, 97, 134 n.30, 154–5, 161, 165, 167, 188
Sypher, Wylie 171–2
systematic 6

Tabernacles festival   34
Tartuffe (Moliere)   186-7
The Tempest (Miranda)   23, 54, 144, 187
tenor   55
Thackeray, William Makepeace   143
theme of descent and ascent   34
Thomas, and Jews. *See also* irony
  in 4:43-6:71   130-6
  and ironization of irony   122-8
  and symbolic narrative   128-30
tokens/scars   36-7
Torrance, Robert   174
Tovey, Derek   156, 164-5
tragedy. *See also* Pilate, Pontius
  18:33-38a (from politics to truth)   75-6
  18:38b-40 (return to innocence)   76-7
  19:12-16 (capitulation)   80-2
  catharsis   87-8
  character   95-7
  conceptual elements of   100-19
  19:9-11 (confirmation of divinity)   79-80
  19:1-3 (desperate measures)   77-8
  and divine   106-7
  19:22 (epilogue)   82
  fear and pity reaction of audience   83-7
  in Greek and Christian perspective   99-100
  18:28-32 (judicial concerns)   74-5
  knowledge and ignorance in   112-14
  Marxist concerns   102-3
  moral order in   114-19
  18:15-27 (narrative context)   73
  overview   67-9
  and Pilate as dynamic character   69-71
  plot   89-95
  19:4-8 (revelation of divinity)   78-9
  structural elements of   88-99
  tragic clash   103-12
  tragic flaw/hamartia   97-9
  trial narrative   71-3

Tragedy and Philosophy (Kaufmann)   101
tragic clash   103-12
tragic flaw/hamartia   97-9
tragic form   117
tragic guilt   109
tragic hero   48, 53, 65, 67, 82-3, 89-90, 95-8, 109-10, 111 n.156, 116-18, 152, 171, 180, 194
the tragic knot   108
tragic misdeed   109
tragic protagonist   29
tragic reversal *(peripeteia)*   93 n.87
transitive comedy   151 n.78, 189-90
trial narrative   71-3
Trinitarian God   107
Twain, Mark   42, 44
Twelfth Night (play)   166, 176-7, 181-3

Ulysses (Joyce)   148

values
  and beliefs in irony   140-2
  and tragedy   108
Vanity Fair (Thackery)   143
Vinaver, Eugene   28 n.26, 46 n.74
Virgil   28
Voltaire, François-Marie Aroue   146

Waiting for Godot (Beckett)   148-50, 196
Watson, Francis   59 n.120
Watts, Harold   103-4
Wead, David   136-9, 142
wedding at Cana   39-41
White, Hayden   5-7, 11-12, 27
Williams, Raymond   101 n.115, 102-3, 104 n.127, 118, 148
Windisch, Hans   46
The Winter's Tale   187, 189
Wise Blood (O'Connor)   144
Women of Trachis (Sophocles)   112
Wright, Stephen   10 n.39

οἱ Ἰουδαῖοι. *See* Thomas, and Jews